TEMPLAR HOUSES and FORTRESSES
IN THE LATE THIRTEENTH CENTURY

```
0        100       200       300 miles
0    100   200   300   400   500 km
```

POLAND

GERMANY

HOLY

ROMAN

BOHEMIA

EMPIRE

ANTIOCH

Famagusta

Paphos   Limassol   Ruad   Safita

CYPRUS   TRIPOLI

Mediterranean
Sea

Acre   Safed
ʿAtlit
(Pilgrims' Castle)

JERUSALEM   Jerusalem

to same scale

HUNGARY

DY

SLAVONIA

Bologna

Lucca

San Gimignano   ANCONA
TUSCANY   Perugia

Chieti
ABRUZZI
Rome

APULIA

SARDINIA

Castrovillari

CALABRIA

SEA

SICILY

The Trial of the Templars

MALCOLM BARBER

✝

LONDON
The Folio Society
2003

Frontispiece: Jacques de Molay, Grand Master of the Temple, and other leaders, are brought before King Philip IV of France and Pope Clement V, seen here apparently acting in concert, although they were never in accord over the conduct of the trial. The illustration is from *Les Chroniques de France*, which is a vernacular narrative of events from 1270 to 1380. It was produced in the monastery of Saint-Denis, north of Paris, which had long been associated with the French monarchy

Third printing 2005

The Trial of the Templars was first published by Cambridge University Press in 1978. The text of this edition follows that of the 1993 printing published by Canto, with some emendations by the author. This edition is published by arrangement with the Syndicate of the Press of the University of Cambridge, Cambridge, England.

Map and plans drawn by Reginald Piggott

TYPESET AT THE FOLIO SOCIETY IN SABON WITH CLAIRVAUX DISPLAY. PRINTED ON CAXTON WOVE AT ST EDMUNDSBURY PRESS, BURY ST EDMUNDS. BOUND BY HUNTER AND FOULIS, HADDINGTON, IN FULL CLOTH, BLOCKED WITH A DESIGN BY SIMON NOYES

Contents

Illustrations

To my parents

Preface

The trial of the Templars was an event unique in the middle ages. Contemporaries found it scarcely believable that a military religious Order, which for nearly two hundred years had fought for the Christian faith in Syria and Palestine, and which was directly responsible to the papacy, should have been the subject of the shocking allegations made against it by the government of France. Equally unbelievable was the fact that, in less than five years after the arrest of its members in France in October 1307, Pope Clement V found it necessary to forbid 'anyone from now on to enter the Order, or receive or wear its habit, or presume to behave as a Templar'. Although the arrests had been made in the name of the papal Inquisitor in France, Guillaume de Paris, it was obvious both then and since that the prime mover was the French government, led by Guillaume de Nogaret, Keeper of the Seals, acting on the orders of the king, Philip IV, 'the Fair'. The basic facts seem straightforward. The king had obtained information which suggested that the Templars were heretics and blasphemers who denied Christ, spat on a crucifix, worshipped idols, and practised institutionalised sodomy. These activities had been kept strictly secret, often by threats of force, leaving an unsuspecting populace to believe that they were still fully committed to the Christian cause in the continuing struggle with the infidel Moslems. No responsible ruler could ignore allegations of this kind, for they put his very realm in danger, and it was therefore vital to investigate the matter by means of interrogating the Templars and calling witnesses. Resistance from Pope Clement V, who was affronted at the undermining of his own authority, and, later, from a considerable number of the Templars themselves, who mounted a spirited defence, prolonged the trial for five years. However, the French king eventually had his way and the Order was suppressed at the Council of Vienne in March 1312.

The implications of these events are far-reaching. Historians are faced with a range of difficult but fascinating problems. Were the accusations 'true' in any objective sense? What was the internal condition of the Order at this time? Why did the king and his advisers take such a drastic step? Who was really responsible for the accusations within the French government? What considerations determined the actions of the pope in the proceedings? How does the trial relate to other contemporary events in the early fourteenth century?

However, these questions were not the ones I originally set out to ask when I began historical research in the mid-1960s. My initial interest was in the careers of the Masters of the Temple from the time of the original founder, Hugues de Payns (*c.*1119–*c.*1136), to that of Jacques de Molay (*c.*1293–1314). This exercise in medieval proso-pography produced results which were too episodic to form a coher-ent book, but it did draw me into a study of the trial proceedings in which the hapless Jacques de Molay found himself entangled, and which eventually led to his execution on the Ile-des-Javiaux in the River Seine in Paris, in March 1314. Important work had been done in describing and interpreting the trial, and in publishing relevant documents, by a brilliant generation of historians active around 1900. Among these were the French, Charles-Victor Lan-glois, Georges Lizerand and Gui Mollat, the American, Henry Charles Lea, and the Germans, Hans Prutz, Konrad Schottmüller and Heinrich Finke (see the Bibliography, pp. 347–61). Finke was out-standing: his *Papsttum und Untergang des Templerordens* (1907), published in two volumes, one documentary and one interpretative, forms the indispensable basis for any scholarly study. My own work was founded upon these historians, who set the benchmark by which future research on the subject should be judged.

Most of my research for the book was undertaken in the early 1970s, but since then there has been important work in a number of fields relevant to the trial (see the Supplementary Bibliography, pp. 362–4). Most spectacularly there has been a renaissance of cru-sading studies, which has made the attention paid to the events before and during the trial even more crucial than realised at the time of writing. Norman Housley has led the way in presenting the loss of Acre and the withdrawal from the Holy Land in 1291 as less of a turning-point than it was once seen by historians, emphasising instead the continuities of the crusading movement through into the fourteenth and fifteenth centuries. This necessarily forces a re-appraisal of the view of the trial as a kind of coda to an era already drawing to a close. Instead it suggests that perhaps there was much life remaining in the Order of the Temple which, left unmolested, might have adapted to new circumstances in ways similar to that of the late medieval Hospitallers. In turn, this is relevant to judgements about the internal condition of the Order in 1307 and to whether or not it required reform. Need for reform, however, is not the same as heresy, and further research into the personality and motivation of Philip the Fair has led to a greater understanding of those facets of his character which might have persuaded him to believe in the charges against the Templars. Even so, no real consensus has emerged, as the very different conclusions drawn by Robert-Henri Bautier and Elizabeth Brown show. Finally, new research has been done on the trial itself, particularly by Andreas Beck, who has produced a fresh study of the trial as a whole, and Alan Forey and Fulvio Bramato, who have tackled the proceedings in Aragon and Italy respectively. During the same period, newly published documents edited by Roger Sève and Anne-Marie Chagny-Sève on the episcopal proceedings at Clermont, and by Anne Gilmour-Bryson on the Papal State and the Abruzzi and on Cyprus, have added invaluable material to the evidential base available in print. Discoveries by Barbara Frale in the Castel Sant'Angelo archive in Rome promise to revise our views of papal policy during the key period of conflict between Philip IV and Clement V in the summer of 1308. These studies and collections are quite specialist, but the trial has also been incorporated into broader analyses of the major participants. Histories of the Order as a whole by Alain Demurger, Helen Nicholson and myself, of Clement V by Sophia Menache, and of Philip the Fair by Jean Favier and Joseph Strayer, all give substantial consideration to the trial, and offer interpretations of contemporary motivations and perceptions.

This work has led to a new wave of interest in the history of the Temple and its final fate, an interest which had waned since the early twentieth century. However, not all this enthusiasm can be described as scholarly or even historical. The revival of serious work has been accompanied by a burgeoning of the market for solutions to the 'mystery of the Templars', a whole subsection of the publishing industry in which the fraudulent and the opportunistic compete for the attention of the credulous. This too has deep roots, particularly in the masonic lodges of the eighteenth century, the conspiracy theorists of the period of the French Revolution, and the romantic novelists of the nineteenth century, of whom Sir Walter Scott is the great exemplar. Peter Partner's *The Murdered Magicians* provides a serious historical context for this and Umberto Eco's novel, *Foucault's Pendulum*, an appropriately ironic commentary.

Both contemporaries and moderns have been sceptical about Philip the Fair's motivations and the French government's insistence on Templar guilt, but recent interpretations differ in one fundamental respect from those of their predecessors seven centuries ago, in that they have all been tempered by the experiences of the twentieth century. No historian who has lived a substantial part of his or her life in the twentieth century can contemplate the trial and the confessions it produced without drawing on their awareness of the power of state coercion to persuade individuals to confess to actions they have not committed. Two examples illustrate this. The work of Marion Melville has a special immediacy in that she was writing in 1940. She argued that the accusations against the Templars were entirely fuelled by outside interests and noted that we were all familiar with the tactic of mass arrests, followed by false accusations and confessions gained by torture. Norman Cohn, writing of the development of the European witch-craze in *Europe's Inner Demons*, gives a chapter to the accusations against the Templars, which he sees as a stage in this phenomenon. Similarly facing the problem of so many Templar confessions, he admits that in the past it may have been difficult for some to believe that the charges could be fabricated and that the confessions could all be untrue, but adds that the Stalinist trials could now leave us in no doubt that this was quite credible. One reviewer of *The Trial of the Templars* called this 'moralising' (presumably referring to my single remark in the original Preface – see p. xv), and it is true that it is perhaps undesirable for the historian to make moral judgements on the past. However, no historian can step outside his own time (any more than could Philip IV, Clement V or Guillaume de Nogaret), and our interpretation of the trial cannot help but be affected by our knowledge that the application of sufficient physical torture and psychological pressure can produce confessions to whatever is required. Indeed, they may even convince the victim that he is actually telling the truth.

This is the twenty-fifth anniversary of the publication of this book and I am particularly pleased that The Folio Society should have chosen this time to publish such a splendid edition. I owe especial thanks to Kit Shepherd, Neil Titman and Emma Ellis, the editorial staff who have made this possible, and to Sara Ayad for her excellent picture research.

MALCOLM BARBER

Preface to the First Edition

I wrote this book for two main reasons. Firstly, because the trial of the Templars was an affair of considerable importance in the middle ages which has been unjustly neglected by historians writing in English, and secondly, because I believe that the event has some relevance to the world of the late twentieth century, so many of whose peoples have been, and continue to be, oppressed by regimes which use terror and torture to enforce conformity of thought and action.

I have received ungrudging help from many people in the writing of this book, but I should particularly like to record my thanks to Dr Bernard Hamilton of the University of Nottingham, Professor J. C. Holt of the University of Reading, and above all, to my wife, Elizabeth, the value of whose encouragement, support and criticism cannot be adequately expressed. I should also like to thank Mrs Janet Cory and Mrs Audrey Munro for the typing of the manuscript, Professor Lewis Thorpe, the editor of *Nottingham Mediaeval Studies*, for kindly granting permission for the reuse of material from my article 'Propaganda in the Middle Ages: The Charges against the Templars', which appeared in 1973, and the Syndics and editors at Cambridge University Press for their interest in the work.

M.C.B.

READING, 1977

Introduction

The Templars were a military religious Order, founded in the Holy Land in 1119. During the twelfth and thirteenth centuries they acquired extensive property both in the crusader states in Palestine and Syria and in the west, especially in France, and they were granted far-reaching ecclesiastical and jurisdictional privileges both by the popes to whom they were immediately responsible, and by the secular monarchs in whose lands their members resided. They also functioned as bankers on a large scale, a position facilitated by the international nature of their organisation. But most of all they bore a large share of the responsibility for the military defence of the crusader states in the east, to which they owed their origin and on account of which they had become so famous and powerful. However, in 1291, the Christian settlers of the east were driven out of Palestine by the Mameluks of Egypt, and the Templars were cut adrift from the main purpose of their existence.

Suddenly, in the early hours of Friday 13 October 1307, the brothers of this Order residing in France were arrested by the officials of King Philip IV in the name of the Inquisition, and their property was taken over by royal representatives. They were charged with serious heresies encompassing the denial of Christ and spitting on the crucifix, indecent kissing and homosexuality, and idol worship, carried on in secret receptions and chapter-meetings of the Order. In October and November, the captured Templars, including Jacques de Molay, the Grand Master, and Hugues de Pairaud, the Visitor, almost unanimously confessed their guilt. Torture was freely used upon many of the prisoners. Molay then repeated his confession before a public assembly of theologians from the University of Paris. For his part King Philip wrote to the other monarchs of Christendom urging them to follow his lead and to arrest the Templars in their own lands, for the confessions had proved them to be manifest heretics.

The reigning pope, Clement V, at first saw the arrests as a direct affront to his authority, for the Templars were responsible to the papacy, and although, the previous summer, there had been discussions between the pope and the king concerning the condition of the

Order, Clement had not actually authorised the arrests. However, after his initial anger, he was forced to accept the situation and, instead of resisting, endeavoured to put himself in charge. On 22 November 1307 he issued the bull *Pastoralis praeeminentiae*, which ordered all the monarchs of Christendom to arrest the Templars and sequester their lands in the name of the papacy. This bull initiated proceedings in England, Iberia, Germany, Italy and Cyprus. Two cardinals were then sent to Paris to interview the leaders of the Order personally. But, once in front of the papal representatives, Molay and Pairaud revoked their confessions and urged the rest of the Templars to do the same.

By now the pope had become highly suspicious of the whole affair and, early in 1308, he suspended the inquisitorial proceedings. Philip IV and his ministers were obliged to spend the next six months in an attempt to force the pope to reopen the trial, both by the marshalling of public and theological opinion in France, and by the implicit threat of physical violence against the pope himself. This campaign culminated in a meeting between the pope and the king at Poitiers in May and June of 1308, in which, after much debate, the pope finally agreed to set up two kinds of inquiry: one by a papal commission into the Order itself, and another consisting of a series of provincial councils, held at diocesan level, to investigate the guilt or innocence of individual Templars. Furthermore, a general council of the Church was arranged, to be held at Vienne in October 1310, to make a final decision in the matter. Meanwhile, three cardinals were sent to Chinon to hear the depositions of the leaders of the Order who were imprisoned there, only to find that they had reverted to their original confessions.

The episcopal inquiries, which were largely dominated by bishops closely associated with the French monarchy, seem to have begun work in 1309, and it appears that in most cases the Templars repeated their confessions, once again under pressure from extensive torture. The papal commission investigating the Order as a whole did not begin its sittings until November 1309. Initially it appeared that the familiar pattern of confessions would be followed, but at first falteringly and then with gathering momentum, the brothers, led by two able Templar priests, Pietro di Bologna and Renaud de Provins, began to mount a defence of their Order and their way of life before the commission. By early May 1310 almost six hundred

Templars had agreed to defend the Order, denying the validity of previous confessions whether made before the inquisitors in 1307 or the bishops in 1309. Pope Clement, seeing that no immediate end to the proceedings seemed in prospect, postponed the Council of Vienne for a year until October 1311. It was to crush this increasingly confident Templar defence that Philip IV took drastic action. The Archbishop of Sens, a royal nominee, reopened his episcopal inquiry against individual Templars within his diocese and, finding fifty-four of them guilty of being relapsed heretics, handed them over to the secular authorities. On 12 May 1310 the fifty-four Templars were burnt at the stake in a field outside Paris. Of the two leading defenders, Pietro di Bologna mysteriously disappeared, and Renaud de Provins was sentenced to perpetual imprisonment by the Council of Sens. With the exception of a few brave individuals, the burnings effectively silenced the defence, and many Templars returned to their confessions. The hearings of the papal commission eventually petered out in June 1311.

In the summer of 1311 the pope collected together the evidence sent from France, as well as the material slowly coming in from the other countries where proceedings had taken place. In essence only in France and in those regions under French domination or influence were there substantial confessions from Templars. In October the Council of Vienne at last opened, and the pope pressed for the suppression (although not the condemnation) of the Order on the grounds that it was now too defamed to carry on. Resistance among the fathers at the council was however considerable, and the pope, pressed by the military presence of the King of France, only achieved his will by imposing silence on the council to be broken only under pain of excommunication. The bull *Vox in excelso* of 22 March 1312 suppressed the Order, and *Ad providam* of 2 May granted its property to the other great Military Order, the Hospital. Soon after, Philip IV extracted a huge sum of money from the Hospitallers in compensation for his costs in bringing the Templars to trial. As for the individual Templars, in some cases they had to submit to heavy penances including perpetual imprisonment, and in others, where they had admitted nothing, they were sent to monasteries of other Orders to spin out the rest of their lives. The leaders eventually came before the papal representatives on 18 March 1314 and were sentenced to perpetual imprisonment. Hugues de Pairaud and Geoffroi de Gonneville, the Preceptor of Aquitaine, accepted their fate in silence, but Jacques de Molay and Geoffroi de Charney, the Preceptor of Normandy, loudly protested their innocence and asserted that the Order was pure and holy. At once, the king ordered that they be condemned as relapsed heretics and, on the same evening, they were burnt at the stake on the Ile-des-Javiaux in the Seine.

The aim of this book is to trace in detail the course of these events, to examine the motivation of the chief participants, and to assess the extent to which the charges brought against the Order were justified.

1: The Participants

THE ORDER OF THE TEMPLE

The great period of crusading endeavour spanned the two centuries between 1095 and 1291, the high middle ages of thrusting population growth, great economic expansion, dynamic social change, political consolidation and blossoming cultural achievement. Men certainly still talked of undertaking a crusade as late as the sixteenth century, but it was during the twelfth and thirteenth centuries that it existed as a vital and living concept which touched the lives of almost everybody in western Christendom. During this time the Christians of the west underwent a whole range of reactions towards this most emotive of rallying cries, from the exaltation and excitement of the capture of Jerusalem by the First Crusade to the growing bitterness and disillusion of the thirteenth century when so many crusading efforts ended in defeat and failure. The Military Order of the Knights of the Temple of Solomon was essentially a creation of these two centuries, shaped and formed by the early crusading enthusiasm which carried it to great heights of fame, wealth and power, but finally pulled down, humiliated and suppressed as the crusading ideal became muddied and twisted by misuse and constant failure.

In the years that followed the capture of Jerusalem in 1099, the Franks gradually consolidated their territories, but they were always short of men, for many of the original crusaders returned to the west, while the crusader states never attracted sufficient new settlers to defend their lands adequately. As a result, pilgrims, who came each year to visit the shrines of Palestine, were often attacked by brigands and Moslem raiders, for the crusaders were unable to spare men to protect them.[1] It was this situation which led to the foundation of the Order of the Temple. Its modest beginnings in 1119 are described by William, Archbishop of Tyre:

> In the same year, certain noble men of knightly rank, devoted to God, religious and God-fearing, professed the wish to live in chastity, obedience and without property in perpetuity, binding

themselves in the hands of the lord patriarch to the service of Christ in the manner of regular canons. Among these, the first and most important were the venerable men Hugues de Payns and Godefroi de Saint-Omer. Since they did not have a church, nor a settled place to live, the king conceded a temporary dwelling to them in his palace, which he had below the Temple of the Lord, to the south side. The canons of the Temple of the Lord, under certain conditions, conceded a courtyard which they had near the same place, to be used for the functions of the Order. Moreover, the lord king [Baldwin II] with his nobles, as well as the lord patriarch with his prelates, gave to them certain benefices from their own demesnes, some in perpetuity, some on a temporary basis, from which they could be fed and clothed. The first element of their profession, enjoined on them for the remission of their sins by the lord patriarch and the other bishops, was 'that they should protect the roads and routes to the utmost of their ability against the ambushes of thieves and attackers, especially in regard to the safety of pilgrims'.[2]

They gathered about nine companions, as well as gaining the support of important visiting crusaders like Hugh, Count of Champagne, and Fulk V, Count of Anjou, but they did not achieve wider fame until the Council of Troyes in 1129, which gave the Templars official recognition and commissioned Bernard of Clairvaux to draw up a Rule systematising their early observances.[3]

The Rule contains seventy-two articles which created the Order's basic structure. There were initially two main classes: knights and sergeants or serving brothers. Entrants had to be old enough to bear arms, so there were no oblates as in more conventional Orders.[4] There were to be no associated houses for women, for 'it is very dangerous to join sisters, since the ancient enemy has driven many from the right path to Paradise by the society of women'.[5] The total rejection of women was symbolised by white. 'To all professed knights both in winter and summer we concede white vestments, if they can be obtained, that those who have placed behind them the dark life should know themselves to be united to their Creator in purity and whiteness. What is whiteness but perfect chastity? Chastity is the security of the conscience and the health of the body.'[6] The sergeants or serving brothers wore a black or brown mantle, reflecting their

more lowly social station.[7] Married brothers were allowed affili-
ation to the Order, but they were not permitted to wear the white
habit. At their death their property was left to the brethren, and the
wife was to receive a portion for her maintenance. However, she
must leave the property itself, since brothers who had 'promised
chastity to God' should not remain in the same house as women.[8]
Since the Templars were not ordained, they at first employed outside
priests as chaplains, but during the twelfth century, a separate class
of brother priests was formed.[9] Like other great monastic Orders,
the Temple was allowed property: 'Therefore, justly we judge, since
you are called knights of the Temple . . . that you should have
houses, lands and retainers and possess serfs, and justly rule them,
and the customary service ought to be specially rendered to you.'[10]

The Templars who had been present at the Council of Troyes had
prepared the way with an energetic and successful recruiting campaign in France and England, most of them, like Godefroi de Saint-
Omer, leaving for their homelands with this aim in mind. Hugues de
Payns himself travelled through Champagne, Anjou, Normandy and
Flanders, and he visited England and Scotland.[11] Apart from new
recruits, the Order also began to receive pious grants in the form of
land, grants which established for it a solid economic foundation
in the west, especially in France, and confirmed the initial character
of the Order as being primarily French. However, within a comparatively short time the idea of a Military Order also established itself in
Languedoc and in the Iberian peninsula, where the proximity of the
Moslem enemy kept the crusading movement in the forefront of
people's minds. The potency of this ideal of 'fighting monks' in the
twelfth century is illustrated by the addition of military functions to
the Order of the Hospital, which had been established in the east as
a charitable foundation since at least the 1070s,[12] and the creation
of new Orders in imitation, in Spain and Portugal, where between
1164 and 1170, the Orders of Calatrava, Santiago and Alcántara
were established, while in 1198, the Order of the Teutonic Knights
was officially confirmed by Pope Innocent III.

The expansion of the Temple was given immense impetus by its
close association with Bernard of Clairvaux. In the early 1130s he
responded to a request of Hugues de Payns by writing a tract justifying the concept of a fighting monk. In a sense, his purpose in
writing 'In Praise of the New Knighthood' was to sell the idea of

what he calls 'a new type of knighthood' to western Christendom.[13] The Templar was 'a fearless knight, safe from all sides, who, as the body is covered with iron, so is the soul by the defence of the faith. Without doubt, fortified by both arms, he fears neither demon nor man. Nor indeed is he afraid of death, he who had desired death.' Motivation was what mattered. 'If the cause of the fighting is good, the consequence of the fighting cannot be evil, just as the end will not be judged good when the cause is not good, and it has arisen from an unjust intention.' This sharp contrast could be demonstrated by looking at the secular knights of the time, engaged in their vexatious wars.

> You cover your horses with silks, and I do not know what hanging rags cover your breastplates; you paint your banners, shields and saddles; you decorate your bridles and spurs all over with gold and silver and precious stones, and with such pomp you hasten to death with shameful fury and impudent foolishness. Are these knightly insignia, or are they rather ornaments for women?

The causes of their wars were trivial and frivolous, moved by the irrationality of temper or the appetite for vainglory, or the desire for earthly possessions. The Templars did not adorn themselves, but took no heed of their appearance, for they were often unwashed, their hair covered with dust, and their faces burnt by the sun. They did not carry swords without reason, for their purpose was to smite evil-doers, for when they killed a malefactor, 'it is not homicide, but malicide'. Because their motive was pure, they knew no fear, throwing themselves upon their enemies, whatever the odds, as if these enemies were so many sheep.

St Bernard characteristically catches the mental attitudes and mood of the first half of the twelfth century. Men with little education and no aptitude for the contemplative life of the more traditional Orders, men whose main skill was fighting, were attracted by the combination of frequent action and potential salvation which the Templars had to offer. The Templars embodied many of the deeply held beliefs and attitudes, indeed instincts, which had motivated men to undertake the risks of the First Crusade. In a sense, they were the living justification of the crusade, and while western Christians retained their faith in the righteousness of the crusades, they were eager to back the Military Orders with land and money, and even their own lives. But such success had its own built-in dangers. If Christians needed a personification of the crusade in the form of a tangible Order on which they could lavish support, they were also in equal need of a scapegoat on which they could concentrate their anger when the ideal of the crusade became tarnished. The Templars were irrevocably tied to the crusading movement, and their fortunes rose and fell with that movement.

The papacy too greeted the new Order with enthusiasm. Three bulls issued between 1139 and 1145 defined the position of the Order towards the papacy and the secular clergy. *Omne datum optimum* of 29 March 1139 approved the Templar Rule and took the Order and its houses under papal protection; it granted the Order free disposal of the spoils taken from the infidel, permitted a chaplain in each house, allowed oratories for the use of members and for burials, and gave the leaders the right to expel unworthy or useless members; it forbade the election of an outsider as Master, or the changing of the statutes, except with the consent of the Master and chapter, or homage to be exacted from members of the Order or tithes to be taken from the Order. *Milites Templi* of 9 January 1144 awarded indulgences to benefactors of the Temple and permitted the divine office to be celebrated in a region under interdict when the collectors of the Order were there. *Milicia Dei* of 7 April 1145 allowed the Order to build its own chapels and to bury its dead in their churchyards.[14]

The growth of the Military Orders was part of a wider monastic revival which found particular expression in the Carthusian and the Cistercian Orders. The First Crusade made an important contribution to the climate of religious enthusiasm, in which society as a whole participated, and helped to generate the right atmosphere for the expansion of these Orders. It is not surprising that eventually the crusades should produce Orders of their own. By the middle of the twelfth century their material success was very evident. The Temple acquired estates with their serfs, their animals, their mills, their wine-presses; they acquired moorlands with their sheep; they acquired liquid capital. Very soon the numbers of fighting knights were relatively small in relation to the large body of officials, bailiffs, craftsmen, servants and benefactors who had either joined the Order or become associated with it. The European estates of the Templars became a vast supply organisation for the crusade in the east, providing men and regular contributions called responsions. Very soon the Order also began to finance lay crusaders. The assumption of this banking role was natural, for monasteries had traditionally guarded valuables and been able to lend money. The Templars had the added advantage of owning numerous strongholds in the west and in the crusader states, in which cash, bonds and deeds could be stored, and when it was necessary to move the money armed men were available. During the Second Crusade, the Templars lent Louis VII the large sum of 30,000 *solidi*, and when Philip II left for crusade in 1190, he arranged that during his absence the receipts from the royal demesne should be deposited at the Templars' house in Paris.[15]

During the twelfth century the Templars therefore developed into an international corporation, administering estates and handling large sums of money belonging to the crowned heads and leading lords of Christendom. But most of all they had become identified with the defence of Outremer. In 1172, Theoderich, a pilgrim visiting Jerusalem, described this with naive awe.

> It is not easy for anyone to gain an idea of the power and wealth of the Templars – for they and the Hospitallers have taken possession of almost all the cities and villages with which Judaea was once enriched . . . and have built castles everywhere and filled them with garrisons, besides the very many and, indeed, numberless estates which they are known to possess in other lands.[16]

It seemed natural that, in that same year, the Angevin King Henry II should entrust to the care of the Templars money deposited in expiation for the murder of Becket, which was to pay for the support of two hundred knights in the Holy Land for a year. Again, in the king's testament of 1182, the Templars and the Hospitallers were granted 5,000 silver marks each, while the Grand Masters were to be the joint custodians of another 5,000 marks for the general defence of Jerusalem.[17]

The responsibilities of the Military Orders became even more extensive in the thirteenth century, for weak or absentee kings wielded little power, while after the mid-century the upper baronage of Outremer found it increasingly difficult to maintain the expensive castles needed for defence.[18] Only the Military Orders had resources great enough to fulfil this function adequately. In 1217–18, for instance, the Templars built the huge Pilgrims' Castle ('Atlit) on the coast between Haifa and Caesarea, and in 1240 began to rebuild Safed in Galilee.[19]

The Templars achieved equal fame as warriors; it was largely owing to the skill of the contingent of Templars which accompanied Louis VII on the Second Crusade in 1147–8 that he was able to reach the Holy Land at all.[20] Seventy years later, Jacques de Vitry, Bishop of Acre, could say of them:

> At the will and command of their leader, they proceed to battle, not in an impetuous or disorderly fashion, but prudently and with all caution, being the first to go forward, the last to retreat . . . which is why they became so dreaded by the enemies of the faith of Christ, that one used to pursue a thousand and two, ten thousand.[21]

The Moslems too appreciated their value to the Christian cause. Ibn al-Athir, who was a close observer of Saladin's career, described the Templars and the Hospitallers as 'the fiery heart of the Frankish forces'.[22] After the victory over the Franks at Hattin in 1187, the usually merciful Saladin ordered the decapitation of captured Templars and Hospitallers because they were 'more vigorous in the war than all the rest of the Franks' and he wished to deliver the people from their wickedness.[23]

The growth of the Order was reflected in the Rule. It seems that from about the 1140s the Rule was translated into French and new clauses were later added to cope with particular situations. The French Rule outlines the hierarchical structure of command with the Grand Master at its head and the Seneschal as his deputy. The Order's possessions were divided into provinces. Ten are mentioned in the Rule: Jerusalem, Tripoli, Antioch, France, England, Poitou, Anjou, Portugal, Apulia and Hungary. Each had its own Master and commander who headed a local hierarchy of commanders or preceptors of individual houses. During the thirteenth century a new post was created, second only to the Grand Master himself, that of Visitor of the Order, who was, for practical purposes, the commander of the Templar possessions in the west.[24] The Grand

Master wielded immense power, for the brothers owed him absolute obedience. Most of the important decisions were taken in chapter-meetings, but it appears that the composition of the chapter was very largely at the discretion of the Grand Master, for only the Seneschal had the automatic right of attendance. At the death of a Grand Master a special chapter had to be held in which his successor was elected in accordance with detailed and complicated rules.[25]

The chapter-general held at Jerusalem dealt with weighty matters, but weekly chapter-meetings, which were compulsory for the brothers, were held in local preceptories. General business was dealt with at these chapters, and offenders were also disciplined in accordance with the penal enactments of the Rule. This often involved only minor penances, but more serious offences like simony, treason, heresy, sodomy or the revelation of secrets of the chapter were reserved for higher authority.[26] The weekly chapter was also empowered to admit postulants to the Order. If a majority of the brethren agreed, the candidate was brought into chapter, and, having confirmed his desire to join, was examined by two or three senior brothers.

> They should ask of him if he has a woman, wife or fiancée, and if he has ever made vow or promise to another Order; and if he has a debt to any man . . . which he cannot pay, and if he is healthy of body, if he has not any hidden malady, if he is anybody's serf.

The candidate was then brought before the Master or the presiding officer and admonished:

> Good brother, you ask a very great thing, for of our Order you only see the surface which is the outside. For the surface is that you see we have beautiful horses and harness and eat and drink well and have beautiful clothes, and it seems to you as if you would be much to your ease there. But you do not know the harsh commandments which are within: for it is a hard thing that you, who are master of yourself, should make yourself serf of another.

The candidate then vowed obedience, chastity and poverty, and to follow the good usage and customs of the house, and promised to strive to help conquer the Holy Land. He was then admitted to the Order, the mantle was placed on his shoulder, and with a psalm and prayers, each brother came forward and kissed him on the mouth.[27]

However, while a small band of ragged idealists can be absorbed into society without disruption, an Order which had grown as large as that of the Temple could not exist long before coming into conflict with other vested interests, especially when papal privilege, popular esteem and economic success began to encourage an independence of mind, even an arrogance. The papal privileges made the Temple independent of the local clergy and theoretically of the secular powers, a situation much resented by William of Tyre.

> When they had kept to their proper purpose for a long time, fulfilling their profession discreetly enough, they withdrew themselves from the lord patriarch of Jerusalem, from whom they had received the institution of their Order and first benefices, neglecting 'humility which is known to be the guardian of all the virtues, and indeed spontaneously sits in a place from which it cannot fall', and denying him the obedience which their predecessors had shown. To the churches of God they caused great vexation, taking from them their tithes and first-fruits, and disturbing them in their possessions without just cause.[28]

In 1179 at the Third Lateran Council, William of Tyre led an attack by the secular clergy on the Military Orders, and the council legislated to restrict abuse of Templar privilege.[29]

The Templars were also beginning to suffer some popular harassment. As early as 1160, the pope had found it necessary to issue a bull restraining people from pulling Templars from their horses, treating them dishonestly, or hurling abuse at them, and this bull was frequently repeated thereafter.[30] Between 1199 and 1210 Innocent III several times warned that violence was not to be done to the Templars, their men or their property, and he condemned bishops who by their provocation had caused Templars to fight fellow Christians and had even imprisoned some members of the Order.[31]

The Templars were no more amenable to secular authority in the Kingdom of Jerusalem. William of Tyre recounts four incidents in which they conflicted with the monarchy and each time puts the worst possible construction on their motives. At the siege of Ascalon in 1153 the Grand Master is said to have prevented any but his own men from entering the city when the walls were breached, which led to the temporary failure to capture the city. William maintained that the Grand Master had done this so that the Order could obtain most of the spoils, since it was customary for those who entered first to hold what they could capture. In 1165 the Templars surrendered 'an impregnable cave' beyond the Jordan to the Moslem general, Shirkuh. King Amalric hanged about twelve of the Templars responsible, although the brothers could claim ecclesiastical immunity. Then, in 1168, the Grand Master refused to support Amalric's third attack upon Egypt, and that attack failed. For William the refusal was 'because the master of a rival house [the Hospital] seemed to be the promoter and the leader of the affair'. Finally, in 1173, the Templars killed an envoy from the Moslem sect of the Assassins who had been to Jerusalem to negotiate an alliance with King Amalric, presumably because the king had agreed to release the Assassins from payment of an annual tribute of 2,000 gold pieces to the Temple. Although the Grand Master pleaded clerical immunity, the king arrested the knight responsible for the murder, and had Amalric not died in 1174, William of Tyre says that he would have taken up the matter with the leaders of Christendom.[32]

Although the Archbishop of Tyre's prejudice against the Templars is well known,[33] and various interpretations may be placed upon the events described, the incidents nevertheless suggest how the Order may have begun to provoke resentment. During the thirteenth century criticisms such as those voiced by William of Tyre became more frequent. The papacy, for instance, became less generous in its support. In 1207 Innocent III condemned the Templars for their pride and their abuse of their privileged position. He complained to the Grand Master that 'yielding to the doctrine of demons, they mark the sign of the cross on the chest of any vagabond', that

> moreover they do not care about adding sin to sin like a long rope, alleging that whoever, having collected 2 or 3 *denarii* annually for them, will have joined their fraternity, cannot lawfully be deprived of ecclesiastical burial, even if they are excommunicate; and through this, adulterers, manifest usurers and other false criminals excommunicated from the Church, are, by insolence

Bernard, Abbot of Clairvaux, who was canonised in 1174, was a key figure in the western Church from the 1120s until his death in 1153. He was highly influential at the Council of Troyes in 1129, where the Templars received their first Rule. This late fourteenth-century Italian painting emphasises his continuing reputation over two centuries after his death. Such impeccable early credentials made it impossible to claim that the Temple was corrupt from the outset. *Below*, Bertrand de Got, Archbishop of Bordeaux, was crowned pope as Clement V at Lyons in November 1305, after a vacancy which, because of deep divisions among the cardinals, had lasted for sixteen months

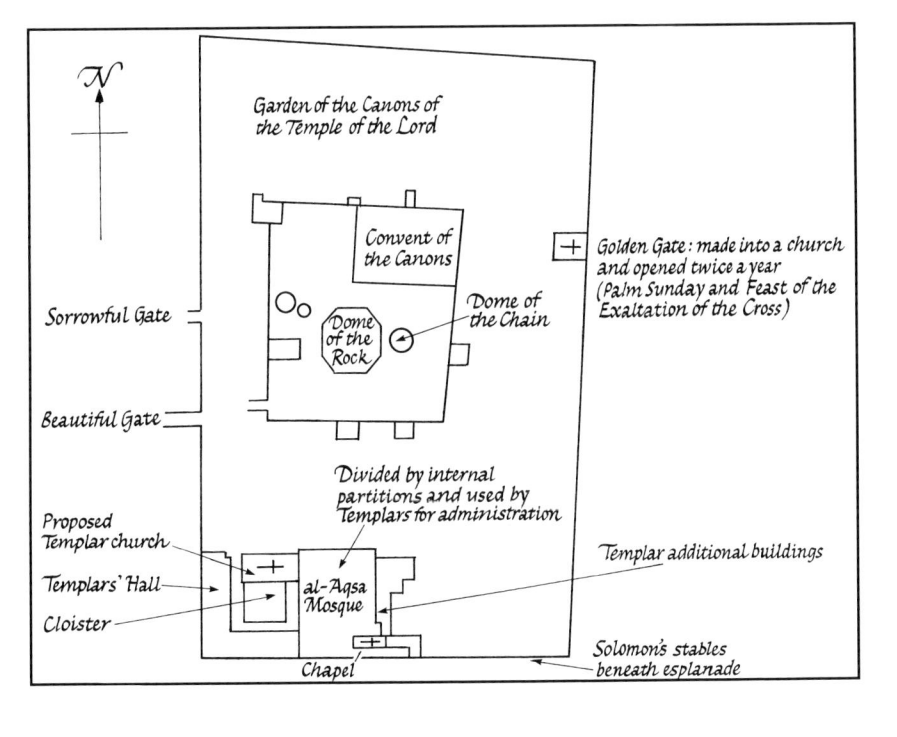

In Jerusalem, the first Templars were given shelter in the al-Aqsa Mosque on the Temple platform, which the crusaders believed to have been the Temple of Solomon. They took over the whole of the southern part of the platform in the mid-1120s when King Baldwin II moved his base across the city to the Tower of David

Garden of the Canons of the Temple of the Lord

Convent of the Canons

Golden Gate: made into a church and opened twice a year (Palm Sunday and Feast of the Exaltation of the Cross)

Sorrowful Gate

Dome of the Rock

Dome of the Chain

Beautiful Gate

Divided by internal partitions and used by Templars for administration

Proposed Templar church

Templars' Hall

al-Aqsa Mosque

Templar additional buildings

Cloister

Chapel

Solomon's stables beneath esplanade

of this kind, buried in their cemeteries just like the Catholic faithful.[34]

In 1265, after a dispute between the papacy and the Order, Clement IV wrote to the Grand Master and brothers reminding them that 'if the Church removed for a short while the hand of its protection from you in the face of the prelates and the secular princes, you could not in any way subsist against the assaults of these prelates or the force of the princes'. The Templars would be well advised not to beat against the edifice 'on whose help, after God, you are totally dependent'. The pope suggested that the Templars display greater humility and mildness.[35]

Certainly, by the middle of the thirteenth century the motives of the Templars were often impugned. During Saint Louis's Crusade to Egypt in 1248 the Grand Master, Guillaume de Sonnac, advised the Count of Artois against attacking Mansourah for perfectly respectable tactical reasons. Matthew Paris, however, used this occasion to attack the Temple, and reports that the Count of Artois accused the Military Orders of hindering the crusade for their own profit, because if Egypt were conquered they would no longer be able to dominate the land from which they drew such large revenues.[36] This lack of trust was directed with particular vehemence against Guillaume de Beaujeu, the last Grand Master to rule in Palestine. He cultivated contacts within the Egyptian army who warned him about impending attacks. When, at his request, the Sultan Qalawun offered peace to Acre if each man there would pay a Venetian penny, the Grand Master barely escaped with his life when he announced these terms to the citizens, for they considered him a traitor.[37] On 15 May 1291 Acre finally fell to al-Asraf, Qalawun's son and successor, and Guillaume died fighting to hold a breach in the wall. The survivors fled to Cyprus, where the remnants of the Order set up their headquarters.

The last Grand Master was Jacques de Molay, already in his middle years when he became Master at about the end of 1293. He tried sincerely to re-establish the Christians on the Palestinian mainland. In 1294 and 1295 he visited Italy, France and England in a desperate attempt to gather new supplies and men for the east. He organised shipments of grain and arms and clothing for the brethren in Cyprus and equipped galleys to protect the island. He took part in

naval raids on Rosetta, Alexandria, Acre and Tortosa, and even attempted to establish a permanent base on the tiny island of Ruad,
off Tortosa, from which to launch attacks upon the Saracens. However, in 1302, the vastly superior Egyptian forces wiped out the
small Templar garrison.[38]

This almost total lack of success is in marked contrast to the
rapid growth of the Order after the Council of Troyes in 1129.
There was a growing disillusionment with the whole crusading
movement; repeated failure led many to doubt the value of the crusade, for even the saintly King Louis had failed to achieve victory.
Perhaps God no longer approved of such expeditions; perhaps the
answer was to be found not in militancy but in peaceful conversion.
Moreover, too often in the thirteenth century, the crusade had been
used for narrow political ends, particularly by popes like Innocent
IV. Looked at in broader terms the crusade was a product of the
expansionist society of the early twelfth century, unfettered by
strong political ties. In contrast, in the second half of the thirteenth
century there can be discerned the first warnings of the economic
collapse which was to characterise much of the fourteenth century.
Inevitably, those associated with the movement were adversely
affected by this declining enthusiasm, and ultimately found themselves blamed for failure. In the long term the chief victim was to be
the papacy, but the immediate anger was thrown against its most
prominent crusading protégés, the Military Orders, whose whole
raison d'être lay in a crusade which was no longer supported and a
kingdom which no longer existed. The crusading movement did not
collapse overnight. The Council of Lyons had been convened by
Pope Gregory X in 1274 partly to formulate a realistic plan for a
new crusade, but this met with little support, and even Guillaume de
Beaujeu, Grand Master of the Temple, was not prepared to commit
himself to the idea of a general passage. One of the Templars at the
council compared the crusades to 'a little dog barking at a great one,
who takes no heed of him'.[39]

Nevertheless, although little practical help was forthcoming in
1291, this should not obscure the fact that contemporaries did not
see the losses of that year as so decisive a turning-point as they now
appear in longer perspective. Clement V, who became pope in
November 1305, was determined to bring together another great
crusade. In June 1306 he summoned Fulk de Villaret of the Hospital

and Jacques de Molay of the Temple, to meet him at Poitiers to advise him about this.[40] Jacques de Molay set out for France accompanied by Raimbaud de Caron, Preceptor of Cyprus, who might be thought to possess special knowledge of the matter in hand, and a small escort of knights. He was clearly not intending to live permanently in France, for the other leading Templar officials were left in Cyprus, together with most of the cash reserves.[41] He arrived late in 1306 or early in 1307, and probably visited the pope at Poitiers. He had reached Paris by June 1307, when he held a chapter-meeting of the Order there.[42]

In response to the pope's request for advice, Molay had prepared two *mémoires*. One was concerned with the organisation of a new crusade. He proposed that fifteen thousand knights and five thousand foot-soldiers should be provided by the western kings and a fleet by the Italian cities.[43] This clearly demonstrates his dilemma: limited schemes could only achieve temporary effect, whereas large-scale expeditions were no more than wishful thinking. Yet to admit this would have meant a fundamental reappraisal of the whole role and function of the Military Orders, of which Jacques de Molay, an elderly man, set in his ways and narrowly concerned with tradition, was not capable. His second *mémoire*, which dealt with a proposal to unite the Military Orders, provides ample evidence of Molay's limitations. He noted that this had been discussed at the Council of Lyons in 1274, that after 1291 Nicholas IV had revived the idea, while Boniface VIII had also looked at the scheme, but had rejected it. Molay then attempted to set out a balanced argument, but the whole tone of the work is hostile to the idea. He argued that innovation is always dangerous; that members of an Order should not be compelled to change their rule of life; that the charitable system of the Orders might be threatened; that discord might arise if duplicate preceptories were suppressed. On the other hand the rivalry between the Orders was beneficial, and the existence of two Military Orders had always proved of great tactical advantage. Molay then tried to put the opposing case, but it is thin indeed. He thought that a united Order could defend itself better against lay and clerical attacks, and that the expenses of the two Orders would be reduced by union. He ended by assuring the pope that he would assemble the experienced men of his Order to advise Clement if he so wished, and by maintaining that no other means would be found of financing the crusade so cheaply as through the Military Orders. If the pope intended to assign fixed and regular revenues to the Orders, Molay preferred that they should be granted separately.[44]

Molay offered no constructive suggestions as alternatives, and he showed only the faintest sense that the Templars might be vulnerable; the growth of hostility to the Military Orders seems to puzzle rather than frighten him. But there were others – especially in France – who demanded urgent reform. One of the most vocal was a Norman lawyer, Pierre Dubois. Much of what he wrote was useful propaganda in favour of the policies of the French monarchy, although, except as a royal advocate, he never seems to have obtained an official position. The exact extent of his unofficial connections with high politics remains a mystery. In *c.*1306 he wrote a long tract, 'Concerning the Recovery of the Holy Land'. An integral part of his plan was the union of the Military Orders. These Orders

> have such a great quantity of rents, crops and possessions on this side of the Mediterranean Sea, which for a long time now have made insufficient contribution to the Holy Land. Since on occasions of great necessity these Orders have many times been divided among themselves, and on this account in confusion, and therefore with very great scandal exposed to mockery, it is expedient and necessary, if the cause of the Holy Land is to go forward, to unite them in administration, habit, status and goods, as will seem expedient to a holy council. Those members living in the Holy Land should subsist from their goods there and in Cyprus.

By this means 800,000 *livres tournois* would be raised annually to transport crusaders across the sea. 'Those members who, up to the present, have not been able conveniently to cross the sea and live there, should be driven into the monasteries of the Cistercian Order and other rich establishments, to do penance for their excesses.' Once the annual income gained from these policies is seen, 'the bad faith of the Templars and the Hospitallers will be apparent and it will be clear how, up to this time, for this thing [their wealth], they have betrayed the Holy Land and sinned towards it'.[45] Although Dubois's ideas here relate to both the great Military Orders, there is a brief postscript, apparently added shortly after the completion of the treatise, which is aimed much more specifically at the Templars. Perhaps by the summer of 1307, Dubois had heard of hostile rumours circulating about the Order. Once the union of the Orders had been completed, and the property granted to this new organisation, 'it will be expedient to destroy the Order of the Templars completely, and for the needs of justice to annihilate it totally'.[46]

THE PAPACY

In 1305 the city of Lyons was part of the Empire, but French influence was paramount there. Philip IV owned the suburb of Saint-Just and held suzerainty over the town. The towns of the Rhône–Saône corridor, including not only Lyons, but also Vienne and Avignon, were only in a technical sense outside the French kingdom, for they were continually subject to the creeping expansionism at which the Capetian dynasty had become so adept. In November 1305 this French presence was very striking. Philip IV and his brothers, Charles of Valois and Louis of Evreux, had arrived with large escorts. John, Duke of Brittany, and Henry, Count of Luxembourg, were also there, as were the ambassadors of Edward I of England and James II of Aragon, and clergy from all parts of Christendom. The occasion of this great gathering was the coronation of a new pope, Bertrand de Got, Archbishop of Bordeaux, who, after a conclave at Perugia lasting eleven months, had, on 5 June 1305, been chosen to succeed Benedict XI. He took the name of Clement V.[47] He was a Gascon of modest family, but by 1305 his kin held several important church offices and as pope he was a notorious nepotist. He had become Bishop of Comminges in 1295 and Archbishop of Bordeaux in 1299,[48] and it is likely that this was the summit of his ambition. It was certainly all that he could expect, for he was increasingly crippled by a serious and recurring illness. In 1314, Tolomeo da Lucca, who was able to observe the pope closely during his reign, described how 'for a long time he had been ill with the gripes, as a result of which he lost his appetite. Sometimes he suffered from dysentery, and through that the gripes were eased. Sometimes he suffered vomiting.'[49] But Bertrand was chosen because he was an outsider to the complicated politics and rivalries of the cardinals' college. For the cardinals were acutely aware of the tremendous and shattering events in which the papacy had been involved over the previous decade. Fully to understand these events it is necessary to trace briefly the historical background of the papacy up to the moment of this election.

The role of the papacy as it had been interpreted by the holders of the office in the thirteenth century had largely been conceived in the second half of the eleventh century. In the early middle ages Church appointments had come under lay control, for lay rulers needed the administrative services of a literate clergy, and the Church commanded great wealth as a consequence of generations of pious endowment. Many of the clergy appointed by lay patrons were unsuited to their office, and it was this situation which the reformers, inspired by Leo IX (1049–54) and Gregory VII (1073–85), had sought to change. They had hoped to free the Church from lay control and to create a moral reformation of the clergy, and through them the whole of the Christian population, under papal leadership. They conceived of a united Christendom controlled by the pope, who held his position directly from God, and whose power transcended that of the secular rulers. From Gregory VII onwards the medieval popes grappled with the problems which had to be overcome if this great ideal was to be achieved. It was not to be expected that the secular powers would give up their entrenched positions without a struggle, but in the twelfth century the papacy was the better equipped, both in its intellectual justification and its administrative skill, to push forward its plans. A particularly potent weapon was the systematic application of canon law to papal activities from the middle years of the twelfth century, a result of the development of a school of canon law at the University of Bologna. This gave the papacy a vital advantage over its secular rivals, because from this time both the popes and their administrators were trained jurists, who by means of canon law could apply the theories of papal government to practical matters.[50] As yet, most secular rulers were relatively weak, their administrative organs primitive, while the extent of their control over the lands that they nominally ruled was in places tenuous and almost everywhere uneven. The reformers were able to create new moral standards for the clergy, and the overall suitability and quality of at least the holders of important church offices improved markedly. Moreover, there was then little effective counter to papal claims to the leadership of Christendom; only the German Emperors tried to dispute them at all vigorously, but in the end they could not have felt very satisfied with the results of their efforts.

However, from the early thirteenth century, this situation was beginning to change. With most rulers of any consequence appointment to high ecclesiastical office was often a matter of compromise between king, pope and local electors. More serious, the principle of papal leadership was never fully free of challenge. Alexander III and Frederick Barbarossa had struggled mightily over this issue, and after Innocent III's death in 1216, a new conflict increasingly came to occupy the papacy with Barbarossa's grandson, Frederick II. The Hohenstaufen saw themselves as the heirs of the Carolingians and of the Roman Empire itself, and such a view did not admit papal claims. This theoretical clash was reinforced by territorial problems. The Hohenstaufen laid claim to Italy, and wished, as supposed successors of Augustus, to control Rome. This necessarily led to conflict with the popes, who based their claim to be Vicars of Christ on their tenure of St Peter's See of Rome. This conflict intensified in Frederick II's reign, for he was King of Sicily as well as Emperor. If he had succeeded in his attempted conquest of Lombardy and Tuscany, the Papal State would have been encircled and the grand theoretical claims of the papacy reduced to empty formulae. It was to avoid this curtailment of independence that the thirteenth-century popes fought the Hohenstaufen to a standstill. After Frederick's death in 1250 the papacy found a champion in Charles of Anjou, brother of Louis IX of France, who, with papal subsidies, destroyed the remaining Hohenstaufen and made himself King of Sicily. He proved, however, an equal threat to papal independence, and in 1281 secured the election of a French pope, Martin IV, who became little more than an Angevin puppet. But, in 1282, a popular rising in Sicily enabled the Aragonese to take control of the island. The papacy had been fortuitously freed from this new threat, but equally had suffered a severe blow to its prestige, so close had been its association with the Angevins. The succeeding popes therefore spent much of their time, energy and resources in a futile attempt to recapture Sicily.[51]

These events highlight the essential dilemma of the reformed papacy: the changes desired could not be fully brought about without the means, financial, legal and military, to implement them, but increased resistance produced increased emphasis on these means at the ultimate expense of the end, which slowly faded from the fore-front of the papal mind. During the thirteenth century the papacy centralised its administration: more and more appeals were chan-nelled to the papal courts, more and more benefices were reserved to the papacy, more and more money was collected from an increas-ingly unwilling clergy to finance papal projects. More often than ever before the papacy backed up its commands with the weapons of its spiritual armoury, so much so that excommunication began to lose the bite that had made it so effective in the early years of reform. The inspiring spiritual leadership of an Urban II was being replaced by the political fanaticism and the legal drive of an Innocent IV.

The thirteenth-century papacy was also faced by the growth of heresy. In the early middle ages deviations were relatively minor and none caught the popular imagination, but from the later years of the twelfth century the papacy was forced to recognise a growing ad-herence to heretical belief among wide sectors of society. Most im-portant and dangerous was a heresy, widespread in Languedoc and northern and central Italy, known as Catharism or Albigensianism. Catharism was a dualist heresy. Cathars believed in the existence of two co-eternal principles of light and darkness. To the former they attributed the creation of souls and of angels, to the latter the cre-ation of the visible universe. They believed that Satan had seduced angelic souls and had imprisoned them in material bodies; but that Jesus, Son of the God of Light, had come to free them from this bondage. He only had the appearance of a material body, so he could not suffer or be resurrected since he did not belong to Satan's material world. Jesus had accomplished his mission by establishing the true Church, that of the Cathars. Unfortunately, at the same time Satan had established a false church, the Church of Rome, which postulated the Incarnation, Resurrection and Redemption, and adopted the cross as a symbol of its faith. The logical application of this was the rejection of all the sacraments of the Catholic Church. The only true path was through the Cathar Church in which the souls, imprisoned in their bodies of matter, could be released. This was accomplished by a baptism of the spirit, the *consolamentum*, a laying on of hands by the spiritual elite of this church, the *Bon-hommes* or *Perfecti*. The *Bonhommes* lived chaste, ascetic lives, eat-ing only the least material foods, such as fruit, fish and vegetables, and living off the charity of their supporters, known as *Credentes* or

Believers. The great majority of *Credentes* were unable to sustain lives of such rigour, and they lived in ordinary society, concealing their beliefs when it was necessary and only receiving the *consolamentum* at the point of death.[52] This heresy was therefore much more than an argument over an intellectual conceit or even a fringe reforming movement which had overstepped the mark; to the papacy Catharism was an attack upon the very fabric of Christian society. To take an aspect particularly relevant to the accusations against the Templars: since Satan was the creator of the material world, then he was responsible for the propagation of vile, material beings. Marriage as a permanent union for such propagation was therefore to be condemned.[53] Opponents of the Cathars seized upon this to accuse them of sanctioning sexual unions outside marriage or even of favouring what the Catholic Church regarded as perverted sexual practices which did not result in conception.

Faced with a heresy so far-reaching the papacy was forced to recognise that the Church had no effective means of dealing with the problem. A series of church councils had excommunicated heretics and their protectors, and this had been backed by preaching missions, but Catharism in Languedoc continued to grow in popularity, in some areas becoming quite overtly the religion of the region.[54] Innocent III launched a crusade against the Cathars of Languedoc in 1209, but it proved ineffective in the long term because it was too dependent on the quality of individual leaders, while the knights who took part could only be required to serve for forty days. It was necessary for Louis VIII of France to undertake a second crusade before the south finally capitulated, and that was fought more for the benefit of the Capetian monarchy than of the Roman Church.

The crusade had failed as a means of suppressing heresy, and the papacy was led to develop a new weapon in defence of orthodoxy, the Inquisition. The old methods for dealing with heresy had relied upon certain cumbersome procedures deriving from Roman law. Heretics could either be denounced by a person in authority (*denuntiatio*) or accused by a member of the community (*accusatio*), or the bishop could proceed against a suspect through *inquisitio*, trying to obtain a confession, taking testimony from witnesses and finally making a judgement.[55] These methods were not very helpful against Catharism, for such an approach belonged to the early middle ages, when the Church was troubled only by isolated individual deviants and when legal studies were largely in abeyance. In 1184 Lucius III issued the bull *Ad abolendam* which enacted that bishops or archdeacons were, at least once a year, personally to visit every parish where heresy was thought to exist. If any heretics were found they were to be excommunicated and then handed over to the secular arm, which meant imprisonment and confiscation of property.[56] This established an episcopal inquisition, but the system remained inadequate. It was Gregory IX (1227–41) who developed a really systematic Inquisition which he entrusted to the newly founded Dominican and Franciscan Orders. Gregory IX's statutes allowed a period of grace for heretics to come forward, they called for witnesses to testify against heretics, they set out methods for the interrogation of the accused, and they provided for the reconciliation of repentant heretics and for the condemnation of the stubborn. Those who remained obstinate ultimately could be sent to the secular arm for punishment. This involved the confiscation of property and sometimes death by burning, officially the work of the state. In 1252 Innocent IV allowed the use of torture in the bull *Ad extirpanda*.[57]

A person brought before the Inquisition faced men educated in canon and civil law, trained in theological argument, and experienced in dealing with the cunning. Bernard Gui, the Dominican who between 1307 and 1323 was an inquisitor in the Toulousain, wrote a five-part treatise describing inquisitorial procedure, which is a useful guide to the procedure current when the Templars were brought to trial. When a suspect was brought to Bernard Gui's attention, a citation was sent out. If the person concerned did not appear, he was provisionally excommunicated, a sentence which became definitive after the lapse of one year. The implications of this were serious, for nobody was supposed to have contact with him and if anyone knew where he was hiding he was obliged, on pain of canonical penalty, to tell the inquisitor.[58] The secular authorities were empowered to arrest a suspect. The King of France ordered his officials 'to supply help and suitable advice to the inquisitors and to obey the inquisitors in everything which appertains to the office of the Inquisition'.[59]

The accused had few chances of proving his innocence. He was interrogated by the inquisitor and his assistants and a summary of the proceedings was recorded by a notary. The aim was to establish guilt, either by confession or by the use of testimonial evidence. He was not allowed a defending advocate, even if he could have found one, and witnesses were reluctant to testify on his behalf for fear of guilt by association. Hostile witnesses were allowed to remain anonymous on the grounds that they might otherwise be intimidated, and the accused could only read a précis of their depositions. In contrast to secular proceedings, all kinds of witnesses could be used, even perjurers, criminals and the excommunicate. The accused could only list his enemies in the hope that some names would coincide with the witnesses.[60] It seems however that the inquisitors' real aim was to obtain a confession, for, without the admission of guilt, a heretic could not be reconciled to the Church. If confession could not be obtained spontaneously, compulsion could be used, firstly by imprisonment under increasingly harsh conditions and ultimately by torture, supposedly of a limited kind which did not involve the effusion of blood or permanent mutilation.[61] Once guilt was established, sentence was pronounced in the form of a 'general sermon' held in public. Heretics who were believed to be genuinely repentant were reconciled to the Church, and penances imposed which varied from a monetary fine for minor transgressions to harsh imprisonment, the prisoner chained in irons and fed only a diet of 'the bread of sadness and the water of tribulation'. Sometimes the guilty had to wear badges on their clothing as signs of their infamy, a provision which often led to their molestation. In other cases they had to undertake a pilgrimage. But those who refused to abjure their heresy, or who retracted their confessions, together with the obstinate who refused to confess the errors of which they were accused, were delivered to the secular arm to receive an appropriate punishment, usually death by burning.[62] Their property was confiscated by the secular rulers, and their heirs debarred from holding any public office, usually for at least two generations.[63]

The harsh legalism of the inquisitorial proceedings reflects the changing nature of the priorities of the Catholic Church in the thirteenth century. The papacy presided over a large centralised administrative, legal and financial structure which encompassed a wide range of responsibilities and roles, from the raising of a papal army to fight political opponents in Italy, to the judgement of adultery or usury. This organisation had finally overcome the Hohenstaufen threat and it had rolled over the heretics of Languedoc and created a permanent organisation to continue the work indefinitely. But this had been achieved at a heavy cost to papal prestige. To many people the papacy had degenerated into just another political power, devoid of any moral purpose or lofty spiritual aims. This loss of prestige was doubly important because it coincided with a significant development in the secular world. While the papacy had been locked in battle with the Empire, France and England had been steadily achieving coherence in administration, backed by a growing sense of loyalty towards the monarchy from the general populace. The extent of these changes should not be exaggerated, for the monarchs had many unsolved problems with which to contend, and in the fourteenth century the French rulers in particular were to sustain many set-backs in their efforts to achieve a unified realm. Nevertheless, the papacy was soon to find that the chief opponent of its goal of universal domination was no longer the Emperor, now too weak for any such pretensions, but the more compact secular monarchy of France.

In the last decade of the thirteenth century the state of the Church was reflected in a series of acute crises at its very centre. When Nicholas IV died in 1292 the cardinals took two years before electing the hermit Peter of Murrone, who became Celestine V. This represented a short-lived triumph for those elements in the Church, such as the Spiritual Franciscans, who were in revolt against the excessive concentration of the papacy upon administration and politics during the previous century. It met with predictable disaster, for within a few months the papal administration was in chaos and Celestine was persuaded to resign. At Christmas 1294 Cardinal Benedict Gaetani was elected as Boniface VIII.[64] He was a man of entirely different temper and experience, fully in tune with the lawyer-popes who had preceded him. There is no doubt that he was able, but his personality was flawed by a lack of diplomacy and tact. He was uncompromising and arrogant when he believed himself right, and it was perhaps because of this that the developments of the thirteenth century came to a head during his pontificate. Moreover, he had many enemies. Within Italy he had alienated the powerful family of the Colonna by his excessive favours to his own family, the Gaetani. The groups which the Spiritual Franciscans represented deeply resented the removal of their candidate and blamed Boniface for it. Finally, in 1296, Boniface provoked a headlong collision with the ruler of the most powerful state in western Europe, the Most Christian King of France, Philip IV.

Both Edward I of England and Philip IV were taxing their clergy to finance their war with each other. In February 1296 Boniface issued the bull *Clericis laicos* in which he placed under interdict those who taxed the clergy without the pope's permission, since this contravened a decree of 1215. Boniface's vulnerability at once became evident. Philip IV effectively blocked the receipt of papal taxation from France, while Boniface's Italian enemies called for a council to try him for heresy and simony. The pope seems to have decided that prudent retreat was the best course, and in July 1297, in the bull *Etsi de statu*, he gave the kings the right to decide when the kingdom was in danger and therefore when the clergy should be taxed.[65] The conflict then subsided, but the basic issue of the relative authority of pope and king in the Capetian lands remained unsettled. In 1301 Bernard Saisset, Bishop of Pamiers, on very thin evidence based upon the depositions of tortured servants and some drunken personal attacks upon the king by the bishop himself, was tried and condemned for blasphemy, heresy, simony and treason by the king's officials, without reference to the pope. Boniface reacted to this new outrage upon ecclesiastical jurisdiction, and by implication, upon papal authority, by a series of demands that Philip justify himself, which culminated in the bull *Ausculta fili* of December 1301. It was quite clear and established law that the Roman pontiff had supreme power over ecclesiastical dignities, but the king abused this by impeding collations, dragging prelates and clerics before the royal tribunal and taking the revenues of vacant benefices. The pope was therefore determined to summon a council in Rome to deal with these matters.[66]

Philip's government acted equally vigorously. The bull was replaced by a slanted summary of its main points which gave the impression that the pope was claiming the feudal overlordship of France, while on 10 April 1302 the French Estates-General was called to add the backing of public opinion to what the government was presenting as an attack upon the French people. The king's reply stated that despite the fact that the king and his predecessors had always been recognised as holding the kingdom from God alone, the pope had decreed that the king should submit to him in temporal matters and should hold the kingdom directly from the papacy. The pope had also called to his presence the prelates and university theologians of France for the purpose of correcting the alleged excesses and abuses committed by the king and his officers against the clergy and churches. This was simply a pretext to impoverish and ruin the kingdom by depriving it of some of its best men. The Church of Rome oppressed the Gallican Church by its reservations and arbitrary collations of important sees so that they were placed in the hands of strangers. At the same time the churches had been crushed by financial exactions. These abuses had developed to such an extent under Boniface VIII that they could not be tolerated any longer.[67]

The French clergy now faced an acute dilemma of divided loyalties. They wrote querulously to the pope, telling him of the grave scandals which had arisen in France because the laity no longer held them in any esteem, and they pleaded with him to revoke the edict for the council, that peace might be re-established within the Church of France.[68] Boniface had no intention of another retreat in the ignominious fashion of 1297. The council was held early in November 1302, and was followed by the issue of the famous bull *Unam sanctam* which, basing its arguments and language upon two centuries of papal tradition, set forth uncompromisingly the doctrine of papal supremacy. In the summer of 1303, the pope drew up the bull *Super petri solio*, excommunicating Philip. He intended to publish this on 8 September.[69]

But the government of Philip IV had not been inactive. In June 1303, Guillaume de Nogaret, Philip's leading minister since 1302, framed charges against Boniface, including murder, idolatry, sodomy, simony and heresy. A council should be assembled to try the pope.[70] Nor were these empty words. Assemblies were held in Paris and in the provinces where the pope's crimes were enumerated.[71] In August 1303 Nogaret travelled to Italy with a small escort and, on 7 September, together with members of the Colonna family, burst upon the pope at Anagni. They insulted and threatened him, but the plan did not succeed, for Nogaret and the Colonna quarrelled, and Nogaret had not the resources to take the pope back to France in the face of growing opposition. He was forced to release Boniface. But the pope, now well into his eighties, died the following month.[72]

The new pope, Benedict XI, endeavoured to calm the political climate both by delay and by separating his dealings with Philip from those with his advisers, especially Nogaret. Between March and May 1304 he lifted all sentences upon Philip and on the Colonna, but Nogaret remained excommunicated.[73] From this time therefore

Nogaret retained a personal interest in the demand for a trial, now posthumous, of Boniface VIII, and pursued this goal with great determination until action was eventually taken in 1310 and 1311. This demand became interwoven with the trial of the Templars, and had an enduring impact upon Clement V's policies. Benedict's measures had restored the King and the Kingdom of France to the status which they held before the issue of the bulls of Boniface VIII. But Benedict died on 7 July 1304, and the cardinals were once more forced into conclave to find a suitable candidate for what had now become two almost irreconcilable parties: the Bonifacians and the partisans of France. For this reason they eventually turned to the Gascon Bertrand de Got as a compromise.

Clement was crowned on 14 November in the Church of Saint-Just in Lyons by the Cardinal Napoleone Orsini, leader of the pro-French faction in the conclave. The ceremony over, a solemn procession left the church and began to wind its way through the narrow streets, packed with spectators. The pope rode a white palfrey; his bridle was held on one side by the king's brother, Charles of Valois, and on the other by John, Duke of Brittany. Immediately behind rode the king himself. Suddenly, a section of a wall collapsed under the unaccustomed weight of the spectators and fell upon the papal party. John of Brittany was mortally wounded, Charles of Valois was seriously injured, and Clement was thrown from his horse. Clement was shaken but not badly hurt, but to those who saw and talked of the incident, this seemed a bad omen for the success of the reign.[74] Certainly Clement carried a heavy weight from the past. To invest the pretensions of the reforming popes once more with some kind of reality and to erase with dignity and honour the scandals of recent years needed vision, drive, health, and above all, opportunity, but Clement possessed none of these. Throughout his pontificate illness rendered him inactive from time to time: in August 1306 he was 'on the edge of the tomb', and during September he was unable to conduct business. Again, the following year, while travelling to meet King Philip IV at Poitiers, illness forced him to break his journey for fifteen days at the monastery of Baignes. These attacks became more frequent as he grew older, particularly after 1309.[75]

He had been elected mainly for his negative qualities: he did not appear violently attached to either the French or the Bonifacian party. He was not a French subject and he had attended Boniface's

council at Rome in November 1302, which had been so hostile to
the French monarchy.[76] On the other hand, to the French he must
have seemed potentially more tractable than any remote Italian who
was likely to view French demands more dispassionately than a
candidate from nearer home. The Cardinal Napoleone Orsini, pen-
sioner of the King of France to the extent of 1,000 florins per annum
since 1303, wrote, after Clement's death, that by the choice of the
late pope the cardinals believed that 'the kingdom and the king had
been magnificently exalted',[77] and indeed, it had quickly become
evident that Philip and his government could effectively keep papal
independence within quite narrow limits. The coronation had been
at Lyons despite the pope's initial choice of Vienne,[78] and once the
formalities were completed, Philip and his ministers were on hand to
ensure that French affairs remained the chief papal preoccupation.
On 15 December the number of cardinals was increased from sixteen to twenty-eight, of whom sixteen were Italian, ten French, one
English and one Spanish. It has been calculated that relatives of the
pope and royal partisans from the French clergy reduced the Bonifacians in the Sacred College to a minority of nine.[79] Four of the new
cardinals, Nicolas de Fréauville, Bérenger Frédol, Etienne de Suisy
and Pierre de la Chapelle, played prominent roles in the proceedings
against the Templars, both in the negotiations between pope and
king and in the tribunals which conducted inquiries against the
Order in 1308 and after. At least two were pensioners of the king. In
1306 Etienne de Suisy was granted an annual pension of 1,000 *livres
tournois*, and in October 1308 Pierre de la Chapelle received a payment of 16,000 *petites livres tournois*.[80] Philip also made progress
on specific issues as well. In the following months Clement quashed
the proceedings against the Colonnas for their part in the attack at
Anagni and revoked the bulls *Clericis laicos* and *Unam sanctam*. A
tenth for three years was granted for Philip's Flemish wars. He was
however more circumspect with the more extreme of French wishes:
the canonisation of Celestine V and the inauguration of proceedings
against Boniface VIII. Here can be seen the personal interest of
Nogaret, who was particularly concerned about his continued excommunication.[81]

Throughout 1306 affairs in France continued to keep the pope
fully occupied – he was vitally interested in a negotiated peace between England and France as a prelude to the gathering of a new

The Templars built up a network of preceptories across Latin Christendom. In the
1170s at Cressac in Charente they decorated their chapel with a series of colourful
frescoes. These scenes recall the defeat of Nur-ad-Din, ruler of Syria, near Krak des
Chevaliers in 1163, a campaign in which two local lords, Hugues de Lusignan,
Count of La Marche, and Geoffroi Martel, brother of the Count of Angoulême,
took part

In May 1189, the German Emperor Frederick Barbarossa set out from Regensburg at the head of the largest ever crusading army. In this illustration from Peter of Eboli's *Liber ad Honorem Augusti* (1195–6), he gestures towards the city of Jerusalem, supported by a phalanx of Templars. *Below*, Templar discipline in battle was an essential part of their military reputation. Their distinctive piebald banner, drawn by the St Albans chronicler Matthew Paris, both signalled the way forward and acted as a rallying point. *Bottom*, All monastic orders cultivated an institutional memory. For the Templars, who grew wealthy through donations and financial transactions, their early poverty was a cherished symbol. Both in Matthew Paris's drawing and on their seals, this was encapsulated in the depiction of two knights riding on one horse

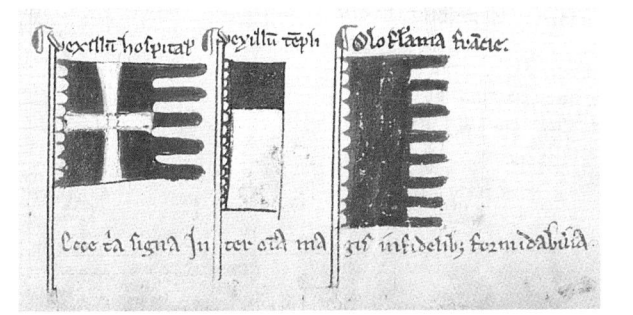

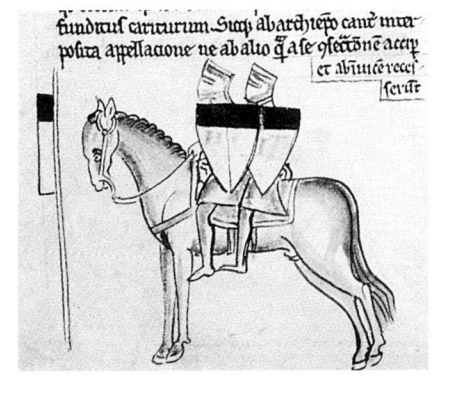

crusade and knew that no progress could be made in either matter if he went to Rome. In May 1306 he met Philip at Poitiers to discuss these affairs and the proposed trial of Boniface. Meanwhile, he proposed that the king abandon the proceedings against Boniface in return for the annulment of all the pope's acts against France. Nogaret was to be absolved but, as a penance, he was to go on a crusade within five years from which he could only return with the pope's permission. But the king rejected this compromise.[82] It was this web of circumstance which finally contributed to Clement's decision in 1308 to set up a papal establishment at Avignon, just outside the Kingdom of France, on a semi-permanent basis.

THE FRENCH MONARCHY

When Philip the Fair became king in October 1285 he was the eleventh member of his family in the direct male line to occupy the French throne, and he represented a tradition which reached back to the accession of Hugh Capet in 987.[83] Initially, the authority of the dynasty had been largely restricted to the royal demesne centred on the Ile-de-France, but the steady enforcement of the rights of feudal overlordship, at first on a small scale against the petty vassals of the royal demesne, and then in conflict with the might of the Angevin Empire during the reign of Philip II (1180–1223), had greatly increased the dynasty's prestige and real power. Philip II's defeat of the Angevin John Lackland had added Normandy, Anjou, Maine and Touraine to the royal demesne. Other gains followed in the thirteenth century. The County of Toulouse fell after the blows of the Albigensian Crusade, finally reverting directly to the royal demesne in 1271. The monarchy had also been strengthened by the support of the Church, which regarded kingship as divinely ordained, and welcomed the protection and peace which a strong king might give. The sacred character of royalty was emphasised by an elaborate coronation ceremony at Rheims, where new kings were anointed with holy oil, which, according to legend, had been brought by a dove from heaven for the baptism of Clovis in 496 and was supposed never to diminish. Moreover, from the time of Robert II (996–1031), a belief had grown up, partly stemming from the predisposition of people to attribute divine origin to the monarchy, that the Capetians had the power of curing scrofula by touch.[84]

To this monarchy Philip the Fair's grandfather, Louis IX (1226–70), added a much more ambitious interpretation of the role of the Capetian kings than had previously been the case, for he believed, more fervently than any of his predecessors, that he had received his throne in trust from God and that it was his duty to govern according to a rigorous interpretation of Christian principles, which should be applied both to his personal life and to the everyday tasks of his office. As a result, he was able to exploit the quasi-religious character of the Capetian kings, to develop the idea of 'theocratic kingship',[85] which, carried to its logical conclusion, was antipathetic to feudal ideas of consent. Ultimately a king must follow his holy duty in endeavouring to achieve the salvation of his people, existing man-made restrictions notwithstanding. Louis IX therefore bequeathed to his successors a very special sacred function, unique to the French monarchy. In his preface to his lives of Louis IX and his son, Philip III, Guillaume de Nangis, a contemporary who was a monk at Saint-Denis, stressed the duties and responsibilities of this function which Philip IV would have to undertake. He sent the work to the king so that 'knowing the vigorous and praiseworthy acts of such princes as your grandfather and father, you should have them as an example of virtue like a mirror, and you should rejoice in the Lord that you have derived your origin from blood so good and praiseworthy'.[86]

Philip IV therefore inherited the raw material which could be forged into what has been called a 'political theology',[87] a means of focusing loyalty upon the monarchy. However, the effectiveness of this would be severely limited without an administrative structure which could match the vaulting ambition implicit in Capetian theory. The simple structure of the past needed expanding. Philip II had already begun this process by appointing salaried officials in the royal demesne called *baillis* in the north and *sénéchaux* in the south. At the same time, at the centre, the old institutions of the household had been enlarged to cope with the increasing flow of documentation which Philip's legal and military activity had provoked, and fixed places of administration were established. Changes were therefore occurring which were ultimately to alter the nature of government, but as yet the basic objectives remained the same. The paid officials, the settled institutions, the embryo capital at Paris, were there so that the kings could utilise the lifeblood of Capetian government: the enforcement of the monarchy's feudal rights. But, after Saint Louis, the French monarchs began to find more and more difficulties in maintaining the system in workable order, for monarchical pretensions had begun to outpace practical means. Philip the Fair was the first of these monarchs to be forced fully to face the new problems which grew out of the very success of the Capetians as feudal monarchs.

It is unlikely that a detailed picture of the personality of King Philip will ever be constructed. Contemporaries seem agreed on his general appearance: tall and handsome, with pale, fair colouring. He was a good knight and hunter.[88] But his personality is screened by a small group of ministers who seem to formulate and execute policy. From the 1290s the dominant figure was Pierre Flote, Keeper of the Seals and head of the Chancery until his death in 1302, and thereafter it was Guillaume de Nogaret, who became Keeper of the Seals in 1307. Nogaret retained his pre-eminence until his death in 1313, but from about 1310 increasingly the royal Chamberlain, Enguerrand de Marigny, seems to have been the most influential minister. Flote, who came from a noble family in the Dauphiné, and Nogaret, who came from near Toulouse and was ennobled by the king in 1299, were lawyers, the leading representatives of the so-called *légistes*, who were so prominent during Philip IV's reign.[89] Closely associated with Nogaret was another lawyer, Guillaume de Plaisians, who often acted on Nogaret's behalf. Marigny is less typical of the ruling coterie. He came from the *petite noblesse* of the Norman Vexin and had had no education comparable to the lawyers. His real forte lay in finance and diplomacy, and he became effective head of financial affairs in 1308. During the last three or four years of the reign, the reorientation of royal policy away from the great juristic battles of Flote and Nogaret seems to have been the consequence of Marigny's influence.[90]

Contemporaries are not very helpful in penetrating the screen formed by these ministers. When they disapproved of the king's actions, most adhered to the conventional line, as, for instance, is reflected by the monk Ives de Saint-Denis, who blamed exceptional currency alterations and heavy taxation 'more on the advice of his counsellors than on the instigation of the king himself'.[91] Some were less restrained. An anonymous writer from the early years of the reign attacked the king because he had surrounded himself with *villani*, thieves and plunderers of all kinds, men who were by nature brutal, corrupt and malignant. These men were a canker which should be purged, if the body politic was to regain its health. Justice was not administered, for the king was almost entirely occupied in pursuing his favourite occupation of hunting.[92] Even more direct was Bernard Saisset, Bishop of Pamiers, who was to pay heavily for his criticisms. He was reported as comparing the king to an owl, which the birds of antiquity had chosen as their king, for none was more beautiful. In fact, it was a worthless bird, good for absolutely nothing. The bishop had allegedly said that 'such was our King of France, who was more handsome than any man in the world, and who knew nothing at all except to stare at men'. He added that 'there was more, since the Kingdom of France would perish during the time of this king, for, when he was Abbot of Pamiers, Saint Louis had told him many times that in this reign the kingdom would perish, since he was the tenth king since Hugh Capet'.[93] In contrast, others idealised him. Guillaume de Nogaret, whose elevation and subsequent landed prosperity stemmed almost entirely from royal favour, offered the following eulogy during the posthumous proceedings against Boniface VIII.

> The lord king was born of the progeny of the Kings of France, who all, from the time of King Pepin, from whose line the said king is known to have descended, have been religious, fervent champions of the faith, and strong defenders of the Holy Mother Church. They have ejected many schismatics who have invaded the Roman Church, nor could any of them have had a more just cause than this king. The king has always in his marriage, both before and after, been chaste, humble, modest of face and in speech, never angry, hating no one, envying no one, loving all. Full of grace, charity, piety and mercy, always following truth and justice, never a detraction in his mouth, fervent in the faith, religious in his life, building basilicas and engaging in works of piety, handsome of face and graceful in manner, graceful even to all his enemies when they are in his presence; through his hands, God affords clear miracles to the sick.[94]

Modern opinion seems now to view Philip as the controlling power in the reign, the director of overall policy and, at times, even the supervisor of much detail, and he is no longer regarded as a nonentity dominated by his ministers. His servants were chosen by him and none dominated affairs throughout the entire reign.[95] Philip IV's apparent aloofness can perhaps be seen as a studied attempt to emphasise the priestly qualities of kingship so strikingly exemplified by his admired grandfather.

By 1285 the strength of the Capetian king was evident: a general acceptance as feudal overlord in France, the support of the Church which elevated him to a quasi-religious figure, membership of a venerable and ancient line, now indisputably legitimate Kings of France. But the weaknesses of this inheritance only became clear as the reign progressed. Four major fiefs remained outside the royal demesne, and each presented special problems which did not prove amenable to the feudal solution so ably propounded by Philip II and Louis IX. These fiefs were Flanders, Gascony, Brittany and Burgundy. The peculiar problems of the last two showed themselves most markedly during the fourteenth and fifteenth centuries, but Flanders and Gascony offered more immediate difficulties.

The position of Gascony had been created by the Treaty of Paris (1259) which had been negotiated between Louis IX and Henry III. Henry III gave up his dynasty's claims to the lost lands of the old Angevin Empire, but was confirmed as the Duke of Gascony, holding it in fief from the King of France. But there remained the temptation for the French monarchy to try to subjugate this fief, as it had done so often before, or at least make it more amenable to central authority. Opportunities presented themselves frequently, for under feudal law the Gascon vassals of the English king had the right to appeal to their overlord's court, the *Parlement* of Paris, if they felt that they had been unjustly treated. However, French intervention had far wider implications than with most other fiefs, for it brought conflict not simply with the Duke of Gascony, but also with the King of England, who could call upon resources outside the duchy and could mobilise allies on a European scale. In 1295 the latent rivalry which stemmed from the anomalous position of the fief showed itself in a violent sea battle between Gascon and Norman sailors. The usual feudal response followed. Philip cited Edward I, in his capacity as duke, to appear before his *Parlement*; Edmund of Lancaster, the king's brother, was sent in his stead. It was agreed to put the main fortresses of the fief of Gascony under the control of the

French royal officials for a forty-day period while an inquiry took place. Provocatively, the French officials, following the methods of feudal encroachment which typified past Capetian policy, were slow to hand back the fortresses. War followed. Between 1294 and 1296 the French king's forces occupied most of Gascony and the following year even assembled a fleet to invade England. Although in 1298 a truce was mediated by Boniface VIII, and a marriage alliance negotiated, the basic problems remained.[96]

Throughout the conflict Edward had been deeply occupied with Welsh and Scottish affairs, and had therefore largely relied upon subsidising continental allies, the most important of whom was Gui de Dampierre, Count of Flanders. Flanders was heavily feudalised, but also had important cities which owed their wealth to the textile industry based on English wool. Power was contested between the urban patriciate and the craft guilds, and if the French crown wished to assert its power there, it had to take account of all these factors. The French crown pushed its alleged rights with extreme rigour. A tax of a fiftieth, imposed in the Flemish towns as a contribution towards the war with England, helped to push the count into alliance with England. This provoked the French counter of an invasion of Flanders and defeat for the Flemish in 1297. When Edward made peace in 1298, Gui was left isolated. The French therefore had little difficulty in occupying most of the major cities of the county in 1300 and it seemed that Flanders would soon be annexed. But the count had traditionally looked for support among the craft elements in the towns, for the patricians, the ruling oligarchies of the towns, were always determinedly pro-French. Attempts by the French occupying forces to extract further tax from the urban communities served only to exacerbate class conflict, for the patricians passed on the brunt of these new demands to the crafts. The result was the revolt known as the 'matins of Bruges' on 18 May 1302, in which a large number of the French were massacred. This opened a long and expensive series of wars for the French monarchy. In July a powerful French army was defeated by the Flemings at Courtrai, and Pierre Flote was killed. This serious reverse was never fully compensated for, although at Mons-en-Pévèle in August 1304, the Flemings were forced to retire, and the Treaty of Athis-sur-Orge (June 1305) was imposed upon them. In theory the conditions were harsh – the destruction of town defences, the count to pay a heavy indemnity, the people of Bruges to go on a pilgrimage of expiation – but the treaty was never fully implemented, for the French monarchy did not have the strength to strike the decisive blow. Despite the occupation of certain towns as guarantees, despite two conferences at Tournai in 1311, despite even the annexation of Douai, Béthune and Lille to the royal demesne, Flanders could not be completely subdued, and the problem dragged on to face Philip's successors.[97]

The existence of the Gascon and Flemish problems entailed expenditure on a hitherto unprecedented scale for which the French monarchy of the thirteenth century was not prepared. The situation had been complicated at the outset by the inheritance of large debts from the previous reign, incurred when Philip III unwisely undertook a crusade against Aragon, which had expenses estimated at not far short of 1.5 million *livres tournois*.[98] What had in the past been largely a matter of enforcing feudal rights, often in a piecemeal and opportunistic fashion, now contained the potentiality of large-scale and prolonged wars. Such wars demanded finance on a parallel scale. Throughout his reign the root of the problems of Philip IV can be found in this financial weakness. The French monarchy did not receive large regular grants of taxation which would pay for a standing army, but instead was forced to rely upon irregular payments related to specific emergencies and the assembly of a feudal host of dubious efficiency and limited utility for the type of warfare which was now required. Moreover, Philip IV presided over an administration in which specialisation of function, although sophisticated compared with the early Capetians in that household and public expenditure were being separated under the Chambre aux Deniers and the Chambre des Comptes respectively, was nevertheless incomplete. At the same time, the number of salaried officials at the disposal of these organs of administration was insufficient and their attitudes lacked the impersonality of a modern civil service. The violence and disruption of the reign stem from these deficiencies which were imposed by the problems created in the attempts to extend the king's power over Flanders and Gascony. The Templars, among others, were sacrificed as the monarchy thrashed around for an answer. The attack on the Templars must be seen in the context of the methods employed by the French government in an effort to relieve the acute financial problems of the reign.

Above and beyond the resources of his own demesne, the monarch was entitled to ask his vassals for a feudal aid on the knighting of his eldest son and the marriage of his eldest daughter, and these were paid in 1313 and 1308 respectively, but such aids could hardly finance a sustained war effort, and a more general and regular form of taxation had to be found. The ancient liability of all men to defend the realm when called upon seemed at first to be a promising means of creating regular tax returns. An intensive effort was made to collect such taxes in the period 1295 to 1300, and was continued until 1305, but the results were disappointing. At first an attempt was made to collect this tax in the form of a general subsidy as a hundredth or fiftieth of capital or revenue. However, resistance was strong and payment irregular. Officials were often obliged to bargain with local powers and sometimes they were forced to accept a much lower sum than they had originally asked for, simply to gain quick payment, for when a campaign was imminent delay could be very damaging. From 1300 the government had explicitly to accept that the payment was in lieu of military service, and did not try to collect taxation as a general subsidy. Even so, it was still necessary to sugar the demands when dealing with the nobility. Some lords were allowed to summon their own contingents for the royal army, and after the government had fixed the tax required, they were allowed to collect at a higher rate to their own profit. Sometimes officials had to say that they were collecting without prejudice to ancient immunities in deference to those lords who claimed themselves exempt. Negotiations with individual lords or with assemblies of notables often involved some sort of concession, such as the confirmation of noble privileges, the promise of exemption from all other taxes or from forced loans, or a specific prohibition on collection if a peace was made. Under Philip IV schemes of general taxation were still inextricably linked to particular wars and campaigns; the government failed to provide regular sums for annual budgets irrespective of the state of the country. A clear sign of recognised failure can be seen in the fact that after 1305 the government tried to avoid this kind of taxation, collecting only two general taxes on laymen on this basis until 1313.[99]

It was not, however, necessary to pay such attention to the sensibilities of those lower down the social scale, where violence and arbitrary action by royal tax-collectors was common. This seems to have been especially true of those parts of the south that had been forcibly subdued as heretical areas during the thirteenth century. There is a record of a series of complaints made by nine communities in the Toulousain in 1298, concerning the financial exactions imposed upon them by the royal clerk Pierre de Latilly and the royal knight Raoul de Breuilli during the previous year.[100] The case of the village of Laurac, a community of probably less than five hundred people situated near Castelnaudary in the present *département* of Aude, is typical. One Tuesday in the autumn of 1297, two agents of Latilly and Breuilli, a notary, Raimond Durand, and another man known as Simonet, appeared in the village, accompanied by a band of about twenty-four sergeants. They had come to levy money which they claimed the community owed the king. At once they went briskly into action, taking securities from houses, even including clothes and bedding, and in some cases turning out the inhabitants, locking their houses and confiscating the keys. According to witnesses from the village, they then summoned fifty or sixty notables to the local *hôtel* and explained what payments they required. One man who refused to go was punched in the back. The consuls and notables were then obliged to go to Toulouse to appear before Latilly and Breuilli themselves, although when they got there, they were met by another royal notary, Guillaume de Gaudiès, who told them they would not leave the city until they had agreed to make a composition for the sums demanded. After some time, they gave in, agreeing to pay the immense sum, for a community so small, of 25,000 *sous toulousains* over the next five years, or alternatively 30,000 *sous toulousains* (or 3,000 *livres tournois*) in the course of the next ten years. It was now necessary for the agreement made by the consuls to be ratified by the rest of the community, and fifteen days later, Durand, backed by his men, again descended upon the village, where, at midday, he assembled the heads of each household – between 150 and three hundred persons in all – in a room in the place where pleas were usually heard for the royal court. When Durand told them what the consuls had agreed, there was a great deal of noisy discontent, from which there emerged a general refusal to pay. Durand therefore shut them up in the courtroom, with his sergeants guarding each exit. They were still there in the early hours of the morning. At length, Durand came back and told them that they would not leave until they had confirmed the agreement. This seems finally to have ended the opposition, and each man filed past Durand, Bible in his hand, and swore an oath to adhere to the agreement.

But the officials were not yet finished with Laurac, for Durand's sergeants came back twice more. On the first occasion they claimed 37.5 *livres* for the expenses of Durand and his men, and when this was not paid the consuls and eight other villagers were taken off to Durand's residence at Avignonet, where they were subjected to the usual threats. Then Durand told them if they could not pay, his brother-in-law would lend them the money. The brother-in-law turned out to be an agent for a usurer in Toulouse, who charged them 15 *livres* for a loan of 37.5 *livres*. The second time that the sergeants came was to collect the first instalment of the composition which had fallen due. The community could not pay, and therefore the usual procedure of confiscations of movables, grain and animals was put into motion, in lieu of direct payment.

The complaints of Laurac and the other eight communities were so vociferous that an inquiry was instituted into the matter in 1298, and it seems clear from the defence put forward that Latilly and Breuilli were unrepentant, for it was claimed that if seizures had been made then they were justified, for such action conformed with 'law and local custom' when those in debt to the king refused to make quittance. The consuls had agreed to pay, however, 'without threats or violence', and if the heads of households had been held for a time it had been 'scarcely one hour' and had been at the request of the consuls 'because the community did not understand the form of the *taille* to be imposed for the purpose of paying the composition'. Clerks and notaries who were present when the consuls and notables were taken to Toulouse claimed that the deputies from Laurac had, when taking leave of the commissioners, a very satisfied air and thanked them effusively. One said that there was joy on their faces, for they rejoiced at being the first in the Toulousain to have made a general composition. This contrasts strangely with the witness from Laurac, who said that 'there were some who, from sadness and grief, were crying when the composition was made'.[101] Although the inquiry does seem to have resulted in an initial lifting of pressure in this region, it seems to have had little permanent effect, for neither Latilly nor Breuilli appear to have been condemned, and there is reason to believe that by 1303 new financial exactions were being made in the south, albeit on a some-what different basis.[102]

A second possible method of raising money fairly regularly was to pick upon one particular group and lean heavily in this direction. In this way the clergy suffered very badly under Philip, paying either a tenth of their income or annates or both, on twenty-four occasions between 1285 and 1314. In proportion to their numbers the clergy contributed more towards Philip's wars than any other single social group.[103] The urgency and violence of Philip's measures against Boniface VIII gain in clarity when examined in this way. The origin of this proportional tax upon the clergy can be found in the crusades, for successive popes had taxed the clergy to pay secular expenses for these expeditions, and soon monarchs began to take these taxes directly as a matter of course; the papacy had led the way in the misappropriation of the Church's incomes. In 1215 the Lateran Council had allowed taxation of the clergy on condition that papal permission was first acquired, and this formality had been adhered to under Louis IX and Philip III.

Under Philip IV collection became more and more arbitrary as financial needs became desperate. There were frequent bitter complaints about the methods employed by the royal officials.[104] In 1295 Guillaume Le Maire, Bishop of Angers, complained about the operation of legal sanctions on *amortissements*, or new property gained by the Church. Guillaume called the royal officials 'officials of hell', who seize everything old or new, asserting that it is all new. 'How in these times the Church is oppressed and tortured, indeed stripped to the bone, when things are newly acquired, I have not the ability to describe. Certainly the wisdom of Solomon or the fluency of Demosthenes, the most eloquent of orators, would not be sufficient for this.' Another abuse was the exploitation of vacant sees. The king was entitled to the revenues of some sees during vacancies, but royal officials seem to have pushed this right to its limits. Guillaume cites the cases of the sees of Tours and Angers, where carpenters and woodcutters had been especially brought in to cut down valuable forests belonging to these sees, 'so that everything could be destroyed before the election'.[105]

Matters had not improved by 1299 when Guillaume was again outraged by the violent collection of tenths. Royal sergeants 'with a multitude of armed men, rushing up to abbeys and the houses of canons and other ecclesiastical persons, break into houses and doors, cellars, chests and barns, take what they can find with them, and sell it at a great market, so that they can have the money immediately'. They seized horses belonging to the clergy, almost, it appears, from underneath them.

> It recently happened at Angers that a certain archpriest, a worthy man, the chaplain of the Bishop of Angers, and his clerk, going to the episcopal residence of the Bishop of Angers on his business, had dismounted from their horses. These men having dismounted, having scarcely taken their feet out of the stirrups, certain sergeants of the lord king were present, as they said, who at once took and led away the horses with them.

Only an expensive monetary pledge could redeem the horses, together with the payment of 10 *sous* expenses.

> Not being content with these excesses, after a few days, going to the house of this archpriest and breaking violently into his room, they took away his books. All of these things were most injuriously done, when the archpriest owed no tithe, since in the previous year, for which two tenths were asked, his benefice had been vacant through death and for it a settlement was made with the collectors of the lord king on the annates of the benefices.

For this a fine of 110 *livres* had been paid to the collectors.[106]

Ostensibly some attempt was made to curb the royal officials. In 1299, in response to complaints from the Archbishop of Tours, the king ordered his *baillis* in Tours and Cotentin to moderate their methods.

> If because it is ordered by our curia that the temporalities of a prelate are to be seized, you are to be content for the main seisin with one manor and another small part, unless perhaps it is ordered that the seisin be extended to the greater part by stages for obstinate contumacy or the audacity of disobedience, not however proceeding to the seisin of the entire temporality, except when this is stated expressly in our letters, or unless the harshness of the action requires it.[107]

An observer might be pardoned for mistaking this as a piece of tactical advice rather than an admonition for exceeding lawful authority.

During 1303 and 1304 the government's methods at last provoked clerical resistance on a wide scale, for the clergy felt strong enough to put up a series of conditions before payment, conditions which suggest the first germination of a movement which might be called 'constitutional'. An assembly at Bourges in 1304 had voted its tenth with conditions: it should be collected by the clergy, 'good money' should be restored (after the violent monetary alterations of the previous years), ecclesiastical jurisdiction should be respected, new acquisitions by churches were to be allowed, the privileges of the Church of Bourges should be confirmed, and finally the temporalities of some of the churches in the province which had been seized should be restored.[108] It is not easy to judge the extent to which this resistance may have inhibited the government from making clerical tenths a regular, annual payment of a steady kind during the rest of the reign. The danger point seems to have been passed by 1305 and both Benedict XI and Clement V proved amenable in granting tenths, but the clerical ideas may have remained in the back of governmental minds and encouraged the search for other sources of income.

Nevertheless, the clergy continued to believe that they were being despoiled, for there were many more complaints during the church council held by the pope at Vienne in 1311–12. The Abbot of Saint-Pierre, in the diocese of Tarbes, was not alone when he claimed that for his failure to recognise that the temporalities of the monastery were held from the king, the *sénéchal* of Bigorre had sent forty sergeants as a garrison who had devastated the place. He himself was dragged on foot to Tarbes, where he spent a long time in prison. After his release he found that the temporalities had still not been restored, that the monks and other ecclesiastics at the monastery had been expelled, that the movable goods, including the sacred vessels, had been carried off, that horses were being grazed in the precincts of the monastery, and that the divine offices had been suspended.[109]

It is evident from governmental dealings with the clergy that the king was not averse to the use of force when and where it was necessary and if it was politically possible. The forced loan was a frequent expedient, especially during the war with England between 1294 and 1297. Individual merchants and urban communities often faced this threat and some preferred to make an outright gift of a smaller sum than was demanded as a loan, since they knew it was unlikely that the loan would ever be repaid. One such individual was a clerk called Jean Croissant to whom Philip wrote in September 1302, asking for a loan of 300 *livres tournois*. The king began by explaining how the needs of the kingdom had involved him in expenses 'without count and without number', and how he himself had made great personal sacrifices in his devotion to the cause. Croissant should therefore make the loan 'by reason of the love and fealty that you have for us and the kingdom', but adding that if he crossed him in this matter he would incur the royal indignation for ever. The loan should be paid into the Louvre at Paris without delay, for 'we know for certain that you can do this easily, either through yourself, or through your friends'.[110] The royal treasury succeeded in raising 630,000 *livres tournois* by this method during the reign.[111]

There were other, at this time, comparatively minor sources of income. The *maltôte* was a tax on commercial transactions, which produced 16,000 *livres tournois* from the Italian merchants in the kingdom in 1295, and proved also to be another means of tapping the wealth of the towns. Certain occupations, like moneylending, were taxed, patents were sold for the export of certain goods, and on a small scale there was the beginning of sales of patents of nobility. As yet however none of these incomes can be seen as more than supplementary.[112] The fact was that regular organised taxation was foreign to the concepts of an age which still saw monetary exactions as exceptional and in response only to some special need, in particular imminent danger from warfare.

With the failure to establish a regular countrywide basis for taxation, or perhaps even the failure to recognise the proper use and value of such a system, the government cast around for other temporary expedients. Alteration of the coinage proved too tempting to resist. Capetian France had inherited the system of *livres*, *sous* and *deniers* of the Carolingians of which only the *deniers* or silver pennies were real money, the *livres* and *sous* being money of account. From the late twelfth century the Italian city-republics issued a silver *gros*, worth a *sou*, and from the mid-thirteenth century, a gold coin, a florin, worth a silver pound *gros*. In France, Louis IX created the *gros tournois* in 1266. But the relationship between real money and money of account was not fixed, and Philip IV exploited this anomaly. Between 1295 and 1306, Philip repeatedly debased the coinage, either by changing the relationship between money of account and specie or by new minting. The silver *gros tournois* which ought to have been valued at 9 *deniers* in 1303, given that under Louis IX it was valued at 12 *deniers* or a *sou*, was in fact issued at 2 *sous* 2 *deniers*.[113] In May 1295 a royal ordinance explained that the king had been obliged to issue a money 'in which perhaps there will be lacking a little of weight, alloy or condition, which our predecessors, the Kings of France, had, in settled times, been accustomed to observe'.[114]

The crown as debtor undoubtedly benefited, but the crown as tax-collector began to lose. A *gros tournois* of 1295, worth 1 *sou*, would fetch 3 by 1305.[115] Therefore, in June 1306 the king blandly announced that he was returning the money to its state at the time of Saint Louis and that from 8 September the weakened *gros tournois* would be worth only its intrinsic value. In one arbitrary act, the money circulating in the kingdom depreciated two-thirds. Riots took place in Paris. According to the chronicler Jean de Saint-Victor, 'the citizens of Paris, especially the paupers and ordinary people, who rented houses, on account of a three-fold rise in rents, caused conspiracy to be made first against the landlords of the houses and afterwards against the king'.[116] Ironically, the king was forced to take refuge in the Templar fortress in Paris, while outside the mob refused to allow any victuals or other necessities to be brought in, or anybody to go in or out, until the king spoke with them about the matter, although the king, plotting secret flight, had no intention of doing this. Frustrated in their attempts to see the king, the rioters turned their attention to a rich Parisian called Etienne Barbete, who they believed had advised the king to make the return to good money. They broke into his houses and burnt them, and destroyed his goods. The king was only able to restore order by armed force, and many people were killed. Those who were thought to be responsible were captured and hanged in January 1307. Little attempt seems to have been made to ensure that justice was done, for the real purpose was to deter others. Jean de Saint-Victor commented laconically that 'by chance some who were innocent were hanged; others however, not wishing to run any risks, sought safety in flight'.[117] There was unrest in the provinces too. In Châlons a riot was incited by 'the great and rich persons' of the town against the royal ordinance prescribing the return to strong money. The local *prévôt* and some royal officials were violently attacked, and sustained many injuries. In 1310 the inhabitants of Châlons were heavily fined for their rebelliousness, being sentenced to pay 2,000 *livres tournois* to Girard de Presles, the *prévôt*, and 10,000 *livres tournois* to the crown.[118] However, despite discontent of this kind, the government continued to alter the currency in the years after 1306, according to the needs of the moment. In 1311 the Parisian *denier* was doubled in value; in 1313 there was another return to 'good money'.[119] For all the problems which the weakening of currency had brought, the return to good money nevertheless seems to have been a mistake. In the late thirteenth century the price of precious metals had been consistently high, and any sustained attempt to maintain the value of money of account in relation to precious metals at the standard set under Louis IX in 1266 was bound to leave the king short of stocks of precious metal; the necessity of finding a new source of this may ultimately have resulted in the arrest of the Templars in 1307.

There was one further expedient: rich groups were singled out who could be despoiled without public protest. One such group were the 'Lombards', merchants and bankers from the Italian city-republics. Two Lombards, Albizzo and Musciatto Guidi, filled the role of receivers of taxes for the crown in the 1290s, as well as acting as royal treasurers at various periods during the reign. In 1294 they advanced the king money on the basis that they would be repaid with future taxation; they secured loans from other Italians in France of 600,000 *livres tournois*; in 1297 they lent the king 200,000 *livres tournois* of their own money. But Philip found it easier to despoil the Lombards and seize their assets than to establish them in a settled position through which he could expect steady, if less spectacular, monetary profits. There was a general arrest of Lombards in 1291, and throughout the 1290s individuals were subject to seizures, heavy fines and expulsions. From 1303 they were used less and less in the royal service and finally in 1311 all their goods and debts were appropriated and they were arrested.[120] According to a royal ordinance of that year, they caused 'the inhabitants of this kingdom to be devoured by usury, our money to be destroyed and our ordinances to be violated'.[121] The Jews also suffered. In 1295 the Jews of the *sénéchaussée* of Beaucaire were

The great tower of Safita (Chastel Blanc) was the centrepiece of a large *enceinte* built by the Templars in the Nusairi Mountains on the southern borders of Tripoli from the early 1170s. The earthquake of 1202 caused serious damage, so most of the present building is dated to the early thirteenth century

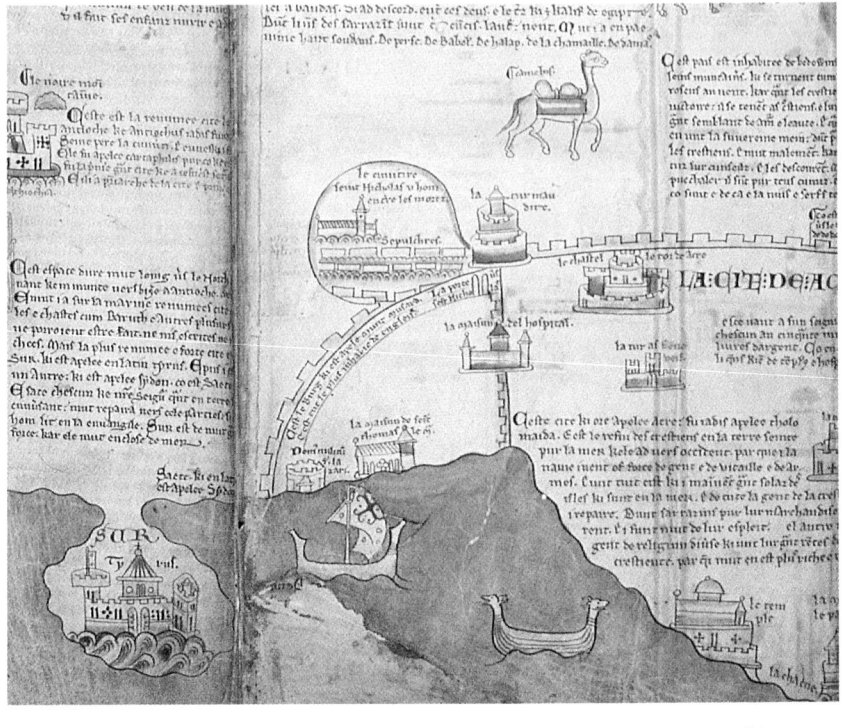

After the loss of Jerusalem in 1187, the great Latin institutions were unable to re-establish their headquarters in the city. Therefore, from the 1190s until the fall of the Latin states in 1291, they developed their enclaves in the great coastal city of Acre. The Templars were situated along the seashore in the south-west corner, as shown in Matthew Paris's plan, *c*.1255. *Below*, Matthew Paris was well placed to receive news of events. This is his depiction of the heavy Christian defeat by the Egyptians and the Khorezmian Turks at La Forbie, near Gaza, in October 1244. On the right, the Templar standard-bearer tries to flee, while still retaining the banner, which was supposed to remain visible at all costs

forced to hand over all 'usurious' profits and to reveal the details of their financial contracts.[122] Their financial power had however been waning for a generation, for Christian bankers were taking over many of their functions. On about 22 July 1306 all the Jews were arrested and their property seized, and they were expelled from the kingdom.[123]

The position of the Templars bears certain similarities to that of these other minority groups. They were unpopular and rich, and they were even more deeply involved in a royal financial administration which appears to have been seeking the removal of outside agents, than even the Lombards and the Jews. From the early thirteenth century the French Templars acted virtually as royal treasurers, working in close co-operation with the *baillis* and *sénéchaux*. For much of the century the treasurer of the Temple at Paris was, for practical purposes, also the treasurer of Capetian demesne finances. In the royal account of 1202, the Temple is shown as the central depot for the surplus revenue derived from the *prévôtés* and *bailliages* of the royal demesne, and the place from which are paid out the expenses not covered by the local officials. Under Saint Louis, the royal treasure was kept at the Temple. The *tablettes* of the royal Chamberlain, Jean Sarrasin, show a constant movement between the Temple treasury and the various services of the royal household. Between February 1256 and November 1257 alone, Jean Sarrasin received from the Temple sums in excess of 84,000 *livres parisis*.[124]

However, during the first half of the reign of Philip IV, the Templars apparently became less crucial to the ordering of affairs. Philip III had already tried and failed to stop the Templars acquiring property in *mainmorte*, and Philip the Fair also attempted to enforce this prohibition by confiscating the property acquired by the Order since Louis IX's confirmation of their possessions in 1258.[125] It is doubtful whether the Templars were being especially victimised, for other ecclesiastical bodies of this period faced the same problems. The Order did however lose its dominant position within royal financial administration, for between 1292 and 1295, the bulk of the royal treasure was transferred to the Louvre, probably as part of the reorganisation of the royal administration. There was nothing sinister about this, for the crown continued to employ the Templars on less regular financial commissions, and in the financial crisis which followed the defeat at Courtrai in 1302, the Templars once more took over part of the royal financial administration. In July 1303 the Visitor of the Temple in France, Hugues de Pairaud, was ordered to collect the war subsidy for the kingdom, except for the *sénéchaussées* of Toulouse and Rouergue.[126] Pairaud was among those who had supported the French monarchy against Boniface VIII in the previous month, and in June 1304 the king made a general confirmation of Templar property in France.[127] The Order retained an active role in the royal financial system as late as 1306, for on 6 November the king had authorised the Templars to pay the wages of some of the soldiers who had served in Flanders.[128] The French monarchy was rationalising governmental functions, and the changes which the Templars experienced as royal financiers were in a large degree a result of this process. During the same period, a greater degree of specialisation was similarly achieved in judicial administration and in the royal chancery.[129]

Despite the practical constraints imposed by the actual implementation of policy, Philip IV was in no theoretical way restricted in what he could do. Six times between 1290 and 1314 the king summoned representatives of the three orders of the realm, the Estates-General.[130] The members were not allowed to debate the policies which the king's ministers propounded to them: the king used the Estates as a vehicle for making his wishes known to the people, and as an expression of French unanimity in the eyes of outsiders, when challenged by Boniface VIII or affronted by the Flemings or the Templars. In fact, throughout the reign the real pressure for such assemblies came not from the French people, who preferred to settle matters on a local basis, but from the monarchy itself, which saw the Estates as a potential means of centralisation. The king's subjects themselves often showed considerable reluctance when ordered to attend. Sectional interests were sometimes afraid that their position might be compromised, for they would, by their attendance, become associated with royal policy, and perhaps forced to express this in written form. The clergy were placed in a particularly embarrassing position in the assemblies of 1302 and 1303, which were aimed specifically at Boniface VIII. The obvious answer was to avoid attendance, a ploy concerning which the French government was well aware, for in the convocations of December 1302 for the proposed meeting the following year, it was stressed that the clerics named were 'to appear personally, all excuses having been put aside'.¹³¹ Further convocations issued in June 1303 were equally peremptory. In a not untypical citation the clergy of Rouergue were told by the king that he could in no way consider to be faithful or friendly to him and his kingdom, those who failed him in this matter. If they did not set out on the journey to Paris within eight days of the order being given, his officials were authorised to seize all their temporal goods.¹³² Those clerics who had genuine difficulty in coming to the assembly hastened to make their excuses. Dragon, Abbot of the Benedictine monastery of Aurillac in the Auvergne, could not come because he was laid up at the castle of Beauvoir with a broken leg, but he was so frightened that his excuse would not be believed that he called in the *bailli* of the Auvergne to witness the fact, and procured two doctors and a surgeon to swear that he was not to move for a month. Another abbot, Paris, of the Cistercian foundation of Longuay (Haute-Marne), was sufficiently alarmed to attempt the journey, although he was almost eighty years of age. But when he reached Troyes he gave up and sent a procurator instead.¹³³

The pretensions of the French monarchy did not lack supporting theories. The theocratic conception of kingship and the refusal to recognise any temporal superior provided a firm base for developing a theory of Capetian sovereignty, which crystallised during the disputes with Boniface VIII. Much of the literature produced was in the form of anonymous pamphlets, which were almost certainly inspired by the government,¹³⁴ but by far the most cogent treatise was written late in 1302 by the Dominican Jean de Paris. Jean rejected the derivative nature of secular government which was so fundamental to the views of the papal reformers. For him a kingdom was 'the government of a perfect community ordained for the common good by one man'. He sharpened this definition by examining each part in turn. 'Government' was the genus. 'Community' was added in order to differentiate from a government in which each rules himself, either by natural instinct as in brute beasts, or by reason as was the case with those who chose to lead a solitary life. 'Perfect' was meant in the sense of self-sufficient, and was to be distinguished from the family, which could only sustain itself for a short time, and could not provide for all the needs of life in the way that a community could. By 'ordained for the common good' he meant to differentiate from oligarchy, tyranny and democracy, where, especially in the case of tyranny, the ruler is interested only in his own good. 'By one man' was included to differentiate from aristocracy or the rule of the best men according to virtue, on the one hand, and what he calls *polycratia* on the other, meaning the rule of the people through plebiscite. 'For he is not a king except that he rule alone, as the Lord said through Ezekiel: "My servant David will be over all and there will be one shepherd over them."' The function of the priesthood was separate from this, for this was the spiritual power, given by Christ to the ministers of the Church for the purpose of administering the sacraments to the faithful. It was not possible to reach the supernatural goal of eternal life for which man is finally ordered, simply through human nature, and therefore leadership in this sphere cannot belong to the king whose responsibility is the care of the government of human affairs. There is then a clear separation or dualism in which the royal power derives directly from God, for this royal power existed before papal power; indeed there were kings in France before there were Christians. 'To say that the power of kingship first came directly from God and afterwards from the pope is completely ridiculous.'[135] For Philip IV and his government, those who were part of this community had the obligation to contribute to its well-being; it was convenient to support this with the traditional medieval conceptions of the organic nature of this community, but now the community was not that of Christendom as a whole, but that of 'the chosen people' under 'the Most Christian King' of France.[136]

The loose collection of feudal and ecclesiastical lordships was being welded together into the Kingdom of France, focused upon the monarchy itself. It is, however, typical of the ambiguities of this reign that it is unlikely that anyone had a very clear idea of what this kingdom was in terms of a concrete geographical area. Frontiers in the modern sense of a line running between two different states did not exist in the fourteenth century.[137] Such vagueness made it all the more imperative that the crown should receive proper respect. This is clearly expressed in Philip's personal conception of his role: the kingship was a trust given to him, as it had been to his grandfather, by God. The king was elevated above the ordinary man however high his social standing, however influential he was in the royal council, and the achievement of the canonisation of Louis IX in 1297 symbolises this whole attitude.

*

By 1307 Philip IV had experimented with almost every financial expedient known to medieval rulers, yet he had failed to achieve the financial security which he sought. This was especially frustrating, as the undoubted power of the Capetian monarchy had been effectively and publicly demonstrated in the conflict with Boniface VIII. The election of Bertrand de Got seemed to confirm this victory over the papacy, for Clement V looked a pale representative of the vigorous Hildebrandine tradition. It was to this pope that the Order of the Temple looked for protection and support, but the failure of western Christendom to organise a new crusade in response to the losses of 1291, undermined the Order's functional role, and made it vulnerable to criticism and attack. Such criticism was not new, but while the Templars were able to sustain their efforts on behalf of the crusade, it was at least contained. Potential sources of conflict are therefore clear. The French monarchy needed specie, especially because of the return to good money in 1306; the papacy, although still an essential element in the political structure and religious life of western Christendom, was, under Clement V, seemingly a pliant instrument; while the Order of the Temple, closely linked to both of them, seemed to have outlived its usefulness. At the same time, the means to accomplish a spoliation of the Temple were at hand in the form of the Inquisition, developed by the papacy, but in France controlled by the monarchy. The spread of heresy had been one of the major issues of the thirteenth century, and the conversion of the Temple's unpopularity into 'heretical depravity' was a task for which the counsellors of Philip the Fair were well suited. The trial of the Templars grew out of the conjunction of these circumstances.

2: The Arrests

'A bitter thing, a lamentable thing, a thing which is horrible to contemplate, terrible to hear of, a detestable crime, an execrable evil, an
abominable work, a detestable disgrace, a thing almost inhuman,
indeed set apart from all humanity.'[1] This high-flown rhetoric forms
the opening of King Philip IV's secret orders to his *baillis* and
sénéchaux throughout France, dated 14 September 1307, instructing
them to make preparations for the arrest of the members of the
Order of the Temple throughout the kingdom. To the king's great
astonishment and horror, persons 'worthy in the faith' had recounted to him the criminality of the brothers of the Temple who,
'entertaining a wolf under the appearance of a lamb', have again crucified Christ; indeed they have brought 'injuries more grave than
those he underwent on the cross'. These men, while professing to be
Christians, in fact, when they were received into the Order, denied
Christ three times and spat three times on his image. Then, stripped
of their secular clothing, and brought naked before the senior Templar in charge of their reception, they are kissed by him on the lower
spine, the navel, and finally on the mouth, 'in shame of human dignity, according to the profane rite of their Order'. Moreover, by a
vow of their profession, they are then obliged to indulge in carnal
relations with other members of the Order, 'being required without
the possibility of refusal'. Finally, 'this unclean people forsake the
font of life-giving water' and make offerings to idols. Throughout
the document the massive verbal onslaught is maintained. By their
words and deeds, they 'defile the land with their filth, remove the
benefits of the dew and infect the purity of the air'.

At first the king admitted that he had doubted the truth of the
accusations, because he felt that informers of this kind and carriers
of rumours so unfortunate might have been acting more from 'the
malice of envy, or the stirring of hatred, or the roots of cupidity, than
from fervour of the faith, zeal for justice, or the compassion of charity'. But so great was the accumulation of accusations and so probable did the arguments put forward begin to appear, that 'violent
presumption and suspicion' was aroused. The king therefore had a
meeting with the pope and took consultation with his council of

prelates and barons as to the best means of finding out the truth of the matter. As a result of these discussions, reinforced by a request from Guillaume de Paris, papal Inquisitor in France, 'who has invoked the help of our arm', the king decreed that every member of the Order be held in captivity and reserved for ecclesiastical judgement, and all their goods, both movable and immovable, be seized and kept, without being diminished, in royal custody. Even though it was probable that some of the knights would be found innocent, such an inquiry would be to their advantage because such bad repute now adhered to them all. Philip's self-image is clear: 'We who are founded by the Lord upon the watch-tower of regal eminence to defend the liberty of the faith of the Church, and exert, before all the desires of our spirit, the augmentation of the Catholic faith.'

The actual arrests were planned as a simultaneous dawn swoop, to take place in the early hours of the morning of Friday 13 October.[2] The operation, perhaps benefiting from previous seizures of this kind against the Jews and the Lombards, was successful to a high degree, given the vast problems of co-ordination and secrecy which were involved. A small number of Templars did escape, twelve according to official sources, although there seem to have been at least twelve others;[3] but only one of the escapees, Gérard de Villiers, Preceptor of France, was a figure of any importance, and for some, like the knight Pierre de Boucle, the respite was only temporary, for although he discarded the Order's mantle and shaved off his beard, he was still recognised and taken into custody.[4] Two others, Jean de Chali and Pierre de Modies, who had made off together, were later apprehended in the striped clothes which they had adopted as a disguise,[5] and one serving brother, Renaud de Beaupilier, who had shaved off his beard and lain low in the Order's preceptory at Virecourt in the Duchy of Lorraine, outside French territory, was nevertheless eventually found, apparently some years after the arrests.[6] Another Templar, the Preceptor of the Auvergne, Imbert Blanke, was captured in England and later played a leading role in the defence of the English Templars.[7] Those who fled may have been worried about the growth of unfavourable rumours, or perhaps were frightened that crimes that they had committed or planned, crimes not necessarily connected with the French king's accusations, would be exposed. An official source claims that Hugues de Châlons (the nephew of Hugues de Pairaud, Visitor of the Order), who had eluded the royal officials, had been party to a plot to kill the king, although this may not have been anything more than an attempt to smear Pairaud by association.[8] Although one Templar, picked up begging in Paris in November 1309, had fled as much as fifteen days before the arrests,[9] most of the Templars seem to have been taken by surprise. For many of those who did escape there seems to have been little or no advance warning; witnesses describe them as fleeing 'at the time of the arrests'. Jacques de Molay, the Grand Master himself, had the previous day occupied a place of honour at the funeral of Catherine, the wife of Charles of Valois, the king's brother, for he had held one of the cords of the pall,[10] while a new recruit was received as recently as eleven days before the arrests, apparently unaware of any impending catastrophe.[11] Philip IV's complaints against the Order, which must have been common knowledge, do not in themselves seem to have been regarded as a warning, for recruitment to the Temple had by no means dried up in the months before October 1307. When, in 1310, the Templars were given the opportunity to defend themselves, several declined on the grounds that they had only been in the Order a short time, and seven of them mentioned specific periods varying from six months down to 'a month less two days'.[12]

In the early fourteenth century no one would have disputed that cases of heresy appertained to the Church or that they fell under the jurisdiction of the ecclesiastical authorities in one form or another. The motivating force in the arrests evidently came from the French government, but in a strict sense, the action preserved the forms of legality, for Philip IV had been careful to explain that he was following the just request of Guillaume de Paris, the Inquisitor in France, who held his authority as a deputy of the pope. However, Guillaume was a French Dominican, so closely involved with the royal power that he held the position of royal confessor.[13] In an effort to meet the ever-growing administrative needs of the French monarchy, the Inquisition was becoming, through its leader in France, another arm of state power. In the arrest of the Templars, the Capetian monarchy, as it had done so often in the past, made strenuous efforts to retain the outward forms of legality, for its whole position rested upon such forms as were expressed in the feudal structure, while nevertheless exploiting the legal processes for its own predetermined ends. However, the full extent of the inquisitor's power was vague.

In 1290, Pope Nicholas IV had granted the Dominican Prior in Paris power to enquire into heresy in France on his own behalf or on behalf of others,[14] but it is unclear how far this power had been transmitted to Guillaume de Paris. In 1308, at Poitiers, the pope did admit that he knew well 'that the inquisitor had general letters of his predecessors on the matter of the Inquisition',[15] but was no more specific than this.

Moreover, Philip's claim to have consulted the pope concealed the fact that Clement had not been asked or even advised about the matter of the actual arrests. There is no doubt that the king and the pope had discussed the matter at least in general terms. Romeus de Brugaria, a university master at Paris, in a letter to King James II of Aragon dated 26 October 1307, wrote that he had been present at such discussions six months before,[16] while another witness, Jean Bourgogne, the Sacristan of Majorca, who was King James's procurator at the papal court, reported a recent meeting at Poitiers between the king and the pope in a letter of 14 May 1307.[17] The pope himself when reviewing the background of the affair at Poitiers in 1308 mentioned also that the king had raised the matter at Lyons,[18] which perhaps refers to the papal coronation there in November 1305.[19] However, it is unlikely that the French government had formulated any specific plans against the Templars as early as this, even though talk hostile to the Order could well have been in general circulation at this time. The question of the Templars had certainly been among the major topics on the agenda of the French government since at least the spring of 1307, for not only was it broached at Poitiers in early May by the king himself, but also the pope had received royal embassies since that date.[20]

However, although the French government may have been pursuing the matter with some intensity, the pope claimed in 1308 that at the Lyons meeting he had said that he did not believe the accusations against the Templars, while at the more recent Poitiers discussions, he could not remember what he had replied. He did nevertheless assert categorically that the king did not proceed in the arrests of the Templars 'through letters of the pope'.[21] Clement was almost certainly being less than frank about his recall of the Poitiers meeting. On 24 August 1307 he had written to the king referring to the talks that they had had at Lyons and Poitiers. Initially, 'we could scarcely bring our mind to believe what was said at that time', but since then 'we have heard many strange and unheard-of things' about the Order, and therefore after consultation with the cardinals and 'not without great sorrow, anxiety and upset of heart', the pope had decided to institute an inquiry. Indeed, according to Clement, Jacques de Molay and many preceptors of the Order, on hearing of the accusations, had several times strongly petitioned him to institute an inquiry 'concerning those things, falsely attributed to them so they say, and to absolve them if they are found innocent, as they assert, or to condemn them, if they are found guilty, which they in no way believe'. In the meantime, the pope undertook to inform the king of any developments, although he specifically asked that Philip make reciprocal arrangements, by sending him information 'fully, wholly and instantly'. However, the pope had in the same letter already made it clear that there was no need for haste over affairs currently outstanding because at the moment he was ill. In September he intended to follow his physicians' advice, by taking several preparations and undergoing a purging. He expected that he would be sufficiently restored to health to receive ambassadors by about the middle of October,[22] and indeed at that time, Hugues de Pairaud, the Visitor of the Order, and several other Templars were present in Poitiers, near where the pope had taken up temporary residence, apparently to refute the allegations of the King of France, when the pope was fit enough to see them.[23] Here perhaps is a small indication that Clement feared precipitate action on the part of the French monarchy and was hoping to stifle such plans by means of an inquiry, by an exchange of information, and by excusing delay on the grounds of illness. The idea of setting up an inquiry, however, argues strongly that Clement was not at that time thinking of sanctioning a general arrest of the members of the Order. A month later, on 26 September, thirteen days after the secret royal orders to arrest the Templars had been sent out, Clement was still asking Philip for information,[24] which suggests both a lack of decisive progress on the part of the inquiry and ignorance of the French plans.

For their part Philip, Nogaret and Plaisians were never able to assert unambiguously that the pope had actually authorised their actions on 13 October, although they did try by innuendo to suggest that Clement had been a party to the affair. At Poitiers in May 1308, during prolonged negotiations between Philip IV and Clement V over the affair, Jean Bourgogne reports Plaisians as claiming that the king had acted on the authority of the pope, an assertion which Clement strongly denied.[25] Plaisians does not however seem to have stated specifically that the pope had authorised the arrests, and it seems unlikely that he would have missed such an opportunity if the means had been available. Indeed, after the arrests, Philip and Guillaume de Paris made excuse for this unilateral action on the grounds that they were forced to act to protect the orthodox faith from the spread of heresy,[26] while late in October the pope wrote to the king in tones of great indignation at what he regarded as the king's contemptuous treatment in not consulting him.[27] At the same time Philip, in letters to King James of Aragon of 16 and 26 October, in which he tried to encourage James to follow his example, described events as if they had been instigated by the French government rather than by the pope.[28]

Evidently the king had become impatient with papal prevarications. His financial needs were acute and the tide of rumour was running strongly. The leaders of the Order were fortuitously in the Kingdom of France, but could at any time have decided to return to Cyprus. It must have seemed that the pope intended to do nothing and that the government would be cheated of its spoils; so Philip acted, perhaps urged on by the more intemperate members of his government such as Guillaume de Nogaret. The action was justified on the familiar ground that 'vehement suspicion' had arisen against the Order, a phrase used both in the secret orders to the royal officials and in later self-justificatory documents and speeches emanating from the French government. Without the existence of vehement suspicion, even the questionable legal device of acting through the papal inquisitor without actually informing the pope lost its validity.

There are of course no objective means of determining vehement suspicion, and in view of the fact that the French government relied upon sources of a distinctly disreputable and shabby kind to establish the case for suspicion – a weakness which the royal ministers were later to find embarrassing – it is hardly surprising that the pope was sceptical and not inclined to take swift action against the Order. There was, by the early fourteenth century, a predisposition to believe ill of the Order, whose popularity had waned throughout the thirteenth century, but it is impossible to pin down the source (if such existed) of something as elusive as rumour and scandal-mongering. Contemporaries, in making similar searches, were often equally confused. The Florentine chronicler Giovanni Villani attributed the origin of the stories to a renegade Templar, the former Prior of Montfaucon, 'a man of evil life and a heretic', who was condemned to perpetual imprisonment for his crimes by the Grand Master. In prison he met one Noffo Dei, a Florentine 'filled with every vice', and these two men conspired together in the hope of financial gain and release from prison by denouncing the Templars to the king. Villani, never an admirer of the French ruler, adds, with satisfaction, that both came to a bad end, for Noffo was hanged and the prior was stabbed.[29] There is however no other evidence to back Villani's story, and it seems that he has confused the Templar proceedings with the near-contemporary trial of Guichard, Bishop of Troyes, in which Noffo Dei figured among the bishop's accusers.[30] Possibly one source of the earliest rumours can be found in southwest France. During the hearings which followed the arrests, a Templar called Gérard Laverhna, Preceptor of Andrivaux in the diocese of Périgord, while being interrogated at Cahors, said that he was terrified that he would be killed, 'because it had been said to him that he would lose his body, because he was that man through whom the secrets of the Order were first revealed'.[31] Much later in the trial, during the hearings of 1311, an outside witness, a Franciscan called Etienne de Néry, testified that he had been present at Lyons on the day of the arrests when a certain secular clerk had been captured while carrying two sets of closed letters from 'the Master of Passages' at Marseilles to the Grand Master. These letters warned that grave accusations had been made against the Order by the king and the pope, and exhorted the Grand Master to try to keep the king 'propitious and favourable' to the Templars. The Master of Passages said that he had found out that the accusations came from certain captured Gascon knights. According to him 'those statutes of the Order, which had been made at the Pilgrims' Castle, had already been revealed'.[32]

On 27 November 1309 a Templar called Ponsard de Gizy attempted to make a defence of his Order. One method he adopted was one of the few possible lines of defence offered by inquisitorial procedures: an accused man could name his enemies in the hope that these names coincided with his denunciators and thus argue that they had acted not from zeal for the faith, but out of malice and evil disposition. Ponsard named four men: 'These are the traitors who have told lies and falsehoods against those of the Order of the Temple and called them disloyal: Guillaume Robert, monk, who has put them to the torture; Esquin de Floyran, de Béziers, Comprior of Montfaucon; Bernard Pelet, Prior of the Mas-d'Agenais, and Gérard de Boyzol, knight, who comes from Gisors.'[33] Two of these men are known to have been responsible for articulating these rumours in high places. Bernard Pelet was sent to England by Philip IV in October 1307, in an unsuccessful attempt to convince King Edward II of the Templars' guilt,[34] while Esquin de Floyran claimed for himself the role of prime mover in the whole affair.

In a badly spelt and semi-literate letter, dated 28 January 1308,[35] after the Templars had been arrested and sweeping confessions extracted from them, Esquin wrote to King James II of Aragon, recounting his role in the affair.

> Let it be manifest to your royal majesty, that I am the man who has shown the deeds of the Templars to the Lord King of France, and know, my lord, that you were the first prince of the whole world to whom, at Lérida, in the presence of Brother Martín Detecha, your confessor, I previously revealed their activities. For which you, my lord, did not wish to give full credence to my words at that time, which is why I have resorted to the Lord King of France, who has investigated the activity and found [it] clear as the sun, certainly in his kingdom, so that the pope has been convinced fully of the affair, and the other princes, namely the King of Germany, and the King of England and King Charles, and also the other princes.

But the purpose of his letter was not merely self-congratulation; his primary motives are clearly mercenary.

> My lord, remember what you have promised to me when I left your chamber at Lérida, that if the deeds of the Templars were found to be evident, you would give to me 1,000 *livres* in rents and 3,000 *livres* in money from their goods. And now that it is verified and when there is a place, think fit to remember.

Part of the king's vehement suspicion therefore came from such as Esquin de Floyran, but the case was reinforced by the organised use of spies and informers. According to Guillaume de Plaisians, the king had authorised twelve men to enter the Order in various parts of the kingdom and, in the report of Jean Bourgogne, 'boldly do what they told them and then come out'. They told the king that the accusations were true.[36] Information was gathered from discontented elements within the Order. The first Templar to testify in public after the arrests of 13 October was a priest called Jean de Folliaco who, in his deposition of 19 October, claimed that he had told 'the curia of the *prévôt* of Paris, the seat then being vacant, that the said Order was not pleasing to him, and that he would freely leave it, if he dared or was able'. He maintained that there were extant documents about this, sealed with the *prévôt's* seal, and also that he had, at another time, confessed to the Bishop of Paris.[37] Jean de Folliaco was later to be found among a group of picked Templars who could be trusted to repeat their confessions and, with them, was brought forward to testify before the pope at Poitiers in the summer of 1308.[38] A serving brother called Etienne de Troyes was another such case. He told the pope that

> being led to the King of France before the capture of the Templars, he did not dare to reveal that secret, but seeing however that the king intended to prosecute that affair strongly, he had confessed the above-mentioned [i.e. the errors of which the Templars were accused] in the presence of the king and his confessor and the Lords P. de Chambili and Guillaume de Martigny and afterwards had repeated it in the presence of the Bishops of Bayeux and Coutances.[39]

At Poitiers in 1308, Plaisians also recounted that Jacques de Molay himself had appeared before the royal court 'wishing to excuse himself and his Order', but had only provided further evidence against it because 'he said words which, although they were premeditated, nevertheless . . . were clearly inspired by heresy'. Apparently Molay had explained that brothers who feared punishment did not confess their sins, but were nevertheless absolved by him in chapter, 'although he was', said Plaisians, 'a layman and did not have the keys'.[40]

Having once committed himself to decisive action, the king seems to have been hoping that he would be able to present the pope with a *fait accompli*. The weakness of the case based on vehement suspicion was to be vastly strengthened by the acquisition of confessions from the Templars themselves. On 22 September 1307 Guillaume de Paris wrote to the Inquisitors of Toulouse and Carcassonne exhorting their co-operation in an inquiry against the Templars. The letter is in the same hyperbolic and elaborately rhetorical style which marks the French chancery under Nogaret and characterises the apologia for the more disreputable acts of the reign. The crime of the Templars was 'most wicked', 'a burning shame to Heaven', 'a bitter thing, a lamentable thing'. As a result, 'the land will surely be moved and all the elements disturbed, the divine name held in contempt, the truth of religion confounded, the stability of the Christian faith broken'. The king had taken council secretly, not only with the inquisitor, but also with the pope, first at Lyons and then at Poitiers. Papal knowledge of the coming arrests is thereby implied, but not explicitly stated. Enquiry had since then elicited vehement suspicion against the Order, especially with regard to its shameful reception, and the king ordered that the Templars be brought before ecclesiastical judgement. Guillaume de Paris therefore asked his fellow inquisitors to make vigilant enquiry of the men brought before them by the king's officials, 'on our behalf, on the contrary more on apostolic behalf'. Their depositions were to be carefully recorded and sent to the king and the inquisitor 'under sealed enclosures' without delay. Meanwhile the fullest possible publicity should be given to the affair through the Franciscans and others who should convey the details to the populace.[41] In the service of the King of France, Guillaume de Paris not only set in motion the machinery for the arrest of the Templars within the area of his own immediate jurisdiction, but also took it upon himself to organise similar action in the south. He could not come south himself, 'being impeded by various matters and by infirmity of body', but not apparently by any lack of authority.

Explicit instructions of a practical kind had also accompanied Philip's orders to his officials, issued on 14 September, to prepare for the arrest of the Templars. The first task was to make a secret investigation of all the Templar houses, suspicion being removed by broadening the inquiry to include all other religious houses in the area, on the pretext that a tenth was about to be levied. On the day of the arrest the royal officials should be accompanied by leading *prud'hommes* of the *pays*, to whom an explanation of what was happening should be given under an oath of secrecy. After the arrests, detailed inventories should be taken of the property and proper guards set up to protect it. The prisoners should be well guarded and placed in isolation and, if necessary, torture should be used to extract the truth. They should be told that the pope and the king had been informed by several witnesses of the methods used at their reception and profession, and then promised pardon if they confessed the truth and returned to the faith of the Holy Church. But otherwise they should be told that they would be condemned to death. Then the order repeats the details of the charges on which they are to be questioned.[42]

The royal instructions clearly indicate that the prisoners were to be terrorised by threats and torture in advance of their official appearance before the inquisitors. It is not difficult to imagine the fear and panic of the victims, many of whom had been wrenched from quiet, rural preceptories, and pitched into harsh captivity. Not all the Templars were fighting knights, fresh from battle with the infidel; many were involved in the routine agrarian and domestic tasks to be found on the estates of any landowner in medieval France. An inventory of the house of Baugy taken by Jean de Verretot, royal *bailli* at Caen, in accordance with the royal instructions, gives a typical picture. There were only three Templars, the preceptor and two companions, none of whom are identified as knights. They presided over a mixed farm of cattle, pigs, sheep, horses and fowls, and arable crops of wheat, barley, rye, oats and peas. The estate had the usual domestic and agricultural equipment, including a mill. Twenty-seven persons are listed as 'domestics and servants' who were not members of the Order, including a chaplain and a clerk, and the expected complement of ploughmen, swineherds and shepherds. The estate seems to have had a manor house, a kitchen, a cellar, a dormitory and a chapel, and the inventory lists everything in these buildings from the ornaments on the altar to the saucepans. Mention of a 'blue surcoat belonging to the wife of my Lord Roger de Planes and which is in pledge', contained in a chest in one of the rooms, indicates small-scale financial activity. But no weapons are recorded and there was no money, for the preceptor said that it had been sent for a quittance. Despite the detailed nature of the inventory no impression is left of a military establishment or of any kind of fortification.[43]

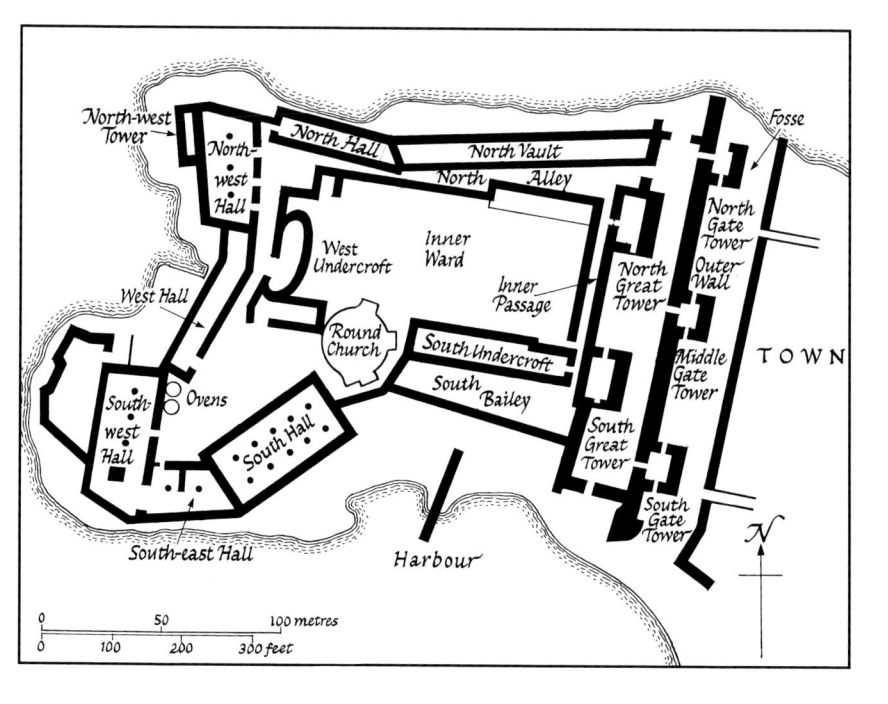

In the thirteenth century only the Military Orders had the resources to build large-scale castles. 'Atlit (Pilgrims' Castle) is situated on a spur of land south of Haifa, jutting out into the sea. It was built between 1217 and 1221, and abandoned in August 1291, after the fall of Acre the previous May

In the second half of the thirteenth century the Templar lands in Italy became increasingly important as a source of supply for the beleaguered crusader states. The frescoes of the Templar Church of San Bevignate, built between 1256 and 1262 at Perugia, just outside the Porta Sole, illustrate this continuing commitment. *Left*, the protection of pilgrims is shown by the Templar ship on the west wall, which also symbolises the Church as a whole within which the faithful can gain salvation. *Right*, Below the ship, a lion threatens a group of white-robed Templars, protectors of the Church against its enemies. *Below*, more traditionally, as at Cressac, there is a battle scene in a long frieze across the west wall, perhaps showing the Templar sack of Nablus in 1242, in which the knights burnt a mosque in the town

The depositions of the Templars questioned at Paris confirm this impression, for they include those of shepherds, stewards, agricultural workers, a keeper of mills, a master carpenter, a granger, a vendor of wines and a ploughman.[44] One of the shepherds, Pariset de Bures, was forty-five years old at the time of the arrests and had not entered the Order until reaching the age of thirty-two, while the carpenter, Eudes de Wirmis, was sixty years of age and had only taken his vows sixteen years before.[45] Clearly they were not recruited as fighting men and it is doubtful if they had ever seen a Moslem. In the 115 depositions resulting from the hearings in Paris which give the age of the examinee, sixty-nine Templars said that they were forty years old or more. One, Gautier de Payns, was eighty years old – incredible longevity by medieval standards – and another, Albert de Rumercourt, a priest, had entered the Order three years before at the age of sixty-seven.[46] The average of the 115 depositions is 41.46 years. These predominantly middle-aged and mostly pacific men were bullied and threatened by Nogaret's ruffians and subjected to the rack or the strappado if they resisted. Not surprisingly only a tiny minority of the surviving depositions, both in Paris and in the provinces during the period October to December 1307, contain any assertion of innocence by the Templars.

There are 138 depositions surviving from the hearings which took place in Paris in October and November 1307, including the confessions of the Grand Master and the other leaders. Only four of these Templars – none of them of any importance in the hierarchy – were able to resist the pressures exerted upon them, although Raimbaud de Caron, Preceptor of Cyprus, at first claimed that he had never heard or known anything bad or shameful against the Order, but on a second appearance, presumably after torture, made a full confession; and Raoul Moyset, although prepared to accuse others, claimed that nothing 'was done or said that was against God or good customs' at his reception.[47] Ninety-four depositions survive from provincial hearings held between October 1307 and January 1308.[48] Here again, resistance was isolated only. Eight Templars at Renneville refused to admit any of the accusations, and one at Caen at first wished to confess nothing, but the next day changed his testimony to accord with the other twelve confessions there.[49] Elsewhere, only at Chaumont was there any resistance, and here the circumstances were rather unusual. Two German Templars, travelling

from Paris, a priest called Corrand de Mangoncia, and his companion a serving brother called Henry, were captured by royal officials
as they tried to flee into Imperial territory. Both strongly denied any
improprieties within the Order. Corrand had been received thirteen
years before by the Master in Germany. He had asked three times
to be admitted for the remission of his sins and for God and Holy
Mary. In Germany it was the custom to shut the doors against enemies, but honest persons were free to enter at receptions. The Master three times asked Corrand to deliberate well on the matter and
then he returned and again asked for admission. He then swore to accept the rules of chastity, obedience and poverty. The Master finally
enjoined secrecy on Corrand and 'nothing else was said or done'.
Concerning the denial of the cross, spitting on it, the improper kisses
and several other things, 'he said with a red face and great sign of
indignation that he knew nothing and had never done any of them'.
The serving brother, who was examined through a German inter-
preter, 'wished to say nothing except good'. The inquisitor of the
region, Raoul de Lineyo, wrote to Philip IV that the serving brother
was not tortured 'because of his illness, which greatly afflicted him'.
Moreover, although there was a public notary present, the inquisitor
refused to attach his seal to the depositions since there had been
no confessions. The inquisitor had nevertheless written the letter
because urged to do so by Henri de Claciaco, the royal knight
deputed to look into the matter of the Templars in this region.[50]

Undoubtedly most of the Templars were subjected to intense
questioning, probably prevented from sleeping, fed largely on bread
and water, and physically humiliated. A Templar knight called Ato
de Salvigny, Preceptor of La Chapelle in the diocese of Cahors, was
imprisoned in irons, and kept on bread and water for four weeks
before his confession at Carcassonne.[51] Géraud Beraud, a knight
from Limoges, although not directly tortured, had his feet permanently shackled, and when moved from place to place in a cart had his
hands tied as well.[52] Pierre de Conders, a knight who had been Preceptor of Gentioux in the diocese of Limoges, told the pope and
cardinals at the hearing of the summer of 1308 that they had wanted
to torture him, but on seeing the instruments he had confessed at
once.[53] Modern studies of subjects who have been brainwashed
show that the more ostensibly violent facets of physical torture need
not necessarily have been applied for the requisite results to have

been achieved. Subjects have their emotions worked upon until they reach an abnormal condition of anger, fear or exaltation, and then efforts are made to maintain this condition. Ultimately the subject becomes hysterical and is much more open to suggestions which he normally would have completely rejected. Will-power and courage may simply hasten this process, for the effort is likely to exhaust the brain. In the words of one authority on brainwashing, 'Granted that the right pressure is applied in the right way and for long enough, ordinary prisoners have little chance of staving off collapse; only the exceptional or mentally ill person is likely to resist over very long periods.'[54] It is possible that some Templars therefore, at least temporarily, came to believe the accusations made against them, whether there was any truth in them or not.

However, close questioning and physical debilitation were not invariably used or systematically applied. Torture of a more crude kind was also extensively used. The rack and the strappado were the most common, but some Templars also had flames applied to the soles of their feet. The rack consisted of a triangular frame upon which the victim was tied. The cords which bound him were attached to a windlass, and when this was turned the joints of the ankles and wrists were dislocated. The prisoner subjected to the strappado had his hands tied behind his back and attached to a rope thrown over a high beam. He was hauled up to the ceiling and allowed to fall with a violent jerk, stopping within a few inches of the ground. Sometimes weights were attached to the victim's feet or testicles to add to the shock of the fall. A fifty-year-old Templar knight, Gérard de Pasagio, later testified that the royal *bailli* of Mâcon tortured him 'by the hanging of weights on his genitals and other members'.[55] Torture by burning involved securing the prisoner's feet in front of a fire, fat was rubbed into them and the flame applied. A board was placed between the fire and the victim's feet during periods when the interrogators wished to question the subject. Bernard de Vado, a priest from Albi, was tortured by this means, a process so vicious that a few days afterwards the bones of his feet dropped out.[56]

Although the depositions commonly end with the formula that the subject 'had told the pure and entire truth for the safety of his soul' and that he had not spoken as a consequence of 'violence, or from fear of torture, or imprisonment, or any other reason', it is clear from evidence presented in the period 1308 to 1311 that many Templars were subjected to tortures of this kind soon after the mass arrests of 13 October. Pierre Brocart, who described himself as a farmer (*agricola*), aged fifty, provides an example. He was examined at Paris on 21 October 1307, and confessed to spitting on the cross and obscene kisses, and said that the practice of homosexuality was enjoined on him. He swore on oath that none of the above pressures had been brought to bear on him. Yet the following year in the summer of 1308, when he was asked about torture he said that 'he was stripped and tortured a little, but he said no more nor less [than his confession in 1308] during tortures'. He added that 'those who placed him in torture were completely drunk'.[57] On 24 October 1307 a fifty-three-year-old brother, Jean de Cugy, who had been keeper of the Templar mills at Paris, similarly asserted on oath that his confession was freely made. He had told the Inquisitor Guillaume de Paris that the Visitor in France, Hugues de Pairaud, had taken him behind an altar and kissed him on the base of the spine and the navel, had threatened to have him put in prison for the rest of his life if he did not deny Christ, had forced him to spit at a cross (although in fact he had spat on the ground), and had told him that he could have sexual relations with other brothers in the Order. Yet the following year in the hearing before the pope and cardinals, although he maintained his confession and still insisted that he had not spoken under duress, he admitted that he had been tortured. He claimed that initial resistance by him had been the result of a prohibition on speaking about these things made eight days before the arrests by Brother Pierre, Preceptor of the house at Paris, 'but he could not sustain any torture, and at once when he was placed in this position, confessed everything'.[58] Iterius de Rochefort, Preceptor of Douzens in the diocese of Carcassonne, was tortured many times after his arrest because although he had confessed to the denial, the spitting, the obscene kisses and the incitement to homosexuality during the first session of torture, his interrogators apparently believed that he knew more and pressed for information about other things such as idol worship, about which he knew nothing;[59] while a knight called Gérard de Saint-Marcial, from Limoges, initially refused to confess, but seems to have been broken by torture and made a full confession. He had not been tortured after this, but had been kept on bread and water for three weeks.[60] In February

1310 a Templar called Jacques de Soci claimed that he knew of twenty-five Templars who, until that time, had died 'on account of tortures and suffering'.[61]

The direction of proceedings which ostensibly had been authorised by the Inquisition was therefore clearly determined by the royal will. In Paris where this will was most felt it was not necessary for the royal officials to make themselves too conspicuous; here Guillaume de Paris personally took the leading role, questioning the first thirty-seven witnesses during the first week of hearings between 19 and 26 October. The confessions of these men, which included those of Jacques de Molay and Geoffroi de Charney, Preceptor of Normandy, set the pattern for the remaining hearings.[62] In the provinces the participation of the royal officials was more direct and explicit. At Bayeux a royal knight, Hugues de Castro, presided; at Chaumont, a royal knight, Henri de Claciaco, had asked the inquisitor to send his account of the arrest of the two Germans to the king; at Caen, two royal knights, Hugues de Chastel and Enguerrand de Villers, were present; at Carcassonne and Bigorre, the royal *sénéchaux* for these regions were prominent among those present; the hearings at Cahors in January were held by the *sénéchal* of Périgord and Cahors. The text of the hearings at Sens has not survived, but in March 1309 a Templar priest, Gautier de Bures, testified that he was examined 'by the *bailli* of Sens and afterwards by the late Archbishop of Sens. He was reconciled by the Bishop of Orléans, since the see at Sens was then vacant.'[63] The see of Sens was not filled until May 1309, so this testimony clearly refers to the hearings of the autumn of 1307. It indicates that the royal orders instructing the officials to interrogate the Templars before their appearance in front of the ecclesiastical authorities were being carried out.

The success of these methods was almost total. A confession to some or all of the charges outlined in the royal order of 14 September was extracted from 134 of the 138 Templars questioned at Paris. These 134 depositions cover an immense variation of age, length of service and status. In contrast to the eighty-year-old Gautier de Payns, Pierre de Sivry thought that he was sixteen or seventeen years old.[64] Raoul Moyset, aged sixty-five, had been in the Order forty-five years, while Nicolas de Sarra, aged twenty-six, had been a member only since 16 August 1307.[65] Although Albert de Rumercourt

had only entered the Order on reaching the age of sixty-seven,
Ansell de Rohaire and Elias de Jocro were both thirteen when they
were received.[66] Even in 1311 Elias de Jocro was described as being
too young to have a beard.[67] Confessions were made by both the
greatest, Jacques de Molay, the Grand Master, and Hugues de
Pairaud, the Visitor in France, and the most humble, such as Raoul
de Grandeville, who had care of the ploughs in the Templar house of
Mont Soissons.[68] In seventy-three of these cases, from the evidence
of these or other hearings, it is possible to designate status specifically: fifteen were knights, seventeen priests, and forty-one serving
brothers or sergeants. From other descriptions, it is almost certain
that another twenty-eight were serving brothers, while the remaining thirty-seven, even though only their names are given, are unlikely to have been any higher in status. Their average length of
service was 14.2 years and their average age of entry 28.7 years.[69] In
these circumstances the four dissenters could be ignored or forgotten, for the range of confessions is comprehensive and far-reaching
in its scope and implications, amply justifying the criterion of vehement suspicion even though it lacked an objective definition.

The individuals mentioned serve to demonstrate the point. Gautier de Payns had been ordered to spit on a cross, which he did,
once, and he was kissed by the receptor on the navel and the mouth.
Intercourse with women was forbidden to him, but permission for
carnal relations with the brothers was offered. He believed that all
other entrants were received in the same way. Pierre de Sivry was
ordered by Hugues de Pairaud to deny Christ three times and to spit
on a cross. He was kissed on the navel and the mouth. As has been
seen, Raoul Moyset would admit nothing on his own account, but
had heard from others of orders to deny Christ and spit on the cross.
He himself, he seems to have thought, constituted a special case
which had no general application to the practices of the Order,
for he believed that his receptor, a priest called Daniel Briton, had
spared him these things because he had brought Raoul up and
because he was very young at the time. Nicolas de Sarra obeyed the
order to deny an effigy of Christ crucified three times and to spit on
it. He was then stripped and kissed on the base of the spine, the
navel and the mouth. Albert de Rumercourt was ordered to deny
Christ and spit on the cross, but, completely terrified, had protested
that as he had brought all his goods to the Order, namely 4 *livres* of

rent from land, why must he do this? In contrast to Raoul Moyset, the preceptor had therefore spared him, 'since you are an old man'. He added that if he had known what the Order was like before he was received, he would not have entered 'for all the world'; on the contrary he would rather have cut off his head. Ansell de Rohaire confessed the denial and the spitting, and described the encouragement of homosexuality. Elias de Jocro had been led behind the altar by his receptor and shown a picture in a certain missal, 'but he was so young that he did not then know whose image it was'. He had told the receptor that he believed in Jesus Christ and the Virgin, but the receptor replied he was wrong. Still protesting his beliefs, 'he was sharply beaten by this receptor, and afterwards was placed in prison for a day without drink and food'. He finally gave in and admitted his wrong belief, since they had threatened him with prison again, 'because he wished to go out and go to his father's house'. He could not remember what had happened concerning the alleged illicit kissing, only that he was tormented by the brothers. Raoul de Grandeville admitted spitting and denial, and maintained that his receptor had called Christ a false prophet. He was then stripped to his shirt and kissed on the base of the spine, the navel and the mouth, and homosexuality was enjoined upon him.

Most Templars were concerned to show themselves as innocent victims of a system over which they had little control, while satisfying their interrogators by making a reasonably comprehensive confession. They therefore admitted that illicit acts had been enjoined upon them, but claimed that they had only participated unwillingly. Renaud de Provins, Preceptor of Orléans, who was brought before the inquisitors on 7 November showed more ingenuity than most in achieving this double objective. He had been received fifteen years before in the chapel of the Templar house at Provins. Many of his friends and relatives waited at the door of the chapel and round about, while Renaud was received inside the closed building. After he had sworn to maintain the orthodox statutes and observances of the Order, one of the brothers showed him a missal with a cross depicting the image of Jesus Christ and asked him, 'Do you believe in him?' He replied that he did not, and at once, one of the other brothers present, called Hugues, said to him, 'You speak well, since he is a false prophet.' Renaud, however, knew in his heart that he did not believe in the image, but in him whose image it was. Then another of the brothers told Hugues to be silent, adding that they would instruct him properly concerning the Order's statutes. Renaud believed that they had discontinued the illicit facets of the ceremony because of those who were waiting outside the chapel and also because it was late. Meanwhile, he himself was deeply disturbed by what had occurred and had been unable to eat that day, and within three days he became ill, a condition which lasted until Advent, during which he had to eat meat because he was so weak. At last he confessed to a Dominican brother called Nicolas, of the convent of Compiègne, who told Renaud that he was displeased with him for entering the Temple when he had several times proposed to enter the Dominican Order. Renaud himself had never seen a full copy of their statutes, and there never was any attempt to show him this; he therefore believed that those who had confessed errors spoke the truth.[70]

If the 138 depositions taken at the Paris hearing are looked at overall, it can be seen how sweeping were the confessions. One hundred and five admitted that the denial of Christ was enjoined upon them in some form, but many adopted a formula which was to become common in the course of the trial; they did it *ore et non corde*, by the mouth only, for they did not believe it in their hearts. One hundred and twenty-three confessed that they had spat at, on, or near, some form of crucifix, at the orders of their receptors, but several claimed that they had spat on the floor or the ground, or that they had only pretended to spit. In 103 cases Templars admitted that they had been indecently kissed, usually on the base of the spine or the navel. There are occasional variations: one Templar, ordered to kiss the receptor's navel, refrained from doing so, because 'he was scabby on the stomach', and in fact only touched him with his nose.[71] Kissing on the mouth, which was even admitted by those who denied all else, cannot be taken as indecent, for it was a standard part of a legitimate reception and – in the homage of 'mouth and hands' – was an essential element in lay feudal relationships in France.[72] In 102 cases there is an explicit or implicit statement that homosexuality among the brothers of the Order was encouraged, although some witnesses would only say that they were told that the brothers had communal beds. One Templar believed that the purpose of this arrangement was carnal, but another professed not to know why.[73] Only three Templars admitted actually having homosexual relations with other brothers, one of whom, Guillaume de Giaco, a serving brother in the household of the Grand Master, claimed that while he was in Cyprus, he had had carnal relations with Molay three times in one night. Another member of Molay's household, Pierre de Safed, said that he had been carnally abused by a Spanish brother called Martín Martín, whom he had not resisted because of the Grand Master's order on the subject during his reception.[74]

However, the Parisian hearings produced little in the way of idol worship. Only nine Templars knew anything of this; all had seen a head, between one and twelve times, worshipped in chapter-meetings, in places as far apart as Paris and Limassol. However, it had appeared in several guises: it had a beard, was painted on a beam, was made of wood, silver and gold leaf, and had four legs, two at the front and two at the back.[75] The most graphic description came from a loquacious serving brother called Raoul de Gizy. He had seen the head in seven different chapters, some of which had been held by Hugues de Pairaud, the Visitor. When it was shown, all those present prostrated themselves on the ground and worshipped it. It had a terrible appearance, seeming to be a figure of a demon, called in French *un maufé*. Whenever he saw it, he was filled with fear and he could scarcely look at it without trembling. However he had never worshipped it in his heart.[76]

With some variations, the pattern was repeated in the provinces. At Cahors, for instance, most witnesses agreed with the first to be examined, Pierre Donaderi, the son of a burgess of Cahors. He had been received about thirty years before. After making entrance he went to one side, stripped off his secular clothes, and dressed himself in the clothes of the Order. He returned to the preceptor who was receiving him and found that he was standing 'like a four-legged beast on knees and elbows' and that he, Pierre Donaderi, had to kiss him on the spine and the navel. He then spat on a cross and denied Christ many times.[77] At Carcassonne, a brother called Jean de la Cassagne had found, in his reception, the preceptor laid out on a bench, and he and others being received kissed him on the anus. He then took a seat and they kissed him on the navel, 'his clothes being between as above'. The preceptor then took from a box a large brazen idol in the shape of a man, wearing something that looked like a dalmatic. The idol was placed on a chest and the preceptor said to them, 'Here is a friend of God, who speaks with God, when he wishes, to whom you must bring thanks, since he has led you to this state, which you desire greatly, and he fulfils that desire.' The brothers worshipped the idol, genuflecting before it, and while they were doing this a crucifix was shown to them and they were told to deny it and spit on it. He did not know what the idol was, although it seemed to him to be a demon. In 1300 he went to Rome and there made a full confession, so that a penance was imposed on him. When he was asked why he consented to do the things that he described, he said it was because of 'stupidity, and simplicity, and his age'. He was twenty-two years old at the time.[78] In this region the confession of idol worship was more common. Other Templars questioned after Jean de la Cassagne had seen, variously, an idol like a bearded head which was the figure of Baphomet, a figure called Yalla (a Saracen word), a black and white idol, and a wooden idol.[79]

The rank and file received no inspiration from their leaders. Eight days after the arrests, Geoffroi de Charney, Preceptor of Normandy, an office which made him one of the foremost dignitaries of the Order, and a man with more than thirty-seven years' service, admitted that his receptor, the then Master in France, Amaury de la Roche, had told him that Christ was a false prophet and was not God, and that on the Master's orders he had denied Christ three times, 'by the mouth and not in the heart', and had kissed the Master on the navel. He had heard moreover that Gérard de Sauzet, a former Preceptor of Auvergne, had told an assembly of brothers at a chapter-meeting that 'it was better that they join with brothers of the Order than engage in sexual intercourse with women', although Charney himself had never been required to do this. He agreed that he himself had received one brother into the Order in the way that he had described, but after that, realising that the ceremony was 'wicked and profane and against the Catholic faith', he had conducted receptions in accordance with the original statutes of the Order.[80]

This was a distinguished scalp for Philip's government, but more important was the confession of the Grand Master himself, Jacques de Molay, on 24 October.[81] The Grand Master must have been in his sixties by this time and throughout the trial his conduct was that of a confused and frightened man, advanced in years and worn down by the pressure of the king's officers. He was out of his depth in the circumstances of the trial and never provided any decisive leadership at this time of crisis. Although in the years that followed he was to chop and change, first retracting and then confessing again, he was never able to erase the impact of this first confession, for it was an event cleverly stage-managed by the French government to achieve maximum propaganda effect in the right quarters.

He told the Inquisitor, Guillaume de Paris, that he had been received forty-two years ago at Beaune in the diocese of Autun, by Humbert de Pairaud, Master in England, and Amaury de la Roche, Master in France. He continued that

> after many promises had been made by him concerning the ob-servances and the statutes of the said Order, they had placed a mantle on his shoulder. And the said receptor [Humbert de Pairaud] caused a certain bronze cross to be brought into his presence, on which was the figure of the Crucified, and he said to him and ordered that he deny Christ whose image was there. He, although reluctant, did it; and then the same receptor ordered him to spit on it, but he spat on the floor. Asked how many times, he said on his oath that he did not spit, except once, and concern-ing this, he remembered well.

Although he denied the charge of homosexuality, he extended the implications of his reception to the rest of the Order, by admitting that nothing had been done to him which had not been done to others, but he himself had taken few receptions. When he had received new members he had left the irregular part of the ceremony to others, although fully intending that the same manner of recep-tion that he had undergone should be imposed.[82]

But the king was not finished with the Grand Master. There was a need to give this confession the maximum possible publicity. Slow communications and the absence of widespread literacy did not mean that any medieval ruler, especially a feudal monarch, could be indifferent to public opinion, and indeed, as will be seen, the charges themselves were framed with the intention of provoking widespread disgust and fear of the Templars throughout all levels of society.[83] On Wednesday 25 October, therefore, Molay, together with other leading Templars – Gérard de Gauche, Gui Dauphin, Geoffroi de

Charney and Gautier de Liancourt – was brought before an assembly
at the Templars' house in Paris. Prominent among those present were
the canons, the religious and secular masters, and the bachelors and
scholars of the University of Paris.[84] The ground had been carefully
prepared, for the day after the actual arrests, before any confessions
had been extracted, Nogaret had gathered a similar group in the
chapter room of the Cathedral at Notre-Dame, and had described
the accusations against the Order. On the following day, Sunday the
15th, a larger and more varied crowd had been harangued on the
subject by various royal officials and members of the Dominican
Order.[85]

The university men had been gathered together again on the 25th
to hear Molay repeat the confession he had made to the Inquisition.
The Master confessed on behalf of himself and the other leaders
present that, although the original foundation of the Order a long
time ago was noble and had been approved by the Holy See to fight
the enemies of the faith and to aid the Holy Land,

> nevertheless the cunning of the enemy of the human race, who
> was always seeking that which he could devour, had led them to a
> fall of such perdition, that for a long time now those who were
> received in the Order denied the Lord Jesus Christ, our Redeemer,
> at their reception, not without the sad loss of their souls, and they
> spat upon a cross with the effigy of Jesus Christ, which was
> shown to each of them at the reception, in contempt of him, and
> in the aforesaid reception they committed other enormities in the
> same way.

He had not wished to reveal these things, he said, 'on account of fear
of temporal penalty, and in case the aforesaid Order should be
destroyed, in which case they would lose the honours of the world,
the status and riches which they had'. These things had been brought
out through the efforts of the Most Christian King Philip of France,
'the bringer of light, to whom nothing is hidden'. He and the Templars were truly penitent, and asked that the gathering intervene
on their behalf with the pope and the king, so that they could be
absolved and receive penance according to ecclesiastical judgement.
It was probably immediately afterwards that Molay wrote the
'open letters' described by contemporary chroniclers, exhorting all

the other Templars to confess because they had for so long been misled by error.[86] On 26 October the university men heard the other
leaders make similar confessions, together with picked Templars
such as Jean de Folliaco, who seems to have been among Philip's
informers in the Order in the months before the arrests.[87] In all,
thirty-eight Templars, including knights, priests and sergeants, confirmed that they had been received in the improper way described by
the Grand Master.[88]

The events of these two days had been no mere academic exercise,
for at the medieval university many of the great issues of religion,
society and government were thrashed out, and the conclusions
reached had a clear relevance to the problems of the day. For the
King of France the university was doubly important, for it provided
him with both theoretical backing for his regime and able staff for
his administration. In the early fourteenth century, Paris was one of
the leading European universities and could command international
influence and respect. Molay's renewal and reinforcement of his
confession therefore gained greater impact because of the nature of
his audience. Indeed, his confession, his public statement before the
university men, and the open letter have a neatness and orderly pro-
gression which suggest detailed manipulation by Guillaume de Nogaret. The effect would be to create scandal on a scale too great to be
easily forgotten, both among the general populace and among any
Templars who might have been contemplating resistance.

Molay may, of course, have been tortured, and in this way compelled to follow a pattern already determined by Nogaret. In the
spring of 1308 a Catalan living in Paris wrote to a correspondent in
Majorca of a melodramatic scene in which Molay was supposed to
have ripped off his clothing to show burns and cuts upon his arms,
legs, back and stomach, but the circumstances in which this scene
was supposed to have taken place – a declaration by Molay from a
platform before a Paris crowd – suggest that this account owes more
to imagination than to reality.[89] Moreover, a document by an anonymous jurist, which can probably be placed in 1310, and which
discusses a number of juridical points in response to what seems to
have been a series of questions emanating from the French government, claims that Molay had said that he confessed 'from fear of
pain' and had not therefore actually been tortured, and that he had
in fact 'asked sometimes to be tortured, lest his brothers said that

he had freely destroyed them'.[90] Although this piece of evidence probably comes from government sources, there was not necessarily any reason why they should have taken pains to conceal torture, since in 1252 Pope Innocent IV had authorised the use of torture by the secular authorities in such proceedings.[91] It is more likely that, in the eleven days which had passed since his arrest, other methods of a less crude kind had been used to wear down any resistance by Molay. Techniques akin to modern methods of interrogation seem likely to have been employed: continuous questioning (possibly in relays), the physical discomfort of prison, and debilitation resulting from lack of food and sleep. Show confessions in other trials, especially in the twentieth century, have been brought about in this way.[92] This technique frequently involves promises as well. Possibly Molay was offered his personal freedom once the affair was over. Nearly two years later, indeed, when the proceedings were still dragging on, Molay asserted to the papal commissioners who were questioning him that 'it seemed to him very surprising if the Roman Church suddenly wished to proceed to the destruction of the Order when the sentence of deposition against the Emperor Frederick [the Second] had been delayed for thirty-two years'.[93]

The king seems to have adopted the same, apparently prearranged, timetable in informing other rulers of the arrest of the Templars and in urging them to follow suit. On 16 October, for instance, he had written to James II of Aragon, 'in order that you equally may arise in the faith'.[94] Following the Grand Master's confession and his appearance before the university masters, Philip wrote again to James reporting this progress, in a letter dated 26 October, immediately after the event.[95]

Meanwhile in France, many Templars had already confessed; now others followed suit, for the Grand Master had removed their strongest motive for resistance by ordering them to submit. Among these confessions was that of Hugues de Pairaud, the Visitor of France, an office which made him virtual overlord of the Templars' houses in Europe, and placed him second only to Molay. Moreover, he had been a Templar even longer, having joined forty-four years before. His family too had close connections with the Order. Humbert de Pairaud, who had received Molay, was his uncle, and two other Templars, Hugues de Châlons and a certain Pierre, are mentioned as nephews of Hugues.[96]

The confession of this man therefore reflected upon the Order as a whole, but especially upon the Templars living in France, because as peripatetic ruler of the western lands, he conducted many receptions, held frequent chapter-meetings, and inspected Templar houses. The Grand Master is seldom mentioned as being present at receptions; but taking, for instance, the 138 depositions made at Paris in October and November 1307, Pairaud was the receptor in fifteen of these, over a period stretching back twenty-two years, and he is mentioned as being present at two other receptions, one of which had taken place as long as forty years before, while another Templar said he had been received at Pairaud's orders.[97] No other living leader had been so closely connected with the mode of reception around which the accusations were concentrated.

It was a temptation for the lesser Templars to try to pass the blame for illicit receptions on to such a man. All but one of the fifteen Templars received by him admitted one or more of the charges as a consequence of Pairaud's role.[98] At chapter-meetings he held, he was accused of bringing in a head for worship. Guillaume d'Arreblay, for instance, testified on 22 October that Pairaud had brought a head made of wood and silver and gilded on the outside into two chapter-meetings, and that the brothers had worshipped this head.[99] Even his visitations were seen as a cause of corruption. Mathieu de Bosco Audemari, Preceptor of Clichy in the diocese of Beauvais, in his deposition of 20 October, claimed that Pairaud prevented him from celebrating divine service by taking away the chalice and other ornaments from the chapel.[100]

Pairaud's confession, made on 9 November, was in these circumstances as significant as Molay's. It was also more sweeping. After he had made many promises to observe the statutes and secrets of the Order, the mantle was placed on his shoulders and his receptor led him behind the altar, where he showed him a certain cross on which was the image of Jesus Christ crucified and ordered him to deny him whose image was represented there and to spit on the cross; he then, although reluctant, denied Jesus Christ, by the mouth, and not in the heart. He did not actually spit on the cross and made the denial only once. No obscene kisses had taken place during his reception. He admitted that he had received many other brothers in the way that he had described. After the usual promises concerning the statutes and secrets of the Order, he led them to a secret place and caused himself to be kissed on the lower part of the spine of the back, on the navel, and on the mouth, and afterwards caused a cross to be brought into the presence of whoever it was and told them that it was necessary, according to the statutes of the said Order, to deny the Crucified and the cross three times and to spit on the cross and the image of Jesus Christ crucified, saying that, although he ordered them [to do] this, it was not done from the heart.

Some had refused to do this, but they had all eventually made the denial and spitting. He also stated that 'he said to those whom he was receiving that if any heat of nature urged them to incontinence, he gave them licence to cool off with other brothers'. He did these things because they were 'the usage of the statutes of the Order'.

The inquisitor then tried to press Pairaud further. Asked if receptions conducted by others on his orders followed the same mode, he replied that he did not know, since only those present were aware of what happened. Moreover, he did not believe that all the brothers were received in the same way. There seems here to have been an attempt to limit the scope of his testimony to his own personal conduct, but the king's men were keen to ensure that the implications of what the Visitor was saying be applied to the Order as a whole. The notarial record continues that 'afterwards on the same day' he said that 'he had understood badly and said on his oath that he well believed that all were received in the same way as each other; and this he said to correct his word and not to deny it'. Clearly threats or torture had been used to force the issue.

The Inquisitor, Nicolas d'Ennezat, a Dominican, now turned to the matter of idol worship and asked about the head which had been mentioned in various depositions. Pairaud agreed that he had

seen, held and stroked it at Montpellier in a certain chapter and he and other brothers present had adored it. He said however that he had adored it with the mouth and for the purpose of feigning, and not with the heart; however, he did not know if the other brothers worshipped with the heart. Asked where it was, he said that he sent it to Pierre Alemandin, Preceptor of Montpellier, but did not know if the king's people had found it. He said that the head had four feet, two at the front part of the face and two at the back.[101]

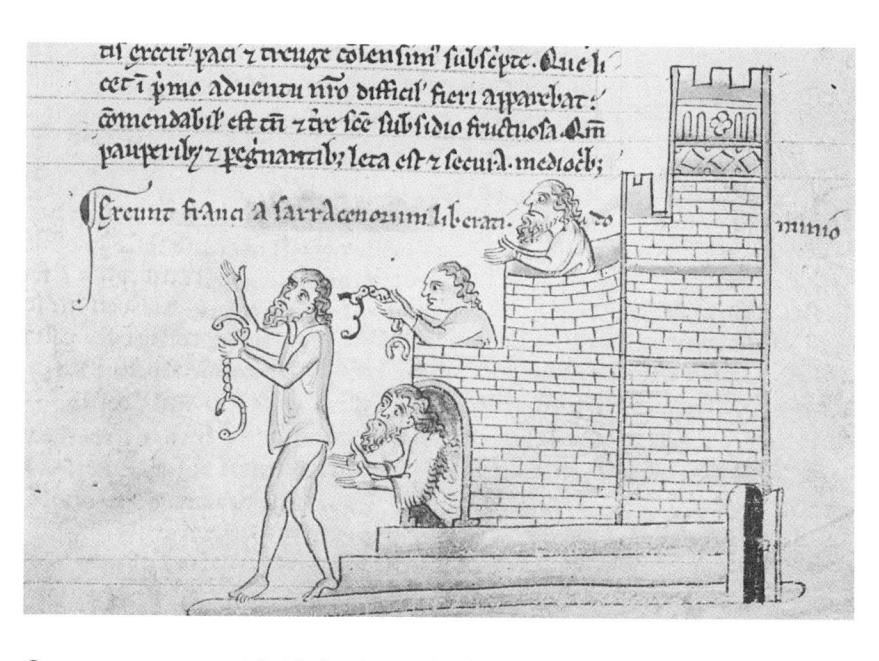

Capture was a perennial risk for those who fought in the east. The Templars themselves often refused to be ransomed but, together with the Hospitallers, they did help to negotiate the release of other Christian prisoners, acts in keeping with their charitable role. However, the long periods some Templars spent in Moslem hands could be exploited by their accusers to suggest that some had been influenced by Islam. *Below*, the sudden arrest of the Templars in France in October 1307 caught most of them by surprise. The leaders were imprisoned in the Temple itself, a large fortified enclosure to the north of Paris

Pope Clement V soon realised that he could not reverse the arrests of October 1307, so he decided to try to take over the proceedings himself by issuing the bull *Pastoralis praeeminentiae* (22 November 1307), which ordered a general arrest of the Templars in Latin Christendom. This shows the version sent to Edward II of England, received 14 December

Two other high dignitaries were interrogated soon after, and both seem to have been tortured in order to add their confessions to the formidable dossier which had already been compiled. Raimbaud de Caron, Preceptor of Cyprus, seems to have travelled to the west with Molay's embassy to the pope in 1306. Initially, on the morning of 10 November, he asserted that he had never known anything bad or shameful in receptions, except that before he was received, a brother had shown him a crucifix and told him that it was necessary to deny Christ, but this had not been done. He claimed that this had taken place in the presence of his uncle, the Bishop of Carpentras. The French officials were evidently not satisfied, for here the interrogation seems to have stopped, and the notarial record states that he was brought back the same day at about noon, and that he then admitted the denial of Christ three times after his reception and that he was told that homosexual relations were permitted within the Order.[102]

Geoffroi de Gonneville, Preceptor of Aquitaine and Poitou, was examined on 15 November. He too was unwilling to make a complete confession. When he was asked to deny Christ, although he was terrified, he argued with his receptor. The receptor told him:

> Do this boldly; I swear to you in peril of my soul that it will never be prejudicial to you with regard to mind and conscience; since it is the way of our Order, which was introduced as a result of a promise of a certain evil Master who was in the prison of a certain sultan, and could not escape unless he swore that if he were released, he would introduce that custom into our Order, that all who were received henceforth should deny Jesus Christ, and thus it has always been observed; and on account of this you can properly do it.

After further argument however, the receptor relented on condition that Gonneville swore, 'on the holy Gospels of God', not to tell other brothers that he had been spared. The denial was not therefore enforced and the spitting was on the receptor's hand and not the cross. Apparently the receptor had been inclined to be lenient because Gonneville's uncle was an influential person among the counsellors of the King of England.

The record here suggests that Gonneville had been questioned in advance of this appearance before the Inquisition, presumably by the king's officials in accordance with the royal instructions of 14 September. He seems to have resisted, and it must be assumed that he was tortured to produce the equivocal statement recorded above. 'Asked why he delayed in speaking to such an extent, since he had been asked to speak the truth at another time', he explained that he had confessed the sin to a Templar chaplain and believed that a privilege granted by the Holy See gave such chaplains the power to absolve him. Rather feebly he added that he had thought that the errors were shortly to be removed from the Order.

He himself had received only five brothers and had spared them as he himself had been spared, but he soon heard rumours that action was about to be taken against him because of this. Because of this situation, when one day he spoke with the king at Loches, he was tempted to reveal all these things to him,

> that he might give him advice on what he could do, and take him in his custody, and he should leave the Order; but afterwards considering that many preceptors and others of the Order had given him many things for his journey, and that he already had money and goods of the Order, it was not good that he should destroy them in this way.[103]

The leaders' confessions, together with the mass of supporting material gathered from the lesser members of the Order, would seem fully to vindicate the arrests of 13 October. When a leader second in authority only to the Grand Master admits the denial of Christ, spitting at a crucifix, obscene kisses, the encouragement of homosexuality, and the worship of a monstrous head, and, from his position of authority, states that such practices were a general rule in the Order, the isolated resistance of the four who confessed nothing – Jean de Châteauvillars, Henri de Hercigny, Jean de Paris and Lambert de Toysi – could have little impact.[104]

The striking success of the royal administration in extracting damning confessions would seem to indicate that the affair would be quickly settled, perhaps by Christmas 1307. The temporary alleviation of the royal financial problems was already being tackled; the king's officials had taken over the Templar estates and were busy making detailed inventories of what had been obtained.[105] However, outside France much of the rest of Christendom was sceptical. To be the grandson of Saint Louis was not in itself sufficient evidence of personal and political probity when viewed in the context of the attack at Anagni or the blatant pressure exerted on the cardinals' college prior to the election of Clement V. Moreover, Philip IV's financial problems were hardly secret; arbitrary seizure, massive debasement, and burdensome taxation had characterised his reign. On 30 October Edward II replied to the letters concerning the arrests sent to him by Philip, by saying that he and his council found the accusations of 'detestable heresies' of this kind against the Order matters of astonishment 'more than it is possible to believe',[106] while just over a fortnight later, on 17 November, James II of Aragon wrote that Philip's letters had caused 'not only astonishment but also disquiet' because the Order had hitherto rendered great services against the Saracens.[107] Neither monarch was prepared to follow Philip's lead in their own lands. Undoubtedly these kings shared part of a wider cynicism. Early in November a correspondent of James II, Christian Spinola, living in Genoa, had written to the king, saying that he had heard of the charges against the Templars, but he believed that 'the pope and the king did this in order to have their money and because they wished to make one single house of the Hospital and the Temple and all the other brotherhoods, of which house the king intended and desired to make one of his sons the ruler'.[108]

Not only kings had been favoured with Philip's letters; among the other persons was the Catalan medical doctor Arnold of Villanova, a layman who strongly supported the Spiritual Franciscan view of the imminent destruction of the world in preparation for a new utopian society, when the Holy Spirit would supersede the decadent Church. On 19 February 1308, at Marseilles, he replied to a letter from James II of Aragon, telling him that he had received news of the Templar heresy from Philip IV. But Arnold was one of the few not to profess astonishment at the affair, for although he would have agreed with the French king about the wickedness of the Templars, he did not see the discovery of the heresy as a miraculous act by a pious and Christian king, but as the prelude to the revelation of much greater apostasies, including those of kings and princes. In September 1307, God had decided upon the reform of the people because Christians had been blatantly denying the life of Christ and seeking the delights and riches and honours of this world with no less fervour than barbarians or pagans.[109]

The disappointing reaction of parts of Christendom was not in itself, however, crucial to Philip's plans; more important was the need to coerce the pope into acquiescence. And here Philip IV and Guillaume de Nogaret underestimated the sick pontiff. Clement's immediate reaction was one of great anger, in which his customary circumspection in dealing with the French monarch was thrown aside. On 27 October 1307, even before Hugues de Pairaud's confession, he wrote to the king that his ancestors 'learned in ecclesiastical discipline' had recognised that it was necessary to submit 'all things appertaining to the religion of the faith to the examination of this [Church], whose shepherd, that is the first of the apostles, was ordered by the words of the Lord: "Feed my sheep" '. After this relatively mild rebuke the letter gathers pace and power. 'The Son of God himself, the bridegroom of the Church, wished, established and ordained that this see be truly the head, the queen and mistress of all churches; and the rules of the Fathers and the statutes of the princes confirm this itself.' Indeed 'the princes of the Romans at the time when the ship of Peter was riding to and fro through many dangers in the midst of the sects of diverse heresies' recognised that in matters appertaining to the faith, everything was left to 'the examination and judgement of the Church' and that nothing appertained to them in such matters 'except reverence to the Apostolic See and obedience when they were required by it'. But the king had defiantly seized the persons and goods of the Templars. 'These things are the occasion of painful astonishment and sadness to us, because you have always found in us such benevolence before all the other Roman pontiffs who in your time have been head of the Roman Church.' Despite this, and despite the agreement made between pope and king to communicate to each other any information gained on the matter, 'you perpetrated these attacks upon the persons and goods of people directly subject to the Roman Church'. The pope now came to the climax of the letter: 'In this action of yours so unlooked for, everybody sees, and not without reasonable cause, an insulting contempt of us and the Roman Church.' He was therefore sending Cardinals Bérenger Frédol and Etienne de Suisy to examine the matter in more detail directly with the king. The persons and goods of the Templars were to be handed over to these cardinals who would receive them on behalf of the Roman Church.[110]

3: The Papal Intervention

When Clement had received news of the arrests of 13 October, he was staying some distance outside Poitiers. He hastened into the city, arriving on Sunday the 15th, and ordered a consistory to be held the next morning. This was a tribunal in which the pope and cardinals heard matters of complaint and accusation brought for settlement at the papal court. The urgency of the situation was underlined when the Cardinal Pierre de la Chapelle, who had been travelling to Poitiers, but who had stopped some distance away because of illness, was ordered to resume his journey at once. At Poitiers the extent of the royal action had been forcibly brought home to Clement, for Hugues de Pairaud, who had been attending the papal court, together with sixteen or seventeen other Templars, had actually been seized at Poitiers and carried off to the neighbouring town of Loches. Only the *cubicularii* or treasurers of the Order, who had presumably been in the papacy's direct employment at this time, were left in Poitiers, 'on account of reverence' to the pope, according to a later witness.[1] For several days Clement held a secret consistory inside a guarded room, and probably during this time he decided to challenge the French king on the issue. Perhaps he encouraged the Templars, for an anonymous correspondent at the papal court, probably one of the Templar treasurers, says that Clement told them to comfort themselves and not to despair or give way to terror. He promised to find a good remedy for the affair and to make provision for them, but above all they were not to take flight. The Preceptor of Lombardy, apparently the senior Templar present, had replied that they had no fear as long as the pope continued to guard them and grant them fair judgement, for they were good Catholic Christians, firm in the faith, having at all times been prepared to die for that faith, or to perish in Saracen prisons. Never in the 190 years of their existence had they been afraid of death.[2] Soon after, on 27 October, the pope wrote aggressively of 'the insulting contempt' of Philip's action.

The first reaction of Clement V to the Templar arrests had therefore been one of anger and wounded pride. But through his anger he saw the fundamental issue very clearly. The independent action of a secular monarch, albeit by the nominal authority of the papal Inquisitor in France, could only be construed as a frontal assault on the authority of Clement V and the tradition which he represented. To Clement, although he felt some sympathy for the Order, as his somewhat emotional assurances to the Templars in the October consistory show, it was not simply, or even primarily, the Order which was at stake, but in some senses the papacy itself; and the tenacity with which he battled with his weightier opponent in succeeding years must be interpreted in these wider terms. Clement was fully prepared to sacrifice the Order for these greater objectives with the consequence that from this time it became little more than a pawn in the continuing conflict between pope and monarch. One of the most tragic aspects was that the great majority of the Templars, and in particular their Grand Master, Jacques de Molay, untutored in European power politics and isolated from the outside world by their close captivity, never really comprehended this basic reality, and most of them continued to place a pathetic faith in the efficacy of papal action on their behalf. At no time during the seven years which the trial lasted was this faith to be justified.

The French government had, however, pre-empted the pope; it was clear that he could not reverse Philip's action. Moreover, since Guillaume de Paris had technically instigated the arrests, it was at least arguable that they conformed to the letter, although hardly to the spirit, of the law. Clement therefore tried to make the best of the situation by emphasising his own higher authority. As a result, on 22 November 1307, he issued the bull *Pastoralis praeeminentiae*. This marks a decisive point in the trial, for by this means Clement irrevocably committed himself to a central role and effectively prevented the hasty end to the proceedings which Philip would have preferred. If Clement had been prepared fully to accede to the coup of 13 October, then it is likely that some quiet, although undoubtedly disreputable, settlement would have been arranged to Philip's material advantage, and the Order would have been dissolved. But this bull ensured that the major part of the proceedings would be conducted in public with the consequent effects upon both the contemporary and later reputations of the principals involved.

The central aim of *Pastoralis praeeminentiae* was to order all Christian rulers to arrest the Templars in their lands and to take over the Order's property in the name of the papacy. The pope claimed that rumours about the state of the Order had come to his ears as long ago as the end of 1305, just about the time that he had been crowned. He had been disinclined to believe these stories, the content of which he relates, but on account of them the King of France, at the request of the inquisitor of that country, had arrested the Templars and taken their property into safe custody. Then the Grand Master 'spontaneously confessed in public in the presence of the most important ecclesiastical persons in Paris, the masters of theology and others, the corruption of the error of the denial of Christ in the professions of the brothers, introduced at the instigation of Satan, in contradiction to the original foundation of the Order'. Many other Templars in various parts of the Kingdom of France had also confessed, including one knight who had appeared personally before the pope. 'From which things, if in the field where the Order was planted, which field was thought to be virtuous and to shine forth in a mirror of great sublimity, diabolical seeds were sown, which may not be fit, our bowels are disturbed with a great commotion.' However, Clement was not prepared to commit himself to a judgement. He continued: 'But, if the premises are proved not to be true, and this is discovered, the turbulence will cease, and, according to the will of God, joy will arise; which is why we propose to investigate the truth of the matter without delay.' He had heard many accusations of criminal acts against the Templars and for this reason his conscience urged him to pursue his duty in this. The rulers were therefore ordered 'prudently, discreetly and secretly' to arrest all the Templars in their lands, and to guard and take an inventory of their property.[3] Ultimately the effect of this was to promote action, ostensibly in the pope's name, to a greater or lesser degree, in England, Ireland, Castile, Aragon, Portugal, Germany, Italy and the crusader kingdom of Cyprus, where the Templar headquarters remained.

Philip the Fair had been kept informed of the pope's intentions. A few days before the issue of the bull, on 17 November, Arnaud de Faugères, the papal chaplain, had been despatched to Philip to tell him of the proposed general arrest of the Templars.[4] The king's inner feelings can only be guessed at. He had not succeeded in coercing the pope fully to accept the arrest and confessions of the Templars, and he may have been rather surprised at the ferocity of the pope's reaction as expressed in the letter of 27 October, but he had caused the pope to take the matter seriously and to initiate proceedings on a wide scale, something which he had signally failed to achieve before 13 October. Moreover, he had extracted the Grand Master's confession with its attendant publicity, and he had gathered a substantial body of other confessions. He seems therefore to have been prepared in some degree to conciliate the pope, perhaps with a view to achieving his aims in co-operation with the pontiff, an attitude which was not unjustified given Clement's past record and the issue of *Pastoralis praeeminentiae*.

Officially at any rate Philip was prepared to allow Clement to take over the proceedings. A letter of Clement to the king dated 1 December acknowledges this and tells Philip that he is sending two cardinals, Bérenger Frédol and Etienne de Suisy, to oversee affairs on his behalf.[5] A royal letter of 24 December confirms the arrival of the cardinals, asserts that the persons of the Templars are being handed over, and promises that the administration of Templar property will be kept clear of that of the crown.[6] But even in the official correspondence there are signs that the public face of the monarchy did not accord with its private activity. Clement V, in his letter of 1 December, was considerably irritated by rumours circulated by some royal counsellors and passed on to the papal court, that the affair of the Templars, both with regard to persons and property, had been entirely handed over to Philip IV. These sources claimed that there were actually apostolic letters from the papal court authorising the king to take over. The pope made it clear that no such documents existed, but it is never easy to erase such rumours completely.

Documentary evidence of what was really happening during the period in which the pope was attempting to grasp control of the trial is sparse, but two letters from France, one to Aragon and one to Majorca, which detail rumours and stories current at the courts of Paris and Poitiers, reinforce the feeling that beneath the surface the French government was maintaining pressure on the papacy, while ostensibly co-operating with justifiable papal demands for control of the proceedings. Neither of these letters can be relied upon in its entirety, but they are perhaps indicative of certain trends and attitudes.

Both date from the spring of 1308. One appears to have been written by a Templar, Bernardo de Baynuls, who describes himself as *camarer* or treasurer of Cornela, and is addressed to Arnaldo de Baynuls, Preceptor of Gardeny in Aragon, to whom he was probably related. Both the description *camarer* and the addressee suggest that Bernardo was one of the papal treasurers who had been allowed to remain at Poitiers during the October arrests, and that he was therefore in a position to pick up rumours, if not exactly inside information, from the papal court. According to Bernardo's information the two cardinals sent to Paris by the pope to obtain the transfer of the persons of the Templars had failed and had returned to Poitiers empty-handed. The pope had at once ordered them to return to Paris and had threatened to excommunicate the king and place his land under interdict if he did not comply with his promise. As a result of this, the Grand Master and 250 other Templars were placed at the disposal of the papal representatives, although no actual physical transfer took place. Papal determination may have been reinforced by events inside the Curia, for Bernardo de Baynuls had heard stories of discontent among the cardinals. The first ten cardinals created by Clement told him that they were resigning, since they did not believe him to be the true pope. When the disconcerted pope asked how they had reached such a conclusion, they replied that they believed that the pope was the lord of the whole world, above secular rulers, yet now they saw him dominated by the King of France and allowing the destruction of a respected Order. Therefore they did not wish to remain as cardinals while Clement acted in this way. The pope thereupon had sent the cardinals to Paris to demand the delivery of the Templars.[7]

If indeed the writer was a Templar this story may contain a strong element of wishful thinking, for throughout the trial many of the Templars remained obstinately convinced that their salvation would come from the papal Curia. Moreover, there is no other evidence to suggest that even one cardinal was prepared to sacrifice his lucrative post on behalf of the Templars, especially not the collection of French political appointees and papal relatives whom Clement had elevated. However, the writer may well have picked up a general sense of dissatisfaction in the Curia with Clement's policies towards the French king, which would help to explain the course of events between December 1307 and February 1308.

The other letter – which is anonymous – was sent to one Bernard F. in Majorca, and again deals with the visit of the two cardinals to Paris, apparently to gain information about the Templar proceedings from the inquisitors themselves. In Paris the royal counsellors

and the inquisitors told them that they believed the truth of the accusations, and the cardinals returned to inform the pope. Clement
was sceptical: had they heard this from Templars themselves? The
cardinals agreed that they had not, but they had listened to the
affirmations of theologians, jurists and royal counsellors, and believed them to be absolutely true. The pope then held a consistory
in which he wished the Templars condemned if the accusations
were really true, but urged that compassion nevertheless be shown
for them. However, he sent the cardinals again to Paris, so he
appears far from convinced. Their first task was to interview the
Templars personally. In Paris they delivered the papal demands to
the king and he made the Grand Master and many other Templars
available to them. When the Grand Master was asked whether his
confession was the truth, he said that if all the inhabitants of Paris,
rich and poor, were assembled, they would see a much greater
error. There then followed the scene in which Molay is supposed to
have torn off his clothing to show the physical evidence of torture
and then to have asserted that the whole Order was without sin. At
this the cardinals wept bitterly and were unable to speak. When the
king's counsellors asked for judgement, the cardinals said that they
could not act against those who were not guilty. As a consequence
the king's counsellors became alarmed at the prospect of allowing
the papacy custody of the Templars and once again took control of
their persons. While this drama was being enacted Philip IV was
travelling to Poitiers and was told of the incident *en route*. He
returned hastily to Paris within two days, and wrote to the pope
that he must condemn the Templars; otherwise he would treat him
and the cardinals as heretics. But the pope was not intimidated.
Before he would condemn innocent people, he would rather die
himself. Even if they were guilty, as long as they showed repentance
he would forgive them, give them back their possessions and make
a new Rule for them.[8]

As with the letter of Bernardo de Baynuls, much that the writer
has to say seems intrinsically unlikely, for the gestures are too heroic
to accord with the known facts about the personalities involved.
Nevertheless the letter records a dramatic event: given the opportunity to appear before papal representatives, Jacques de Molay
revoked his confession. There is confirmation of this. According to a
series of anonymous replies to a set of questions on the juridical

aspects of the case, questions which probably emanated from the royal government, Molay had persisted in his confession for two months or more before retracting, saying that he had confessed from fear of torture.[9] Indeed, Molay may have gone further. The renegade Templar priest Jean de Folliaco testified before the pope at Poitiers some months later, in the summer of 1308, that he had heard that some brothers had revoked their confessions and believed that they had done so because 'the Master of the Order or someone acting on his instruction sent through certain wax tablets to the brothers from room to room, before the king and the cardinals entered, that all should revoke their confessions'. In substance the words on the tablets were 'Know that the king and the cardinals will come to this house tomorrow; some brothers have revoked their confessions, you should revoke and return these letters to the bearer.' A brother who had been received a month before the arrests carried the tablets, and he took them away when they had been read out.[10] A serving brother called Jean de Châlons, who was also prepared to repeat his confession at Poitiers in June 1308, gives some confirmation of this. A priest called Renaud had persuaded more than sixty Templars by means of 'secret writings' (in this version, parchment with a lead seal) to revoke their confessions, saying that if they did not the Order would be destroyed, and he, Jean, had been pressed to revoke also, although he had resisted. Jean de Châlons believed that the driving force behind the letters advising revocation was the Dean of Langres, Jacques de Molay's brother.[11] Meanwhile, Hugues de Pairaud, the Visitor and the other leader of major stature, had been invited to dine with the cardinals, whom he presumably knew personally as a result of his previous work in administering the Order in France. During the meal he too revoked his confession.[12]

Almost until the very end Molay's main hope centred upon papal intervention, and although he clearly held an exaggerated view of papal freedom of manoeuvre, his revocation before the papal representatives in the last days of 1307 set in motion a series of events which caused serious obstruction to the plans of Philip the Fair. His faith in the efficacy of papal action may well date from this time. He certainly seems to have believed that he would receive a fairer hearing before the papal representatives, and perhaps if the royal officials had implied in October that he would be treated leniently if co-operative, he now felt he had been tricked and that the trial was not to be rapidly brought to an end. He seems to have been prepared to risk the possibility that he might be regarded as a relapsed heretic in order to grasp his chance once free of the royal officials and French inquisitors.

The two Catalan letters, therefore, although embroidered with highly coloured thread, do provide a strong sense of changing mood. The seemingly watertight case against the Order had begun to spring leaks, and the papal view had considerably sharpened. Both sides now dropped their lukewarm co-operation. Some time in February 1308 Clement suspended the activities of the inquisitors and announced that he was taking the matter into his own hands. He later explained that he had become suspicious of the great power wielded by the king in the affair, and after the revocations of certain Templars had become doubtful about the whole case.[13] The French government, which had no legal way of wresting control of the proceedings from the pope, or of revoking the suspension, now began a concerted campaign to coerce Clement into changing his mind. The first six months of the year 1308 saw the development of a grim battle between king and pope, fought in the characteristic style of Philip's administration, by means of propaganda, bullying and intimidation, which culminated in a personal confrontation between Philip and Clement at Poitiers in the summer of 1308. Inevitably Clement suffered, as his predecessors had suffered, from a lack of material force with which to oppose the king, so for much of the period the pope was pushed on to the defensive; but nevertheless, at the end of the day, Philip IV can hardly have been completely satisfied with the results that he had obtained after the expenditure of so much effort.

If the king had had any real intention of handing over the persons of the Templars to papal custody, the suspension of the inquisition quickly changed his mind. His greatest asset was now the control which he retained over the persons and property of the Order. Clement V was painfully aware of his weakness. On the night of 13 February Oliviero di Penne, Preceptor of Lombardy and the senior Templar among the treasurers to whom Clement had given his assurances in October 1307, fled from the unguarded hospice in which he was lodged. The next day the pope called a consistory and, apparently in a state of great agitation over the escape, ordered that all the Templars be kept in custody, and that the cardinals were to enquire as to how the escape had happened. A reward of 10,000 florins was offered to whoever could find the escapee. Clement took the escape so seriously because, as he said, the King of France and the other rulers would ask, if he could not guard one, how could he guard two thousand?[14] His unease continued into the spring. He is reported as suddenly saying in a consistory in April that it was necessary to make a decision about the goods of the Temple. The jurist Jean le Moine, who was present, pointedly replied that first some decision should be reached concerning the persons.[15] The pope had no means of forcing Philip IV to give up either the persons or the property of the Order. Moreover, he was virtually a prisoner in French territory, for if he had left for Rome (even assuming that the city was a safe place for the papacy at this time), it would have been tantamount to conceding the field to the French king.

Philip's government at once set out to exploit these circumstances by attempting to create a climate of opinion in France so hostile to the Templars and to anyone who appeared to be lending them support, that the pope, surrounded by the French cardinals he had promoted to please King Philip, would feel so isolated that he would reactivate the inquisitorial proceedings. Philip's government was experienced in such matters: the technique of mobilising French public opinion had already been developed against Boniface VIII. Three methods were employed: the circulation of anonymous writings attacking the pope; the framing of a series of questions to the masters of theology at the University of Paris concerning the conduct of the participants in the affair, evidently designed to provide intellectual and theological respectability for the actions of the French government; and the calling together of the Estates of the realm, where representatives of the French people could be directly harangued by the king's ministers.[16]

The attacks upon the pope cannot be traced directly to the government, but they must have been government-instigated. Two anonymous examples, one dating probably from the beginning of 1308 and the other more likely from April or May, purported to be expressions of the discontent of the French people at the papal role in the trial. They may have been written by Pierre Dubois, the Norman lawyer, who, although he never held a post in French government, would certainly have been prepared to accept freelance employment of this nature, although the many echoes of these works found in the speech made later by Guillaume de Plaisians at Poitiers in June 1308 suggest that it is equally likely that the author was one of the lawyers of the royal administration.[17]

The first of these, written in the vernacular, claimed that the people of France had always been more devoted and obedient to the Holy Church than any other people, and they demanded that the King of France, who had access to the pope, should show him that he had greatly angered them and caused great scandal, 'because he only appears to have punished in words' the iniquities of the Templars. Their confessions are such that no believer can doubt them, and this is why the French people cannot understand the delay. Perhaps the Order has used its wealth for bribery to prevent action being continued, which shows how a single sin can be the cause of many sins. A lawgiver should dispense justice to all to whom it appertains, but the pope has already shown himself corrupt, for he has granted benefices 'from the affection of blood' to his relatives and to his nephew the cardinal, to an extent which outruns more than forty popes of the past, even including Boniface VIII. As a result more than two hundred masters of theology and law, each of whom is a far more able ecclesiastic than the pope's nephew, have less clerical property together than this man. The sees of Rouen, Toulouse and Poitiers have been granted out to papal relatives.[18] 'But . . . Our Lord commands that justice be done to the small as to the great and without exception or favour of person.' Indeed, Aquinas considers such bias a mortal sin. The real culprit however is not he who fills these benefices, but he who chooses them, for he has abused his position, just like a servant of the king who provides his master with his nephews as champions to fight for him or as doctors to tend him, rather than the best men available. By analogy, the pope, as God's servant, has committed a similar abuse. The people will ensure that after the present pope's death, these nephews will be deposed and replaced 'by the great masters in theology'. By his nepotism the pope has denied those who had rights of election. Indeed, whoever temporises 'through gift or promises, through fear, love or hatred, is the son of the devil and by this alone denies God who is true justice'. The king should tell the pope therefore to take care that he is using his great lordship in the proper way, for it is important that the right persons receive ecclesiastical benefices.[19]

While the first tract concentrates upon papal nepotism, the second diatribe, in Latin, is more closely concerned with society's treatment of heresy and the relevance of this to the Templars. The people of France cannot accept that the Templars' error is in any way like other heresies, which make avowal to the Catholic faith, claiming to differ only in certain articles; in such cases the laws 'are known and speak expressly against the intention of the king'. The people of France see these Templars as a special case and therefore believe that they should be placed entirely beyond the power of the Church. The author is really saying that the case was beyond the scope of ecclesiastical jurisdiction, and he draws a dramatic parallel to demonstrate this. Moses punished a similar apostasy of the sons of Israel, who had worshipped a golden calf, by ordering: 'Each take his sword and kill his neighbour.' 'In this way he caused to be killed, so that the matter would be perpetually remembered and feared, twenty-two thousand, least of all having asked the consent of Aaron, his brother, who was high priest established by the order of God.' The case is then taken to its most extreme point. 'And if "all [things] which are written and done", as the Apostle says, "are written and done for our instruction", why therefore should the king and the Most Christian prince also not proceed against the entire clergy, if, God forbid, they thus erred or were sustaining and favouring errors?' In this context the demands of Philip IV could be presented as essentially moderate.

The discourse gathered momentum. 'Are not all these Templars homicides or *fautores*, sustainers, accomplices and receivers of homicides, damnably uniting with them apostates and murderers?' Should they not suffer a punishment such as that meted out by Moses? If they did not, it could only encourage others to transgress, for pardon should not be too lightly given. A potential objection that Moses could be regarded as a priest, based on the Scriptural quotation 'Moses and Aaron in their priesthood', is then countered. Moses was only a priest in so far as the giving of law is the giving of something sacred. If he was a priest for any other reason he would not have had a high priest over him, nor would he have caused so many people to be killed, for the Lord said to the prophet David: 'You will not build a temple to me, because you are a man of blood.' The Scriptures made it manifest that the execution of justice should not be delayed and that the king was fully entitled to take matters into his own hands, 'unless the teaching of the Scriptures might be reversed through the false judgements of men by showing that Antichrist has already come and by denying God, according to the witness of the Apostle, by acts so perverse'.[20]

Material like this was so extreme that the government's action could be made to seem restrained. This view was later to be manipulated by the king's minister, Guillaume de Plaisians, before the pope at Poitiers, to suggest that the king, by asking the pope to act, rather than taking the matter completely into his own hands, was himself acting with great forbearance, and was indeed more conciliatory than the mass of his people. In fact the impression created is false, for had the king felt himself on secure legal ground, he would not have hesitated, nor would he have spent so much effort pressurising the pope. The insecurity of the royal legal position was demonstrated in the spring of 1308, when the king put seven questions relating to the juridical problems of the case to the masters of theology at the University of Paris.

The questions were probably posed some time in late February after the papal suspension of inquisitorial activity. No one doubts, the king says, that it is the Church's function to preach the faith and to instruct the people, nor that the Church is responsible for deciding when persons are in error and for bringing them to penitence and reconciliation. Moreover, it is accepted that if those in error continue contumacious, or relapse into their former ways, they are to be handed over to the secular arm and punished according to temporal justice. The Church may not judge or condemn them temporally, but prays for the relapsed. The first question arises when a secular prince or the people exercising jurisdiction hear heretics and schismatics blaspheme the name of God and disregard the Catholic faith. Should the prince then exercise his powers of justice against them, or, if the matter is not public, institute inquiries, even though he is not specifically empowered to do so by the Church or anyone else, when it is evident that a criminal act has been committed and that a great scandal is arising? Or is the authority of the secular power restricted by the New Testament, that the prince ought not to intervene except at the request of the Church? Secondly, and more specifically, can the prince proceed against the Templars when it has been found that some of them have been affected by horrible and abominable heresies, even though they are members of the religious? Can they not be seen primarily as knights rather than clerks?

Among the accusations brought against the Templars in 1307 was the claim that they worshipped idols in the form of heads. A few Templars gave vivid descriptions, which in fact seem to be based on reliquaries which they had seen in the Order's churches and elsewhere. These two late twelfth-century head reliquaries of Frederick Barbarossa, *right*, and St Eustace, *below*, must have been the type of object they had in mind

During the twelfth century the Church strove to combat heresy, first by preaching and legal procedures, then, in the thirteenth century, by crusade and, from the 1230s, by the use of inquisitors. Heretics who were regarded as contumacious or who had relapsed might be handed over to the secular arm, where they were burnt to death. *Below*, the Albigensian Crusades (1209–29) were specifically aimed at the dualist Cathars of Languedoc. This fourteenth-century illumination shows the expulsion of the inhabitants of Carcassonne after its fall to the crusaders in August 1209. The framing of the charges against the Templars was clearly influenced by inquisitorial experience of combating dualism

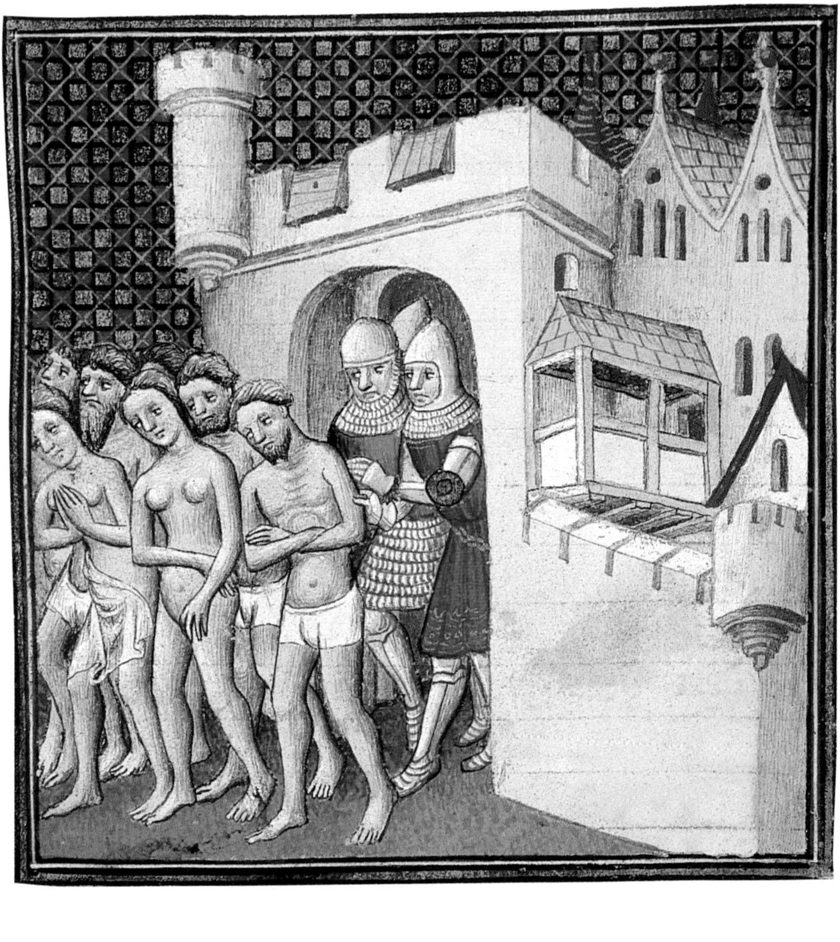

Thirdly, can this Order be condemned, since the Master and the other leaders, as well as more than five hundred other Templars, have confessed their crimes, especially as confessions have been received from every part of the kingdom, and as those who confessed did not know that others had done the same, nor had they any idea of the manner of the confessions, nor whether it was necessary to wait to see if they similarly confessed in other regions, before the Order could be condemned? Fourthly, since new entrants were forced to apostasise against the faith in secret ceremonies in which only two or three persons were present, and these persons might be dead, whether, if the truth cannot be forced from such Templars, they should still be held as Catholics? Fifthly, whether if ten, twenty, thirty or more Templars have not confessed but have denied the crime, they ought to retain their status as members of the Order, or whether the Order can be condemned because so many witnesses have deposed against it? Sixthly, are the goods of the Templars rightly to be confiscated by the prince in whose land they are situated, or are they to go to the Church, or be applied to the use of the Holy Land for which they were originally collected? Seventhly, and last, if it is decided that the goods should be applied to the use of the Holy Land, who should administer them? Should it be the Church, or should it be the temporal princes, especially the King of France, in whose lands the Templars have primarily resided over a very long period and who, together with his predecessors, has had the special guard and custody of the goods from ancient times?[21]

During his long and often violent reign Philip IV was driven to many desperate measures as he and his ministers struggled to create an administrative and financial structure commensurate with the king's needs and ambitions, but he never forgot the value of legal procedures in the development of Capetian power. The pope had objected because, as he was to say, he was suspicious of the great power held by the king in the affair.[22] These questions represent an attempt to meet Clement on his own ground by suggesting that because of papal negligence he, Philip, had been forced to take action to maintain the integrity of the Catholic faith.

The Parisian masters took their time over replying. It is possible that they wanted a period for reflection; it is probable however that they did not view with any enthusiasm the prospect of telling the king that, on certain central issues, he was in the wrong. Their reply is dated 25 March, and they explained that they had taken so long because many of their important members had been absent until recently, and they did not wish to proceed with such an important matter without them. They thanked the king for his forbearance. Their circumspection can be seen in part of the preamble to their reply. 'The Most Christian kings of the illustrious Kingdom of France are known to have shone, from the beginning of the kingdom itself, not only with the magnitude of their power, but also in the goodness of their customs and the Christian piety of their faith.' The king, 'following the praiseworthy customs of your holy predecessors, inflamed with zeal of the faith, nevertheless wishing indeed to defend the faith with the proper rule of reason', has amicably asked their opinion, even though he could have ordered them, 'his insignificant clients . . .'

However, in answer to his questions on how far he could proceed against subverters of the faith without 'usurpation of the law of another', they had this to say. In the first case, they did not think that a secular prince could imprison, examine or punish heretics except by direction of the Church, unless notorious danger were imminent and then only when it was certain that the secular action would receive ecclesiastical ratification, and when the heretics were handed over to the Church as soon as the means presented themselves. Nor could they find anything in the Old or New Testament to support a contrary view. Secondly, the Templars must be regarded as clerks and therefore exempt from secular jurisdiction, since 'a knighthood ordained for the defence of the faith is not impeded in the religious state'. If individuals have not obligated themselves to a proper Order but have only agreed to observe a heresy, then they cannot of course be held religious, but in that case it is for the Church to judge whether they have professed properly or not. Indeed by reason of the crime, everything which that crime touches appertains to the Church, until the Church directs otherwise. Thirdly, they agreed that the extent of the confessions received ought to be enough to condemn the Order, or at least be justification for an extensive enquiry, since they created vehement suspicion against all members either as heretics or *fautores* of heretics. Fourthly, when suspicion is so strong against the Order as a whole, those who have not confessed nevertheless ought to have 'safe provision' made for them, because it is still to be feared that there is a danger of others being infected, although such persons are not to be condemned as heretics. The fifth question, which asked whether the limited number who have denied the accusations ought to have the law and constitution of the Order provided for them, they felt had already been answered by articles three and four. The sixth and seventh questions offered the greatest problems if the king was not to be offended. Here, the masters prudently hedged. The gifts made to the Templars were not handed over to them 'principally and as to lords, but rather as ministers for the defence of the faith and the aid of the Holy Land' and therefore should be used for this purpose. However, the guard of the goods 'ought to be administered in the way which best expedites the said end'. The concluding paragraphs of these carefully worded answers perhaps convey something of the unease which these masters must have felt.

> Here therefore, most serene lord, are those things which we have concluded in agreement and have written as well as we can, very much wishing from the heart to obey the royal orders and also to be truthful; would that, as we desire, they are acceptable to your royal majesty, because we have very freely furnished diligent study to labour towards that which may be agreeable to so great a Highness. And would that such injury to the faith, of which you are the principal fighter and defender, which is so scandalous and so horrible to all the Christian people, be quickly conquered in accordance with your holy desire.[23]

There was scant justification for unilateral action by Philip IV in this, but the university masters had said that the confession might justify condemnation, in this way providing the king with further support for his campaign against papal dilatoriness.

In 1302 and 1303 Philip had called the Estates-General to marshal support and spread propaganda against Boniface VIII. Between 24 and 29 March 1308 he again sent letters of convocation to the clergy, nobles and towns to attend a meeting of the Estates. The clergy were especially asked for their aid to defend the faith against the sacrileges of the Templars. The archbishops and bishops received personal letters, telling them that provincial councils were to be held by the metropolitans as a preliminary to the Estates and that a procurator was to be chosen from each diocese.[24] The great nobles too received personal letters, reminding them of their fealty to the king, but with little more detail than this.[25] The most virulent language was reserved for the towns, which serves to emphasise the propaganda nature of the exercise. Our predecessors, the king says, were always concerned before all other princes to drive out heresies and other errors, 'defending the most precious stone of the Catholic faith, as an incomparable treasure, from robbers and brigands'. Therefore 'giving heed to the rock from which we are cut, inheriting the characteristics of our predecessors', he was striving to defend the Catholic faith not only from overt enemies but more especially from secret ones, because these were by their very nature the more dangerous. It was by means of the Catholic faith that they all subsisted, and anyone striving to attack this faith was trying to kill Catholics by depriving them of the hope of achieving the Kingdom of Heaven.

> Christ is the way to us, the life and the truth; who then can deny him, by whom and in whom we subsist, who is not acting to destroy us? Everyone considers that he loved us so much that for us he did not fear to assume flesh and to undergo the most cruel death in the flesh. Let us then love such a Lord and Saviour, who so loved us before, we who are one body to reign equally with him; let us strive to revenge his injuries.

The Templars, by denying Christ and the sacraments, forcing new entrants to spit on and tread the cross underfoot, kissing one another in vile places and adoring an idol in place of God, are such attackers; indeed they say that their false rite allows them to act against nature, doing things which even 'brute beasts' refuse to do. These enormities have been proved throughout the whole kingdom and beyond the sea too, a fact made patently clear by the confessions of the leaders. The king proposed to confer personally with the pope in the near future with the purpose of extirpating this heresy. The towns were therefore ordered to send two men to Tours three weeks after Easter to assist the king in the name of their communities.[26]

Extra administrative effort was mobilised in an effort to overcome the resistance of the king's subjects to such assemblies. The *baillis* were ordered to expedite matters as quickly as possible, and were given permission to multiply the documents needed under the seal of the *bailliage* if they were insufficiently supplied by the chancery.

Delay would be regarded as serious misconduct.[27] The *baillis* seem to have responded with alacrity; the *baillis* of Amiens and Mâcon, for instance, were transmitting their orders by 7 and 8 April.[28]

The call for participation bit very deep. Local studies have shown that the towns called upon to send representatives might be very small, since the king apparently expected deputies from 'all the towns where there are fairs or markets'.[29] In the *bailliage* of Troyes, for instance, there were six such places, including communities such as the town of Ervy, which, although it had obtained a community franchise in 1199, did not have a mayor or an elected council, but had been ruled by a *prévôt* appointed by the Count of Champagne. It is difficult to imagine Ervy as an important town in Champagne, let alone in the Kingdom of France as a whole. Nevertheless, on 4 April, the *bailli* of Troyes, the king's regional official, sent Pierre Veriauz, the *prévôt* of Ervy, a copy of the king's instructions to be read before the assembled inhabitants. He ought then to arrange that suitable candidates be sent to the meeting of the Estates. Their diligence and loyal obedience would be the means of avoiding the reproaches of the king and protecting themselves from all damage. Pierre Veriauz duly carried this out and on 28 April assembled the bourgeois of Ervy and arranged for two of their number to be sent to the Estates-General at Tours.[30]

Like an estimated seven hundred other urban deputies,[31] the two bourgeois from Ervy dutifully appeared at the assembly, for Philip's command met a very full and docile response from the towns. The small town of Gien on the Loire, for example, chose two of their number, Etienne Cartier and Jean Galebrun, from the forty electors who formed the most 'qualified' part of the population of the town. They were elected

> in order to go to Tours, or wherever it pleases our lord the king, to listen and to take in the wish, ordinance and establishment of the king our lord and his noble council touching the ordinance, absolution or condemnation of the Templars and all other things that it is pleasing to the king our lord and to his said council to ordain and to establish and to do all the other things which loyal procurators could and ought to do.

To do this they gave them 'full power and special mandate', pledging their property as a guarantee that they would abide by what was done by the procurators or even what was done by one of them.[32]

Some of the nobles and clergy were less anxious to please. Many sent proxies on the grounds of illness or the pressing demands of their affairs, including several great nobles who had been personally convoked, for example Arthur, Duke of Brittany, and his son Jean, *Vicomte* of Limoges, and Robert, Count of Flanders, who could not be present because of his arduous affairs (for which he was sad), together with his son Louis, Count of Nevers.[33] Political circumstances played the dominant role here, but others too could not work up enthusiasm for an institution like the Estates-General which lacked deep roots among the French aristocracy. These included the Counts of Forez, Auvergne, La Marche and Angoulême, Périgord, Astarac, Comminges and Valentinois, and the *Vicomtes* of Turenne, Narbonne and Polignac.[34] While most pleaded illness or business reasons couched in conventional formulae, Jean de Lévis, Lord of Mirepoix, maintained, in a letter dated 16 April, that he could not come because the notice given was too short.[35] For some however there really were serious problems: the abbot who was head of the Premonstratensians was visiting houses of the Order in remote parts of Germany, while the Abbot of Joug-Dieu in the diocese of Lyons could not leave because his presence was necessary to defend his monastery from its enemies.[36]

Others were not as pleased as the bourgeois of Gien to go 'wherever it pleases our lord the king'. The Abbot of Vilmagne, near Montpellier, had been told to go to Poitiers, where he arrived apparently exhausted after a long and arduous journey, only to be told that the meeting was in fact at Tours. But he would go no further, and contented himself with sending three deputies from Poitiers.[37] Despite the king's anxiety to ensure a large attendance to exert maximum pressure on the pope, there appears to have been administrative indecision as to the exact place. The Archbishop of Narbonne, who was in Paris with the other royal counsellors, sent many of his suffragans to Poitiers, and of the 140 procurations to the clergy, seventeen had the wrong place indicated, mostly from the ecclesiastical province of Narbonne.[38] The fact that this mistake emanated from a counsellor who was very close to the king suggests that the government had not yet a clear idea as to the exact use of the Estates. Possibly the pope could be more easily overawed if the meeting were held at Poitiers where he was in residence, but past experience suggested that opposition from the clergy, or at least a section of it, was a possibility, and the close proximity of the pope might have encouraged this. Even in their replies to the letters of convocation there are signs of this, for some clerical procurators were sent, not with fully delegated powers as in the case of the loyal bourgeois, but 'saving and reserving' the authority of the Holy See, or 'without prejudice to the Holy Roman Church'.[39] It was safer to hold the meeting at Tours, within easy reach of the pope, and then to select representatives of the Estates who could be relied upon to support the king, and take them to Poitiers afterwards. The Bishop of Cahors, for instance, who was not able to attend personally because of his arthritis, stated expressly in his reply to the king that his procurators would appear on his behalf 'at Bourges, Tours and Poitiers, in curiae and parliaments and convocations made and to be made by the most holy father Clement, our Lord High Pontiff, and the Lord King of France, and the venerable father the Lord E., Archbishop of Bourges'.[40] The bishop here refers to the provincial council to be held by his metropolitan, the Archbishop of Bourges, for the purpose of choosing a procurator; the actual meeting at Tours itself; and what seems to have been the planned end, the meeting with the pope at Poitiers by the king, accompanied by representatives of his realm.

These manoeuvrings show clearly that the primary function of these representatives was to accord with royal policy. In this context the calling of delegates from such a wide range of apparently minor market towns is not to be interpreted as a democratic tendency, but rather the opposite. The absolutist trend of the French monarchy in the early fourteenth century is reflected in this attempt to extend royal power and disseminate royal propaganda to even the most parochially minded sectors of society.

Unfortunately there are no records of the proceedings at Tours. If the Estates had met at the appointed time – namely Sunday 5 May, the three weeks after Easter stated in the royal letters – then the assembly was in being for ten days. On Wednesday 15 May the king gave licence for the deputies to return to their homes.[41] Doubtless they were equipped to spread the word even to such as Ervy or Gien, for they would have listened to the speeches of the royal ministers, probably Nogaret and Plaisians, describing in the violent rhetoric of Philip's regime the heinous crimes of the Templars. Obediently they declared that the Templars merited death for their crimes.⁴²

By 18 May the king had returned to Paris, but soon after, as promised when he convoked the Estates, he set out to meet the pope at Poitiers.⁴³ Not all the deputies were given licence to disperse, for a good number accompanied the king, their expenses being paid by a special tax.⁴⁴ The royal entourage was formidable. Jean Bourgogne, James II's procurator, who is a valuable eye-witness to the meetings of the king and pope at Poitiers, wrote that Philip brought with him his brother, Charles of Valois, and his sons, as well as barons and prelates and representatives of the cities and important towns. This small army reached Poitiers on 26 May,⁴⁵ and must in itself have been a powerful instrument of intimidation to a pope with no comparable armed force. Boniface VIII had been physically attacked by Nogaret in faraway Anagni in an attempt, almost successful, to carry him off to France to be put on trial. Clement V must have felt more acutely than ever before the grave disadvantage of having no settled place of residence from which he could face the French king, and his experiences during June and July 1308 may well have persuaded him to create a new (if temporary) papal seat at Avignon soon after.

Outwardly, however, the king presented a smiling face. While his servants quarrelled with the cardinals' men over lodgings, for Poitiers was already overstretched by the presence of the papal court, the king humbly prostrated himself at the pope's feet.⁴⁶ Clement, for his part, received the king with every sign of favour. He was pleased, he said, at the king's arrival, for two reasons in particular: firstly, because he wanted to see Philip personally before he set out for Rome, and secondly, because the king had come on account of the important matter of the Holy Land.⁴⁷

Outward appearance did not deceive the experienced observer. Jean Bourgogne told King James in a letter dated 26 May, the day of the king's arrival, that it was not known how long Philip would stay but 'it is believed that it will not be a short time', since the pope had suspended from 25 May until 24 June the *audientia causarum*, the court in which the pope heard pleas, and the *audientia litterarum*, in which defendants' objections to proceedings against them were considered.⁴⁸ Jean Bourgogne found it almost impossible to see the pope on Aragonese business. Over a week before, the procurator had tried to talk to the pope while he was out riding.

He said to me that I should return that day after lunch, which I did. And through a certain servant he told me that I should return the next day, which I did. And on the morrow when he was due to ride, seeing me he called me and excused himself on account of the multiplicity of affairs, since he had not heard me, that I should return on the morrow, namely Sunday . . . I returned on the Sunday and the Monday and several days after and I have not yet spoken to him.[49]

Clement was clearing away the ordinary affairs of papal administration so that he could give his full attention to his meeting with the King of France. Jean Bourgogne was to become more and more frustrated in his attempts to gain an audience.

Clement V was well aware that this was the culmination of the pressures which the French government had been building up since the suspension of the inquisitorial proceedings against the Templars in the previous February. On 29 May the pope held a public consistory in the royal palace at Poitiers. The cardinals and the royal counsellors were present, together with a large crowd of ecclesiastics and laymen. Guillaume de Plaisians, the royal minister, rose, and having ascended a platform, presented the royal case against the Templars, in a long and forceful speech, delivered, according to Jean Bourgogne, in the vernacular,[50] presumably to be understood by the widest possible audience. It is almost certain that the authorship of this speech, as well as that of a second discourse delivered in mid-June, belongs to Guillaume de Nogaret, but he could not make the speech himself because he remained personally obnoxious to the pope as a result of his role in the attack on Boniface VIII at Anagni.[51]

Plaisians began with a panegyric on the victory just accomplished on behalf of the defence of the Catholic faith, namely the exposure of the 'perfidious Templars', the greatest of the victories accomplished by the Lord. He uses the formula 'Christ conquers, Christ reigns, Christ rules' as a prelude to the account of how Philip the Fair, as Christ's vicar on earth, had achieved the victory over the Templars.[52] In order to show this victory to the pope the king had come with all his court and representatives of the body politic, 'not intending to assume the part of accuser, denunciator, instructor or promoter in the form of a trial against them', but, together with his prelates, barons and people, to act 'as zealots of the Catholic faith, defenders of the Church, the wall of Jerusalem, and the purgers of heretical depravity'. Plaisians then began to 'elucidate' the victory, as he put it. 'At the beginning of the war, the said victory was horrible and terrible, in its progress pleasing and marvellous, in its end clear, well known and undoubted'. Nothing else remained to be done except for the expulsion of the Order by the pope.

It was 'horrible and terrible' for the king and ministers for four reasons: firstly, the initial denunciations were from men of low status to move an affair so great; secondly, because of the great status and the riches and power of the accused; thirdly, because of the inhumanity of the crimes, sufficient to subvert divine and human nature; and fourthly, because of the links of love and devotion by which this Order had been bound to the king and his predecessors under whom they had enjoyed special grace and favour.

However, despite these first problems, the affair was 'pleasing and marvellous' because of the events which, by God's miracle, had followed. God chose ministers for his victory who were acting not for themselves but for Christ, 'throwing aside from themselves all cupidity and vainglory'. In this regard Plaisians would state the intention of the king with regard to the Templars' property. No one else living has dared to do a thing as great as this accomplished by the king, who is obliged to do this for many reasons, but 'most importantly since he swore on oath in his coronation'. Moreover, 'Christ is seen to act miraculously, as from the Kingdom of France chosen and blessed by the Lord before the other kingdoms of the world, he has elevated you [i.e. Clement V] as successor of the apostle Peter, and you are present at this time in the aforesaid kingdom with your curia.' Now both king and pope could join together to wage war for the Lord. In addition, all the leaders of the Order from various parts of the world had been brought into this kingdom 'under the cover of another cause' so that they could 'be led to justice'. Even before their capture the Master and the other leaders, 'in excusing themselves to the king and in hiding their errors', had confessed manifest heresy against the sacrament of the keys and sacramental confession. Then, after they were captured, many Templars, 'in fear of the crimes of which they were accused, despairing of Christ's mercy', killed themselves. The others, 'with few exceptions', have, throughout the kingdom, spontaneously confessed, independently of one another, even though they have not been questioned from 'fixed particulars'. The Master himself had confessed in a public speech before the University of Paris, while certain Templars at Uzès and Carcassonne had been brought to their confessions by 'manifest miracles'. They had long persevered in these confessions in the presence of bishops, their officials and other religious men, and in the presence of the clergy and the people. Some, however, after maintaining their confessions over many months, revoked them, 'having colluded on this among themselves', as the cardinals who had been sent to Paris knew. They had also received comfort through messengers and letters from certain persons in the Kingdom of France. Some of these comforters were corrupted by money, others acted from confused motives, but all could justly fear punishment as *fautores* of heresy. After the general confessions many had spontaneously confessed to further enormities, some before the Archbishop of Sens, others before the Bishop of Mâcon.

After this miraculous progress it was finally possible to say that the heresy stood 'clear and undoubted'. The Order had been convicted by many witnesses, the many confessions received made the matter plain, its public reputation throughout the world 'acclaims' against it, it is not only clear in law but to all men, the evidence is recorded by public instruments and authentically sealed, it had been convicted by 'the certain report of a prince so great and so Catholic, minister of Christ in this affair' (i.e. Philip IV), and by many Catholic bishops, and by the acclamation of the barons and people of the kingdom.

Plaisians had tried to show how the affair had developed through its various stages. Although the king had first doubted that such things could be true, he had been convinced by overwhelming evidence, and had therefore been obliged to act as a sacred duty of kingship. At the same time Plaisians had tried to overcome the weaknesses of the case, by meeting known objections. He admitted the low status of the original denunciators, explaining that this was one of the reasons why the affair had initially been horrible and terrible. He blandly asserted that the king was not attempting to gain the Order's property, but with his ministers was acting as God's instrument, the favoured ruler of a chosen people. The confessions themselves, on which so much of the case rested, he maintained had been spontaneous and independent and had not been obtained by leading questions.

He then proceeded to make a final attempt to clinch the case by adducing arguments which, he claimed, made the matter undoubted, even without the preceding points. From a time 'for which the contrary memory does not exist', the people had believed that something illicit was being committed in the secret ceremonies of the Templars, a view sustained by the fact that they refused to reveal these secrets to the bishops. They held chapters and meetings at night, 'which is the custom of heretics', for those who act evilly hate the light. Their guilt shows too in the results of their activity, for by their defection the Holy Land is said to have been lost, and they are said to have often made secret agreements with the sultan. They did not give hospitality or alms, or offer other works of charity in their houses, for their whole aim was acquisitive, by means of litigation and contention. They had promised to act in this way, legally or illegally, as certain depositions show. Some Templars, having broken out of prison, give further proof of guilt, for they have taken to robbery in the woods, and pillage along the roads, and threaten the lives of the judges and ministers of the affair. In many places they have built castles against the Church, and stolen goods and dissipated them, even sacred vessels. None or few have presented themselves to defend the Order, 'even of those who were living outside France', despite the issue of a general order by the pope. Indeed, many of those in Spain have actually crossed over to the side of the Saracens.

From these points the evidence is therefore very clear, nor could 'anyone who is a true Catholic and wishes to avoid the danger of favouring heresy' doubt these things, which have been made 'miraculously manifest by God' by means of the king, Church, barons and people of France. On the contrary, 'if a brute animal brought this so clear and proved, it would not be disputed further'. The cause of the faith should in this way be protected, especially by the pope, who is loosed from all restraints in a case such as this.[53]

Plaisians's 'elucidation' therefore reached its climax on a threatening note; it must have been tempting to a pope, surrounded by potentially hostile forces, to have capitulated there and then. Moreover, there is some evidence to suggest that the oral version of Plaisians's discourse, as reported by Jean Bourgogne, who was present, implicated Clement more directly in the development of the affair and pressed him more strongly than the official written version of the text suggests, as well as including more circumstantial detail. Possibly the written version gives only the substance of the speech, and it was strengthened for the actual delivery. However, much of the extra material reported by Jean Bourgogne is not based on very firm ground, and perhaps it was simply intended to help create a generally excited atmosphere which would not have been receptive to a reasoned papal reply.

According to Jean Bourgogne, Plaisians related that when the king had first heard of the accusations against the Order, he had spoken about them directly with the pope, first at Lyons and then at Poitiers, and sometimes through messengers. Jean Bourgogne reports: 'And in this affair he [i.e. the king] had proceeded by the authority of the letters of the lord pope.' This was tantamount to saying that Clement had authorised the arrests, and it is nowhere included in the official version of Plaisians's speech. Plaisians too laid greater stress upon the purity of the king's motives: God had chosen Philip 'who is God's vicar in temporal things in his kingdom'; he is not moved by cupidity as some evil-speakers would have it, as he has enough property already, and more than that of any other Christian prince. He has committed the goods to faithful persons, who were not his officials, to be used 'on the passage to the Holy Land, for which they had been given', even though he could legally have confiscated them. Concerning Molay's admissions before capture, Plaisians explained that he had confessed to lay absolution of Templars. The revocations he ascribed explicitly to certain persons within the Church – in the official version he is much vaguer – who had received Templar bribes (an idea already implanted by one of the anonymous attacks on the pope). Plaisians gave details of some of his more general statements: the additional confessions before the Bishop of Mâcon, for instance, had included urinating upon the cross. Further testimony as to guilt came from royal spies who had been placed in the Order.

Finally, Jean Bourgogne reports a much more direct hectoring of the pope than does the official version. Since the victory is clear and undoubted, then it only remains for the pope to condemn the Order. He is urged by king and people not to delay, but to act with the speed that the affair requires. He should also relax the suspension on the inquisitors so that they could proceed against individuals, condemning those who merited it, but bringing those who are penitent back into the fold. If the pope delays further, however, the king cannot neglect to take revenge for these injuries to Christ. Indeed, he has had great difficulty in restraining his people, 'who, hearing these insults, these blasphemies and these injuries brought against Jesus Christ, have risen up and wish to attack the brothers of the Temple, without waiting for any judgement'. The pope should take heed of this, for the Kings of France have spilt their blood for the Church – both Saint Louis and Philip III died in its service – and so have the barons and people. This too is the kingdom where the study of theology flourishes, 'the divine wisdom', by which 'the whole of the Church of God is illuminated'. When therefore the king, prelates, barons and all the people of this kingdom ask for a quick expedition of this affair, holy father, 'it should please you to expedite it at once! Otherwise it will be necessary to speak another language to you!'[54]

Jean Bourgogne also reports further speeches endorsing what Plaisians had said. Gilles Aicelin, Archbishop of Narbonne, compared the Templars with the Midianites who had perverted Israel, although there never was a more perverse heresy than that of the Templars. Various pagans and heretics denied that Jesus Christ was God, but did accept that he was a prophet and a holy man. The Templars both deny him to be God and claim that he was a false prophet. It was necessary to act quickly against this danger, otherwise it would spread across the world like Arianism, which began as a spark in Alexandria, but, because it was not put out, created a huge conflagration. He was followed by Egidio Colonna, Archbishop of Bourges, and by representatives of other elements in the community: a member of the baronage, a citizen of Paris, who spoke for those who understood the French tongue, and a citizen of the Toulousain, speaking for Toulouse and Montpellier in the language of the south and west, the land of Languedoc.[55]

But although the ring was tightening around him, the pope did not concede. It was now his turn to reply. Backing his statements by quotations from Amos and Malachi, he agreed upon the necessity to hate evil and to love good, incumbent upon all prelates, but especially upon the pope. Nevertheless it followed that this should be justly done. Before his election as pope, he had known little of the Templars, for few nobles of his native region had entered the Order. However, after he had become pope he had got to know many of them, valuing them as good men. If nevertheless they were guilty of such things as had been spoken of, then he hated them. When these things were established before him as judge, he would proceed against them. He and the cardinals should act quickly, 'but not however precipitately, but honestly and maturely' as befitted the Church of God. He said this in Latin, repeating it in the vernacular for all to understand. Clement made much less of the meetings which he had had with Philip than had Plaisians. They had talked about the Templars at Lyons, but the pope could not then believe the accusations, while at Poitiers he could not even remember what he had said. But the pope knew that he had never sent letters authorising the king to arrest the Templars.

He, as pope, had high status, as head of a Church founded first upon the blood of Christ and next upon the blood of the Apostles, but despite this status and despite the beautiful and precious clothes and other exterior things, he had a burden to bear. He had never believed that the King of France was moved by greed, since, 'as was proposed on his behalf' he does not intend to appropriate the goods, 'but that they should be placed at the disposition of the Church in the matter of the Holy Land'. Jean Bourgogne wryly notes the papal skill at turning Plaisians's statement to his own advantage, when he comments, 'This "at the disposition of the Church" the lord Guillaume had not said.' The pope then stated that he would proceed quickly in the matter, and that he would give a forty-day indulgence to whoever would say five times per day, *Pater noster*, and seven times, *Ave Maria*, that God would give him grace to proceed in the matter in such a way as to be to the honour of God.[56]

Effectively therefore the verbal onslaught of the French government had failed to move the pope. Plaisians was obliged to embark upon a second long discourse on 14 June, and this time the tone was even more overtly threatening. The opening words are ominous.

Most holy father, you know that it is written by the Lord, our master, maker of the world, who did not make sin: 'Which of you reproves me for sin?' For speaking to the people of the Jews, he delivered this word as an example to his future vicars in the Church of God, lest on account of the height of their dignity they should disdain, if, as men, they should have sinned, to be reproved for sin.

Sometimes they still 'scorn to receive kindly any advice in conduct from small persons' which would prevent a scandal from following, but 'the Lord is able to reveal things through small persons . . . which should be profitable to the great'.

In this context Plaisians came once more to the central issue of the Templars. 'A powerful noise resounds to God and you who hold his place: the weed can already be separated from the fruit, followed by the lifting and putting on the fire.' The king, 'not as accuser, denunciator or special mover, but as the minister of God, fighter for the Catholic faith, zealot of the divine law', has taken action to defend the Church. Although many have suggested that he can take action on his own to 'extirpate the perfidy of the Templars', and this is known 'according to the precept of God and the institution of the holy fathers', he is a respectful son, and addresses three requests to the pope. Firstly, that he be careful to instruct the ordinary prelates of the kingdom, as well as of other kingdoms, to take action against the individual persons of the Templars in their dioceses; secondly, that the suspension of the inquisition be revoked; and thirdly, that the Order of the Templars, which in fact ought to be considered a condemned sect, be totally removed from the Church by apostolic provision.

These requests had been answered by the pope only in very general terms, and nothing specific had been declared; 'as a result of this you will know that the minds of the listeners who were present were greatly astonished, and there has been generated among all a grave scandal.' For some suspect that the pope wishes to protect the Templars and that this has been made known to them, while others, 'seeing that you reply as if in doubt', themselves doubt the sin of the Templars even though it is clear and certain. To overcome scandal and effectively prove his love for justice and goodness the pope must act, for already the devil 'has furtively taken from you the sheep of the Temple and turned them into wolves', and he will be trying to steal those who remain in the flock. Do not be caught asleep by this robber, but be vigilant.

If the pope does not act, then the princes and people will act in default of him, for all live by the Catholic faith, and any attempt to deny or pervert it is an attack on the life and substance of all. 'If therefore the right hand, namely the ecclesiastical arm, is deficient in the defence of this sacred body, may not the left arm, namely

temporal justice, rise to the defence?' Indeed, if both arms are deficient, then the people should come to the defence of the faith. 'From
the foregoing it therefore follows that you give to another your
glory in the service of God, which was to you shameful.'

There followed a second confusion from the delay of the pope,
because it gave the enemy the opportunity of victory. Delay indicted
the pope as a *fautor* of the Templars' crime. Here Plaisians drew a
parallel with Anastasius, in himself a good pope, but one struck
down by God and repulsed by the clergy as a *fautor* because he acted
half-heartedly against heresy. He quoted what had happened to
another prelate, to whom God had said, 'I wish that you were warm
or cold, but since you are neither warm nor cold but tepid, I begin to
vomit you from my mouth.' Delay will cause double confusion, for
the heresy of the Templars, which was once secret, is now known,
and could spread. Already the souls of the weak have been troubled
in the faith. As well as this, the discipline of the Church will be
brought into contempt, because of its failure of application. The
truth of the error of the Templars is clear and the quick execution of
justice must not be impeded. Nor is it necessary to trouble about
how these crimes have been found out, even if they had been discovered in the presence of the laity and not the inquisitors. 'All
which the affair touches, all are called to the defence of the faith.'[57]

The menace is direct and obvious. The king can act on his own
authority if necessary. He can leave the pope isolated by ensuring
that the French clergy break off their allegiance. He can take steps
to indict the pope as a *fautor* of heresy and even to depose him.
Indeed, the pope was virtually irrelevant, since the Templar crimes
had been found out and proved already, and it did not therefore
matter on whose authority this had originally been done. Philip had
thus dropped all pretence that the arrest and trial had been in co-
operation with the pope, and was now arguing that, where heresy
is manifest and threatens all, any member of the Christian community has the right to act in lieu of the established authorities. Even a
century later this view, taken to its logical conclusion, would have
represented a very radical conciliarist opinion of church government, and it is doubtful if it would have been held by any large
sector of educated opinion in 1308. But then it is doubtful if Philip
took this view at all seriously; certainly a French subject who argued
in the same way with regard to the French monarchy would not

have met with a very friendly reception. Moreover, if Philip had really held this view of papal irrelevance, why had he posed the questions to the masters of theology, encouraged the scurrilous tracts, and called the Estates? Why was he at Poitiers at all, debating the case with the reluctant pope, if Clement's position was so weak? Indeed, the conclusion of Plaisians's speech seems to suggest a note of desperation at the failure to move an obdurate pontiff.

There now followed an exchange between the pope and Plaisians which serves to emphasise this point. Clement maintained the traditional view – unchanged by Plaisians's harangue – that ecclesiastics could not be judged by laymen and that judgement could not be pronounced without mature reflection. Plaisians replied that heretics like the Templars were of less value than the Jews or Saracens and that it was lawful for every Christian to put them to death. The pope agreed that it was permitted for Christians to hate them and avoid their company, but not that they could kill them unless it were granted by the Church or unless they were openly at war with Christians. Moreover, even if the Templars of France were heretics, he could not condemn the entire Order for this. Clement returned to his original position: he could not take any decision until the members and the property of the Order were handed over to him. Then, if they were found innocent, he would set them free; if not, he would put them beyond the Church. The king could only say that he would have to take counsel, and that he would reply another day.[58]

4: The Papal and Episcopal Inquiries

The public harassment of the pope, the climax of six months of intensive activity by the French government, had not succeeded in forcing Clement to revoke his decision to suspend the activities of the inquisitors in the trial. Despite the fact that King Philip effectively controlled both the persons and the property of the Templars, and despite the fact that the papal Inquisitor in France, together with most of the north French episcopate, could be mobilised on behalf of the French government, Clement's stubbornness was still an implacable barrier to further progress in the proceedings. This is testimony to the continued importance of the papacy, and indeed of the personalities of individual popes in European politics, and suggests that caution should be exercised before charting prematurely the decline of papal power after the disasters of the pontificate of Boniface VIII. Philip IV still needed Clement V, for all the outrageous language of Guillaume de Plaisians.

The king therefore decided to make a placatory public gesture. On 27 June he had seventy-two Templars brought to Poitiers so that they could testify in person before the pope. Philip maintained that the previous December he had not been able to release any of the Templars when they had been demanded by the pope, seemingly because of the problems presented by the fact that they were scattered all over the kingdom.[1] Between 29 June and 2 July these Templars appeared before the pope and the cardinals concerned with the case, at first in secret, and then, on 2 July, in public, when their depositions were read out and translated in full consistory.[2] Not all these depositions have survived, but it is possible to trace the names of fifty-four of the Templars concerned, of whom forty have left full depositions confessing to some or all of the crimes of which the Order was accused; and three others in a later testimony in 1310 admitted that they also had made confessions before the pope and cardinals at Poitiers.[3] Only one, a priest from Périgord, Jean de Valle Gelosa, asserted that although he had appeared before the pope, he had confessed nothing in his presence.[4]

Among the first to be heard, on 29 June, was the priest Jean de Folliaco, who had been the first witness in the Parisian hearings of October 1307, where he had asserted that he had told the curia of the *prévôt* of Paris before the arrests that the Order was not pleasing to him, and had claimed that he would have left it if he had dared.[5] Now Folliaco embellished this testimony. After he had made the standard profession of chastity, obedience and poverty, and had sworn not to leave the Order and to keep its observances and secrets, he was taken into the oratory of the chapel in which this reception had taken place, 'which is a secret place', by Brother Guillaume, Preceptor of the Temple at Paris. Here Guillaume said, 'You are ours; it is necessary that you say after me: You who are called God, I deny you.' Folliaco refused, and the receptor grabbed him by his clothes at the neck, and threatened, 'You are entirely ours, and you have sworn not to leave the Order for any reason; I will place you, unless you speak after me, in such a prison that you will never get out.' Folliaco then shouted as loud as he could, 'I deny you', without mentioning God, for he meant to refer to the receptor, and he had hoped that his shouting would be heard outside. In 1304 he had appeared before the *prévôt* of Paris and made a protest about the Order, proof of which he believed was contained in an official letter. The letter however did not seem to be forthcoming, and in any case Folliaco admitted that he had not actually mentioned any errors of the Order during the protest, but only complained about its austerities. If he had spoken of the errors, he knew that he would have been killed. Even in a confession to the Bishop of Melun, to whom he had apparently bemoaned the possibility of being sent to the east, he did not actually mention the errors.[6]

Etienne de Troyes, a serving brother, was another witness at Poitiers who had spoken to the authorities before the arrests, having confessed the Order's errors before the king and his confessor as well as before other important lay and ecclesiastical lords.[7] He was very explicit about those errors before the pope and the cardinals. At his reception he had been compelled to deny not only Christ, but 'all the apostles and saints of God', his reluctance being overcome by the threat of a drawn sword, which one of the brothers present said that he would thrust into him if he did not do as he was told. In response to an order to spit on a cross three times, he had spat on the ground.

He then stripped himself naked as told to by the receptor, who kissed him on the lower spine, the navel, and three times on the mouth. Next, the receptor gave the novitiate a new shirt and tied a small cord around his waist, which 'he had wrapped around a certain head, which they had for the saviour and helper of the Order, and [which] was especially holy, and [said] he should wear it continuously around himself on top of his shirt'. They then gave him the new clothes of the Order.

He was naturally asked about the head, and he answered in lurid detail. The Order customarily held an annual chapter on 24 June, which was held at Paris within a year of his reception.

> He was in the chapter for three days, in which he waited, and they began to hold the first vigil of the night, and they continued until prime, and at the prime of the night they brought a head, a priest carrying it, preceded by two brothers with two large wax candles upon a silver candelabra, and he [the priest] put it upon the altar on two cushions on a certain tapestry of silk, and the head was as it seemed to him, flesh from the crown to the nape of the neck with the hairs of a dog without any gold or silver covering, indeed a face of flesh, and it seemed to him very bluish in colour and stained, with a beard having a mixture of white and black hairs similar to the beards of some Templars. And then the Visitor [Hugues de Pairaud] stood up, saying to all: 'We must proceed, adore it and make homage to it, which helps us and does not abandon us', and then all went with great reverence and made homage to it and adored that head. And this witness heard it said that it was the head of the first Master of the Order, namely Brother Hugues de Payns. And from the nape of the neck to the shoulders it was completely encrusted with precious stones of gold and silver.

At this chapter, three hundred brothers were sent overseas, and Etienne de Troyes was among them. He stayed in Outremer for two and a half years, and spent another two years in the Order on his return. He then left and re-entered secular life, staying with the 'Count of Brittany' until the count's death. During this time he had visited his mother, and he was seized by the Templars, who kept him for five weeks, 'until his mother redeemed him with 200 *livres*', an agreement being made that he should thereafter be secure from the Templars.

While he was in the Order he had also been importuned by a Brother Paul de Valleceli for homosexual purposes, and when he had strongly refused to be corrupted by 'this vicious sin', the brother 'had struck him on the jaw and had broken three teeth, and he appeared deformed and fractured in the mouth'. Paul de Valleceli had said, 'You do not know the points of the Order. This is one of the points, that a brother should not deny himself to another.' When Etienne de Troyes brought this matter to the attention of Hugues de Pairaud, he was told that the brother had done well, since indeed he ought not to deny himself. Beyond this he had heard that the points concerning the denial of Christ and the other things were in the Rule of the Order, which the Visitor held. Brothers could only be received according to this Rule, which was guarded by the great men of the Order, and the younger men were prevented from seeing it. He believed too that the sacraments, especially that of the altar, were not administered, 'but to deceive the world on great feasts they received the host, it not having been consecrated or blessed'. Eventually he left the Order 'because of the evils and shameful things which he saw done there, and at the prompting of a brother of his'.[8]

Jean de Châlons, a serving brother, who had been the preceptor of two small Templar houses at different times, showed himself equally prepared to make an all-embracing attack on the Order. He had denied Christ because he had been told that if he did not the receptor

> would, within a few days, place him in a pit at Merlan. And he said that this pit or prison was so harsh, that no one was able to live long there, and he saw, after one man had been thrust in there, that he lived only five days, and he was sometimes keeper of this prison, and in his time nine brothers died there from the harshness of the prison.

Anyone who crossed the preceptors, especially Gérard de Villiers, Preceptor of France, was placed in this pit, 'such was the cruelty of the Order'. According to Jean de Châlons the Order was rife with abuses. No one was received unless he had a great deal of money: he himself had given 500 *livres*, and his companion at the reception,

Robert de Malen, had given as much. Very few charitable gifts were made, most of the Templars' possessions being put to their own use. He never saw any correction made in chapter even though he was in the Order for a long time. Apostolic letters were abused indiscriminately, and the Templar clergy 'vexed many'. Gérard de Villiers, who had learned beforehand about the arrests, had fled with fifty horses, and he had heard it said that he had taken ship with eighteen galleys, while another escapee, Hugues de Châlons, had made off with all the treasure of Hugues de Pairaud. All this had been kept secret for so long because individual Templars feared that they would be killed at once if they dared to reveal anything, 'except that the pope and king had opened the way'.[9]

Although these three men provided the most detailed and extensive confessions, all forty of the extant depositions contain one or several admissions, mostly similar to the confessions made during the hearings of October and November 1307: the denial of Christ, indecent kissing, spitting on a crucifix and incitement to commit homosexual acts, all of which were backed by threats if co-operation were not forthcoming. Incarceration in the prison at Merlan was mentioned more than once, a place 'from which no one comes out', said one Templar.[10] Several also mentioned the worship of an idol in the form of a head, although their descriptions varied from 'a foul and black idol' to one which 'seemed to be white with a beard'. Two witnesses claimed that it had three faces.[11]

The Templars who appeared at Poitiers were not of course a random choice. The French government had the Templars at its disposal and there can be little doubt that those selected either had some grudge against the Order or were terrified by threats and torture, and were therefore confidently expected to make the appropriate confession. Both Jean de Folliaco and Etienne de Troyes had, even before the arrests, shown a predisposition to malign the Order, and Etienne de Troyes had actually left its ranks. Of the remainder, five others no longer regarded themselves as members, three describing themselves as 'former' Templars, and one other claimed that he was on the point of leaving when the arrests had been made. Two of the five said that they had not even been captured. None of these claimed that they had been tortured or threatened.[12] Others seem to have spoken less willingly, for nine of them said that they had been tortured, eight others had either been threatened with torture or kept in a harsh prison or restricted to bread and water or shackled, while one, although not actually tortured himself, knew that his companions had been.[13] However, all stressed that their confessions had been freely made and were not a consequence of this ill treatment. The knight Pierre de Conders, for instance, said that

> he had properly confessed the truth, although he was greatly afraid and had been in fear all the time since the arrest. When however it was said to him that he should not be afraid, since he was in the hands of the lord pope, he replied that he had spoken only the pure and bare truth for the safety of his soul.[14]

Three of those who had been tortured – Déodat Jafet, Raymond Massel and Adhémar de Sparres – said in 1310 that they had lied when they had appeared before the pope and now wished to defend the Order.[15]

Nearly 60 per cent of those for whom there is an extant deposition from the hearings at Poitiers can therefore be shown as either apostates from the Order or as having, at some time since October 1307, been terrified by torture, either applied or threatened, or by general rough treatment. Moreover, there is not a single leader of standing among them, for the pope had been told that certain of the leaders were too ill to be brought before him.[16] They remained in prison at Chinon, where in mid-August they were seen by three cardinals on the pope's behalf, but by this time the decisive moment had passed and the gathering at Poitiers had broken up, having already made a number of important decisions regarding the future conduct of the trial. From the fifty-four names of those known to have appeared at Poitiers just over a quarter – fourteen in total – can be positively identified as knights, while there were only three priests. Twenty were serving brothers and the remaining seventeen are not designated, which probably means that they were of lower rather than higher social status. Fourteen are named as preceptors, although only two, Humbert de Corbon and Jean de Crèvecœur, appear to have received any Templars.[17] The title of preceptor does not in itself suggest that its holders were of high status within the Order, for it was not necessary to be a knight to command one of the many small Templar houses scattered throughout France and western Christendom, of which there were at least eight hundred.[18] While status in itself is no guarantee of truth or courage (as the course of the trial clearly shows), in the hierarchical society of medieval Christendom the presentation by Philip the Fair of a selection of Templars more representative of the Order and its leadership would have made a more effective demonstration of the king's conviction of the Templars' guilt and of his willingness freely to hand over their persons to the pope. Only the range of years covered by the confessions is impressive, implying corruption in the Order up to fifty years before on the one hand, and on the other as recently as two years before.[19]

Nevertheless, the pope appeared to find the selection acceptable. He reported that he had enquired of some of the Templars himself, 'not a small but a great number, not men of light but of great authority, formerly priests, preceptors, knights and serving brothers'. These men spontaneously and freely made confessions 'to us and our brothers' at first in secret and afterwards in the presence of the whole college of cardinals, and 'it was manifestly clear with respect to the persons making these confessions that the said crimes and enormities were true'. The Templars asked humbly for mercy and although Clement was indignant at what he had learned, they were absolved, since it was his duty to bring back into the bosom of the Church those who had confessed and were genuinely repentant.[20] It is however almost impossible to tell how far Clement was really convinced. Not all the witnesses had confessed; the priest Jean de Valle Gelosa had not done so,[21] and it can be surmised that there were others. Even the pope was careful not to assert that all the seventy-two Templars had confessed, saying in the bull *Subit assidue* of 5 July that 'some of them' confessed, a statement which accords with the notarial record of the depositions, which states that they wished to adhere to their depositions 'except a few'.[22] What is indisputably clear is that Philip had provided the pope with a respectable reason for reopening proceedings, without at the same time making Clement appear obviously humiliated and browbeaten by pressure. The production of the seventy-two Templars was for Philip a means of enabling a pope, who could not bear to be seen to have wilted under the harangues of Guillaume de Plaisians, to save face. Clement could now say that the Templars had been returned freely by the king,[23] and this, at least superficially, accorded with papal authority over an exempt Order. Moreover, further hesitation would, in the light of these new public confessions, have made Clement more vulnerable to Plaisians's hint that the pope was a *fautor* of heresy. The news was soon available in the courts of Christendom. On 11 July Jean Bourgogne reported to King James that the previous day more than fifty of these Templars had abjured their heresy before the Cardinals Pierre de la Chapelle, Bérenger Frédol, Etienne de Suisy and Landolfo Brancacci, and had been absolved and reconciled to the Church, thus being ready to stand punishment and penance decreed by the Apostolic See.[24]

At about the same time, the king put forward, probably in secret, a number of propositions regarding the future position of the persons and goods of the Templars. It is difficult to date these propositions exactly, but since they were presented in a way which allowed Clement at least nominal authority, did not violate his stated position in principle, and are written in a tone far removed from the rhetorical violence of Plaisians, they probably coincide with the new, more compromising policy which the handing over of the seventy-two Templars represents. A brief letter from Philip to Clement V in which the king officially remits the Templar property to special curators appointed to administer it, dated 27 June, the same day on which the first group of Templars appeared before the pope,[25] perhaps helps to confirm this, since the setting up of such special curators was an element agreed in the negotiations between pope and king which arose from the royal propositions.

In these propositions the king conceded that the persons of the Templars should be placed in the hands of the Church, but 'since they cannot be safely guarded except by royal power, that meanwhile they be guarded by the hand of the king at the request of the Church'. The prelates should then be allowed to do 'what appertains to them' (i.e. to begin inquiries against the individual persons of the Order). The property needed more detailed arrangements. This should be used for the Holy Land 'in accordance with the intention of the donors of the goods', and the overall surveillance for this purpose should be by the bishops in whose dioceses the goods were situated. The actual administration should be done by 'good, faithful and discreet persons' named by both the king and the bishops, accountable to the king's officers and the prelates. The pope himself would provide superintendents who would hear the entire account annually. After the accounting the money collected from this property 'cannot be usefully and safely guarded in certain respects except by royal power'. The king would provide safe places for it and the information regarding the account would be sent to both the prelates and the papal superintendents. The king would guarantee that the money would be put to no other use than the Holy Land, with the advice of the Church and the king.[26]

Clement seems to have agreed broadly to these proposals, but in his reply he considerably tightened the detailed provisions. The Templars would be returned directly to the pope and then the prelates would be allowed to take part. The Templars would be guarded 'by royal power at the request of the Church', but should be available when required 'without any difficulty'. The metropolitans in each province, together with persons nominated by the pope, should deal with the individual persons of the Order, but the leaders were reserved to the pope, 'in order that from these he might be in a position to judge the whole Order'. With regard to the goods, if the Order were suppressed, then they could only be used for the Holy Land, as should the proceeds at present being taken. The pope would appoint a curator of the property for each diocese, and the local bishop another, who would administer the goods on behalf of the Templars, while an inquiry was pending. The king would deliver the goods 'which he has seized and held' to these administrators. The king, however, could suggest the names of curators in secret to the pope, and these would be appointed. These administrators would render account before the bishops or persons deputed by the pope, but again the king could make secret propositions regarding the persons appointed 'if he believes that the matter will be expedited' by this means. The pope though would also appoint his own persons to audit the accounts. The money rendered in these accounts was to be put in a safe place, and the amounts concerned to be fully documented, so that it could be kept for the Holy Land. Only moderate expenses would be permitted apart from this. The pope himself would not spend the money except in the cause of the Holy Land, unless it became necessary to restore it to the Order. Clement did not wish by these provisions that any prejudice should arise to the king, or any persons in his kingdom, concerning any rights which they had on the Order's property at the time of the arrests. Finally, the pope agreed to restore the powers of the inquisitors in France, suspended since February, who would act in association with the ordinaries, although this concession was granted with obvious reluctance, for the pope felt that it seemed 'against his honour' to do so. He concluded by saying that this situation was to appertain 'until there is an arrangement concerning the Order and its goods'.[27]

Substantial agreement seems at last to have been reached, for, significantly, the papal reply had stated that 'the High Pontiff intends, before the king leaves Poitiers, to make provision in a reasonable and honourable manner concerning those things which touch on the whole Order of the Templars', and indeed the arrangements which were to determine the course of the trial during the next four years were encompassed in official form in a series of bulls issued in July and August 1308, after the examination of the seventy-two Templars had been completed. In the bull *Subit assidue* of 5 July Clement explained why he had suspended the powers of the inquisitors: Guillaume de Paris, the papal Inquisitor in France, although almost a neighbour of the pope, had told Clement nothing of the plans for the arrests, and this fact, combined with proceedings conducted 'in precipitous haste', had aroused great suspicions in the pope's mind. Clement however was prepared to accept the explanations since offered by the king, the inquisitor and the prelates of France that it had been necessary to act quickly because of the danger of irreparable damage to the faith. He had not initially been inclined to believe in the accusations, but the depositions of the Templars whom he had recently heard had convinced him. Since it was not possible for the pope and the cardinals to examine every Templar individually themselves, Clement was now prepared to relax the suspension and allow the archbishops, bishops and inquisitors to begin inquiries against individual Templars. These inquiries would have power of ecclesiastical censure and could sentence individual Templars.[28] On the same day Clement specifically restored the powers of Guillaume de Paris, although he could not forbear to tell him that he had justly incurred papal wrath.[29] On 13 July the pope laid down that the episcopal inquiries should consist of the bishop, together with two canons of the cathedral church, two Dominicans and two Franciscans.[30] Jean Bourgogne learned that the pope was intending to make similar provisions for inquiries of this kind in the other countries where the Templars had been arrested.[31] Officially the Templars were to be handed over to the Cardinal Pierre de la Chapelle on behalf of the pope, but in practice they were left under royal control, to be produced when the ecclesiastical authorities required.[32] Between 9 and 12 July, Clement officially instituted the agreed provisions for the administration of the Templar property through curators.[33]

The final arrangements were made in a series of bulls dated 12 August 1308, although it is likely that at least one of them was issued a few days later.[34] *Faciens misericordiam* sets out the pope's version of the proceedings thus far. About the time he had become pope he had heard secretly that the Templars 'had lapsed into an unspeakable wicked apostasy, the vice of detestable idolatry, the execrable act of sodomites and various heresies'. He was at first unwilling to listen to these accusations since

> it did not seem likely or credible that men so religious, who were believed principally to shed their blood often in Christ's name and frequently to expose their persons to the danger of death, and who most often showed great and many signs of devotion, both in the divine offices as well as in fasts and other observances, should be so forgetful of their salvation that they would perpetrate such things.

But then King Philip, to whom these facts had been told, 'not from avarice, since he intends to claim or appropriate nothing from the goods of the Temple' but 'with the fervour of the orthodox faith, following the clear footsteps of his ancestors', sent a great deal of information to the pope through messengers and letters. Clement then indicates that this scandal was reinforced by the witness of an important Templar knight, presumably the same man referred to in the bull *Pastoralis praeeminentiae* of November 1307.[35] The knight described the denial of Christ, the spitting and 'other things which are not licit nor accord with human honesty'. Clement now felt it was his duty to listen to these accusations, for the testimony of the noble Templar was swelled by that of 'the dukes, counts and barons and other nobles, also the clergy and people of France' who had come before the pope. Finally, these crimes seemed to have been proved by the many confessions of the Master, preceptors and brothers before many clerics and inquisitors in France. The Order's infamy had now grown so strong that it could be tolerated no longer 'without grave scandal and imminent danger', and this led Clement to enquire of the seventy-two Templars presented to him at Poitiers.

He had wished also to enquire of the leaders of the Order, but illness had prevented their appearance at Poitiers, and he had sent three cardinals to hear them at Chinon, to whom the leaders had also made extensive confessions. The bull finished by reiterating that provincial councils were to be set up to enquire against individual Templars.[36]

Clement was not however satisfied to leave matters entirely in the hands of the provincial prelates. The bull also created another form of inquiry: an inquiry against the Order as a whole and not against individuals within it. Eight commissioners were named to

> go personally to the city, province and diocese of Sens, and by a public edict of citation to be made by you [i.e. the commissioners] in the places in which it will have been seen by you to be expedient, having called those who should be summoned, you make inquiry of the truth with diligence, on our authority, against the said Order, on the articles which we have sent to you enclosed in our bull, and in other things which your prudence will see to be expedient.

Should anyone interfere with the commission's activity, 'you are to restrain by ecclesiastical censure, appeal having been disregarded, invoking in this . . . the help of the secular arm'.[37] The activity of the papacy following the hearing of the seventy-two Templars was completed by a third important bull, *Regnans in coelis*. Here Clement gave full vent to the atmosphere of calamity which characterises his pronouncements during July and August 1308.

> But, oh, grief, a new and calamitous voice, setting forth the enormity of the malignity of these brothers swelled up to us, indeed more truly disturbed our hearing. For this voice, the messenger of lamentation and sorrow, immediately agitated in the listeners a horror of mind, disturbed their souls and furnished to all believers in the Christian faith the bowl of new and ineffable bitterness; and while, as necessity demands, we bring forth the course of this matter, our spirit is racked by anguish, and our tired limbs decay, having been broken in strength by too much grief . . . For what Catholic, hearing this, could grieve so much and not burst into mourning? What believer, learning of a terrible

event of this kind, would not emit bitter sighs and utter words of lamentation and sorrow, since the whole of Christendom is participant in this grief, and this matter torments all the faithful?

But 'a healthy remedy' was available; this was to call a general council, in which both the Order and the individuals would be considered. It would assemble on 1 October, two years hence, and would look not only at the affair of the Templars, but also at the possibility of giving aid to the Holy Land in the form of a revived crusade, and at the general question of church reform. The council was to be held at Vienne in the Dauphiné.[38]

The suspension of the inquisitors had been lifted, two inquiries – one against individuals, one against the Order as a whole – had been instituted, and a general council had been planned to consider the results of this increased large-scale judicial activity against the Templars. The French government now appeared determined to capitalise upon Clement's apparently conciliatory mood. Six months of increasingly frenetic effort had, at one time, seemed likely to have been frustrated simply by papal stubbornness. Now the façade seemed to have cracked; if Clement was ready to co-operate concerning the Templars, then it was now time to revive other outstanding matters at issue. Like a blackmailer, Nogaret could always see something more to be had. Guichard, Bishop of Troyes, who had been accused, among other things, of poisoning the late queen, had been cleared of his alleged crimes the previous year. The king now sent to Clement asking for a new inquiry

considering that the crimes of the bishop constitute an attack on the divine majesty, on the royal majesty as well as the Catholic faith; that they were a grave and dangerous example if they were left unpunished; that there was there a grave peril and imminent scandal for the children and relatives of the queen: for, if the Church did not exact vengeance for such crimes and did not provide a course of justice, they could not, although moved by just sadness, obtain reparation for so great a sin.

Clement now ordered the Archbishop of Sens to seize Guichard and, on 9 August, charged the archbishop, together with the Bishops of Orléans and Auxerre, to begin an inquiry against him.[39]

More important, both to Nogaret and the pope, was the inter-weaving of the trial of the Templars with the proposed proceedings against Boniface VIII.[40] Although between 1307 and 1310 these proceedings are less prominent than the Templar affair, they worried the pope much more deeply, for if successful they would strike at the very root of papal prestige and papal continuity. Now, on behalf of the king, Plaisians asked again for the canonisation of Celestine V, for the bones of Boniface to be exhumed and burned, and for Noga-ret to be absolved from the excommunication that he had received for his part in the attack at Anagni. He also pressed the pope to reside permanently in France. On the issue of Celestine's canonisa-tion, Clement was quite encouraging, promising an inquiry into the miracles reported concerning him. But he was less positive on the other requests. He could not deny justice in the case of Boniface, but maintained, according to a sixteenth-century translation of a con-temporary French manuscript, that the late pope 'in his government did manifestlye shewe that he was a good man and a catholique of great industry, and therefore one worthye of reverence and honoure; whereupon, he saide that he marveled that the kinge would aske that what he asked; also he requested the kinge to cease from this pur-pose'.[41] Clement remained intransigent towards Nogaret. According to Tolomeo da Lucca, he spoke of Nogaret 'with detestation', and would not grant the absolution.[42] As for staying in France, he said that he would not remain there long, both because he intended to go to Rome, and because the cardinals were suffering financially from living in 'an angle of Christandome'.[43] However, for all his personal dislike of Nogaret and pious statements about an imminent journey to Rome, the French were correct in sensing that Clement was in general conciliatory. The king left Poitiers about 24 July,[44] but his ministers remained to keep the pressure applied, and, on 12 August, Jean Bourgogne reports that the pope held a public consistory, in which he said that he would proceed in the matter of the 'grave propositions' made against Boniface, on 2 February next.[45]

On Tuesday 13 August Clement at last departed from Poitiers where, since 26 May, he had been pinned by the urgency of French affairs and the intimidating presence of French troops.[46] The fact that the pope was then able to leave suggests that the French gov-ernment had achieved its political objectives. The pope had certainly failed to wrest physical control of the persons and goods of the

Templars from the king, and this was an important failure, for in practice the property remained at Philip's disposal despite the papal reservations concerning the Holy Land. Moreover, proceedings against the Templars had been restarted. Nevertheless, it had by no means been a complete capitulation. The proceedings had been reactivated in such a way as to ensure that there would be no final decision on the matter for at least two years and that then this decision would be taken in a great council of the Church presided over by the pope. There is every indication that in October 1307 Philip the Fair had hoped to end the affair of the Templars within a matter of weeks, or at least months, rather than years, and that when this immediate objective was blocked by an angry pontiff, he had called upon all his resources to force the pope to condemn the Order and close the matter in 1308. But he had not been able to do so, for Clement had shown that he regarded the matter as still open, and for all his lamentations, he would not unequivocally condemn the Templars. Provisions which he had made regarding the Order's goods were still essentially temporary and did not preclude the possibility that these goods might still actually be returned to the Order. In the face of intense pressure, Clement, despite the flaws in his character, had not relinquished the principle that the Order was an ecclesiastical body and that final judgement lay with the pope.

It was now, however, nearly three years since Clement's coronation. He had not visited Italy, let alone Rome, but had been forced to perambulate France, constantly occupied and attentive to the affairs of the French court. The king was now calling for his permanent residence in France, where Clement knew that he would be able to bring further unpleasant pressure on two central issues – the Templars and Boniface VIII – which the pope had managed to delay, but which he knew would not simply disappear. These factors must have weighed heavily on the pope's mind in the late summer of 1308, and in combination they seem to have determined the decision to leave Poitiers and to set up a semi-permanent establishment at Avignon. At least Avignon was on the route to Italy and, although near France, was not actually in the kingdom, and was well away from the centre of Capetian power in northern France. In 1274 Pope Gregory X had bought for the papacy an enclave in the Comtat Venaissin which contained the city of Avignon, so although the surrounding territory appertained to Charles, King of Naples, and therefore remained in the French sphere of influence, Avignon was technically a papal city. On 12 August Clement made his decision known to the world; the court would reassemble in the new centre on 1 December.⁴⁷ The stifling blanket of pressure exerted by the servants of the French king would be perhaps partially raised, and the papacy might be less vulnerable to the kind of direct confrontation with French armed force which might have manifested itself at Poitiers if the pope had tried to leave the city. At the same time Clement would have at his disposal a more stable and more fully documented administration. French affairs were of course certain to retain their paramount position, but the business of the rest of Christendom would flow more easily to a spot so conveniently placed in its geographical centre. In mid-August the papal court at Poitiers therefore broke up. Clement, with a small group of cardinals, intended to go to Bordeaux, but first there remained a piece of unfinished business, and for a few days he remained within four or five leagues of Poitiers in order to see it through.⁴⁸

Clement had made one exception to his general plan for proceedings against individuals at diocesan level. The leaders of the Order were to be reserved for papal judgement. On 14 August, the pope sent three cardinals to Chinon – Bérenger Frédol and Etienne de Suisy, both Frenchmen close to the king, and an Italian, Landolfo Brancacci – to see these leaders. Chinon was, according to Jean Bourgogne, about sixteen leagues from where the pope was staying, and Clement intended to remain there until the cardinals reported back.⁴⁹ Between 17 and 20 August, they interrogated the most important leaders, Raimbaud de Caron, Preceptor of Cyprus, Geoffroi de Charney, Preceptor of Normandy, Geoffroi de Gonneville, Preceptor of Poitou and Aquitaine, Hugues de Pairaud, the Visitor, and on the final day, Jacques de Molay. Nogaret, Plaisians and the gaoler of the Templars, Jean de Jamville, who was to assume a prominent role during the investigation of the papal commission between 1309 and 1311, were present, and this intimidating line-up brought predictable results, for in essence the leaders repeated their confessions of the previous October and November, giving added weight to the confessions of the lesser Templars at Poitiers. These were mature men, none of whom had served for less than twenty-eight years, and four of whom had been Templars since their middle teens, over forty years. They had risen to occupy key positions of command, and their renewed confessions were indeed damning for themselves personally and for the Order as a whole. None admitted everything, but between them they admitted the denial of Christ, spitting on a crucifix, the encouragement of sodomy, and the worship of an idol in the form of a head. On certain details they prevaricated – Gonneville, for instance, diluted his confession by repeating his claim that his receptor had spared him the denial and the spitting, provided that he kept the matter secret – but the collective result of the cardinals' hearing was a further vindication of the accusations. Molay, in addition to his own confession, asked the cardinals to listen to that of a serving brother. Finally, each of the leaders, having abjured the heresy, was reconciled to the Church.[50] The cardinals then returned to the pope, who found that 'the Master and brothers have transgressed on the premises, although certain of them in more and some in less'.[51] Philip was evidently pleased, for in September he himself wrote to King James of Aragon stressing the confessions of 'more than sixty Templars, knights, priests, preceptors and others, who were greatly in authority in their profane Order' at Poitiers, and the renewed confessions made 'more fully than before' by the leaders at Chinon, all of which should encourage King James to take further action in his own lands.[52]

His pleasure would have been more muted if he could have foreseen the problems which lay ahead. By inaugurating a whole new series of inquiries Clement had opened up another wide range of possible means of delay. After the flurry of activity at the papal chancery in July and August, there seemed little immediate indication that either the pontifical commissioners or the episcopal inquisitions were about to begin. Jean Bourgogne, who had no axe to grind in the Templar affair, described the vacation from 12 August until 1 December as 'very long', and became increasingly concerned about completing his monarch's business before the pope left the region of Poitiers.[53] Once again Clement was employing the most effective tactic at his command – that of delay and prevarication. Throughout the trial Clement can be seen reacting to Philip's initiative, for the positive action came from the French rather than the papal side. The dynamic, reforming papacy of Gregory VII, Urban II and Innocent III had often had to fight grim battles for its independence, but these had been on the heroic scale between participants of roughly equal power, a giant battle between the two competing universal powers of Papacy and Empire, whereas Clement found himself driven into a sordid and essentially unequal struggle in which he could only manoeuvre and wriggle, and from which he could never decisively break free.

A letter written by Clement to Philip, dated 6 May 1309, gives some indication of the torpor induced by the administrative obstacle course which the pope had set up the previous summer. The pope says that he has received royal letters complaining about the papal arrangements made at Poitiers, and as a result he will deal with each individual 'doubt', as he puts it, very fully. The king had become agitated because so little had followed from the Poitiers meeting, and if something was not done soon there could be 'sad and dangerous consequences', indeed already 'the most grave evil' had resulted from the delays, because many Templars had revoked their confessions, while the people clamoured against pope and king saying that they were interested only in pillaging the Templars' property. The pope was indignant, claiming that he had allowed no delay, having prosecuted the affair 'without any neglect', despite the onset of illness during the journey between Poitiers and Avignon. He had taken only a small amount from the movable property, which was insufficient even to cover the expenses of the cardinals engaged in the affair.

The king and some of the French prelates were also concerned at the lack of clarity in some of the papal documents issued at Poitiers governing the new proceedings, and the pope turned to answer a number of specific points arising from this. He had to agree with the king that the letters relating to the episcopal inquiries against the Order in Lyons, Bordeaux and Narbonne had not been sent out, and he promised to despatch these at once. Nor had the papal commission authorised to enquire into the Order as a whole been able to open its proceedings. Clement acceded to the request that the commission could begin its work in the province of Sens, since the majority of the Templars of the French kingdom were held at Paris, Tours or Sens, and agreed that the commission need not move from province to province collecting evidence, but would remain at Sens – a pronouncement which really meant that the king had ensured that the commission would sit in Paris, the most important city in the province, and therefore under the close scrutiny of the French government. Clement would not however concede that the commissioners could make individual enquiries, for conflict might arise 'from the diversity of the inquisitions'. Moreover, the pope told the king, if he allowed the division of the commission, 'it would seem that we were appearing to condescend to your wishes in everything in this matter'.

The king also asked a number of questions about procedure which the pope had left vague in his instructions. Need Templars who have been moved from their original diocese at some time in the past be returned for the episcopal inquiry, since this would be a cause of delay? Whether Templars previously examined on a smaller list of articles of accusation than the one authorised by the recent bulls need be examined again? What should be done about those who first confessed but have since revoked their confessions? What should be done about those who are obstinate and have not confessed, but are strongly suspected? Carefully, the pope dealt with the points: there need be no unnecessary transfer of Templars for the episcopal inquiries; Templars formerly examined by the pope and cardinals need not be examined again, and those who had already been examined by prelates or inquisitors could be absolved or condemned as appropriate, if it was felt that sufficient enquiry had been made. Clement stressed that papal plenitude of power would normally forbid the actual sentencing by a provincial council of those examined by the pope, but in order to expedite the affair in this case he was prepared to allow it, reserving only the leaders of the Order. Clement did not however reply in detail to the questions about those who had revoked their confessions or were proving obstinate, but promised to deal with such questions of procedure more fully elsewhere. Philip had also tried to intervene in the arrangements being made for other countries. He wanted to know why certain German prelates, who could well afford it, had been exempted from contributing towards the inquisitors' expenses, and why the pope had not written to any countries other than France and England about the persons and property of the Order, for the business would not be complete unless there was a uniform procedure.[54] The pope had apparently been frustrating royal objectives by organised administrative inefficiency.

It was probably soon after this that Guillaume de Baufet, Bishop of Paris, sent out instructions in his diocese for the proper conduct of the inquiries against individual Templars, for these instructions made detailed provision for dealing with the problems raised by the king concerning Templars who revoked or who could be regarded as obstinate. Possibly Clement V had ordered the bishop to construct a model for procedures which could be used in other dioceses. On the day appointed, the Templars were to be brought before the bishop or inquisitor and to swear on the holy gospels to tell the pure and full truth concerning both themselves and others. They were then to be asked about the time and place of their reception.[55]

The bishop then details the mode of interrogation in a way which reflects the general methods of the Inquisition in dealing with heretics.[56] For those Templars who deny the charges, there should be several interrogations, and careful note should be taken to see if there are any differences in the answers given. They are to be questioned about the time and place of their reception and the person who received them, and about those who were present at the reception, and the manner of that reception. Then they should be asked whether they were taken to any secret place after the public reception and, if so, what was done there, how it was done, and who was present. If they knew of anybody who had been present who was still alive, he should be asked if he was available to testify; and if he could not be brought to the inquiry very easily, a letter should be sent to the local prelate in whose city or diocese he was detained, so that a deposition could be taken from him. Such a Templar should be guarded in secret and in full custody. Similarly, he was to be asked whether he had seen anyone else received and the same details were to be investigated.

The instructions next explain the treatment which should be handed out to those who persisted in their denials even after questioning on this close pattern. They are to be put on 'a restricted diet, namely bread and water and a few other refreshments, unless infirm, weak or for any other reason in need, in which case more may be administered to them'. If they still have not told the truth, nor have been convicted in any other way, they should be shown the confessions made by the Grand Master and the other leaders, contained in the apostolic bull, and they should be told of the great number of Templars who have freely confessed. If there is a Templar who has a good record of persevering in his confession he should be sent to talk to them in an effort to convince them. Finally, if this is not efficacious, torture should be threatened and the instruments shown to them. As a last resort torture should actually be applied, at first lightly, and always in accordance with proper procedures, that is in the presence of an appropriate cleric and 'without excess'. They should not receive the sacraments except for confession, in which case a confessor should be deputed 'who might properly put them in fear, and diligently exhort them, in order that they might return to speaking the truth, on account of the safety and well-being of their soul and body'. The confessor should not however allow the sacrament of absolution or ecclesiastical burial, if the Templar concerned persists in his recalcitrant state.

In contrast the treatment of those who have confessed and persist in their confessions is much gentler. They are to be absolved, and 'treated kindly both with regard to the sacraments and to prison and food'. Nevertheless they are still to be kept in safe custody. Those who had at first denied and then afterwards confessed, although they are to be treated with some suspicion because of this, are to receive the sacraments and be absolved, and are not to be fed according to a harsh regime. 'And concerning perjury, which they may have incurred when they first denied, they can be absolved and a salutary penance enjoined.' Every encouragement was therefore to be given to ensure that they persisted in their confessions. The final group were those who had revoked their initial confessions, and here the treatment was to be much the same as for those who denied throughout, with the sacraments removed from them, except for confession.

These instructions, like others of their kind, show very clearly that the aim of the inquisitorial process was to lead the accused along the path of penitence and reconciliation. Torture could be justified on these grounds, for the sufferings of the body were as nothing if the soul was to be damned. The records of the actual proceedings of the episcopal inquiries have unfortunately largely been lost, and what is known of them has mainly to be gleaned from references made later by the witnesses who appeared before the pontifical commission investigating the Order as a whole. The papal letter of May 1309 would suggest that little had been done by this time, since for some dioceses the requisite papal authorisation had not even been sent out. However, some episcopal inquiries seem to have begun proceedings at about this time, for the Bishop of Clermont interrogated sixty-eight Templars between 4 and 10 June

1309,[57] and a remark by a Templar called Guillaume d'Arreblay, Preceptor of Soisy in the diocese of Meaux, in February 1311, that enquiry had been made of him thirteen months before his appearance at the Council of Sens – which can be dated May 1310 – suggests that this inquiry began about the spring of 1309.[58]

The inquiry at Clermont heard confessions from thirty-nine Templars, but pressure to the extent suggested in the instructions of the Bishop of Paris does not seem to have been applied, since the remaining twenty-nine asserted their innocence. At the end of the hearing the Templars were divided into two groups, those who had confessed repeating their confessions, those who had not done so persisting in their denials, the latter 'protesting that if in the future they, from fear of torture or prison or other things or mortification of the flesh, should confess what others had confessed, they did not wish to be believed'.[59] But torture, threats and humiliation were freely used elsewhere. In the Parisian diocese, Jean de Furnes, a serving brother, had been tortured for three months before appearing in front of the bishop, and had been 'infirm of reason' from the tortures for a year. He told the papal commissioners in November 1309 that he had falsely confessed to the sin of sodomy, because of the fear of this torture being repeated. Etienne de Domont had also been at Paris, and seemed unable to make a coherent deposition before the papal commission in February 1311, as 'he seemed to be in great fear on account of a deposition made by him in the presence of the Bishop of Paris, since he had been tortured for two years or more before his deposition'. A serving brother from Clermont, Robert Vigier, told the papal commissioners in February 1310 that he had previously confessed before the Bishop of Nevers, in Paris, because of violent torture, and because he had heard that three of his companions had died as a result of such torture.[60] The physical control of the Templars was ruthlessly exploited by the king's men. At Poitiers, Humbert de Puy had been tortured three times on the orders of Jean de Jamville, the Templars' gaoler, and the *sénéchal* of Poitiers. When he would not confess what they wanted he was placed in a tower at Niort and kept there in chains and on bread and water for thirty-six weeks. He then confessed before the official of Poitiers, the bishop's chief judicial functionary, and the dean. Jean Bertald was 'tortured a little' before confessing to the official and the dean.[61] Further south, in the Bishopric of Saintes, three serving brothers testified to the papal commission in March 1311 that they had been tortured or threatened. Guillaume d'Erée had at first denied all the accusations when he had appeared before the Bishop of Saintes, but threats and a regime of bread and water had changed his mind. Thomas de Pamplona had confessed 'on account of the strength of the many tortures previously brought on him at Saint-Jean-d'Angély . . . that he believed the confession made by the Grand Master to be true and that he adhered to it'. Pierre Théobald had acknowledged some of the accusations in the presence of the Bishop of Saintes from fear of the kind of tortures imposed on him for the six months previous to this.[62] In the diocese of Périgord, Consolin de Saint-Jorio had only confessed to the bishop because of tortures the previous year and because he had been kept for about six months on bread and water and left without adequate clothing when his shoes, surcoat and hood were taken away. Eighteen others who were with him also alleged torture and starvation.[63]

Equally sinister and equally indicative of the determination of the royal gaolers to ensure that the Templar confessions were repeated before the bishops was a document shown to the pontifical commission in February 1310. A Templar called Jean de Couchey exhibited a letter, sealed with two seals, 'of which however the characters were not clear'. The letter had been given to the brethren held at Sens by a clerk called Jean Chapin, at the time the Bishop of Orléans came to examine them; it said that it was from Philippe de Voet and Jean de Jamville, the Templars' gaolers, to Laurent de Beaune, the former Preceptor of Epailly, and other brothers imprisoned at Sens.

> We make known to you that we have obtained that the king our lord sends you the Bishop of Orléans to cause you to be reconciled. In consequence we require you and pray you to hold to the good confession that we have permitted you, and that you behave so devotedly and so graciously in regard to the said Bishop of Orléans that he has no reason to say that through you we have caused him trouble nor that we have caused him to hear a lie; we authorise Jean Chapin, our beloved clerk, in whom you will be pleased to believe, since he will speak to you on our behalf and whom we send to you in our place.

The letter concluded with the ultimate pressure to conform. 'And know that our father the pope has ordered that all those who have confessed before the inquisitors, his delegates, and who do not wish to persevere in this confession will be condemned and put to death by the fire.' The commissioners called Philippe de Voet before them and asked him about the letter, but were blandly told that he did not believe the letter had been sent. Moreover, his clerk held his seal at various times, and it had never been sealed at his mandate or with his consent. He had never in any way tried to induce the Templars to say anything 'except the pure truth', and wished the brethren them-selves to be asked about this. Both Jean de Couchey and Laurent de Beaune were then brought forward, and they agreed that Voet had never told them to say anything except what was 'good and true'.[64]

The Templars therefore were as firmly under the control of the king in the summer of 1309 as they had been in October 1307. Royal custodians guarded the prisoners and, when necessary, tortured and bullied them, even appropriating for themselves the right to threaten them with death as relapsed heretics. Moreover, royal nominees largely chaired the episcopal inquiries. During Clement's reign, the king induced the pope to use his powers of reservation in favour of royal supporters in many cases – the Archbishop of Sens and the Bishops of Bayeux, Auxerre (twice), Orléans, Cambrai and Cahors were all chosen in this way – while royal rights in local elections ensured that the king retained paramount influence in many other sees.[65] At least in the northern parts of his kingdom, and in many places elsewhere, the king had effective control of the higher clergy.

If the Poitiers arrangements had failed to deliver the Templars themselves from the king's power, they were equally impotent as a means of wresting the property from the royal grasp. Theoretically the goods were to be kept to help the recovery of the Holy Land, and in August 1308 the pope had written to individual prelates ordering them to hand over the goods to the special commissioners whose task was to administer them, an order which, if disobeyed, carried the penalty of excommunication.[66] In January 1309 Philip IV claimed that he had complied with these arrangements. In a letter to the dukes, counts, barons, *sénéchaux, baillis* and other officials of the kingdom, he described how, a short while ago, he had extended his hand to the Templar goods 'wishing to counteract the danger and dissipation which appeared' and 'not intending to deprive the Order of the Templars of the possession and ownership of the said goods, but on behalf of the Order, if good should be found, otherwise to conserve the goods for the aid of the Holy Land'. Afterwards, in agreement with the pope, he had transferred control to the curators and administrators deputed for the purpose. 'We have caused the goods, movable and immovable, which had been taken and held by our people, to be handed over in full, and have caused the said curators and administrators to be protected and defended by our people, when necessary.' He therefore ordered that everybody should similarly give up any such property held, to the proper authorities.[67]

In practice however, when the matter is investigated at a local level, it can be seen that the royal administrators had no intention of complying with the order. By Easter 1309 – only six weeks after the royal letter – the former Templar Preceptory at Bonlieu in the diocese of Troyes had been leased out by the royal officials of the region on the authority of Jean Guérin de la Villeneuve-Le-Roy, the royal administrator responsible for Templar property in the *bailliages* of Troyes and Meaux. In return for an annual rent of 200 *petites livres tournois*, Henri de Bar from Onjon and Jacques Biaulus d'Isles gained a six-year lease on the three Templar houses appertaining to the Preceptory of Bonlieu and their dependencies. Exempted from the lease were the woods not in communal use, the ponds, the rights of *formariage*, *mainmorte* and high justice, the profits of which apparently would still go to the royal treasury. The movable property on the estates was valued and then granted 'at the guard and peril' of the lessees, to be returned in full at the end of the lease or to be paid for. If the administrators of the property so chose, the movables would have to be paid for in any case, a provision which suggests an inclination to sell the Templar movables where possible.[68] No provision was made for the possibility of the Templars being found innocent or for any decisions of the Council of Vienne, scheduled to meet in October 1310, regarding the property. It is hardly likely that this was a unique case, for in a letter to the king of December 1310 Clement V himself confirmed that the practice was quite general. 'On the subject of the administration of the property of the Temple in your kingdom, the pope knows well that all was lost and dissipated, which he had foreseen when he was at Poitiers.'[69] It was a sad recognition of the pope's inability to prevent the royal administration from doing as it wished with the Templar property.

Since Philip controlled the property and persons and strongly influenced the episcopal inquiries, he ought to have been equally sure of his ground with regard to the papal commission which was to enquire against the Order as a whole. Earlier in the year he had sent Clement a list of individuals who should compose the commission and asked that the pope make no changes,[70] and certainly the king's men were well represented on the eight-man commission. The president was Gilles Aicelin, Archbishop of Narbonne, who had already attacked the Templars in public when he had supported Plaisians before the pope at Poitiers in 1308, and who can certainly be numbered among Philip's inner counsellors. Both Guillaume Durant, Bishop of Mende, and Guillaume Bonnet, Bishop of Bayeux, were royal partisans, the former being a member of a strongly royalist family, while the latter was a royal nominee to the see. Between 1309 and 1311, when the commission sat, both Gilles Aicelin and Guillaume Bonnet were frequently absent on royal business. Renaud de la Porte, Bishop of Limoges, had less direct links with the crown, but it is unlikely that he was in any way anti-royalist, for such bishops, as the case of Bernard Saisset had shown, could not survive long in early fourteenth-century France. Half the commission therefore consisted of French prelates. Of the remainder neither Matteo di Napoli, the Apostolic Notary, nor Jean de Montlaur, Archdeacon of Maguelonne, are quite so distinctly royal nominees, but the other two, Giovanni di Mantua, Archdeacon of Trent, and Jean Agarni, *prévôt* of the Church of Aix, were clearly within the French orbit. Giovanni di Mantua was the auditor of Pietro Colonna, a leading pro-French cardinal from the family which had helped Nogaret attack Boniface VIII, and Jean Agarni was a former procurator of the Angevins of Naples at the Roman court.[71] However, Jean Agarni never took part in the proceedings, because he was involved in collecting a papal tenth in the south of France, and was therefore excused.[72]

The commission was undoubtedly composed in the way that the king desired, but nevertheless the course of events seems to suggest that it was the king and not the pope who was placing obstacles in its path. The commission did not open its sessions until 8 August 1309, at the monastery of Sainte-Geneviève, a year after papal authorisation, when letters were sent to the prelates of the French kingdom explaining its function and citing the Templars and other witnesses to appear on 12 November in the episcopal hall at Paris at the hour of prime. The prelates were to ensure that this citation was read in public to the clergy and people of their dioceses in the cathedrals, the great collegiate churches, the schools and the official curiae of the cities and dioceses, and also in the principal houses of the Templars and in the places where the brothers were held captive.[73]

On Wednesday 12 November the commissioners assembled in the episcopal hall. But only five of them were present: Matteo di Napoli and Jean de Montlaur were inexplicably missing. Notaries were sent to Matthew's home in Paris to see if he was there, but on arrival they were told that he was with Geoffroi du Plessis, notary to the Apostolic See, at Valles in the diocese of Paris. Letters came from Jean de Montlaur to say that he had been taken ill on the journey to Paris and that the commission should proceed without him. Since the papal bull of authorisation allowed for the possibility for as few as two members being present, the commission proceeded. But nothing happened. They waited patiently until the hour of terce but none of the Templars appeared. Eventually, they ordered Jean, apparitor of the curia of the official of Paris, 'to proclaim in a loud voice' that if anyone wished to appear on behalf of the Order then the commissioners were prepared to hear them kindly. But all the shouting of the apparitor was useless; there was no response. Accordingly the five commissioners decided to adjourn until the next day.[74] It had not been an auspicious beginning.

The same charade was repeated on Thursday, Friday and Saturday, and again on the Monday and Tuesday of the following week. On Tuesday a check on the replies received to their citation sent out the previous August showed that many of the prelates and their officials had not even bothered to reply. Even the Bishop of Paris had not sent a satisfactory answer, despite the fact that the commissioners were using the episcopal hall for their proceedings. Accordingly an adjournment was arranged until Saturday 22 November, and a letter was sent to the Bishop of Paris to expedite the commission's order with all speed. He should require the royal gaolers to bring any Templars who wished to say anything on behalf of the Order before them, 'but only if they wished to come voluntarily'. At last, on the Saturday, the Bishop of Paris made a personal appearance. He had gone to the places where the Grand Master and the Visitor were held and had the original apostolic letters and bulls which had created the commission, and the commission's own citations, read out to them and to the other brothers who were there. Molay and Pairaud had said that they wished to appear before the commission, and 'some of these brothers expressly said that they wished to defend the aforesaid Order'. Accordingly Philippe de Voet and Jean de Jamville were ordered to bring them to the episcopal hall, and on the same day produced seven Templars, including Hugues de Pairaud.[75]

In a city where several hundred Templars were being held, it had taken the papal commission a week and a half to cause any of them to be brought out, even though the citation had been sent out three months before and the commission itself created over a year ago. The inference is clear. Philip's servants controlled the persons of the Order, and the French government was reluctant to allow them to appear. Probably Philip was concerned because, despite the composition of the commission in his favour, its course was less predictable than the episcopal inquiries, for it was clearly designated a papal body, and in December 1307 some Templars had retracted their confessions before such a body even though the clergy concerned had been closely associated with the French monarchy.

5: The Defence of the Order

As the hearings of the commission opened, any fears that King Philip may have had that the Templars were about to embark upon any kind of defence must have been quickly dispelled. It was soon revealed that the Bishop of Paris had been somewhat disingenuous, for the Templars did not seem to be aware of the reasons for their appearance. The proceedings began when

> a certain person in secular habit came into their presence, who was said to have come on behalf of the matter of the said Templars. Asked by them his name, status and the reason for his arrival, he replied that he was called Jean de Melot, and that he was from the diocese of Besançon, and he showed a certain seal on which the aforesaid name seemed to be engraved, which seal he asserted to be his. He said also that he was from the Order of the Temple and that he had worn the habit of the Order for ten years, and that he had left that Order, and that never, swearing on his soul and faith, had he seen or heard or known anything bad about the above-mentioned Order.

He added that he had come to the commissioners 'prepared to do and seal whatever they wished'. However, further enquiry elicited that he had not come with the intention of defending the Order, but only because he wanted to see what was to be done about the Templars, and in particular to ask the commission to make provision for him personally 'since he was a pauper'. Jean de Melot must have been a depressing sight as the first witness.

> And since he was seen by the lords commissioners, from looking at and considering his person, gestures, actions and speech, to be very simple, or stupid, or not fully in control of his mind, they did not proceed further with him, but persuaded him to go to the Bishop of Paris to whom it appertained to receive such fugitive brothers in the diocese of Paris.[1]

Voet and Jamville then brought in six Templars. The first was a knight called Gérard de Caux, who was more ordered but almost equally pathetic. He had come 'because he believed, on account of certain words spoken by the Bishop of Paris and others in the publication of the said edict, that the commissioners wished him to come to their presence, and that they wished to be informed by him about the deeds of the Order, or to enquire from him whence he had come'. The commissioners explained that there was no necessity for him to come, for they were not enquiring against individuals, but against the Order as a whole. Templars should come if they wished to defend the Order. 'However, asked whether he wished to defend the said Order, he finally replied, after many words, that he was a simple knight, without horses, arms or land, and he could not, nor knew how to, defend the Order.' The other five replied in much the same manner; they could not defend the Order since they were *simplices*.[2]

The next witness was more eminent. Later the same day, 22 November, Hugues de Pairaud was examined. If any proper defence was to be offered it must surely be by this man, and by Jacques de Molay, who himself testified the following week on Wednesday 26 November. These were the two most senior Templars, and many members of their Order, of lesser rank but greater courage, showed later that they believed that the defence should stem from these leaders. But once again Philip IV must have been little troubled, for Pairaud made no effort to defend the Order, while the Grand Master, confused and ill, succeeded only in making himself look ridiculous. For both these men the ultimate hope was that they would gain a personal hearing from the pope himself, since he had reserved their cases, and, all else having failed, they were concerned lest they might blight this last chance. This is very explicit in Pairaud's testimony. Pairaud said that he had come because the Bishop of Paris had told him that the commissioners would listen to whoever wished to come before them 'on behalf of the activity of the Order', and also because he wished to ask them to insist, 'in respect to the pope and the king', that the Templars' property should not be dissipated, but applied to the aid of the Holy Land. He also said that he personally had many times discussed the state of the Order with the pope and the three cardinals sent to interview him and others, and 'he was at this time prepared to speak when he was in the presence of the lord pope', but not before the commission.[3]

But the commissioners had not finished on this first Saturday of hearings, for now secret information came to them that some men who had come to Paris to defend the Order had been detained. Jean de Plublaveh, *prévôt* of the citadel of Paris, confirmed that on the orders of the king's council, seven men wearing secular clothing had been held by him. He had been told that they were Templar fugitives who had come to Paris with money to find advocates and advisers for the defence of the Order. However, the *prévôt* had tortured two of them, but they had not admitted this. The commissioners had the seven men brought before them. The first to testify was a Pierre de Sornay from the diocese of Amiens, who said that he had been a Templar for three months before the arrests, but had avoided capture because he had fled fifteen days before. He had neither known nor heard anything perverse or evil about the Order. He had come to Paris at this time to earn some money, since he was 'an obscure and ignoble pauper', and he had hoped to find service. He had not come to defend the Order, nor did he wish to. The other six men also denied any wish to defend the Order, although two of them said that they had been in the service of certain Templars from the County of Hainault and had been sent by them to find out what was happening in Paris and then to report back. Since Pierre de Sornay was the only Templar, he was detained, but the commission ordered that the other six be set free.[4] Saturday 22 November had been a long and fruitless day for the commission, beginning with the half-truths of the Bishop of Paris and ending in the confusion of Pierre de Sornay, bereft of subsistence and reduced to scraping for a living around Paris.

The next witness was Jacques de Molay, who appeared on Wednesday the 26th, after the commission had been forced to suffer another blank day on the Monday when no Templars were presented to them. Molay's appearance was considerably more dramatic than that of Pairaud. Asked if he wished to defend the Order, he replied that the Order had been confirmed and given privileges by the Apostolic See and it was unbelievable that the Roman Church now wished to destroy it, especially since the sentence of deposition on the Emperor Frederick II had been postponed for thirty-two years. He was prepared to defend the Order, although he was not confident of his ability to do this, and certainly doubted if he could do so on his own. However, 'he would otherwise regard himself as vile and miserable and would be so regarded by others if he did not defend the Order, from which he had received so many advantages and honours'. He thought that it would be difficult, since he was in the captivity of the lords pope and king, and had nothing to spend on the defence.

> On account of this he asked that help and advice be given to him towards the aforesaid defence, saying that it was his intention that the truth about those things which were imputed to the said Order should be known, not only among those belonging to the Order, but also in all parts of the world by kings, princes, prelates, dukes, counts and barons.

Since the affair was 'arduous' and he had only one serving brother with whom he could take counsel, the commissioners told him to deliberate 'well and fully' about the defence, bearing in mind the confessions which he had already made against both himself and the Order. Nevertheless they were prepared to receive him as a defender and also to concede him a delay for fuller deliberation. He ought to know, though, that 'in cases of heresy and the faith it was necessary to proceed simply, summarily and without the noise of advocates and the form of judges'.

In order to enable Molay to make a proper defence the relevant documents of the case were now read out, including the apostolic letters both regarding the aims and powers of the commission and relating to the affair in general. Suddenly, during the reading of these documents, when they came to the material relating to his confession at Chinon before the three cardinals in August 1308, Molay was seized by violent emotion. He twice made the sign of the cross before his face and seemed to be 'greatly astonished about the things which were contained in the aforesaid confession and other things contained in the apostolic letters mentioned above'. Molay claimed that he would have something else to say about this, if certain other persons were present, presumably meaning the cardinals who had heard his confession at Chinon. The commissioners were affronted by Molay's manner and told him they were not there to receive a battle challenge. Molay replied that he had not intended that, 'but it may please God that that which was observed by Saracens and Tartars should be observed against such evil-doers in this case, for the Saracens and Tartars cut off the heads of evil-doers that they found or split them down the middle'. The commissioners replied chillingly that 'the Church judged those heretics who were found to be heretics and left the obstinate to the care of the secular arm'.

Molay's emotional and almost incoherent manner seems therefore only to have alienated the commissioners. In his confusion, Molay turned for help to, of all people, Guillaume de Plaisians. Plaisians had entered the episcopal hall uninvited, as the commissioners were careful to stress, but his presence indicates that it was almost impossible to respect the secrecy of the depositions. It became evident that both Plaisians and Nogaret had direct access to the hearings and were even prepared actively to intervene if it suited them. Plaisians now asserted how he esteemed the Grand Master 'since they were both knights' and therefore 'he had to take care in case he [Molay] blamed or lost himself without cause'. Molay then said that he now saw clearly that unless he deliberated properly he would 'quickly perish by a noose of his own making'. At the Master's request, a delay until Friday was conceded, or longer if he wished.[5] Molay seems to have been crushed by his two years in prison. He does not seem too sure when he had confessed and when he had revoked, or whether he should defend the Order and, if so, how to go about it. A forty-eight-hour respite could do nothing to change that.

While Molay was preparing his defence, a much freer flow of Templars was being allowed before the commissioners. On Thursday 27 November they heard twelve. At first sight they appear as uncomprehending and as frightened as previous witnesses. Raoul de Gizy had come 'because the Bishop of Paris had said that those who wished to come to the commissioners could do so, and because he wished to see them'; Jacques Verjus said that he was an *agricola* and did not know how to litigate; Jean de Villecerf was a pauper and wished to persist in his confession made before the Bishop of Paris; Aymon de Barbonne was a poor man and not able to defend the Order; Etienne de Provins had only been in the Order for nine months before the arrests and did not wish to defend it, but 'if the Masters wished to defend it they should do so'; Guillaume Boscelli could not make a defence since he was a poor man and not a clerk; Nicolas de Celles wished to persist in his confession 'as long as it was pleasing to God and the Virgin Mary'; Jean de Furnes 'did not wish to quarrel with the lord pope and the King of France'.[6] But although none was prepared to offer a defence of the Order, some of them did begin to show what, in the light of later events, may be interpreted as signs of a changing spirit among the captured Templars now that the papal commission had come into full operation. Jacques Verjus added that 'if he knew or could, he would freely defend the Order'. Aymon de Barbonne complained that 'he was tortured three times, and with a *cucufa* in his mouth, water was applied to him, and he was on bread and water for seven weeks'. He would freely defend the Order if he could, but he was not able to do so since he was in captivity. He had guarded Molay's room for three years in Outremer and 'knew nothing bad about the Master or the Order'. He did not know what was to be done 'since his body grieved and his soul mourned, and he had suffered many bad things on behalf of the Order'. He would not say anything more 'since he had been in captivity a long time'. Guillaume Boscelli would freely speak the truth if he were outside prison, while Jean de Furnes stressed that torture had made him confess things that were not true.

The impetus for these slight but significant signs of resistance seems to have come from the second witness of the day, Ponsard de Gizy, Preceptor of Payns. When he was asked if he wished to defend the Order he replied that all the articles imputed to the Order were false, and 'everything he or other brothers of the Order confessed concerning them in the presence of the Bishop of Paris or others was false'. They had said these things 'through violence and on account of danger and fear, since they were tortured by Floyran de Béziers, Prior of Montfaucon [and] the monk Guillaume Robert, their enemies'. Thirty-six brothers had been killed at Paris as a result of torture and many others in other places. He was prepared to defend the Order if provided with expenses from the goods of the Temple, and allowed aid and counsel from two brothers, Renaud de Provins and Pietro di Bologna. He then submitted a document detailing the Order's enemies, as he was permitted to do under the rules of the Inquisition.[7] It seems therefore that Ponsard had talked with Renaud de Provins and Pierre de Bologna while they were in prison, and possibly they had suggested the tactic of naming the Order's enemies. These two men were later to be very prominent in the Order's defence when they showed their legal knowledge and skill as advocates to a degree well beyond that which could be managed by Ponsard de Gizy.

Ponsard was then asked if he himself had ever been tortured. He answered that 'in the three months which elapsed before the confession made by him in the presence of the Lord Bishop of Paris, he was placed in a pit, his hands having been tied behind him so tightly that the blood ran to his nails'. The pit was only one pace in width. If he was again tortured 'he would deny everything that he was now saying and say whatever anyone wished'. Indeed, 'because it only took a short time, he was prepared to suffer either decapitation, or fire, or boiling, for the honour of the Order, but he could not thus sustain long tortures, which he had already endured for two or more years in prison'.

It was not to be so simple. The effect of this brave, emotional statement was quickly countered by Philippe de Voet, *prévôt* of Poitiers and one of the two chief gaolers of the Templars. He produced a letter intended for the pope and the commissioners, which Ponsard de Gizy admitted that he had written, 'because the truth was not searched for in corners', which detailed faults within the Order. Although Ponsard protested that he had written it because he had been angry at some insults addressed to him by the Treasurer of the Order, and although the contents of the letter do not accord with the accusations brought by the French government, nevertheless the credibility of this witness was severely shaken. According to Ponsard's letter the brothers were forbidden (1) to take part in the offertory, (2) to hold children over fonts to be baptised, and (3) to sleep under the same roof as a woman. A poor brother had been imprisoned for contravening these rules. While this was no more than a protest about the Order's discipline, the other allegations were more serious. The Masters who created brothers and sisters of the Order made these sisters promise obedience, chastity and poverty, but when they had entered deflowered them.[8] It was obligatory for Masters to 'force to their wish' other sisters 'of a certain age and who thought that they were entering the Order to save their souls'. These sisters have children by them, and the Masters make the children brothers of the Order, even though the Order's statutes forbid the entrance of bastards. In fact even thieves and murderers can enter, 'if they have a little money'. Preceptors of local houses ask for authorisation to create new brothers 'just as one sells a horse at a market', which means that the Order contains simoniacs and excommunicates. To this is added perjury, for the receptors make new brothers swear on the saints that they have not bought their way into the Order. If a brother annoyed one of the preceptors he bribed the provincial commander to authorise that he be sent to Outremer 'to die there or to a strange land where he knew nobody, and he died there in sadness and in poverty'. Those who abandoned the Order were imprisoned in the event of capture. There had been quarrels within the Order when some brothers accused Gérard de Villiers, Preceptor of France, of having been responsible for the loss of the island of Tortosa and for the deaths of the brothers stationed there. It had been for this reason that Gérard de Villiers had fled, misleading his friends into going with him.[9]

The presentation of this letter seems to have destroyed Ponsard de Gizy's attempt to defend the Order, and instead he now became very frightened that he had exposed himself to further torment in prison. He asked that the commissioners

> make provision in case he was oppressed on account of the afore-said; and the lords commissioners said to the *prévôt* of Poitiers and Jean de Jamville that in no way were they to oppress him because of the fact that he had come to the defence of the Order. They answered that they would not oppress him more on this account.

These first flickers of resistance seem to have been extinguished. The fiasco of Ponsard de Gizy's defence was in no way mitigated when Jacques de Molay appeared again on the following day, Friday the 28th. He does not seem to have used the interval to prepare a coherent statement, but instead made an attempt to avoid committing himself to anything. Asked again if he wished to defend the Order he replied that 'he was a knight, unlettered and poor, and that he had heard to be contained in a certain apostolic letter that had been read to him, that the lord pope had reserved him and certain other important leaders of the Order to himself, and for this reason, at present . . . he did not wish to do anything concerning the afore-said'. When expressly asked if he therefore intended to make a defence or not, he said that he did not, but humbly asked the commissioners to intercede with the pope so that he could be brought before him as quickly as possible, when he would say those things to the pope 'which were to the honour of Christ and the Church'. He could see no reason why the commissioners should not proceed in the affair. Beyond this, 'to relieve his conscience' he wished to say three things about the Order. Firstly, only in cathedral churches did he know of better or more beautiful ornaments and relics or of a better celebration of the divine services by the priests and clergy. Secondly, he did not know of any other Order that had distributed more charitable gifts, for every house gave charity three times a week, by a general ordinance of the Order. Thirdly, he knew of no other Order which had shed its blood so readily in defence of the Christian faith and which was more highly considered by the enemies of the faith. It was because of this that the Count of Artois had wanted the Templars to be the advance guard in his battle-line, and if the count had followed the advice of the Grand Master of that time neither he nor the Master would have been killed in the ensuing battle.[10] But the commissioners were not impressed. All this was of no value for the safety of souls, they declared, where the foundation of the Catholic faith was absent. Molay replied that he knew this to be true and that he believed

> in one God and in a Trinity of Persons and in other things appertaining to the Catholic faith, and that there was one God and one faith and one baptism and one Church, and when the soul was separated from the body, then it would be apparent who was good and who was bad and each of us would know the truth of these things which were being done at present.

Plaisians had been present to confuse the Grand Master the previous Wednesday; now Guillaume de Nogaret intervened. Molay's simple, uncomplicated statement of belief might have seemed convincing. Nogaret told a story which he claimed came from the chronicles of the Abbey of Saint-Denis, that in the time of Saladin, the Grand Master and other leading Templars had paid homage to this sultan, and that Saladin, hearing of a great defeat which the Templars then suffered, said publicly that this calamity had befallen them 'because they were afflicted by the vice of sodomy and because they had violated their faith and law'. Molay was astonished by this story and professed that until then he had never heard it. He recounted a tale of his own. During the Mastership of Guillaume de Beaujeu, 'he, Jacques, and many other brothers . . . young men, eager for war, as is usual among young knights who wish to see feats of arms', murmured against the Master, because, during the truce which the late King of England had made, Beaujeu was careful to maintain the sultan's favour. But finally Molay and the others realised that the Master had no alternative, because the Order held many towns and fortresses in Saracen territory and these would have been lost. Then Molay asked if he could hear mass and the other divine offices and have his chapel and chaplains, a request which the commissioners, 'praising the devotion which he was showing', granted him.[11]

Only one more Templar was heard that Friday: a serving brother called Pierre de Safed. In his opinion the Order had good defenders in the pope and the king and he was satisfied with their defence. He himself did not wish to defend the Order.[12] It must have seemed to the French government that no effective defence was to be offered, even before a papal body. There was no further reason to obstruct the proceedings of the commission, and therefore even before Molay's second appearance Philip IV had issued orders to his *baillis* and *sénéchaux* to send to Paris all Templars who wished to defend the Order, although making sure that they were kept separate to prevent collusion (26 November).[13] Meanwhile, the commissioners, deciding that the episcopate had still not fully co-operated in publishing their citation, adjourned until 3 February 1310, ordering that their citation be made 'under every possible canonical penalty'. On Friday 28 November the papal commission officially ended its first session.[14]

Nevertheless when the commissioners reassembled in the cold dawn of a February morning, Tuesday the 3rd 1310, it seemed as if the proceedings were again to be frustrated, for no Templars were produced. Moreover, the king now seems to have felt the commission to be of little importance any more, for the Archbishop of Narbonne was otherwise employed on royal business, having sent excuses for that day and any other days on which he should be absent. Giovanni di Mantua was ill, but the other commissioners celebrated mass in the Church of Sainte-Marie, and waited. They soon learned that this new delay was 'on account of the inundations of the water, the severity of the weather and other impediments which arose from the shortness of the time fixed by them'. On Thursday 5 February the commissioners ordered Voet and Jamville to bring certain Templars from the diocese of Mâcon before them, since they had heard that they wished to defend the Order, and the next day sixteen Templars appeared. It was soon evident that the recess had effected a radical transformation in the attitude and spirit of the captured Templars, for the tentative rebuttals of such as Ponsard de Gizy had been transformed into an unambiguous willingness to defend the Order among a large section of the Templar rank and file. More and more Templars now saw hope in appearing before a papal body, hope perhaps encouraged by certain individuals such as Renaud de Provins and Pietro di Bologna whose names had been cited by Ponsard de Gizy. On 5 February all but one of the sixteen Templars said that they were willing to defend the Order, some qualifying this by saying that this did not include the bad points or bad men in it if any such existed, while others asserted that they knew of no bad points. Only Gérard le Lorinhe was not prepared to defend the Order, 'since it was very bad and there were many bad points in it'.[15] In the following days they were supported by a rapidly growing number of Templars, including Ponsard de Gizy, who on 20 February again maintained his willingness to defend the Order.[16]

February 1310 was a good month for the Templars. Between Saturday the 7th and Friday the 27th, 532 Templars from all over the kingdom joined the original fifteen in declaring that they wished to bring themselves to the Order's defence.[17] Lambert de Cormeilles, a serving brother, declared that he did not know how to defend the Order, since he was not a clerk, but he would defend it as far as he was able if there was any bad imputed to it. Jean de Chames would defend it, he claimed 'as far as death'. Bertrand de Saint-Paul asserted 'that he had never confessed nor would confess the errors imputed to the Order, since they were not true, and he said that God would work a miracle if the body of Christ should be administered to them and if those confessing and those accusing received it together'.[18] Some pleaded ignorance of the ways of defence, but would do as well as they could; others told stories of torture and death; many asked for the sacraments, as they were good Christians. A few were prepared to defend the Order, but only if they were released from prison, or in some cases, if they could consult the Grand Master. Those who would not offer to defend the Order were in a small minority during this period, numbering fifteen in all, while another twelve would not commit themselves either way, wanting to consult the leaders or leave the whole defence to them. Humbert de Reffiet said he was a poor man and did not intend to defend the Order, but he would approve of whatever the Grand Master did. Jean le Bergonhons stated bluntly that he had not wished to defend the Order, because a year before the arrests he had apostasised on account of a certain woman. One group of four refused a defence because they had been Templars for such a comparatively short time, one of them less than a month, and none more than five weeks, while Jean de Primeyo, a knight from Chartres, who had seen only four or five months' service before the arrests, chose this moment to ask for permission to leave the Order, and Nicolas de Boncelo, a Templar of two months' standing in October 1307, asked specifically to be allowed to enter another Order for the safety of his soul. Some were equivocal. Gérard de Caux, who had already refused to defend the Order when he had appeared before the commission the previous November, 'before everything protested that the things which he said before the commission were in no way intended to sustain error, nor to be in any way against the Roman Church, the pope or the King of France'. He did not feel he could make a sensible response to the commission while he was in prison and the goods of the Temple were being despoiled, and asked to be freed so that he could proceed properly by way of the law before the commission, but he was told that the commission had no power to set him at liberty, even though they were prepared to listen favourably to him whenever he wished to appear. Raoul de Gizy, who had also appeared the previous November, was anxious to say that he intended nothing against anyone, and if the commissioners would free him from prison and restore the Order's goods, he would appear as many times as they ordered him.[19]

But the waverers could not obstruct the ascendancy of the defence. Even the appearance of Jacques de Molay on Monday 2 March failed to dampen the new-found enthusiasm. Asked the usual question as to whether he wished to offer a defence, he replied that his case was reserved for the pope and that when he was released and in the papal presence, 'then he would say what seemed useful'. It was painstakingly pointed out that this was an inquiry against the Order and not against individuals, but this seems to have made little impression, for he simply asked the commissioners to write to the pope so that he and the other leaders should be summoned to his presence, and was told that this would be done as quickly as possible. Neither Geoffroi de Gonneville, Preceptor of Aquitaine and Poitou, nor Hugues de Pairaud, who appeared on the same day, Friday 13 March, was any more forthcoming. Gonneville said that he was 'illiterate and insufficient to defend the Order, nor had he advice', and would only speak before the pope. Thinking that he feared torture, the commissioners tried to reassure him that they would protect him, but Gonneville was as set on the idea of papal reservation as Molay. As for Pairaud, he wished to say nothing in the commissioners' presence for or against the Order except what he had already said.[20] Nevertheless, on the same day, another fourteen humbler Templars joined the ranks of the defenders, bringing the number to 561.[21]

This was a defence of formidable proportions, and the commissioners were now obliged to make good their constant promises to provide the facilities for such a defence. On Saturday 14 March a full list of 127 articles of accusation, which had been drawn up in August 1308 after the Poitiers meeting between the pope and the king, was read out in Latin and French before ninety of those who had volunteered to defend.[22] Meanwhile, on Friday 27 March another thirty-six defenders were added to the list, one of whom, a priest called Jean Robert, said that he had heard many Templars in confession and had never found any of the errors named.[23] This growing confidence converted many waverers to the defence, among them Pierre de Saint-Gresse, who had originally refused to defend because he had only been a Templar for four months at the time of the arrests,[24] Jean de Pont-Evêque, who first of all had said that he could not offer a defence while he was in prison and poverty-stricken,[25] Pontius de Bon Œuvre, who previously had not been able to bring himself to say anything for or against the Order,[26] and Pierre Picard de Bures, who initially had gone no further than expressing a desire to ask the Grand Master's advice.[27] During the last week in March a total of 597 defenders was reached.

This was a number too large to be dealt with within the episcopal buildings, and on Saturday 28 March a mass meeting of the defenders was convened by the commissioners in the garden behind the bishop's house. Here a total of 546 brothers heard the purpose of the commission restated and the articles again read out in Latin, but when it was ordered that they be repeated in the vernacular the brothers refused to countenance it, saying that they did not care to hear such wickedness, which was altogether false, in this way. The commissioners then asked that those assembled name some representatives to put their case, for they could not hear all those prepared to make a defence 'without confusion and tumult'. They were prepared to receive six, eight, ten or more of them as procurators. After some discussion among the Templars, two priests, Renaud de Provins, Preceptor of Orléans, and Pietro di Bologna, Procurator of the Order at the Roman court, described as literate men (*litterati*), put forward a number of points on behalf of themselves and the other brothers. They complained about their conditions: deprivation of the sacraments, loss of their religious habit and all their temporal goods, their vile incarceration in chains, the poor state of provision made for them. All the brethren who had died in prison, except at Paris, had been buried outside holy ground and had been denied the sacraments. As to the question of procurators, they could not see how such persons could be named without the consent of the Grand Master, to whom they all owed obedience. Moreover, almost all the brothers were 'illiterate and simple' and needed the advice of prudent and wise men; they added that other brothers who wished to defend the Order had been prevented from doing so, and named two such men. They finally asked that the Master and the provincial preceptors be assembled with them so that they could consult them about the question of procurators and other matters, and asserted that if these leaders did not agree to this or could not be present with them, they could 'by no means do what they ought'.

But the commissioners would only repeat that they were prepared to hear procurators and remind them that the Grand Master and the other leaders had already refused to defend the Order. They also ordered that the two potential defenders named by Provins and Bologna be brought before them. The Archbishop of Narbonne, as president of the commission, then addressed the assembled Templars, telling them that they must 'arrange things today while you are here, since the affair requires despatch, and the time of the general council approaches'. The commissioners did not intend to assemble like this again, but to proceed in the form given to them. The proceedings would begin again on Tuesday. Meanwhile, the Templars should consult together, and notaries would be sent to record their decision.[28]

Three days later, on Tuesday 31 March, the commissioners

ordered the notaries, who were attached permanently to the commission while it sat, to visit each of the places where the Templars were being kept in Paris, to ask the prisoners if they would establish procurators to act for the defence of the Order, and to record anything which any individual Templar had to say. At the same time they ordered the gaolers, Voet and Jamville, to ensure that the Templars who had spoken on the previous Saturday – apparently two knights, Guillaume de Chambonnet and Bertrand de Sartiges, as well as the priests Renaud de Provins and Pietro di Bologna – be brought before them the next morning, together with other 'discreet and sensible' brothers up to the number of twelve.

The influx of Templars into Paris from the provinces had led to their wide dispersal in many different places throughout the city, including abbeys, episcopal residences and private houses, as well as the Parisian Temple itself. During the following week the notaries visited thirty different places, which contained groups of Templars as large as seventy-five in the Temple at Paris and as small as four in the house of Guillaume de Domont.[29] The private individuals and corporations who housed them heavily exploited their power for their own profit, and sometimes ill-treated them as well. The seven Templars held in the house of the Abbot of Tiron on the island of Notre-Dame complained that their allowance of 12 *deniers* per day was totally inadequate. They were obliged to pay 3 *deniers* for each bed and 2 *sous* 6 *deniers* per week for the rent of a kitchen and cloth. The washing of their clothes cost 18 *deniers* every fifteen days, and logs and candles were charged at the rate of 4 *deniers* per day. If they wished to appear before the commission, they had to be unfettered and chained up again on their return, a service which cost them 2 *sous*, while transport to and from the island was 16 *deniers*. Moreover, the keeper at this house had kept two of the brothers in a dark ditch all night, perhaps because they lacked the necessary money for beds and other necessities.[30]

Despite these problems the notaries found the Templars much more vociferous than at any time since the trial had started, but, apparently for tactical reasons, few were prepared to name procurators as such, maintaining that they had leaders and this was their function. In some houses the notaries were asked why Provins, Bologna, Chambonnet and Sartiges had not been sent to them so that they could deliberate together, claiming that this had been promised by Voet and Jamville.[31] The thirteen brothers at Saint-Martin-des-Champs wanted to consult the leaders of the Order, adding that they were good and just men, and that the Order was free from errors, which they had never heard of before their capture.[32] Twenty Templars at the Abbey of Sainte-Geneviève condemned the articles read out the previous Saturday as 'false and against the faith', and one of them, Elias Aymerici, on behalf of all, handed to the notaries an appeal for Christ's mercy, written in the form and tone of a prayer. They humbly asked God that they 'of weak and miserable flesh' might receive 'truth and justice'. They maintained that the Templars, whose Order had been founded by St Bernard in a general council through the most merciful God, had been arrested by the King of France 'without just cause'. They cried to the Lord, 'You know us to be innocent, cause us to be freed, in order that we might keep to our vows and your mandate in humility, and might do your holy service and your wish.'[33] At the house of Robert Anudei, situated near the pig market in Paris, Raoul de Thauvenay told the notaries that he had seen many brothers received and in every case the reception had been orthodox, new members being received in the name of the Holy Trinity, Father, Son and Holy Spirit, and the Blessed Mary and all the saints.[34] Only occasionally was there a discordant voice. Aymo de Pratimi, one of the twenty-eight Templars held at the house of Jean Rosselli, near the Church of Saint-Jean *in Gravia*, said that he was not able to defend the Order, since he was 'a poor and simple man', but he was not a heretic, nor had he ever done any of the things of which the Templars were accused. He had not seen or heard of any of these errors. He then asked if he could leave the Temple and return to secular life or enter another Order, since the Order in which he was at present did not please him, although he did not specify in what way. Presumably to achieve this release, he wanted to be brought before the commission or at least the Bishop of Limoges.[35]

However, the most important and lengthy statement was made by Pietro di Bologna himself, on Tuesday 31 March, when the notaries visited the largest group of Templars, who were imprisoned in the Parisian Temple. He continued to assert that procurators could not be appointed without the Master's consent, but he was not prepared to let the opportunity pass on this account. The articles in the papal bull were shameful, most wicked and unreasonable and detestable things, and they were lies, false, indeed most false, and iniquitous, and were fabricated, invented and made from new, by witnesses and rivals and lying enemies, and that the Order of the Temple was clean and immaculate, and always was, from all these articles, vices and sins. All those who had spoken or spoke to the contrary, did so both as infidels and heretics, desiring to sow heresy and most foul tares, and these things they were prepared to sustain in heart, mouth and deed, in all the ways in which it could and ought to be done.

The Templars should be freed to enable them to mount a proper defence, and means should be provided for them to attend the Council of Vienne personally. Any confessions which had been made should not prejudice the Order, since they were clearly lies which 'were known to have been spoken from the fear of death and through the grave tortures which they had suffered, and if some of them were not placed in torture, they were nevertheless terrified by the fear of torture, seeing others tortured in this way, and said what the torturers wished'. This should not therefore stand against them, 'since the punishment of one is the fear of many'. Others had been equally corrupted by promises and blandishments. All this was so public and well known that it could not be concealed by evasion. They asked the mercy of God that justice might be done to them, having been oppressed for such a long time without just cause, for they were good and faithful Christians.[36]

On the following day, Wednesday, Pietro di Bologna, Renaud de Provins, Guillaume de Chambonnet and Bertrand de Sartiges, together with a representative of the serving brothers, Robert Vigier, were brought before the commission as had been ordered. The commissioners seem to have decided that these men would be reasonable procurators and, anxious to hasten the affair, wanted to establish this explicitly. But when they asked if procurators had been constituted Renaud de Provins was ready with a prepared statement, which went a stage further than that made by Pietro di Bologna. Bologna had condemned the accusations and asserted the Order's innocence; Provins now began to take the accusers on their own ground by arguing from a judicial point of view, something that the leaders of the Order were either unwilling to do or incapable of doing. First he took care not to commit himself fully. If he should say anything which suggested a joining of issue, it should not prejudice him or those joined with him in this defence, since this was not his intention without advice and money. It seems that the defenders, by the refusal to appoint procurators and formally 'to join issue', were seeking to reply effectively to the charges, while at the same time trying to forestall judgement and therefore possible condemnation, because they were not procurators legally constituted by the Grand Master. The general reluctance to appoint procurators which was emerging from the notarial visits seems therefore part of an agreed tactic, perhaps formulated during the assembly in the bishop's garden the previous Saturday. Provins similarly took care to make clear that it was not his intention to say anything against the pope, the papacy, the King of France or his sons. Nevertheless he went on to argue that they could not appoint procurators without the consent of the Master and chapter, and these men would not dare to offer a defence while they were in the custody of the king's men 'on account of fear and seduction and false promises'. They should therefore 'be placed wholly in the hands of the Church so that neither the people of the king nor his ministers can in any way intervene in their custody' since, 'as long as the cause remains, false confession will remain'. If the leaders would still not consent to make a defence, then 'I ask the assent of their superiors in their defection and negligence.' At the very least therefore Provins could offer a defence himself, but if possible he wanted the attack to be spread on a broader front with the leaders taking an active part which might mitigate the damage caused by their confessions. If this failed, he hoped that the pope himself, as their superior, would be drawn into a direct role. The refusal to appoint procurators seems therefore to have been an important issue: an attempt to have the best of both worlds, the product of much more subtle minds than had hitherto been brought to bear in the Templars' defence.

Provins then asked that certain requests be met: that they be granted money to pay for procurators and advocates and to cover necessary expenses; that such procurators and advocates, and he and his associates, be given security; that renegade brothers be placed in the custody of the Church until the truth of their testimonies could be ascertained; that enquiry be made of those who had been at the death-bed of brothers, especially of priests who had heard their confession, as to whether the late brothers had spoken for or against the Order in their last hours. He then came to the core of the document. 'I say, reverend fathers, that you cannot proceed against the Order *de jure*, except in three ways, or in any one of them, namely by way of accusation, denunciation, or by the office of the judge.' If the intention was to proceed by accusation, then the accuser should appear, and he should be obliged to pay tallage and cover expenses of the prosecution of his suit should it be found that he had brought the case unjustly. If the method was denunciation then the denunciator should be not heard, 'since before the denunciation he ought to have warned us, the fraternity, of corruption, which he did not do'. Finally, if procedure was by the office of the judge, then 'I reserve to myself and my adherents reasons and defences to be proposed in the ordained proceedings, not being restricted in any way on those things which are conceded to myself and the Order.' By picking on specific procedural irregularities, Provins was determinedly exposing the arbitrary nature and questionable legality of the initial arrests in a way in which not even the pope, almost totally concerned with the protection of the theoretical superiority of the spiritual power, had been able to do. At last, pitiful confession had been replaced by coherent and logical argument, and for the first time the Templars were attempting to play a significant part in their destiny, instead of being merely the tools of papal–monarchical conflict.[37]

Meanwhile, the notaries continued to visit the imprisoned Templars. By Friday they had managed to gather a number of spokesmen for various groups, and fourteen of these appeared before the papal commission that day. One of them, Jean de Montréal, presented a document, in French, from which he read a defence of the Order, more emotional than that of Provins, but nevertheless a positive contribution on its own level. He spoke of the Order's honest foundation, its continuance without sin, the orthodoxy of its internal customs and the great processions and feasts before the people. He drew attention to the constant employment by the Kings of France and by the kings of other countries of the Templars as treasurers and in other capacities, arguing that they would not have been chosen unless the Order had been free from error. He reminded the commissioners of the great services the Order had rendered against the Saracens, especially with Saint Louis and the King of England, and he mentioned the gallant death of the Grand Master, Guillaume de Beaujeu, at Acre, together with three hundred brothers. Moreover, they had carried the cross not only in the east, but in Castile and Aragon as well. The thorns of the crown of the Saviour which flowered in the hands of the Chaplains of the Order on Holy Thursday would not have done so if the brothers had been guilty, nor would the heart of St Euphemia have come to Pilgrims' Castle by the grace of God, in the light of which several miracles occurred. Nor would they have been able to acquire such a collection of relics as they possessed. More than twenty thousand brothers had died for the faith in Outremer, and the defendants were prepared to combat any man who spoke against the Order, except the people of the king and the pope. On the back of the documents there was written, 'And if the other side wish to put forward anything we ask for a transcript and a day in which to deliberate.'[38]

The notaries were now sent out again to ascertain that these brothers really did represent the views of the Templars in the houses from which they had come. At the same time the notaries were to tell the Templars that the commissioners did not intend to wait any longer and that they were about to proceed according to the law, being prepared to receive whichever brothers came forward as representatives of the mass of the defenders.[39] But this hustling met with continued resistance. On the Friday afternoon the eleven brothers held at the house of Rabiosse or de la Ragera were told that the commission intended to proceed the following Tuesday (7 April) and were therefore asked whom they wished to represent them. They replied that they did not wish to appoint procurators until they had taken advice,

since it was very dangerous for them to submit at once both the honour of the whole Order and their persons to the defence of four or five persons, because if, in the view of some powerful men, these defenders defended the Order less than sufficiently, and the Order was put aside for the above crimes, although it was an inquiry against the whole Order, nevertheless their persons were in danger who remained at such a time in the said Order, but each was prepared by himself, as far as he could, to defend the said Order.[40]

On Saturday the Templars at the house of the Abbot of Tiron told the notaries that they had already sent the commissioners a document stating that the Order was good and lawful.⁴¹ The consistent theme of these visits however was that the Templars should be allowed to consult with Provins and Bologna and the other spokesmen. Accordingly, the Bishop of Bayeux allowed these consultations to take place in the hope that they could be persuaded to choose these men as procurators by the following Tuesday. The sense of the views gathered by Tuesday was that the Templars were prepared to allow Provins, Bologna, Sartiges and Chambonnet to speak on their behalf, but not that they should be appointed procurators as such.⁴² During a week of intensive activity the notaries had paid a total of fifty-nine visits to Templar prisons in Paris and had collected the views of 537 Templars or their representatives.

On Tuesday 7 April 1310 nine Templars appeared before the commissioners in the chapel next to the episcopal hall. These were Renaud de Provins and Pietro di Bologna, priests, Guillaume de Chambonnet, Bertrand de Sartiges and Bernard de Foix, knights, and Brothers Jean de Montréal, Mathieu de Cresson-Essart, Jean de Saint-Léonard, and Guillaume de Givry. Pierre de Bologna now set out their defence at length. The brothers were making a defence 'not for the purpose of contesting the proceedings, but simply to make a response', for procurators could not legally be appointed without 'the presence, counsel and advice of their Grand Master and chapter'. They all offered themselves 'personally, generally and separately' for the defence of the Order, and asked that they could be allowed to attend the general council or any meeting in which the state of the Order was being investigated. This they fully intended to do when they gained full liberty. They repeated the arguments already put forward by Pietro di Bologna that confessions against the Order were of no validity, since they were obtained by force, and that they would prove this when restored to full liberty, and asked again that Templars 'living dishonourably to the shame of the said Order and the Holy Church' should be apprehended. In a clear reference to the illegal presence of Nogaret and Plaisians at certain of the commission's hearings they requested that 'whenever any brothers are examined, no layman may be present who could hear them or any person whose probity could be doubted'. In the circumstances it is not in any way to be marvelled at that there are those who have lied, but more so concerning those who have kept to the truth, seeing the tribulations and dangers which those who speak the truth suffer continually and the menaces and outrages and other ills which they sustain daily, and the advantages, favourable conditions and pleasures and liberties which the liars have and the great promises which are daily made to them.

He continued that as a consequence 'it is a marvellous thing and greatly astonishing to all that greater faith is placed in these liars who, having been corrupted in this way, have testified such things in the interests of their bodies, rather than those who, like Christian martyrs, for the purpose of sustaining the truth have died by torture'. Similarly, those still living who have sustained the truth 'on the prompting of conscience alone' are as a result 'suffering daily in prison so many tortures, punishments, tribulations and dangers, indignities, calamities and miseries'. In further corroboration of this it was said that

> beyond the Kingdom of France no brother of the Temple in all the lands of the world will be found who says or who will speak these lies, on account of which it is clear enough why they have been spoken in the Kingdom of France, because those who have spoken, have testified when corrupted by fear, prayers or money.

Having attempted to discredit the validity of past confessions, the defenders then brought forward positive arguments in support of the Order. The Order was 'founded in charity and love of true fraternity' and it is

> for the honour of the most glorious Virgin, the mother of our Lord Jesus Christ, for the honour and defence of the Holy Church and for all the Christian faith and for the expulsion of the enemies of the cross, that is of the infidels, pagans or Saracens everywhere and especially in the Holy Land of Jerusalem, which the son of God himself consecrated with his own blood in dying for our redemption.

Their holy Order was 'untainted by all defect and all uncleanliness of any vices, in which there always flourished and flourishes regular custom and salutary observances' which had been confirmed by the many privileges granted by the papacy. A new entrant promises four essentials, 'namely obedience, chastity, poverty and to place all his strength at the service of the Holy Land of Jerusalem'. He is received 'with the honest kiss of peace and, having received the habit with the cross which they carry in perpetuity on the breast, on account of our reverence of the Crucifixion, in memory of his passion, it is taught to them to preserve the Rule and ancient customs transmitted by the Church of Rome and the holy fathers'. This mode of profession is preserved throughout the Order and has been from its foundation to the present day. Anyone who says or believes otherwise 'errs entirely, sins mortally and is altogether discredited by the transmission of the truth'.

Next, the defenders moved to attack the accusations directly. The articles against the Order were 'shameful, horrifying and detestable, both impossible and most foul'. Those who brought such lies to the pope and the king are

> false Christians and altogether heretics, detractors and seducers of the Holy Church and all the Christian faith, because motivated by the zeal of cupidity and the ardour of greed, as these most impious propagators of scandal had searched for apostates and fugitive brothers of the Order, who on account of wrong-doing, just like sickly cattle, were thrown from the fold, that is from the congregation of brothers,

and they have got together and made up these crimes and lies, leading the king and his council to believe them. From these things then 'proceeded much danger', in that the brothers had suffered arrest, spoliation, torture, killing and violence, and had been 'forced through the threats of death' to confess 'against conscience'.

With regard to the actual proceedings, they argued that the commission could not proceed by law in the way appertaining to it, namely *ex officio*, since the Templars 'were not defamed concerning these articles before their arrest nor was public opinion working against the Order, and it is certain that we and they are not in a safe place, since they are and were continually in the power of false liars to the king'. Every day new threats are brought to the Templars, telling them that they will be burnt if they retract. The brothers who have confessed have done so through torture and would freely retract if they dared, and therefore they asked that the commission give them a guarantee of safety so that 'they may return to the truth without fear'. Pierre de Bologna concluded with the usual reservation:

> All these things they declare and say, saving always all defences given and to be given by the brothers of the Temple singularly, specially and generally, now and in the future, for the defence and in the favour of the said Order. And if anything had been given or brought or said which could redound to the damage or prejudice of the said Order, it is altogether cancelled, void and of no value.[43]

Pietro di Bologna was followed by the serving brother Jean de Montréal, who read out a shorter statement specifically on behalf of the Templars detained in the house of Richard de Spoliis. He repeated the arguments that the confessions had been extracted by means of threats and torture, maintaining that the confessions were void in any case, since the Templars were exempt from all lay and ecclesiastical jurisdiction including the inquisitors', and were responsible only to the pope or his representative specifically appointed to deal with Templar affairs. He decorated his case with examples, such as the case of a Templar whose misdeeds had caused his expulsion but whom Boniface VIII allowed to return, saving the justice of the Order, which meant that the man had to eat off the floor for a year and a day; or the time when the castle of Safed was taken and eighty brothers, having been captured by the sultan, refused to deny Christ and were beheaded.[44]

The commissioners were not however prepared to be diverted by the activities of individuals or bodies in the past with whom they had no connection, choosing to base their reply to these arguments on a strict and narrow interpretation of their function in receiving defenders of the Order. They themselves could neither free the Templars nor restore their goods, since it was not they who had captured them, nor they who retained them. This appertained to the pope and the Church. They could not accept that the Templars were not defamed, for the papal bulls showed the contrary. Jean de Montréal's point that they were exempt from the jurisdiction of the ordinaries and the inquisitors was also completely wrong, for the inquisitors had apostolic authority to proceed when they suspected heresy. As for what had been said about the Grand Master, they stressed that he had been called several times, but he only maintained that he was reserved for the pope and would speak when brought before him. The remaining points the commission did not answer in detail, simply saying that 'their power did not extend to these things, but they would willingly ask those to whom these things appertained that they should do what good they could for the said brothers'. They concluded by saying that they were now going to proceed with the inquiry, but that they were prepared to receive any defence at any time, 'even up to the end of the inquiry'. The next Saturday, 11 April, the commissioners fixed the practical details of this proceeding. Pietro di Bologna, Renaud de Provins, Guillaume de Chambonnet and Bertrand de Sartiges were to be received as representatives of the brothers. These four men had therefore become procurators whether they wished to or not, and from this time were present during the questioning of witnesses, and were therefore in a position to take a positive role in the trial.[45] Despite the failure of the defenders to convince the commission of the justice of many of their arguments, they nevertheless had shaken the Templars from their passivity and given them hope that they were not completely doomed. Moreover, they had taken on, with great skill, the task of shaking the distinctly unstable legal foundation upon which their arrests and subsequent trial were based. In the first two weeks of April 1310 the prospects for the imprisoned Templars looked brighter than they had at any time during the two and a half years that the proceedings had continued.

Despite the strictly hierarchical nature of the Temple, it was these four men, two priests and two knights, who now occupied the centre of the stage, while Jacques de Molay and the other leaders, incapacitated by the chimera of papal reservation, took no more active part. Pietro di Bologna was a priest, forty-four years old, who had already seen twenty-five years' service. He had been examined at Paris on 7 November 1307, when he had been described as 'the general procurator of the whole knighthood of the Temple', which seems to have been the basis on which the commission regarded him as having already received the requisite authorisation from the Grand

Master to act as a procurator, albeit in a different context. He had been received at Bologna by Guillaume de Noris, Preceptor of Lombardy at that time, and therefore it seems likely that he was an Italian who possibly had received his education at the law schools of Bologna.[46] These schools produced legal graduates of the highest quality, and this may well be the background to his choice as procurator at the Roman Curia. It would certainly explain the coherence of his arguments, and the respect with which the commission treated the points which he made. However, at Paris in November 1307 he had admitted denying Christ and spitting on a crucifix and had said that the receptor had told him that he could commit homosexual acts with other brothers without sin, although he had never done so. He had been kissed on the mouth, the navel and on 'the vile lower part'. At this time he swore on oath that no pressure had been brought to bear on him, repeating the formula that he had told the pure truth for the safety of his soul.[47] The other priest, Renaud de Provins, had already shown great tactical skill in avoiding making a direct confession when he had appeared at Paris on the same day as Pierre de Bologna, although in doing so he had suggested strongly that illicit ceremonies were the general practice of the Order.[48] He too appears to have been an educated man, for in his deposition at Paris he indicated that he had several times thought of entering the Dominican Order before finally choosing the Temple. He was a little younger than Bologna, about thirty-six years old, and had seen fifteen years' service since his reception in the *bailliage* of Brie.[49] The two knights, Guillaume de Chambonnet and Bertrand de Sartiges, had, in contrast, admitted nothing when they had been examined by the Bishop of Clermont during his episcopal inquiry in June 1309.[50] Both were preceptors of local houses, Chambonnet at Blaudeix in the Auvergne, and Sartiges at Carlat in Rouergue, and both had seen service in the east, Sartiges having actually been received into the Order at the Templar house of Tortosa by the Grand Master of the time, Guillaume de Beaujeu. If they seemed to lack the obvious educational qualifications of the two priests, they compensated by their long experience extending over a generation in France, Palestine and Cyprus. Both men had given over thirty years of their lives to the Order.[51]

On the same day – Saturday 11 April – the first witnesses were sworn in, twenty-four in all, four of whom were not Templars. It is noticeable that at this time, when the Templar defence was at its height, an element clearly hostile to the Order was introduced to the commission. Three of the four seculars deposed, and all three proved to be unfavourable, if unconvincing, witnesses. Raoul de Presles is described as an 'advocate in the court of the king' and seems to have been an important member of the group of lawyers with which Philip IV surrounded himself;[52] Nicolas Symon, an *armiger* or squire, was an associate of Presles;[53] and Guichard de Marsillac was a former *sénéchal* of Toulouse, whose house in Paris was being used as a prison for Templars and who had been involved in torturing them to extract confessions.[54] Fifteen of the twenty Templars came from that same group of seventy-two picked witnesses presented to the pope at Poitiers in June 1308, including the notorious Jean de Folliaco.[55] Only one of these, Jean de Sivry, a priest, was among those who had offered themselves for the defence.[56] None of the remaining five Templars had offered to defend the Order, and all in fact confessed to at least two of the major charges: the denial of Christ, spitting or trampling on a cross, illicit kissing and idol worship. Gérard de Pasagio, one of these five, had left the Order five years before 'on account of its depravities'.[57] It is possible to interpret this one-sided selection of witnesses in the sense of a prosecution case being presented first, although the procedural methods adopted by the commission give no evidence in support of this view. Moreover, if this were the intention, it would seem to be a rather pointless operation, for in the event the commission decided not to listen to the fifteen Templars who had already appeared before the pope,[58] a decision which was in keeping with the papal ruling on the matter in the letter of May 1309.[59] Once again it must be emphasised that Philip the Fair controlled the persons of the Templars, and the selection of this particular twenty, when there were over 590 others prepared to defend the Order actually present in Paris, must be seen as an attempt to 'feed' unfavourable witnesses to the commission in an effort to stem the swelling tide of the Templar defence. The secular witnesses, who appeared first, would be present to stiffen this hostility to the Order.

Raoul de Presles told the commissioners that when he had lived in Laon, about four to six years before the arrest of the Templars, he had been very friendly with Gervais de Beauvais, preceptor of the local house. This brother had frequently said – indeed over a hundred times – that there was a point in the Order so secret that he would rather have his head cut off than tell anyone. There was also a point in the general chapter of the Order which was so secret that if Raoul de Presles or even the King of France should see it, those holding the chapter would seek to kill them, deferring to the authority of no one in this. Furthermore, Gervais had said that the Order had a small book of statutes which he would show to Presles willingly, but there existed another secret book which he would not show for all the world. Gervais then asked if Presles would help him gain promotion to the general chapter, because then he did not doubt that he would quickly become Grand Master. Presles did as requested and asked the leaders of the Order that Gervais be admitted to the general chapter. This was granted and after his entrance 'he saw him in great authority, and that some of the great and powerful men of the Order gave him authority, as Gervais had predicted'. Presles knew nothing of any other articles, except for that which related to the means of compulsion employed within the Order against disobedient brothers. He had often heard Gervais and many others say that no other prisons were as dreadful as those of their Order, and that whoever resisted any command of the preceptors was thrown into such a prison, even until death. This was thin material. Nicolas Symon, the squire, could add nothing more. He was reduced to saying that he knew nothing about the articles 'but he suspected that the said Order was not good', a suspicion apparently based upon the same source as that of Raoul de Presles.[60]

On Monday and Tuesday of the following week the commissioners heard Guichard de Marsillac. His story, like that of Presles, was based almost entirely on hearsay, but it lacked even Presles's plausibility. He claimed that he had heard about article number thirty, concerning kissing on the anus, as long ago as forty years before and he had heard it about five hundred times since, in various places including Toulouse, Lyons, Paris, Apulia and Aragon, from knights, burgesses and many others. It was a matter of public rumour, which he defined as 'that which is referred to publicly in various places and by various persons'. He did not know the origin of the rumour, but asserted that it came from 'good and serious men'. However, the greater part of his deposition concerned the reception of a Templar knight called Hugues, a kinsman of his, and its consequences. The reception, held at the Templars' house at Toulouse, had been completed when Hugues was taken into a room where elaborate precautions had been taken to prevent anyone from seeing in, apparently even to the extent of hanging a curtain across the inside of the door to prevent the inquisitive from peering through the cracks between the door and its frame. After a long period of waiting Hugues emerged in Templar clothing looking 'very pale and as if disturbed and stupefied', in distinct contrast to his happy and enthusiastic demeanour before he had entered the room. When Guichard de Marsillac had asked Hugues about this the next day, all he would say was that he could never be joyful again nor have a peaceful heart. Others whom Guichard encouraged to ask Hugues what was troubling him were no more successful, but one of them, Lancelot de Paspretes, a canon of Orléans, did find out that Hugues had made a seal on the circumference of which was cut *Sigillum Hugonis Perditi* – the seal of the lost Hugues. The canon believed that Hugues was desperate, and Guichard tried to force his kinsman to hand over the seal so that he could break it. He only managed to get an impression however, made by Hugues in red wax, and could find out nothing about its meaning. After Hugues had been in the Order for two months he returned to his kinsfolk with whom he lived for another six months. He then became ill and died, after having made confession to a Franciscan whom Guichard had called. On the second day of his deposition, Tuesday 14 April, Guichard was asked why he thought Hugues had called himself *perditus*. He first replied that he thought this was because of the loss of his soul on account of the things which were said against the Temple, but then he changed his mind and said that he believed it was because of the austerities of the Templars. Guichard had little to add to this: he knew of a Templar who had transferred to the Hospital, and he had heard rumours that the Grand Master, Guillaume de Beaujeu, had been too familiar with the Saracens, a familiarity which had caused the Christians great harm. He did not believe this to be the case however, since he knew that Beaujeu had fought strenuously and died in the defence of Acre in 1291.[61] Guichard de Marsillac never explained, nor apparently was he asked, why ten years ago Hugues had joined an Order about which, according to Guichard's account, public rumour had been rife concerning obscene kisses for more than forty years.

On the same day the first of the Templar witnesses was brought in, a twenty-five-year-old serving brother called Jean Taylafer de

Gêne, from the diocese of Langres. He no longer had the habit of the Temple, but instead wore clothes of coarse grey wool, and his beard had been shaved off. His deposition followed a pattern which was adopted as standard by the commissioners, who took him through all the 127 articles in a systematic fashion, although it was not generally necessary to deal with them individually, for the articles fell into definable groups. The effect of this was to produce much more detailed depositions than had been received during the Parisian hearings of the autumn of 1307, and perhaps incidentally to offer some clues regarding the personality of individual Templars. Jean Taylafer had been a Templar for about three years before the arrests. At his reception, on the orders of Etienne, the chaplain of Mormant where the reception was taking place, he had denied Christ once, although by the mouth and not in the heart, and he had spat near, although not actually on, a cross, which was old and made of painted wood. They threatened that 'unless he did these things, they would put him in such a place that he would not see his hands and feet'. This had taken place about dawn by the light of two candles only, so that he could not see clearly in the chapel. He had been told that he would be more fully informed about the points of the Order afterwards, but he never had been because he did not go to see nor to attend chapters, although he was often reproved for his absence. He had not been to any other receptions, but he believed them to be the same as this, although when he was asked why he believed this, he replied that he did not know. A brother who had since died, who had had experience overseas, had once told him that the Templars trampled the cross underfoot, but he had no direct information on this. In reply to an additional accusation, which formed part of the 127 articles, concerning the practice of lay absolution in the Temple, he asserted that he had heard it generally said that the Grand Master could absolve brothers from their sins, as could the Order's chaplains, but he had never heard this about the other leaders. At his reception he had been kissed on the mouth, navel and on the lower part of the back, as he believed others were. He had been made to swear not to leave the Order, he had had to make profession at once, and the whole thing had taken place in secret behind locked doors, with only Templars present. He believed from secular persons that 'vehement suspicion' had arisen as a result of this secrecy, but he was not certain where or by whom this was said, he simply knew it was before the Templars were arrested. On the day of his reception 'a certain head' had been placed on the altar of the chapel and he was told to adore it. He did not know what substance it was made from, since he had not often gone near it, but it appeared to be an effigy of a human face, red in colour, and as large as a human head. He had never actually seen it adored by anyone, nor did he know in whose veneration it was made. He was given a cord of white thread at this reception which they said had been around the head, and was ordered to wear it on top of his shirt day and night, although he in fact had thrown it away. He asserted that this worship of a head applied in other receptions besides his own. He had been forbidden to reveal anything of what had happened at the reception, an injunction which had been reinforced by talk among the brothers which claimed that anyone disobeying this command would be put in prison in irons and kept there for ever. The only favourable thing that he managed to say was that in the houses in which he had lived, alms had always been given, and he believed that many brothers liberally distributed alms and hospitality. He had heard that those things ordained by the Grand Master beyond the sea were equally preserved on this side of the sea. He had seen many leave the Order, although he did not know for what reason. As for himself, the Order displeased him 'on account of the filthy things and errors of which he had deposed above'. He was actually pleased when he was arrested with the others but now he was less enthusiastic because of the great length of time he had remained in prison. Because of his displeasure with the Order, he had recently given it up and put aside his mantle.[62]

The commission only had time to hear part of a not dissimilar deposition from a Templar from the diocese of London called Jean de Hinquemeta, who was from the same group which had been sworn in on 11 April, when it was decided to recess for Easter, and to reassemble on Thursday 23 April. On that day the Bishop of Bayeux appeared to say that he could not be present for the next month or so, since he had to attend the provincial Council of Rouen.[63] He was not therefore present to hear a new blast delivered by the four Templar defenders, apparently prepared during the recess, and possibly intended to counter these hostile witnesses. Attendance at the actual hearings enabled the defenders to keep in much closer touch with new developments than had been the case when they were incarcerated, and to some degree mitigated the advantage held by the French government in having control of the persons of the Order.

Once again Pietro di Bologna acted as spokesman. In rhetorical fury it was a match for any of the characteristic hyperbole of the royal chancery, suggesting perhaps by its style and linguistic command the common form of training and education received by Pietro di Bologna on one side and Guillaume de Nogaret on the other. The proceedings against the Order had been 'rapid, violent, unlooked for, hostile and unjust, altogether without justice, but containing complete injury, most grave violence and intolerable error', for no attempt had been made to keep to proper judicial procedures. On the contrary

> with destructive fury all the brothers of the Order in the Kingdom of France were suddenly arrested, and led like sheep to the slaughter, their goods and all their things having been suddenly despoiled, delivered up to harsh prisons, [and] through diverse and various kinds of tortures, from which many had died, many were for ever disabled, and many at that time driven to lie against themselves and the Order.

Because of all this violence there had been taken from the Templars completely 'freedom of mind, which is what every good man ought to have'. Once a man is deprived of this free will, he is deprived of all good things, 'knowledge, memory and understanding'. Therefore, whatever might be said by anyone in such a state ought not, nor cannot, be prejudicial. Some brothers had been induced more easily to lie because 'letters were given to them with the seal of the lord king attached, concerning the conservation of limbs and life, and freedom, and all punishments, and carefully decreeing to them good provision and great revenues to be given annually during their lifetime, always saying first to them that the Order of the Temple was altogether condemned'. For these reasons, therefore, whatever the brothers say against the Order is corrupt. 'All the aforesaid matters are so public and well known, that by no evasion are they to be hidden.' The defenders then offered to prove these things at once.

The defenders could put forward 'good presumptions' on behalf of the Order 'against which proofs to the contrary ought not to be received'. No one can be believed 'so foolish and mad who, to the loss of his soul, would enter and persevere in the Order'. Many noble and powerful men of distinguished lineage from many different countries made profession in the Order and remained in it until the end of their lives. If so many men of this kind had known of anything shameful, especially the injuries and blasphemies to the name of Jesus Christ, 'they would all have shouted out, and have divulged all these matters to the whole world'.

They then asked for the documentary material relevant to the case: a copy of the commission's terms of reference, a copy of all the articles, the names of all the witnesses sworn and to be sworn. This last point was emphasised by their declaration that they intended 'to speak against their persons' at the appropriate time, apparently in justification of their previous claims of coercion. They also asked that witnesses who had deposed be prevented from speaking with those who had not yet given their evidence, and that witnesses should swear on oath not to reveal the secrets of their testimony. Whatever was said should be kept secret, for danger and scandal would result if the contrary was allowed to happen. The commission should assure each witness of the secrecy of his deposition, until such time as the information was sent to the pope. The gaolers should be asked about the testimony of brothers who had died in custody, especially those who were said to be reconciled, and Templars who had refused to defend the Order should be asked why, on oath.

The statement concluded with a story intended to demonstrate the purity of the Order. It concerned a Templar knight called Adam de Wallaincourt. This man

> wishing to enter a more severe Order, asked permission and entered the Order of the Carthusians, in which, persevering for a short time, he asked, with long instance of prayer, to return to the Order of the Temple; he was received, saving the discipline of the Order, since he came naked with only a thigh covering from the outer door to the chapter, in the presence of many nobles, relatives and friends, with all the brothers present; and genuflecting in the presence of the preceptor, who was holding the chapter, he asked mercy, and asked again, with tears, that he be admitted into the company of the brothers; he made solemn penance for a

year and a day, by eating on the ground for the weekdays of that year, by fasting on bread and water every Sunday, by going naked to the altar in solemn masses, by receiving discipline at the hand of the priest; and afterwards he recovered the habit and the company of the brothers, according to the statutes of the Order.

They asked that this brother should be brought forward to defend the Order and swear the truth about the state of the Order, 'since it is not likely that such a man, in dishonour of his soul and censure of his body, would have proceeded to such a penance, if the Order was bad; for it was necessary for all the apostates from the Order of the Temple to do penance, before they could be admitted to the company of the brothers'.[64] But this point the defenders could never prove. Apparently unknown to them, Adam de Wallaincourt had been among those who had evaded the royal officials in October 1307, and since there is no record of his taking part in the trial, he presumably made good his escape.[65]

The parade of picked witnesses continued, but it was evident that they were having a less than decisive effect in the face of the increasingly aggressive stance now being adopted by the four brothers, who seem even to have dropped the pretence that the case against them had developed merely because King Philip IV had been misled by liars, and who now appeared to be attacking the monarch directly. Moreover, the list of defenders continued to grow, for on Saturday 2 May another twenty-five brothers from Périgord added themselves to those who had assembled in the garden of the Bishop of Paris.[66] Meanwhile the hostile witnesses remained unconvincing. Jacques de Troyes, for instance, a serving brother who appeared on Saturday 9 May, confessed to the denial of Christ, spitting and trampling on the cross, and obscene kisses. According to him it was the receptor who had stripped himself naked at his reception in front of him and other brothers. He had ordered Jacques to kiss him on the anus, but he had refused, instead kissing him on the bare shoulder. But he also admitted that he had left the Order a year before the arrests, at first claiming that this had been because he was 'captured by the love of a certain woman', but later in his testimony maintaining that he had left 'more on account of the filth of the Order than for the love of the woman . . . since he had and could have this woman in the Order when he wished'. The commission, on this occasion lacking the presence of its two most strongly royalist members, the Archbishop of Narbonne and the Bishop of Bayeux, found this man too much to take. The notarial record says that this witness 'seemed to be very easy and shameless in talking, and in several things that he said he was not steady, but varying and vacillating'.[67]

It would have been characteristic of the French government to employ more than one method to combat the Templar defence. In the spring of 1308 the king had sent a series of questions to the masters of theology at Paris in order to gain a legal basis for his adopted position. The limited value of the reply to the royal case does not seem to have deterred the government from continuing to seek such opinions, for there exists a reply to four questions concerning legal points which had arisen during the course of the trial, questions which appear to have emanated from the French government. The reply is anonymous and undated and therefore cannot be certainly ascribed to the early months of 1310, but the nature of the points raised concerning, for instance, the legitimacy of retracting confessions, and the justification for being allowed to mount a defence, would tend to support this date. Most historians have placed this document early in 1308,[68] by implication associating it with the questions to the masters of theology posed at that time, but the question of defence had not then arisen; indeed the decisions at Poitiers which led to the creation of the papal commission had not been envisaged. Moreover, in the first question, it is asked what is to be done about the Grand Master who had first confessed, then retracted, and finally had returned to his first confession, a situation which did not occur until August 1308, when Molay returned to his original confession during his appearance before the cardinals at Chinon. The document therefore cannot be earlier than 1309, while the contents of the questions suggest a much greater relevance and topicality in relation to the events of early 1310. To place the document after mid-May, however, when the defence collapsed, would be to reduce it merely to an academic exercise. If the questions did originate with the French government this would be an unwarranted luxury for an administration which was essentially interested in academic argument only for its practical application.

Unlike the masters of theology, the individual jurist (the document is in the first person) who answered the questions was completely favourable to the government's position. About the first question concerning the vacillations of the Grand Master, the jurist was in no doubt. He could not weaken by his own witness what 'he has clearly and publicly confessed'. Moreover, his confession had been amply confirmed by the testimonies of many other Templars, and therefore it should clearly stand against him. The explanation for his variations was simple. 'For it is the secret judgement of the Lord, that the master of such great blasphemies against Christ, who lived evilly for so long, delivered so many others to the damned sect . . . may be punished as an example to the world.' The same argument applies to Hugues de Pairaud, 'who is known to have delivered a thousand brothers to the condemnable heresy'. To the second question, as to whether the essence of the profession, which is 'I swear to preserve the statutes and secrets of the Order', ought to be condemned as corrupt, the answer was again affirmative. New entrants erred in their ignorance of the substance of their obligations, and in their acceptance of the demands to deny Christ and other wickednesses. If a shameful condition is introduced then the whole substance is corrupted, and the whole obligation is nullified.

The third question was very pertinent to the defence being mounted. The jurist thought that a defender should not be allowed for individual persons. In relation to the whole Order however, since the Grand Master would not make a defence, he agreed that there was a prima facie case for granting the right to a defender, given that the usual judicial processes were being employed. But in this case the corruption of the Order was clear to the Church from the innumerable depositions of the Templars. 'Therefore the king does not speak as accuser or taking the part of a litigant, but as the minister of God and defender of the faith and champion of the Church.' He shouts to the Church to intervene as 'the son excites the sleeping father, that he might be vigilant against the robbers undermining the house of the Lord, just as the Church is accustomed to require of Catholic princes'. The king is showing 'the wounds of Christ to the Church, in order that it might cure them and expel the putrid flesh from the body of the Church', a duty which the Church required that he perform. The Church's task is to decide whether the clamour is justified, but here there can be no doubt, for the depositions show quite clearly that the Order is depraved. A defender could only be 'for the purpose of defending the errors'. The Church must not delay by proceeding through judicial means in these circumstances, but should proceed by way of provision, and peremptorily cast out the Order because it is a mortal danger to the body of the faithful.

The fourth question asked what should be done if any Templars were found innocent. The jurist thought that it would be almost impossible to find an innocent person 'who was not from conversation or other means struck by the contagion'. Even if no evidence could be found against him because witnesses were dead or the persons concerned were obstinate it would not follow that innocence was proved, 'since grave presumption would always live against him. He would always be a rock of scandal and an abomination to any Catholic seeing him.' It was already clear that the majority of them had sinned, which was sufficient to condemn them all, especially since those sins had been committed by the leaders. He concluded that 'such an Order cannot remain without danger and scandal to the whole Church'.[69]

In summary therefore the confessions were valid, the profession was corrupt, and there was no need for any defence. It was unlikely that any remained entirely uncorrupted within the Order, but in any case this was no justification for failing to act against the Order. The patient attempts by the four defenders to draw attention to procedural irregularities were swept aside, for the king acted from Christian duty inherent in his monarchical position, a duty imposed upon him by the higher spiritual power of the Church, and not as an accuser or litigator. The arguments of Renaud de Provins and Pietro di Bologna were, by implication, irrelevant. The close association of these arguments with those put forward by the defenders gives further credibility to a date of early 1310 for this document. Any attempt to pin down the author of the replies must be purely guesswork, but one possible candidate is Jean de Pouilli, a secular clerk and master of theology, who was strongly opposed to the privileges of exempt Orders, including the Mendicants as well as the Templars. He was deeply convinced of the Templars' guilt, and at about the time of the Council of Vienne in 1312, in reply to some questions sent by a group of prelates to the University of Paris, he argued very strongly that the Templars who had revoked their confessions must be relapsed heretics, which would make them liable to execution. They had confessed by legal means, and they had abjured the heresy and been absolved. If their subsequent retractions did not make them relapsed heretics, then the Church was denying the repentance by which she proved subsequent relapses. Jean de Pouilli was however in a distinct minority in expressing this view, for of the other twenty-one masters who gave their opinion, he was only able to convince two of them that he was correct. The remaining nineteen argued that such persons were 'impenitents', an important distinction which allowed time for further persuasion.[70] This suggests that the views expressed by the anonymous person in early 1310 would not have been fully acceptable to most theological and legal opinion, and that they were provided by a particular individual whose views suited the French government. In no other reign is the twisted legalism by which the Capetians had justified the extension of their power more fully exposed to scrutiny than during that of Philip the Fair.

6: The End of Resistance

Philippe de Marigny, Archbishop of Sens, was the brother of Enguerrand de Marigny, who, as the royal Chamberlain, was Philip IV's principal minister of finance. In 1310 Enguerrand was the rising star of Philip's government, for he was beginning to displace Guillaume de Nogaret as the first minister of the royal council. It seems that Enguerrand had drawn the king's attention to his brother, who, as the former Bishop of Cambrai, does not seem to have been well known to Philip. The previous Archbishop of Sens, Etienne Béquart, had been ill for some months before his death on 29 March 1309, and since December 1308 Philip IV had been pressing the pope to reserve the see and not to nominate a successor without royal advice. This reservation was made on 23 April 1309, and about October, Philip asked for the promotion of the Bishop of Cambrai.[1] In March 1310 Philippe de Marigny granted his brother a fief at Gainneville, especially bought in December of the previous year, as a reward for his generosity.[2] While the papal commission took its course in Paris, the episcopal inquiries could still continue to hear cases against individual Templars. With this new elevation Philip IV now had effective control of the proceedings in the province of Sens, within which lay the city of Paris. In the second week of May 1310 Philip IV utilised this control in the most brutal way to crush the Templar defence. Already, on 4 April in the bull *Alma mater*, Clement had found it necessary to postpone the Council of Vienne for a year from October 1310 until October 1311, because the inquiry against the Order was taking longer than expected.[3] King Philip lost patience. The arrests had taken place in October 1307, yet the matter was still pending in May 1310. Indeed the Templars were actually gaining ground. He therefore turned to the episcopal inquiries, where royal influence was so paramount, and to his nominee, Philippe de Marigny. The pope had provided that the bishops, after conducting examinations of the Templars, could convoke provincial councils to decide the fate of individuals.[4] Only the Order as an Order was to be judged at the forthcoming Council of Vienne; it was therefore quite legal for the episcopal inquiries to proceed to fulfil their appointed functions, independent of the papal commission. Philippe de Marigny now convened a council at Paris to judge the individuals of the province of Sens.

Suddenly it was clear that King Philip was determined to bring matters to a head. On 10 May, although it was a Sunday and the commission was not sitting, the four defenders tried desperately to convince the commissioners that they should block the Archbishop of Sens. In a hastily convened meeting in the chapel of Saint-Eloi in the monastery of Sainte-Geneviève in Paris, to which the hearings had recently moved, Pietro di Bologna recounted how many brothers had come forward to defend the Order before the commission. But now

> they had heard, and from likely conjectures feared and believed, that the Lord Archbishop of Sens with his suffragans, convoked in provincial council at Paris, wished on the following day to make some proceedings against many of the brothers who had brought themselves to the defence of the said Order, in order that, as the defenders said, he might make the brothers from this necessity desist from the aforesaid defence.

As a result, they had prepared an appeal which they wished to read before the commissioners. However, the Archbishop of Narbonne told them that it was not the commission's business to hear appeals, but they were prepared to hear anything said in defence of the Order. Pietro di Bologna then read out a statement which explained that the defenders thought an appeal was necessary because they feared that the Archbishop of Sens and the other prelates of France were about to proceed against the Templars *de facto* even though they could not do so *de jure* while the commission was hearing defenders. If any injury were brought to them at this time it 'would be against God and justice, and would completely overturn the inquiry'. They therefore appealed to the Holy See, placing all the brothers who had offered to defend the Order under its protection. They asked 'the advice of wise men' for the purpose of 'correcting this appeal', and for 'necessary and sufficient expenses' from the goods of the Order. They should be taken, in full security, to the pope to prosecute this appeal. They asked the commissioners to order the Archbishop of Sens and the other prelates not to proceed 'in any new way' against them, and that through the mediation of the commission, they be allowed to go to the Archbishop of Sens to appeal against him, together with one or two of the commission's notaries, since they could not find a notary who was willing to go with them.[5]

Gilles Aicelin, the president of the commission, was, for a man of his temper, placed in an acutely embarrassing position. He came from a Burgundian family with many important connections in the Church. He had been legally trained and since 1288 had been in the royal service. Since that time his career had been closely involved with the Capetian monarchy. He had been made Archbishop of Narbonne in 1290 and had been prominent in the negotiation of treaties and in the conduct of royal embassies. For a period he had been Keeper of the Seals, preceding Guillaume de Nogaret. He had not, however, invariably been in agreement with the king. In 1301 when Bernard Saisset was arrested, he had incurred the king's displeasure by standing out for the bishop's regular and correct treatment in law as a cleric.[6] Nevertheless, he had been no friend of the Templars, having spoken against them at Poitiers before the pope in 1308.[7] To the king, he must have seemed a good choice as president of the papal commission despite the occasional show of independence. But the Templars had been very properly allowed to make their defence before the commission under his presidency, whatever his personal views on the extent of their guilt. Now King Philip was no longer prepared to let this continue. As a member of the king's council, Aicelin must have been fully aware of the royal attitude, and rather than sacrifice himself, he stood aside. He washed his hands of the Templars and the commission. At this vital moment of crisis for the Order, he excused himself from the discussion of Pietro di Bologna's appeal, 'saying that he had either to celebrate or to hear mass'.[8]

It was left to the other commissioners to deliberate among themselves. The Bishop of Bayeux was still absent, but the Bishops of Mende and Limoges, Matteo di Napoli and the Archdeacon of Trent had heard the appeal, and they were now joined by the Archdeacon of Maguelonne. After some discussion they told the defenders that they would make a reply that day at vespers, 'as far as they could and as far as these things appertained to them'. On the Sunday evening they gave their reply. They felt much sympathy for them, but the matter in which the Archbishop of Sens and his suffragans were engaged related to their own council and not to the commission;

these were 'completely different and mutually separate'. They did not therefore see what they could do, for both the commission and the Archbishop of Sens received their power directly from apostolic authority, on account of which they had no means of preventing the archbishop or other prelates from proceeding against individual Templars. They did agree to deliberate further on what might be done, and to have the notaries insert the defenders' request and appeal into the records of the proceedings.[9]

The next day – Monday 11 May – the commission resumed the hearing of witnesses, although the Archbishop of Narbonne remained out of sight. Early on Tuesday morning, during a pause in the examination of a Templar called Jean Bertald, the commissioners were told that fifty-four Templars who had brought themselves to the defence of the Order before the commission were to be burnt that day. The commissioners were now obliged to act if their many weeks of hearings were to retain any semblance of meaning, and if this blatant attempt to intimidate the defenders was to be blocked. They sent Philippe de Voet, one of the gaolers of the Templars, and Amisius, Archdeacon of Orléans, described as a royal clerk, who also seems to have been involved in the administration of the persons of the Order, to ask the Archbishop of Sens to delay his action, since Voet was now maintaining that many Templars who had died had asserted at the end of their lives, 'in danger of their souls', that the Order was falsely charged. If the executions took place the work of the commission would be impeded. Moreover, many witnesses were now so terrified that 'they did not seem to be in their full senses as a result'. Voet and the Archdeacon of Orléans were also told to inform Marigny and his council of the appeal made the previous Sunday by the four defenders.[10] But Philippe de Marigny blandly told the messengers that this had not been signified by the order of the commissioners.[11]

The fifty-four Templars were loaded into carts and taken to a field outside Paris near the convent of Saint-Antoine, where they were burnt to death. The continuator of the chronicle of Guillaume de Nangis says, with some surprise, that 'all of them, with no exception, finally acknowledged none of the crimes imputed to them, but constantly persisted in the general denial, saying always that they were being put to death without cause and unjustly: which indeed many of the people were able to observe by no means without great admiration and immense surprise'.[12] One observer noted that they placed their souls in great danger of damnation, for their constancy might lead *le menu peuple* into the error of believing in their innocence.[13] Those who had refused to confess at all before the provincial council were condemned to perpetual imprisonment, for they could not be counted as relapsed, while those who confirmed their confessions were reconciled and set free.[14] A few days later four more died at the stake, and the bones of the former Treasurer of the Temple at Paris, Jean de Tour, were exhumed and burnt. Soon after, nine more suffered the same fate at Senlis on the order of the provincial council at Rheims.[15]

It is not possible to assemble any realistic list of those who were burnt. There are scattered references in later depositions to seven brothers who were burnt at Paris, and to one other of whom it had been heard that he had been burnt at Paris.[16] Although the notarial record of the commission's proceedings states that all fifty-four 'were said to have brought themselves to the defence of the Order in the presence of the lords commissioners',[17] and the Archbishop of Sens apparently regarded this as revoking their previous confessions for which they had been reconciled to the Church, thus making them relapsed heretics, the evidence obtainable from these eight names does not bear this out. Only four of the eight Templars known to have been burnt – Raoul de Freynoy, Gautier de Bullens, Gui de Nice and Jacques de Soci – can be positively identified as having offered to defend the Temple, while two of the others – Laurent de Beaune and Anricus d'Anglesi – had done no more than ask to be allowed to deliberate with the Grand Master and had not committed themselves to the defence.[18] Moreover, there is no record of the remaining two – Gaucerand, *curatus* of the house of Bure, and Martin de Nice – as having ever appeared before the commission, even though the records of the commission would appear to be complete.[19] While it is clear that the Inquisition did threaten relapsed heretics that they would be handed over to the secular arm,[20] there is some evidence here of indiscriminate burnings, perhaps as a consequence of the haste with which the provincial Council of Sens was organised. Even those who had offered to defend the Order would not necessarily have been regarded as relapsed by a large sector of authoritative theological and judicial opinion.[21] While the burning of relapsed heretics was legal, and the right of this provincial council to make a judgement upon individual cases among the Templars of the province undoubted, this in itself cannot make a faulty decision correct in law, a point which arises quite apart from the obvious impediment of such an action at this time to the work of the papal commission. In the Parisian burnings the Capetian ability to 'adapt' the law to suit its own political ends is again demonstrated.

Nevertheless, the burnings of 12 May were the decisive stroke for which King Philip had hoped. Even beforehand, the commissioners had spoken of witnesses who 'did not seem in their full senses', but after the burnings their terror was much greater. The next day, Wednesday, the first witness to appear before the commission was a Templar aged about fifty, who had been a brother for about twenty years and before that had served the Order for about seven years. His name was Aimery de Villiers-le-Duc from the diocese of Langres. He is described as 'pale and very frightened'. He said

> on his oath and under danger of his soul, bringing on himself sud-
> den death if he was lying in this, and that at once he might be
> drawn into hell body and soul in the presence of the lords com-
> missioners, beating his breast with his fists, and raising his hands
> towards the altar in a most great assertion, going down on his
> knees, that all the errors ascribed to the Order were altogether
> false.

He admitted that he had confessed some errors, but it had been 'on account of the many tortures inflicted upon him by the lords Guil-laume de Marcilly and Hugues de la Celle, royal knights, who had made inquiry with him'. Yesterday he had seen fifty-four brothers 'who had refused to confess the errors' being taken away in carts for burning and he had heard later that they had been burnt. When he saw this he doubted if he would have fortitude to suffer it, saying that fear of death would make him confess that 'all the errors imputed to the Order were true and that also he had killed the Lord if it were asked him'. He pleaded with the commissioners and the notaries not to reveal what he had said to the king's people or to his gaolers, since if they knew, he was afraid that he would suffer the same fate as the fifty-four Templars. The commissioners now decided to suspend the hearings, for Aimery appeared to be 'on a precipice' and 'completely terrified' because of the dangers that seemed to threaten.[22]

Five days later, on Monday 18 May, the commissioners assembled once more, having been rejoined by the Archbishop of Narbonne, for the meeting was held at his house, only to find that they had again been pre-empted. Renaud de Provins came from the province of Sens, and Philippe de Marigny had taken advantage of the adjournment in the commission's hearings to have Provins brought before his provincial council to answer for himself as an individual. The fate of burning seemed to hang over one of the two chief defenders of the Order. The commissioners now made some attempt to stand up for themselves, once more sending Philippe de Voet and Amisius d'Orléans to intervene. It was explained that the commissioners had been deputed by the Holy See to enquire against the Temple by means of summons, and as a consequence of their citation stemming from this clause, brothers of the Order had come forward to defend it. Among these was a priest, Renaud de Provins, who, together with others, had put forward many points for the defence. With these others, he had been ordered to be present to see the witnesses received by the commission and, having assumed the defence, could come before the commission, 'under full and safe custody, as many times and whenever they wished, for the defence of the Order'. The commissioners asked the Archbishop of Sens and his suffragans to take note of this, 'especially because they were said to have called the same Brother Renaud to their presence, to make inquiry against him as an individual brother of the Order, which was said to be unfinished'. Although the commissioners did not intend to impede the Archbishop of Sens in his office, for 'the exoneration of the commissioners, and in order that the truth might be known to them', they signified these things to the archbishop and his suffragans so that they, as experienced men, could deliberate among themselves 'as to how they should proceed in the inquiry against Brother Renaud, who was said to be of their province'.

Such delicacy was lost on the Archbishop of Sens. On the same day at vespers he sent three canons to convey his answer to the commissioners, who, having left the Archbishop of Narbonne, were now sitting in the chapel of Saint-Eloi in the monastery of Sainte-Geneviève. Two years had passed since the inquiry against Renaud de Provins as an individual had begun, and now they had assembled in Paris in order to finish their inquiry against individual members in accordance with the papal mandate. The archbishop 'was not able to assemble the said council whenever he wished', and the canons asked the commissioners 'what they intended by the message which they had caused to be sent to them that day'. The commissioners explained that they had sent the message on the wish and advice of the Archbishop of Narbonne, that the message was 'clear and contained no ambiguity', and that since the archbishop was away in Paris they could not make a further reply at the moment. Anything else they had to say would be communicated after discussion with the archbishop on his return.²³

The commissioners' protest seems to have led to a change of tactics. Provins was swiftly restored to them, for after the three canons had gone he appeared in company with Chambonnet and Sartiges. But now Pietro di Bologna had completely disappeared. He had been separated from them and they did not know for what reason. They were simple and inexperienced men and these events 'so stupefied and disturbed them' that they could do nothing on behalf of the defence without Pietro di Bologna. This was why they asked the commissioners to summon him and find out how and why he had left them and whether or not he wished to continue with the defence. Accordingly, the commissioners ordered Voet and Jamville to bring Bologna before them the next morning. But the next morning there was no mention of Pietro di Bologna; instead, there appeared forty-four brothers who said that they had recently come to the defence of the Order, but now they wished to desist and renounce such a defence.²⁴ There was little that the commissioners could do; on Saturday 30 May, 'on account of many causes acting among them' they adjourned the proceedings until 3 November.²⁵

Tuesday 3 November duly arrived, but only three members of the commission appeared at the monastery of Sainte-Geneviève: the Bishop of Mende, Matteo di Napoli, and Giovanni di Mantua, Archdeacon of Trent. Gilles Aicelin was not even in Paris, for he was on king's business arising from his office as Chancellor; the Bishop of Bayeux was about to be sent to Avignon to negotiate with the pope; Jean de Montlaur, Archdeacon of Maguelonne, excused himself on the grounds of illness; and the Bishop of Limoges had appeared briefly only to leave almost at once on learning in letters from the king that 'it was not for certain reasons expedient to proceed in the said affair until the king's principal *parlement*, which was to be held on 23 January. The three remaining members made a half-hearted attempt to find out if anyone wished to defend the Order, and then adjourned until such time as they had sufficient numbers. Eventually, on 17 December, five members assembled, the Bishop of Bayeux and the Archdeacon of Maguelonne being excused. The letters of excuse of the absentees were read out before Guillaume de Chambonnet and Bertrand de Sartiges, but there was no sign of Renaud de Provins and Pietro di Bologna. They asked that Provins and Bologna be brought to help them since they were 'illiterate laymen', but were told that these two 'had solemnly and freely renounced the defence of the Order and had returned to the first confessions made by them', and that after his renunciation, Pietro di Bologna had broken out of gaol and fled. There is no further evidence as to Bologna's fate, for he appears no more in the trial, but he might have been murdered by his gaolers while in prison. As for Provins, the commissioners said that he could not in any case be admitted to the defence, since he had been degraded from the priesthood by the Council of Sens. They were however prepared to listen to Chambonnet and Sartiges and to allow them to continue to be present while witnesses were heard. But the two knights had lost the stomach for it; they did not wish to be present or to inspect witnesses unless they had Provins and Bologna with them. 'And thus', states the notarial record, 'they left the presence of the commissioners.'[26]

The defence of the Order, which had been ebbing away since 12 May, now dried up almost completely. Although the commission sat until June 1311, few were now brave enough, or even given the opportunity, to speak up for the Order. In the sitting which began in November 1310 the commission heard 215 witnesses, of whom 198 made confessions of some kind, fourteen continued to assert the Order's innocence, and three – a Franciscan, a Dominican and a notary – were witnesses from outside the Order. This is a dramatic reversal of the proportions of late March, when 597 were prepared to defend the Order and another twelve remained non-committal, while only fifteen actually refused.[27] The burnings, together with the removal of the chief defenders, were the major causes of the collapse of the defence, but there remain some hints that the Templars were not so completely demoralised as first appears. The government's physical control of the Templars could still be exploited: only eighty-seven of the 212 Templars who appeared between November 1310 and June 1311 are recorded as offering to defend the Order earlier in the year, even though it seems that there must have been well over five hundred left alive in Paris, who now largely disappear from the records. Eighty-four of the eighty-seven now reverted to their previous confessions. Yet a much larger proportion – twenty-six out of forty-four – of those who on 19 May had come forward specifically to retract their offers to defend were afterwards brought before the commission.[28] It is impossible to know how the remaining vast majority of defenders had reacted to the burnings, for there is every likelihood that the French government picked out those former defenders most obviously terrified by the new situation in which they found themselves. There was, for instance, a particular concentration of Templars who had been absolved and reconciled before the provincial Councils of Sens and Rheims – eighteen from the first group of twenty to appear had been before the Council of Sens[29] – and thus found themselves in exactly the same position as those who had gone to the stake in May, and could therefore be expected to be appropriately cowed. The provincial councils had certainly continued to hear cases against individuals after the initial burnings. On 5 March 1311 six Templars (three priests, one knight and two serving brothers) who had been condemned to perpetual imprisonment appeared before the commission. Renaud de Provins himself was among the three priests who had been 'degraded at the Council of Sens from all major and minor orders, moreover divested of all clerical privilege and deprived of the habit of the Temple'.[30]

Most of those who did testify were anxious to disavow any previous commitment to defend. Many prefaced their testimony by asking that anything they might say 'on account of their simplicity' should not prejudice their persons,[31] a clear indication that the proceedings of the provincial councils and not those of the commission were uppermost in their minds. Others tried to explain away their defence: the youthful Elias de Jocro told the commissioners that he had come to the defence because of 'the bad advice which he had had', Nicolas de Compiègne 'did not know why, except that he saw others offering themselves', and Philippe de Manin said he had done so 'from his stupidity and simplicity'.[32] Some were obviously in terror, and in that terror became confused. Etienne de Domont, a fifty-year-old serving brother, was such a case. He had originally confessed to the denial, the spitting, the illicit kisses and the incitement to homosexuality at the Parisian hearings of the autumn of 1307, but since then, in February and April 1310, he had brought himself to the defence.[33] A year later, on 16 February 1311, he told the commissioners that he had been absolved and reconciled by the Bishop of Paris and did not intend to retreat from the deposition made in his presence. However, when questioned in detail, he described an entirely orthodox reception, maintaining that he had not known, heard or seen any errors in the Order. Asked specifically if anything illicit had occurred in his reception, he replied that 'he could not remember, since many years had passed'. But when the first thirteen articles of accusation were read to him, he said that 'he had spat next to a cross and denied God'. The record then notes that this witness seemed 'of such simplicity' and said these things 'in such a way . . . as was apparent through many circumlocutions' that the commissioners could not place great faith in his deposition. 'He seemed in great fear', the notarial record adds, 'on account of a deposition made by him in the presence of the Bishop of Paris, since he said that he had been tortured for two years or more at Paris before his deposition.'[34] Three serving brothers – Jean de Nice, Henri de Compiègne and Pariset de Bures – actually denied that they had ever brought themselves to the defence despite the fact that their names are clearly noted among the defenders in the notarial record.[35] Apart from the burnings, the sentences delivered by the provincial councils seem themselves to have been used as an inducement. A priest called Gilles de Rontange declared that he did not intend to recede from his confession made at the Council of Rheims, where he was absolved and reconciled and condemned to prison, but was not degraded. He then added that the sentence was remitted by the council, to be fixed by the decision of the *prévôt* of Poitiers and Jean de Jamville 'on account of some reasons'. Apparently in an effort to explain away his previous willingness to defend the Order, he claimed that he suffered from 'double quartan malaria' and when this occurred he did not know what he was saying.[36]

Essentially the 198 confessions centred upon the main charges of the denial of Christ, spitting on a cross, illicit kissing, incitement to commit homosexual acts, and less frequently, worship of an idol. Between them the Templars confessed to denying Jesus, God, Christ, Our Lord, the figure of the Crucifixion, that prophet represented by the image of the Crucifixion, and a cross depicted in a book. They had kissed or been kissed on top of the clothes or on the bare flesh, on the mouth, navel, chest, between the shoulder blades, on the spine of the back, shoulder, anus, thigh, between the thighs and the neck, the nipple (although the Templar concerned could not remember whether it was the right or left), on the back of the neck, the belly, and even on the ankle. They had spat at, on or near various kinds of crosses made of wood, copper, metal or silver or carved in stone, sometimes painted, sometimes depicted in a missal, a picture or a book, or on a mantle or red garment, sometimes held in the receptor's hand or placed on an altar, and in one case on a window. Several witnesses had seen an idol; for one it was simply 'a copper object' and for another it was 'a small picture of base gold or of gold which seemed to have a picture of a woman'.[37] For most, however, it was a head, of varied appearance; for the knight Bartholomé Bochier, for instance, it wore a cap and had a long, grey beard, being made of wood, metal or bone, or human.[38] Guillaume d'Arreblay, Preceptor of Soisy and former royal almoner, had heard that the silver head which he had frequently seen on the altar in chapter-meetings was the head of one of the eleven thousand virgins, but after the arrests, having heard the accusations, he suspected that it was the head of an idol, 'since it seemed to have two faces and a terrible countenance, and had a silver beard'. He agreed though that it was shown on feast days with other relics, and claimed that he would recognise it. This description was so specific that the commissioners asked Guillaume Pidoye, the royal custodian of the goods of the Temple, to search the Temple at Paris for any metal or wooden heads which he could find. After a delay of several weeks, he eventually appeared, bringing the only such object he could find. It was

> a certain large beautiful silver-gilt head, shaped like that of a woman, within which were the bones of a single head, rolled up and stitched in a certain white linen cloth, red muslin having been placed over it, and there was sewn in there a certain document on which was written *capud LVIII*, and the said bones were considered as similar to the bones of the head of a small woman, and it was said by some that it was the head of one of the eleven thousand virgins.

Having committed himself to a double-faced bearded object, Guillaume d'Arreblay would not then admit that this relic and reliquary were the objects to which he had originally been referring.[39]

Some witnesses coloured the accusations with their own highly individual stories. Raynaud Bergeron, a forty-five-year-old serving brother from the diocese of Langres, deposed on 23 February 1311. At his reception seven years before he had refused to enter unless his wife was allowed to accompany him. When the receptor, Laurent de Beaune, came to that part of the ceremony in which the novitiate vowed chastity, Raynaud said that 'he would never do this, nor enter the Order unless his wife remained with him', and walked out. Laurent de Beaune and another brother came after and 'caught hold of him, saying that he was stupid to refuse such and so great an honour, persuading him that he should return, since it was well with him, and he and his wife would be placed and be together in the same house'. Nevertheless, during the ceremony which followed, despite this extraordinary scene, it was enjoined upon him that he should not live with women. Afterwards he was taken to a small room next to the chapel where the denial, spitting, incitement to homosexuality and illicit kissing took place. He then confessed these things to a Templar priest who told him that they were not very sinful and gave him a light penance only, although a Franciscan to whom he confessed refused to absolve him, saying that he should go to the pope. The key, it seems, to this situation was that 'the Preceptor of the said house of Vall de Tor had his goods . . . to the value of 50 *livres tournois* and on account of this they had induced him to enter the Order'.[40]

Hugues de Narsac, a serving brother who was Preceptor of Espans in the diocese of Saintes, seemed especially resentful of the Order's leadership. In his deposition on 8 May 1311 he described how, twenty-five years before, he had been received in an orthodox way, but that two months after the reception he had been forced to deny God, a denial which he rather thinly argued was unavoidable because they all swore to obey their preceptors at the receptions and refusal would have been perjury. He himself had enjoined this denial on brothers he received, although his conscience had tormented him over this and over the fact that receptions were often made by simony through the giving of money and equipment. However, he named four knights who were not forced to do anything illicit because of their nobility and power. He had seen and heard of other incidents within the Order which apparently shocked him. A brother called Jean Godell de Tours together with 'certain other stupid serving brothers' had urinated at the foot of a wooden cross in the cemetery of the house of Balo. Hugues de Narsac thought they were doing this in active disrespect for the cross and rebuked them, telling them that there were other places nearby where they could urinate. He was told that it was nothing to do with him. He had too heard scandal about Jacques de Molay from brothers who had returned from Outremer, although he could not remember their names. They told him that Molay had had homosexual relations with a certain *valet de chambre* of his called Georges, 'whom he loved very much'. This Georges met a sudden death by drowning, and Hugues de Narsac thought that this was divine vengeance for the sin of sodomy, which he believed to be general among the leaders living in Outremer. He then returned to the denial, which his receptor had told him enabled the Order to have more abundance in temporal goods. He clearly felt the leaders directly responsible for he maintained that Molay and others gave lay absolution for disobedience, and that Molay had himself received Templars whom he had kissed not only on the mouth, but also on the navel and at the base of the spine on the bare flesh. He believed that the errors had been in the Order for a long time and had arisen in Outremer, apparently from contact with the Saracens, which was especially the case under another of the Grand Masters, Guillaume de Beaujeu, who had some Saracens in his pay.[41]

A third deposition – that of Bertrand Guasc, a serving brother from the diocese of Rodez, on 22 May 1311 – contains a curious mixture of heresy on the one hand and militant Christianity on the other. Bertrand Guasc appears to have joined the Order after running out of money while on a pilgrimage to the Holy Land. After an orthodox reception in the Templar chapel at Sidon, the receptor ordered him to deny Christ, and when Bertrand refused he threatened to kill him. In the midst of this there was a sudden call to arms, for the Saracens had attacked, and the receptor, the three brothers present and Bertrand Guasc rushed out to defend Christianity, killing twenty Saracens during the conflict. Just before they went out, however, Bertrand was made to swear not to reveal the denial to anyone, and after it was all over he asked what it had been about. The receptor told him it had been a test and a joke. Apart from this Bertrand Guasc had never seen anything illicit in the Order.[42]

Some depositions were of course much fuller than others; one of the most detailed confessions which illustrates the general trend of the commission's hearing in its third sitting was that of Raoul de Gizy, a serving brother of about fifty years of age, who had been Pre-ceptor of Lagny-le-Sec and Sommereux in the diocese of Beauvais and receptor of the king's money in Champagne. In contrast to his nephew, Ponsard de Gizy, Raoul, who deposed on 11 January 1311, had never committed himself to the defence, and in fact he impli-cated the Order in the errors of which it was accused in a way as sweeping as any.[43] He had put aside the mantle of the Order at the Council of Sens, and had been absolved and reconciled by the Bishop of Paris.

He was taken through the articles of accusation in detail by the commissioners, but first, like so many, he was anxious to protect himself. He said, 'before everything', that he did not intend to retreat from his confession made before the Bishop of Paris, which was that originally the Order had been 'a good and holy foundation', but that at some time afterwards the errors of the denial, spitting, homosexu-ality and obscene kissing had been introduced. He then described his own reception, made about twenty-five years before by Hugues de Pairaud, which followed the orthodox pattern. Raoul asked for the bread and water and companionship of the proven men of the Order. The receptor replied that

> he had asked for a great thing, and that he should deliberate well, since he was renouncing his own will, and when he wished to be on this side of the sea it would be necessary for him to be beyond it, and to be awake when he wished to sleep, and to be hungry when he wished to eat, and many similar things.

Finally, after deliberation with the other brothers present Pairaud said that he would receive him, making him vow chastity, poverty and obedience and 'to preserve the good customs and usages of the Order'. He vowed to work for the acquisition of Jerusalem, not to involve himself in the unjust disinheritance of any noble person, and not to leave the Order without the permission of his superiors. Raoul de Gizy then seems to have tacked the illicit part of the ceremony upon the end of this quite regular beginning. He was ordered to deny God and spit on the image depicted in the book upon which he had taken his oath, being told that these things were 'points of the Order'. When Gizy asked how this could be, since the Order was said to be very holy, Pairaud had told him not to trouble himself about it, and so he had denied, 'in the mouth and not in the heart' and spat 'not on the said image but next to it'. He did this 'sorrowing and sad . . . because then he wished greatly to be in the middle of the sea or otherwise dead; and when he went out of the said place, he shed tears bitterly in the sight of all; and although those seeing him cry asked what had happened, he did not wish to reveal it'. Similarly, he had been ordered to kiss the receptor between the navel and the chest, but had baulked at the order to kiss him on the anus, which he was not then forced to do, and he had been told that should 'the heat of nature' require it he could 'cool himself' with his brothers.

Raoul de Gizy had himself received many others in this manner, and he gave details of four receptions which he had conducted in various places in Champagne between seven and fourteen years before. He preserved this manner of receiving because it involved points of the Order, although it greatly displeased him. Moreover, after the receptions, he told those received that 'they should not engage in carnal intercourse', although during the reception he had told them that they could. He had seen four or five others received in this way by Pairaud and Gérard de Villiers, Preceptor of France, and he believed that this method was adhered to generally throughout the Order. He claimed that he frequently told these two leaders that it was wrong for such abuses to be perpetrated and for receptions to be held in secret, but they had replied that it was necessary to continue in this way, since 'they were points of the Order which could not be changed without the Grand Master and his chapter beyond the sea'.

He was equally forthcoming upon the question of lay absolution. After chapter-meetings, the man who had held the chapter, having said the usual prayers, stood at the head of the brothers kneeling before him and said to them in the vernacular:

Good lord brothers, all the things which you omit to say for shame of the flesh or because of the justice of the house, such pardon as I can make you I have made to you with good heart and from good will; and God, who pardoned Mary Magdalene her sins, pardons them you, and I pray you that you pray to God that he pardons me mine; and our brother chaplain will stand up and make the absolution which God grants him and us.

If a priest was present, he then arose and made a general absolution, but if not, the person holding the chapter said, 'If there was a brother priest here, he would make absolution.' However, Raoul de Gizy himself said he did not believe that he was absolved from unconfessed sins by the layman holding the chapter, nor did he believe that the Templars so thought. Confession was done properly three times a year by the Templar priests or others of their licence. When he was asked why the person holding the chapter made absolution in this way he answered that 'it was because there were many who had property and committed other sins which they did not dare to mention, on account of the punishments of the Order or on account of shame of the flesh'.

He knew too about the accusation that the Templars worshipped an idol in the form of a head. He had been present at Paris in a general chapter held by Gérard de Villiers, nine or ten years before. When the chapter had ended, a serving brother brought in 'a certain head of idols' and put it on a bench next to Villiers. Raoul was so terrified that 'it was as if he did not know where he was' and he left the chapter at once, so he did not know what was then done. He did not know what the head looked like, but believed it was bad. He remembered also another chapter held by Villiers and Pairaud in which a head was brought in, in a bag he thought, but other details and names eluded him. They were issued with a small cord at receptions, to be worn above their linen garments, but he knew nothing about this cord touching idols as the articles of accusation suggested, for he wore his as a sign of chastity.

The Order was guilty of neglect in several ways, for the errors were often discussed among the brothers, but they had not corrected them, nor denounced them to the Church. Alms and hospitality were not properly maintained, and in a year when there was a great dearth of wheat in which he, as Preceptor of Lagny-le-Sec, had increased the customary amount of alms given by the house, the other brothers had in fact urged him to diminish it. He knew for certain that Gérard de Villiers had diminished alms in this way.

Throughout his deposition, Gizy seemed, not unnaturally in the circumstances, anxious to please his questioners while at the same time anxious to pass the blame to others, particularly the leaders such as Villiers, Pairaud and Molay. 'He believed that what the Grand Master with his chapter ordained was everywhere preserved in the Order, and great scandals against the Order arose on account of the aforesaid.' Raoul de Gizy himself had confessed all this, before he had known anything about the arrests, at Lyons to a Franciscan called Jean de Dijon, who could be questioned about this, since he was an official of the papal penitentiary. The Franciscan had at first been astonished, but finally absolved him, imposing a harsh penance, saying that he should then try to eradicate the errors from the Order; and in fact when he was near Lyons after this confession, he spoke to Hugues de Pairaud about possible remedies. Pairaud answered that he was waiting for the arrival of the Grand Master from Outremer, and 'he swore, placing his hand on a cross which he wore on his mantle, that, if the Master did not wish to remove the errors, he [Pairaud] should remove them, because he knew well that all the brothers of the Temple would follow him in this'.[44]

Confessions such as this made the use of witnesses from outside the Order a much less urgent consideration for the French government than would have been the case if the majority of Templars had continued resistant. Nevertheless, periodically such a witness came forward to give testimony, as was the case with Etienne de Néry, a Franciscan who was warden of a house at Lyons, and who deposed on 27 January 1311, just over two weeks after Raoul de Gizy. His knowledge of the errors of the Templars dated back twenty years to the time when a kinsman of his called Ancelin Gara entered the Order. The day before his reception, Etienne de Néry and other relatives of Ancelin jokingly told him that on the morrow he would have to kiss his receptor on the anus, and Ancelin had replied that if anything like this was said he would run his sword up the anus of the receptor. As a result, they extracted a promise from him to tell them the way he was received. The next day Ancelin first received the arms of knighthood, and then was led into the house of the Temple. Once there he was taken to a secret place, where the doors were closed, and his kin excluded. After a long delay he returned, now wearing the mantle of the Order, but 'so altered and changed in countenance and disturbed and most sad of heart, as it seemed, having angry and tearful eyes, that his appearance was to this witness and the other friends of his present as if horrible and terrified'. They were especially surprised at this because before he had entered the room Ancelin had been in very good spirits, so they determined that, in accordance with his promise of the day before, they would find out from him how he had been received. However, repeated attempts by Etienne de Néry produced no reply, until eventually Ancelin, in a much disturbed state, told him to speak no more of this. Soon after, Ancelin, having been equipped with arms and horses by his friends, set out for Outremer with the Templars, but to the astonishment of his friends, when he reached Marseilles he abandoned the Order and returned home. He told his friends that he did not care to be in the company of the Templars, that these men were perjurers.

Afterwards, when the Templars were arrested, Artaud Carat, a blood relative of Ancelin, warned him that, for the safety of his soul, he should speak the truth about the things which were said against the Order. Ancelin refused to do this before the Inquisition, but did agree to speak to Artaud. In the presence of a public notary from Vienne, Ancelin confessed that at his reception the Templars had forced him to deny Christ, had told him Christ was a false prophet, and had made him spit and trample on a cross and indulge in 'that horrible kiss'. When Néry heard this he arranged for Ancelin to be arrested, for the affair touched the faith and this confession was not sufficient until it was made before the prelates of the Church.[45]

Nevertheless, despite the crumbling of all organised defence, some brave individual spirits as well as the occasional small group of Templars still attempted to maintain the innocence of themselves or of the Order during the period of the commission's third sitting. Fourteen Templars held out against the pressures placed upon them, although only four of these had previously appeared before the papal commission, of whom three had offered to defend the Order, while the fourth, Audebert de la Porte, a serving brother from Poitiers, had simply asked to have the advice of the Grand Master, to whom he owed obedience.[46] Some indication of the mental anguish and physical effort necessary to maintain the Order's innocence in these circumstances can be gauged from the oscillations of one of these four, Rainier de Larchant, a serving brother from the province of Sens. He had been the second witness after Jean de Folliaco at the Parisian hearings in October 1307, and he had made a sweeping confession, including kissing the receptor on the base of the spine and the navel, the denial of a cross shown to him, spitting three times on this cross, incitement to homosexuality by the receptor and the worship of a bearded idol which he had seen no less than twelve times. Yet in February and March 1310 he had placed himself among the Order's defenders only to retreat from this on 19 May after the burnings, coming forward with forty-three others specifically to renounce his part in that defence.[47] But on 27 January 1311, although he had put aside the mantle of the Order at the Council of Sens, and afterwards had shaved off his beard, and although he had been absolved and reconciled by the Bishop of Paris, he would admit nothing illicit about his reception, and stated that he did not believe that there were any errors in the Order. He claimed that he could not remember if he had confessed before the Bishop of Paris, but did assert that he had been tortured.[48] The other three – Jean de Rumprey, Robert Vigier and Audebert de la Porte, all serving brothers – did admit previous confessions, but explained that these were the result of torture. Audebert de la Porte 'cried a great deal during his deposition and asked that his life be preserved'.

The remaining ten – one knight and nine serving brothers – had not previously appeared before the commission. Six of them, although from different regions (one, Thomas de Pamplona, was from Aragon), were sworn in together on 8 March 1311. They had all appeared before the provincial council of the Bishop of Saintes, and had been imprisoned together at La Rochelle.[49] They had therefore the opportunity of concerting a common policy, although the last of those who appeared, when asked, denied that they had all agreed to depose in this way.[50] They all claimed that their receptions were orthodox – Guillaume de Liège, the elderly Preceptor of La Rochelle, said that he had received between twenty and twenty-five brothers in an orthodox way – while three claimed that their previous confessions before the episcopal inquiry were the result of torture. The first two witnesses were critical of the general conduct of certain Templars: Guillaume de Liège said that 'many of them were proud and some oppressive, extortions being made by them through the abuse of apostolic letters and other ways'; and Guillaume de Torage had, soon after his reception, been told by a

Spanish Templar that he did not believe 'that their Order could last a long time because of their pride, and since acquisitions for the Order were made in whatever way they could, and they were full of cupidity and ambition, nor did they intend to take up arms against the infidel as they ought'.[51] Indeed, the eighty-year-old Guillaume de Liège, who was the first to depose, was the most equivocal of the six, saying that he did not intend to retract from his deposition made before the Bishop of Saintes, who had absolved and reconciled him, and that he had heard that receptors had ordered spitting on a cross and suspected in his heart that it was true, but he had had no direct experience of the accusations. Thomas de Pamplona went into some detail on the question of lay absolution, for he believed that the lay head of the chapter had the power to absolve the brothers of contraventions of the Order's discipline (of which there were forty offences serious enough to justify expulsion or imprisonment), but he did not believe that they were in this way absolved from venial or mortal sins.[52] Another three Templars – Gérard d'Augny, Pierre de Saint-Benoît and Bartholomé de Puy Revell – had also been sworn in together on 15 March 1311 in a group of nineteen Templars. Their depositions also suggest collusion; there was nothing wrong with their receptions, but Gérard d'Augny believed that there were illicit acts in other receptions 'because the Grand Master and others were said to have confessed these things'.[53] Finally, Elias Costat, who deposed on 10 May, seems to have asserted the Order's innocence without even the moral support of others.[54]

Five other Templars attempted to stand up for their Order during this session, but whereas the other fourteen seem to have deposed unhindered, these men were carefully observed by their royal gaolers and their futile efforts were brutally crushed. Three of them – Martin de Montricard, Jean Durand and Jean de Ruivans – came from the group of nineteen who had been sworn in on 15 March, and their depositions followed the pattern of Gérard d'Augny and his companions.[55] For instance, Martin de Montricard, Preceptor of Mauléon in the diocese of Poitiers, said that he believed that in France the brothers 'were received uniformly and well, as he was received and he saw others received, but that in some parts they were received as the Master was said to have confessed'.[56] These men appeared on Monday 22 March 1311, but within two days, on Wednesday, they were brought back and all three then admitted the denial of Christ and spitting on a cross, saying that in their previous depositions they had lied because of their stupidity. All of them asserted that they had not been threatened in any way, or led by anyone to change their depositions, or had even spoken to anyone else about the matter.[57]

The same transformation had occurred with two other serving brothers who had appeared earlier the same year. The depositions of Jean de Pollencourt, who appeared on 9 and 12 January, and Jean de Cormeilles, who appeared on 8 and 9 February, demonstrate the application of this pressure.

Jean de Pollencourt came into the commissioners' presence without the mantle of the Order, which he said had been destroyed, and having shaved his beard, explaining that some prelates and the *prévôt* of Poitiers had told him and other brothers that they could shave. He was about thirty years of age. He had previously been examined by the Bishop of Amiens and had been absolved and reconciled. In answer to the first four articles he said that he had only been to the reception of one brother, Philippe de Manin, where 'he had seen nothing shameful done or enjoined', and he had never attended a chapter, so he did not know if the contents of the articles were true, 'but he did not believe so since he had not seen anything'. He himself had been received about ten years before by Garin de Grandeville, Preceptor and *bailli* of Ponthieu, at La Ronsière in the diocese of Amiens, in the presence of the priest Gilles de Rontange and two serving brothers. Pollencourt then began to describe an orthodox reception largely following the pattern set out by Raoul de Gizy: asking for bread and water and companionship, the necessity for putting aside one's own will, the vowing of chastity and poverty and to conserve the goods of the Order. Then suddenly his courage began to fail, for he broke off the thread of his description and 'said and protested several times that he wished to stand by the confession first made by him in the presence of the said Lord of Amiens and his predecessor, and that then he had confessed that he had denied God in his reception'.

The notarial record describes him as 'very frightened and just as pale', and at this point the commissioners intervened in an effort to reassure him. They told him that 'he should attend to speaking the truth and to the salvation of his soul, not to the aforesaid confession unless it were true'. They assured him that no danger would threaten him if he told the truth, for neither they nor the notaries present would reveal the contents of his deposition.

> He said after some interval, in terror of his soul and under the oath taken by him, that in his reception he had not denied God nor Jesus nor the crucifix, nor had he kissed his receptor, nor others present, except on the mouth, nor was he asked to; nor had he spat on a cross, nor had he been asked concerning the said denial, spitting and any shameful kiss, although he had confessed the contrary in the presence of the inquisitors from fear of death.

He then tried to explain himself. Gilles de Rontange had been in prison with him and had told him and others 'with tears' that 'they would lose their bodies unless they swore to the destruction of the Order, by confessing that they had denied God and that they had spat on the cross'. He went on to say that after he had made this confession before the Bishop of Amiens and the inquisitors, he confessed that it was false to a certain Franciscan deputed to him by Robert, Bishop of Amiens. He had wanted to admit this to the bishop as well, but he had replied that he could not hear him because he was occupied with the other brothers, and the Franciscan absolved him and told him that from then on he was not to make false confession in the affair.

He knew nothing concerning the other articles, declaring that he believed properly in the sacrament of the altar, and that he believed the other brothers did too. They professed at once on entrance (there was no probationary period as was customary with most Orders), and the receptions were held behind closed doors with only Templars present. At his reception he was told to wear a small cord above his linen garments as a sign of chastity. He could on no account reveal to secular persons, or even to other brothers not present, what was done in chapter-meetings, or he would be punished. He was confessed three times a year in chapters. Alms were generally given three times a week in the places in which he had stayed. He believed that the things ordained by the Grand Master and chapter beyond the sea were preserved generally in the Order, and he had heard that the Grand Master and other leaders had confessed some errors. As for himself, however, Pollencourt seems by this time fully to have regained his determination. 'Asked if he knew other errors to be in the Order, he replied in danger and damnation of his soul that he did not, nor had he heard anything about the aforesaid errors before their capture.' He concluded: 'In which certain attestation he said that he wished to persist, whatever happened, wishing rather in this to look after his soul than his body.'

But Jean de Pollencourt did not persist for very long; on Tuesday 12 January he asked to be given another hearing. He said that 'he had lied . . . on the last Saturday gone by, and that he had perjured himself, asking on bended knees and with clasped hands forgiveness from them'. But the commissioners found this volte-face barely credible.

> Since, however, the lords commissioners suspected that this witness had in some way been suborned, they received from him an oath by touching the holy gospels, so that he should speak the truth to them. Asked on the said oath if he had revealed his confession to any persons, and if he had been induced by anyone to revoke this, he answered that he had not.

He had, however, asked Jean de Jamville and his gaolers to bring him back before the commissioners so that he could say something he had forgotten in the above deposition. He then confessed that, at his reception, he had denied God and spat next to a white silver cross on the receptor's order, who told him that these were points of the Order. The receptor had also told him that if any Templars 'wished to join with him carnally, and required him, he ought to suffer this in accordance with the points of the Order'. He had, however, been excused the illicit kiss. He believed that the errors were generally preserved and had seen them in the reception of Philippe de Manin. He even denied the presence of the priest, Gilles de Rontange, at his reception, about which he had made a mistake, having sought advice on the matter. Presumably, Pollencourt knew that Gilles was available to testify and might contradict him. He said too that he had heard about a certain cat who came into the assemblies of the Templars. Finally, he added that 'even if the Order of the Temple was not destroyed . . . he himself did not wish to remain in it, since it was bad'.[58]

Jean de Pollencourt's case indicates that there was little hope for the lone defender. He had been threatened, probably tortured, in

the intervening three days, by men who were well aware of his supposedly secret deposition. Even a witness, still living, who might
have been able to confirm his original testimony, was effectively
silenced, for Gilles de Rontange was bribed to maintain his confession by the mitigation of his sentence received at the Council of
Rheims.[59]

The other serving brother, Jean de Cormeilles, experienced similar treatment: aged about forty-one, from the diocese of Soissons,
he had been Preceptor of Moissy in the diocese of Meaux. He was
not wearing the mantle of the Order, which he had put aside at the
Council of Sens, and he had already been absolved and reconciled
at the Council of Chartres by the bishop. Despite this, he said that
he did not believe in the contents of the first thirteen articles, which
were primarily concerned with receptions, having seen or heard
nothing illicit or shameful. He then specified three receptions at
which he and other named witnesses had been present, one of
which had been conducted by Raoul de Gizy and another by
Hugues de Pairaud. They had all taken place within the last eight
years. He himself had been received twelve years before by Raoul
de Gizy at Chéroy in the province of Sens, and among those present
was Ponsard de Gizy, who had been the first Templar to attempt
any kind of defence of the Order as a whole, and who Cormeilles
said was now dead. He had asked three times for the bread and
water of the Order, had vowed chastity, obedience and poverty, and
to preserve the Order's secrets, swearing upon an open book in
which was a picture of the Crucifixion. The mantle was then placed
on him and the brothers present kissed him on the mouth. Some
instruction of a fairly basic kind followed concerning his general
conduct. To this point he had described an ordinary reception at
which nothing irregular had occurred, but he then gives a glimpse
of the pressures upon him.

> Asked if in his reception there had intervened anything shameful
> or illicit, and especially concerning the contents of the thirteen
> articles, he did not wish to answer, but asked that the lords com-
> missioners should speak separately with him on one side, which
> they did not wish to grant; and he seemed greatly frightened on
> account of the tortures which he said had oppressed him for so
> long at Paris after their capture, in which tortures he said that he

had lost four teeth, and he said that he could not in fact fully remember about those things which he had done in his reception, and asked for time to deliberate more fully.

This time was granted to him and he was ordered to return the following day to complete his deposition. 'And they ordered him, by virtue of the oath taken by him, that he should not reveal this his deposition, and that he should not ask advice from anyone as to how he should depose and how he should answer to the interrogation made of him, and to other things which might be asked from him.' He answered that it was to God alone that he would turn for advice about this.

Cormeilles reappeared the following day, but he now said that his receptor had told him to deny God, and when he objected that this was wrong, he had been told that it was necessary for him to do this and so he had 'by the mouth, not in the heart'. Then the receptor held a wooden cross in his hand and ordered him to spit on it, but he spat next to it and not on it. Afterwards he was told he could enter into carnal relationships with other Templars, but he had never done this nor had been asked to do it, and he did not think that it was done in the Order as a whole. Although the receptor ordered him to kiss him on the anus, he had refused, but he did kiss him, 'on top of the clothes round about the leg'. He had not been told that these were points of the Order, and no other shameful things had occurred. He was now asked, 'since he was as certain yesterday as now concerning what he had done, why had he not confessed these things yesterday?' His explanation was that 'on account of the foulness and horror he shrank from saying the above things'. He had not taken the advice of anyone in the intervening period, but he had asked a priest called Robert, who was in the service of the Temple at Paris, that 'he should say one mass of the Holy Spirit that God should direct him, and he believed that he said it'. He had confessed the errors to a Templar priest, the week that he was received, and had been given absolution and a penance, and after the arrests, he had confessed again to a canon belonging to the household of the Bishop of Chartres. Some signs of the witness's doubts seem to creep in during this part of the deposition, for he asserted that what he had said the day before was true, 'nor did he wish to change anything in it', a statement which could be consistent with his later addition of the illicit parts of the ceremony, but he appears also to have said, according to the notarial record, 'several times that he did not know of the contents in the said thirteen articles'.

He knew nothing about the contents of article fourteen and beyond, only that he believed properly in the sacraments and thought that other Templars did also, that their priests celebrated as they ought, since they were often aided by secular priests, and that he did not believe that the laity could absolve from sin. They were professed at once, so that they could quickly be sent to Outremer, they held secret receptions as a result of which he believed that suspicion had arisen against them, and they wore cords around themselves, but he did not believe that they had touched the heads of idols. They were ordered not to reveal the secrets of the chapter, and if anyone did he was punished, but he did not know how. A Templar could not confess to anyone except the priests of the Order without permission. Those who knew of the errors were negligent, because they had not corrected them or denounced them to the Church, but he believed that they had failed to do so because of fear. Alms and hospitality were consistently given in the houses in which he had stayed. However, when there was a dearth they had to restrict the giving of alms because of the multitude of paupers. Chapters were held secretly and the whole Order preserved what was ordained by the Grand Master and his chapter. He had heard that the Grand Master and others had confessed some errors. He had offered himself to the defence of the Order, 'since he saw that others offered themselves'. 'Asked if he had deposed thus from prayer, order, fear, love, hatred or any material comfort had or to be had, he answered that he had not, but had spoken on behalf of the truth.'[60]

The fate of Pollencourt and Cormeilles illustrates clearly the complete control exercised by the Templars' gaolers, and the ready flow of information from the commission to the French government. In general, Templar confessions were reinforced by the occasional use of outside witnesses, but here too, as among the Templars, there was the exceptional witness who would not fully conform. Pierre de la Palud was a bachelor of theology, a Dominican from Lyons, who deposed towards the end of the hearings on 19 April 1311. He had been present at the examination of many Templars, having heard some confess and some deny the articles, but 'from the many arguments it seemed to him that more faith was to be attached to those denying than to those confessing'. This however was as far as he was prepared to go. He had heard 'many tales by many persons who had examined Templars who had made confessions in their presence, from which stories and others he believed that the illicit contents in the articles, or the major part of them, occurred in the reception of some of the brothers of the Order or after, and not in the receptions of others or after'.[61]

By the late spring of 1311, if not before, the papal commission as a body constituted to hear potential defenders of the Order was serving very little function. The Archbishop of Narbonne had been frequently absent, the Bishop of Bayeux had taken no part in the third session since November 1310, when he had been sent to Avignon to negotiate with the pope on the king's behalf, and the Archdeacon of Maguelonne had been excused on the grounds of illness.[62] Often the commission had been operating with only three members. In November 1310 the king seems to have wanted its work postponed until late January 1311, after his next *parlement*, perhaps with a view to having it wound up.[63] The last three depositions were received on Wednesday 26 May 1311, and then the commissioners wrote to the Bishop of Bayeux at Avignon to ask the pope if the hearings could be concluded. The bishop replied that the pope and cardinals thought that the commissioners had done sufficient, although they would like more information on receptions in Outremer. Guillaume Bonnet then left Avignon and joined the king and the Archbishop of Narbonne at Pontoise, north-west of Paris, where a *parlement* was being held. Gilles Aicelin and Guillaume Bonnet 'could not conveniently put aside the royal *parlement* and go to Paris in order to finish the aforesaid', so the proceedings were closed in Paris by the Bishops of Limoges and Mende, Matteo di Napoli and the Archdeacon of Trent 'at the request of the king' and the commissioners then travelled to the royal abbey at Pontoise where, on Saturday 5 June, they conferred with the king. Here they considered the position: they had heard 231 witnesses, some of whom had deposed about receptions in Outremer, and another seventy-two had been heard by the pope and the cardinals, the general council was imminent, and it was the wish of the pope and the king to bring the matter quickly to an end. Thus in the presence of Gui, Count of Saint-Pol, Guillaume de Plaisians, Geoffroi du Plessis and the five notaries who had recorded its work, the proceedings of the papal commission were officially closed. It had been in session for 161 days spread over nearly two years. All the material gathered, consisting of 219.5 folios, each with approximately forty lines per page, was sent to the pope by special messengers. Two copies had been made; the first was sent to the pope, sealed by the commissioners, and the other was to be deposited in the treasury of the monastery of Sainte-Marie at Paris, where it was not to be shown without special letters of permission from the pope.[64]

7: The Charges

When, on 14 September 1307, Philip IV had issued his secret orders for the arrest of the Templars, he had justified his action on three main grounds: the denial and the spitting, obscene kissing and homosexuality, and idol worship.[1] In July 1308 Clement V finally agreed to reopen the proceedings which had been suspended the previous February,[2] and on 12 August 1308 a fuller and more systematic list of charges was drawn up. This runs to 127 articles, which can be summarised under seven main headings. Firstly, that when a new Templar was received, he denied Christ and sometimes the Holy Virgin and the saints, an act instigated by those receiving him. He was told that Christ was not the true God, that he was a false prophet who had not been crucified for the redemption of the human race, but on account of his sins. There was therefore no hope of receiving salvation through Christ. The new member was then made to spit on a crucifix or on an image of Christ and, in some receptions, to trample or to urinate on it. Secondly, that the Templars adored idols, specific mention being made of a cat and a head, the latter sometimes having three faces. This head was worshipped as a saviour and venerated as a giver of plenty which could make the trees flower and the land germinate. They touched or encircled it with small cords which they wore around their waists. Thirdly, that they did not believe in the sacraments and that the Templar priests omitted the words of consecration during the mass. Fourthly, that they believed that the Grand Master and the other leaders could hear their confessions and absolve them from sin, despite the fact that many of these leaders were laymen. Fifthly, that the Order's receptors kissed new entrants on the mouth, the navel, the stomach, the buttocks and the spine, and that homosexuality was encouraged and indeed enjoined on them. Sixthly, that the Templars sought gain for the Order by whatever means came to hand, whether lawful or not. Donations made to the Order were not used in approved ways, nor were they apportioned to hospitals. Seventhly, that chapter-meetings and receptions were held in secret at night under a heavy guard and that only Templars were present. Brothers who revealed to an outsider what had occurred were punished by imprisonment or death.[3]

In 1307 Philip IV had reigned for twenty-two years. He had around him a settled and reliable group of ministers led by Guillaume de Nogaret. These men had, over the years, developed set techniques for dealing with those who, for one reason or another, fell foul of the regime. Intimidation and violence were backed by an intensive propaganda campaign aimed at harnessing support within France and blackening the name and reputation of the opponent concerned. Once the right climate of opinion was established the Estates were assembled to hear the discourses of the royal ministers on the subject and their members were then sent back to their own regions to spread the word. Boniface VIII had been the most famous protagonist. From Boniface's death in 1303 sporadic but determined attempts were made to associate the late pope with heresy, witchcraft, magic and homosexuality, attempts which came to a head in March 1310, when Nogaret succeeded in forcing Clement V to set up a commission of inquiry.[4] In August 1308 Guichard, Bishop of Troyes, who had incurred the enmity of the king's wife, Jeanne of Navarre, and of her mother Blanche, was accused of having made a wax image of the queen, and of having baptised and stuck pins in it, activities which in 1305 had resulted in the queen's death. He had then made a mixture from snakes, scorpions, toads and poisonous spiders, and had told a local hermit that he wanted it administered to the royal princes. He had done this because he had lost the friendship of Queen Jeanne, who therefore had prevented his return to favour at court, a favour which he had enjoyed up until 1301. An inquiry was begun in October 1308 which opened in characteristic style before an assembly of clergy and people in the garden of the king in Paris. Witnesses were called, many of whom gave incriminating evidence after being subjected to intensive torture. Guichard himself, despite his clerical status, was kept in the royal prison at the Louvre, the appearance of clerical privilege being maintained by giving him an ecclesiastic as a guard. Several hearings were held during 1309, but gradually the case of the bishop seems to have been pushed into the background, and he was still in prison in April 1313. He was finally released later that year and given the see of Diakover in Bosnia, which he never occupied. He died in 1317.[5]

An examination of the charges against the Templars reveals the same flair for propaganda and the same understanding of the susceptibilities of contemporary society at both its educated and popular levels. Such abilities were the special mark of Guillaume de Nogaret, who had instituted the proceedings in the cases already mentioned. The charges were not a random collection. Contemporaries believed them because the ground had already been prepared by the events of the preceding three centuries and by the existence of myths and superstitions which were part of the common heritage of the European and eastern peoples. Indeed centuries afterwards doubts remain about the Templars' guilt or innocence, and, in the nineteenth century, passions on the subject ran so high that attempts were made to forge objects which might link the Templars with eastern heresies, or to adduce proof that the leaders of the Order possessed a secret rule which contained heretical teaching.[6] To examine their contemporary impact the charges will first be looked at as a group and then individual items will be taken to see if they stand on their own.

In June 1233 Pope Gregory IX sent letters to several important German dignitaries in order to stimulate action against certain heretics in the Rhineland. The letters included a detailed description of the rites and practices of the heretics. When a novice entered the sect, the shape of a frog or toad appeared before him, which some heretics kissed on the hindquarters or on the mouth. The novice then went forward to meet a pallid man with very black eyes and an emaciated figure, whom the novice kissed. After the kiss 'the memory of the Catholic faith totally disappears from his heart'. After the heretics had risen from a meal, the statue of a black cat descended backwards with its tail erect, and 'first the novice, next the master, then each one of the order who are worthy and perfect kiss the cat on its hindquarters'. Then each inclined his head towards the cat, and intoned a series of responses. The candles were then extinguished and there followed 'the most disgusting lechery'. However, 'if by chance those of the male sex exceed the number of women . . . men engage in depravity with men'. The candles were then lit again, and from a dark corner emerged a man 'from the loins upwards gleaming more brightly than the sun, so they say, whose lower part is shaggy like a cat and whose light illuminates the whole place'. The Master picked something from the novice's clothing, and said to the figure, 'This which has been given to me, I give to you', and the figure replied, 'You have served me well and will serve more and better. I commit what you have given into your custody.' He then disappeared. The heretics also received the body of the Lord each year at Easter, and carried it home in their mouths where they spat it into a latrine 'in contempt of the Saviour'. Furthermore, they asserted that the Lord unjustly threw Lucifer into the lower world, maintaining that he is the creator of heaven and will return there in glory when the Lord has fallen.[7] The similarity to the charges against the Templars is striking, and indeed the letters might almost have been a text for Nogaret and his men: Christ is denied, the host (rather than a cross) is spat into a latrine, an idol is worshipped (in this case a toad or a black cat) and a devil figure is adored and touched with articles of clothing received from the novice, the mass is perverted, and some engage in obscene kisses and homosexuality.

Gregory IX was not however the first to hear such tales; Nogaret built on a long tradition. In 1022 the monk Adhémar de Chabannes had heard of heretics at Orléans who adored the devil and secretly practised various abominations which so shocked him that he could not bring himself to describe them.[8] Another monk, called Paul, from the Benedictine Abbey of Saint-Père-de-Chartres, his vision clarified by a time-lapse of half a century, was more explicit. The heretics gathered at a certain house and conjured up demons by chanting their names. Once the demon had appeared, usually in the form of a small beast, the lights were put out and 'each, as soon as he could, seized the woman nearest at hand . . . their copulation being regarded by these men as a matter of sanctity and piety'.[9] Not long afterwards, Guibert, Abbot of Nogent, picked up a rather confused variant on this tale which he used against heretics at Soissons in 1114. Among these heretics, he said, men lay with men, and women with women. They assembled in secret places such as cellars and there in the full light of the candles, women with bare buttocks offered themselves to a certain one who was lying behind them. Then the lights were put out and indiscriminate sexual intercourse took place.[10] Walter Map, writing *c.*1182, described a sect which he called Publicans or Paterines, who worshipped a huge cat which descended to them on a rope. This cat they kissed on the feet or under the tail or on the private parts, an act which inflamed them with lust. The usual sexual orgy followed.[11] In his defence of the faith against the Cathars, written in the late twelfth century, Alain de Lille drew on the same tradition, asserting, among his explanations of the name 'Cathar', that they were so called from 'cat' because they kissed the hindquarters of a cat, in whose form, it was said, Lucifer appeared to them.[12]

In 1231 an anonymous chronicler in Trier, talking of various heretical groups in the region, knew some who 'did not believe in [the sacrament] of the body of the Lord' and others who 'kissed a pallid man or even a cat'.[13] Guillaume d'Auvergne, Bishop of Paris between 1228 and 1249, claimed that a black cat and a toad appeared to the followers of Lucifer and that these persons indulged in such abominations as kissing a cat under its tail and a toad on the mouth.[14] Shortly after the trial of the Templars the Inquisitor Bernard Gui included a brief paragraph in his *Manuel de l'Inquisiteur* about heretics who, he said, indulged in sexual excesses and to whom a cat appeared, but he was referring to the Waldensians not to the Templars.[15]

It is evident that these accusations had been part of the stock apparatus of propaganda used for centuries by church and state to discredit religious and political opponents.[16] The medieval versions almost always associate such practices with the Cathars or the Waldensians,[17] and Nogaret may have aimed to taint the Templars by association. It is also likely that the inquisitors, whose training had been directed towards the detection of these particular heresies, would tend to ask questions which would draw the hapless examinee to make confessions along these lines, thereby further strengthening the French case against the Order by means of apparently free confessions. However, most important of all, the charges can be seen to contain many of the elements which were to reappear in the witch-craze of the sixteenth and seventeenth centuries. The Templars were, according to Nogaret, potential witches. Perhaps their great worldly wealth had been acquired with the help of the devil, whom they worshipped; perhaps they had entered into a pact with him. Here is a clear justification for the Christian King of France to confiscate gains made by such base means. None of this is explicit but it is strongly implied. Only one important element is missing. The Templars were not accused of doing active harm on the devil's behalf, the final ingredient in the sixteenth-century picture of a witch.

The connection is made more explicit in the vernacular narrative of the reigns of the French kings, produced at the Abbey of Saint-Denis, known as *Les Grandes Chroniques de France*. The author reproduces a list of eleven articles of accusation against the Templars, which contains certain notable additions to the official indictment of 127 articles.[18] The essence of the main charges is repeated: the denial of Christ, the spitting on the crucifix, homosexuality, and the worship of an idol, which, in this version, was an ancient embalmed head with 'hollow, carbuncled eyes, glowing like the light of the sky'. The Templars are accused of treason with the Moslems, and the wearing of a belt around their body is adduced as proof of this connection. More significant however is the appearance of accusations that the child of a Templar and a maiden was burnt on a fire and the fat taken away to sanctify and anoint their idol, and that dead Templars were burnt and new Templars fed upon their powdered remains. Like the accusations of heretical sexual orgies, these too had been a part of religious propaganda since Roman times.[19] Since the chronicles are a semi-official history of the Capetian kings, and the author would certainly have maintained contact with members of the French government, there seems little doubt that the eleven articles as described in the chronicles were intended as a further element in the royal propaganda machine, couched in the vernacular for wider dissemination.

However, there is evidence that a group of eleven articles, separate from the official list of 127 articles, did exist outside *Les Grandes Chroniques*. At the beginning of the twentieth century, Professor Heinrich Finke published, in his invaluable collection of documents on the trial, a fragment from a series of interrogations of Templars, which he had found in the Vatican Archives.[20] The fragment contained twenty-five depositions, not all of which were complete, beginning in the middle of number sixty-four and ending halfway through number eighty-eight, and it was undated. Despite the imperfections of the document, it is clear nevertheless that these Templars were being interrogated on a list of eleven articles. The answers in the depositions extant from this hearing provide further proof that the articles were part of the continuing tradition of literary cliché which had dominated accusations against the heretics since the early eleventh century, and in this sense *Les Grandes Chroniques* may have been offering a crude version of an official list of eleven articles which seemingly existed at some time during the trial, although there does not seem to be any direct connection between the two versions.

Finke's Vatican depositions include the denial of Christ and the associated charges, but besides these, seventeen of the Templars questioned in this hearing admitted that the brothers adored or genuflected not only before an idol in the form of a head, but also before a cat, variously coloured black, white, brown or red, which ten of them said that they kissed on the anus or the buttocks. Some thought that the cat had come on behalf of the devil, and one said that it disappeared after it had been adored. Although the accusation that the Templars adored a cat appears in the main list of 127 articles, they were not charged with the obscene kissing, and indeed nowhere else in the extant trial records do any Templars admit this charge.[21] Under interrogation, five of these Templars also admitted the presence of women at their receptions, whose presence and origin they could not explain, but who they believed were not truly women but devils in female form who had used their special powers to enter the locked chamber in which the receptions took place. Two of the five admitted that they and other brothers present had had sexual intercourse with the women. The impression that these interrogations were attempting to establish a more explicit link with sects alleged to be devil worshippers in the tradition of those already described is reinforced by the questions on the denial of Christ, which elicited replies describing not only spitting on the cross, but also urinating on it while it was on the floor and, uniquely for the trial records, the dragging of the cross for a few paces, 'in contempt of Jesus Christ', a practice which was also associated in the popular mind with the Moslems.[22] Moreover, the idol in the form of a head, which according to these witnesses had up to four faces, was also described by one Templar as having two small horns and possessing the ability to reply to questions put to it.

It is not however possible to draw conclusions too sweeping from these two pieces of evidence, for the list in *Les Grandes Chroniques* has no surviving official counterpart and the depositions printed in Finke are only a fragment of a much larger inquiry for which no date exists. Since the records of the papal commission are complete, it is most likely to have been an episcopal inquiry (indeed, most of the witnesses originate from Provence, Vienne and Annecy), a surmise strengthened by the requests of the Templars for absolution, requests which they were less likely to have made if they were testifying about the Order as a whole. The year would then almost certainly be 1310.[23]

A belief in sorcery and magic, in an ability to control and harness natural forces, is common to many societies in many periods, but in the course of the thirteenth century in western Christendom the practice of these arts began to develop specifically heretical connotations. In 1258 Pope Alexander IV laid down that inquisitors could only act in relation to sorcery when clear heresy was involved,[24] but new theories of the second half of the thirteenth century began to tie certain magical acts much more firmly to heretical belief, slowly creating a mental climate which accepted the idea of witchcraft, of a sorcerer who had a pact with the devil. In the early fifth century, St Augustine had not believed it possible for devils to change the soul or the body into bestial form, but only that they could create a phantasm which might appear to others in bodily shape.[25] This view was reiterated in legislation: the famous canon *Episcopi* of the early tenth century spoke of women 'seduced by the illusions and phantasms of demons' who believed that they rode upon certain beasts at night; but such beliefs were heretical, since 'it has been written of our Lord, "All things have been made by him" '. Therefore whoever believes that anything can be made, or that any creature can be changed into something better, or worse, or can be transformed into another shape or likeness, except by God himself who made everything and through whom all things have been made, is beyond doubt an infidel.[26] In contrast, Thomas Aquinas, who died in 1274, assigned demons a much more positive role in human affairs. He said that some would have it that there were no demons except in men's imagination, but the true teaching was that demons did exist who could take action which caused human distress.[27] Although Aquinas presents no systematic picture of a world of witches, it is significant that the earliest writers on witchcraft used many quotations from his works, gathering together scattered references to form the foundation of a whole body of theory.[28] Soon after the Templar trial, Pope John XXII, often obsessively concerned about supposed attempts on his life by means of magical practices, several times urged his inquisitors to be diligent in searching out those who worshipped or invoked devils, or who used the sacraments of the mass or the consecrated host for sorcery or witchcraft. In 1326–7 he spoke of persons who entered into 'a pact with hell', having made offerings to demons whom they adored. In return the demons provided them with aid in attaining their wicked desires.[29] This pope was convinced that there were persons, masquerading as Christians, who were joined to the devil by secret alliance.

The Templars were therefore brought to trial when attitudes towards magic and witchcraft were crystallising and new authorities coming to dominate thinking on the subject. Taken as a group Nogaret's charges can thus be seen as a means both of inciting popular hatred and vicarious excitement and of satisfying the intellectual who felt himself to be above the violence of the emotions and superstitions of the mob, and to need a detailed theoretical structure before arriving at the same conclusion.

Individually the accusations are equally potent: the denial of Christ alone was an indictment sufficient to destroy an individual or group so convicted, as its appearance in so many previous accusations of heresy indicates. The disrespect for the cross can be linked with the Cathars, for, according to the Dominican Moneta of Cremona, the Cathars believed that, since Christ was not God-made-man his material body could not have been crucified. This was the work of Satan, who had tried to kill what he believed to be a material body. The cross could not therefore be an object of veneration.[30] In the popular view, however, it was the Moslems who most obviously treated the cross with contempt; stories of Moslem armies dragging a crucifix through the streets were quite common in the west.[31] The Franciscan Fidenzio of Padua, who was in the Holy Land in the late thirteenth century, claimed that Christian boys captured by the Moslems were made to spit upon crucifixes and pictures of the Lord.[32] The charges concerning the crucifix might suggest penetration by either Catharism or Islam or both.

Those who framed the charge that the Templars worshipped idols, and who elicited confessions that the main objects of veneration were a cat and a magic head, aimed to exploit certain persistent popular beliefs. In general terms they were implying that the Templars were corrupted by Islam, pandering to the idea, long since rejected by the educated, that the Moslems worshipped idols.[33] More specifically they seem to have intended to exploit the contemporary view of the cat as the devil incarnate. In his collection of stories, assembled mainly as preaching material, the German Cistercian Caesarius of Heisterbach, writing in the 1220s, maintained that 'the devil on account of his rapacity is compared to a cat and a lion, who are very much alike in appearance and in nature, especially in their lying in wait for the souls of simple persons'.[34]

It was, however, the head which was the centre of the most spectacular stories, and here perhaps not even Nogaret was fully aware of the rich vein of folk memory which he had struck. Several witnesses said that they had seen a head, although its form varied widely.[35] However, two depositions made before the papal commission sitting in Paris in the spring of 1311 are of particular interest, and have been the object of detailed analysis by M. Salomon Reinach.[36]

The first of these was made on 1 March by an Italian notary called Antonio Sicci di Vercelli, who was not a member of the Order, but who had worked for the Templars for about forty years in Outremer. He had heard many times at Sidon that a lord of that town loved a noble lady of Armenia:

> He had never known her carnally while she was alive, but at length he secretly had intercourse with her when she was dead in her tomb, on the night of the day on which she had been buried. When he had done this, he heard a certain voice saying to him: 'Return when it is time for birth, because you will find a head, offspring to you.' And I have heard that when the time had passed, this same knight returned to the tomb, and found a human head between the legs of the buried woman. Again he heard the voice saying to him: 'Guard this head, because all good things will come to you from it.'

He claimed that at that time a Templar called Mathieu le Sarmage was Preceptor of Sidon, and that he had made himself the blood-brother of the Sultan of Egypt.[37]

On 12 May a Templar knight from Limoges, called Hugues de Faure, produced a variant on this tale. Sidon had been bought by Thomas Bérard when he was Grand Master, but he had not heard that any lord of Sidon had been a Templar. However, he had heard in Cyprus, after the fall of Acre, from Jean de Tanis, a secular knight who was *bailli* of Limassol, that

> a certain noble had deeply loved a certain damsel of the castle of Maraclea in the County of Tripoli, and since he could not have

her in her lifetime, when he heard that she was dead, he caused her to be exhumed, and had intercourse with her. Afterwards he cut off the head for himself, and a certain voice rang out that he should take good care of the said head, since whoever saw the head would be totally destroyed and routed.

He covered the head and placed it in a chest. Since he hated the Greeks, he then exposed the head to the Greek castles and cities and 'all were at once ruined'. Some time after, he set out for Constantinople to destroy that too, but the key to the chest in which the head was kept was secretly stolen from him by his former nurse, who wanted to see what was in the chest. She opened it and discovered the head, and at once a storm sank the ship. The only survivors were the sailors who told the story. 'It is said that from then on there were no fish in that part in which the foregoing had occurred.' However, Hugues had not heard that the head had come into the Templars' possession, nor did he know about the head described by Antonio Sicci.[38]

Finally, a third witness, Guillaume April of the diocese of Clermont, although he knew nothing about the other two stories, had heard it generally said in Outremer that in ancient times, before the Orders of the Temple and the Hospital had been founded, there sometimes appeared on the sea, in a whirlwind at a place called Satalia, 'a certain head after whose appearance boats which were in the said whirlwind were imperilled'.[39]

M. Reinach has shown that the medieval origins of this story can be traced at least to Walter Map, writing in the late twelfth century, although Walter does not connect its events with the Templars. The principal in Map's tale is a young shoemaker of Constantinople, who had attained such a mastery of his craft that great nobles came to him for personal fittings. This mastery, together with marvellous prowess at sport, gained him wide fame, and one day a beautiful maiden with a large entourage came to order some shoes. The shoemaker was so overwhelmed by her that, although he realised that social barriers made her unapproachable, he thought at least that he would sustain a milder rebuff if he gave up his craft and took up the nobler profession of a soldier. Attaining great skill in this field too, he approached the maiden's father for her hand, but was not accepted. Violently angry, he took to piracy as a means of avenging his humiliation and soon came to be greatly feared. However, he heard that the maiden had meanwhile died, and hastening to the funeral he took note of the place of interment. That night he returned, broke into the grave, and violated the corpse. Then he heard a voice telling him to come again to this place, when he should see what offspring had been produced. When he returned, he received a human head from the dead woman, which he was forbidden to expose to anyone except an enemy whom he wished to kill. He kept the head in a locked chest and caused great havoc among his enemies when he used its power. Eventually, he was given the opportunity to marry the daughter of the Emperor of Constantinople, who was also the heiress. After some time she demanded to know what was in the chest, and one day opened it while he was asleep. Waking him up she thrust the head into his face and he was killed. Horrified, the princess caused the head and its keeper to be thrown into the sea, an act which caused a great storm which, when it subsided, left a great and treacherous whirlpool in that spot. The place is now known as the Gulf of Satalia.[40]

Two near-contemporary writers also include similar stories in their works. Roger of Howden, describing the return of Philip II of France from Palestine in 1191, recalled the tale while they were passing 'the Isles of Yse'. The hero is a knight and the result of his necrophilia is a stillborn son. A voice told him to cut off the head, for it could be used to destroy enemies who gazed upon it. After some years of successful use, his wife found the head while he was away and threw it into the Gulf of Satalia, where, when it was lying face upwards, it caused a terrible storm.[41] Gervais of Tilbury, writing *c.*1210, again identified the Gulf of Satalia as the site of the head, which he believed to be that of the Gorgon whose head Perseus had thrown into the sea. However, local traditions, he says, tell of a knight who loved a queen and who had intercourse with her after her death. The product of this union was a monstrous head, again possessed of destructive power if a person looked directly at it. At length, while he was at sea, the knight fell asleep, and his mistress, curious to know what he kept in a chest which he always carried, stole the key, opened the chest and was at once struck dead at the sight of the head. When the knight woke he found his mistress dead and the chest open, circumstances which caused him to look on the head. The result was that both he and the ship were lost. During the next seven years when the face of the head was turned upwards, it constituted a great danger for sailors in that region.[42]

The essence of this tale stems from the ancient legend of Perseus and Medusa, and various versions of it were commonly known in antiquity in places as far apart as Persia and Italy. Ovid provides a detailed literary form, but this in turn is based on pre-existing oral versions. It is to be expected that different regions and periods produced changed emphases, but the tale has a universal appeal and a hardy durability which enabled oral versions to survive even among the peasants of nineteenth-century Tuscany.[43] The appearance of the story among the depositions of the Templar trial is therefore only a minor incident in the overall history of this piece of folklore and it cannot by any stretch of the imagination be directly connected with the activities of the Order. It was however a useful weapon in fourteenth-century France, for it contained several elements which struck a response in the collective folk memory. Two features in particular are worthy of mention: the idea that the living and the dead can conceive and the belief in the possession of the evil eye.

Many societies have shared a belief in ghosts and their ability to have sexual intercourse with the living. The basic structure of the so-called 'haunted widow' myth is that a husband dies but returns to have intercourse with his wife. She conceives and usually gives birth to a monster of some kind, often a head, which in some cases is endowed with destructive powers. A tale from the Indians of British Columbia serves to demonstrate this. The daughter of a chief loved a certain youth, but her father refused them permission to marry. One night her brothers secretly murdered the youth and buried him, with his horse, in a wood. The girl mourned him, not knowing his fate, when he reappeared, covered with blood and with icicles in his hair, and carried her off. He slept with her in a grave in the wood, and nine months later she gave birth to a great stone which at once struck her brothers dead.[44] A belief in the power to 'fascinate' with the evil eye, thus causing damage and destruction to the object of the eye's gaze, is probably even more widespread, and seems especially to have been associated with witches and magicians.[45] Medieval men were familiar with the idea from Scripture.[46] Once again, literary sources can be found in the ancient world, most notably in Plutarch.[47]

The other charges were also significant for contemporary society.

The reference made in the charges to the small cords supposedly worn by the Templars with which they touched these idols, may, as the eleven articles suggest, have been associated with beliefs about Islam, but there is a connection also with Catharism again, for inquisitorial records of the late thirteenth century show that the Catholic Church believed that the wearing of such cords was a sign of having received the *consolamentum*.[48]

As with so many of the charges framed against the Templars, the accusation that they omitted the words of consecration in the mass can be understood on more than one level, depending on the status and attitudes of the listener. The popular mind was accustomed to attacks upon Cathars, especially concerning their alleged rejection of the sacraments of the Catholic Church stemming from their denial of the doctrines of the Incarnation, Resurrection and Redemption.[49] Bernard Gui provides a near-contemporary official statement of what people should believe on this issue. These heretics, he said, believed that they were all empty and devoid of meaning.[50] 'They abuse and disparage all the sacraments of the Church, especially the sacrament of the Eucharist, saying that the body of Christ is not in it.'[51] Once again the potential link with Catharism was established.

Nogaret, of course, may have had a more specific end in view. If the Templar priests omitted the words of consecration, no sacrifice was offered and Christ was not corporeally present in the church. In this case Templar masses spoken on behalf of patrons, living or dead, would have had no spiritual value, and lay benefactors had made their very considerable material sacrifices to the Order for nothing. The vast Templar lands had been granted under false pretences. This again is an effective way of rallying an influential sector of public opinion – the landholding class – to the side of the French government, and of justifying the seizure of the Templars' property. Nogaret could leave others to speculate on the possible reasons for this behaviour. Perhaps the Templars feared damnation if they took communion in the wilful state of mortal sin implied by the worship of a head or a cat. Unconsecrated bread was a possible way of avoiding this. Perhaps it went further than this. The Templars might have considered the sacrifice of Calvary of no consequence and therefore went through an empty form of worship simply to cover up this fact; the alternative of secret conversion to a heresy of some sort or even to Islam then presents itself.[52]

One further motive might perhaps have been adduced, a motive which would provide an effective link with the idea that the Templars were witches in league with demons. It was widely believed that the consecrated host was proof against witchcraft because no devil could bear to look at it. This belief may conveniently be demonstrated by a twelfth-century story about the wife of Geoffrey, Count of Anjou, taken from Giraldus Cambrensis. The countess seldom went to church, but even when she did, she never remained during the celebration of the secret canon of the mass. The count and others remarked this with astonishment, and therefore one day when she went to leave at the usual time, at the count's command she was stopped by soldiers. At this, she seized two of her four small sons under her arm and flew out of one of the high windows of the church, never being seen again.[53] Perhaps few people tried to delve for these implications, but all at least would have been aware of the central importance of the mass in Catholic worship, that the mass made the sacrifice of Christ available to the men and women who were present at it.[54] If this charge could be pressed successfully, then the whole of Christendom would be incited against an Order which acted in a way so contrary to such a fundamental aspect of medieval life.

The internal confession and absolution of sins would serve to reinforce the suspicions which the other charges had provoked, for the instigators of such crimes would not wish any of the Templars to reveal what was happening to an outside confessor. Although many Templars maintained during their testimonies that they had confessed to outside priests as well as to Franciscan friars, there does seem to have been some truth in this accusation. During the trial in England it became clear that some Templars did not distinguish between sacramental absolution by priests and the absolution of the local Master or preceptor for infringing internal regulations of the Order. Although the reasons for this seem to have been quite innocuous and unconnected with heretical belief, this practice could easily be associated with the Templars' supposed general contempt for the sacraments.[55]

The charge of homosexuality was an obvious accusation to direct against an all-male celibate Order, and it would be surprising if the Templars, any more than other monastic Orders, were completely free of it. Nogaret may have included the charge for this reason only

The Paris Temple was the Order's largest complex in the west. It formed a large walled enclosure with a prominent tower, seen in the background of this fifteenth-century miniature depicting the execution of heretics. This was the administrative centre of the Templar lands in France and the site of its most important bank. *Below*, Laon, north-east of Paris, was one of the many smaller Templar preceptories, probably established in the early 1140s. The twelfth-century church has a narthex leading into a hexagonal chapel

The first Templar preceptory in London was at Holborn, but sometime between 1155 and 1162 it was moved nearer to the Thames, just south of the Strand. The Round Church was built in English Transitional style and consecrated by Heraclius, Patriarch of Jerusalem, in 1185. The new chancel was consecrated in the presence of Henry III in 1240. *Left*, on the floor of the Round Church are effigies of lay associates of the Temple. Among them is William Marshal, Earl of Pembroke and Regent of England during the minority of Henry III, who had arranged for his burial in the London Temple but here again contemporary reaction was conditioned by attitudes more deep-seated. The Church had always taught (probably erroneously) that homosexual practices had brought the wrath of God upon the city of Sodom.[56] Ecclesiastical writers and the framers of civil law throughout the middle ages had therefore been careful to condemn such acts lest divine vengeance fall upon their land. St Basil and St Augustine had warned novitiate monks and nuns of the dangers,[57] and in 538 and 544 the Emperor Justinian issued laws against homosexual practices.[58] More recently, St Peter Damian in the *Liber Gomorrhianus* of 1051 had attacked homosexuality, quoting Leviticus 20:13: 'If a man lie with mankind, as he lies with a woman, both of them have committed an abomination: they shall surely be put to death; their blood shall be upon them.'[59] Even more pertinent to the case of the Templars are the laws promulgated in 1120 at the Council of Nablus in the Kingdom of Jerusalem. In a frontier land where there was constant danger of infidel attack, it was easy to interpret disasters as divine punishment for the sins of the flesh. One of these sins was sodomy, and four of the council's twenty-five canons dealt with the subject. Proven sodomists were to be burnt. Those who hid the fact that they had been forced to commit sodomy and allowed this to happen a second time were to be regarded as sodomists themselves. Those who voluntarily came to penitence must renounce 'that abominable wickedness' on oath, and if they transgressed again and asked for penance they were to be expelled from the kingdom.[60]

The implications are clear. The sins of the Templars had led to the fall of the crusader states in 1291. If speedy action was not taken the wrath of God would equally fall on the Kingdom of France, which sheltered the perpetrators of these 'unnatural acts'. Church and people must combine to eradicate such a danger. This was a concept most could understand. The Templars became scapegoats not only for the failure of a crusade to which most people were no longer prepared to subscribe, but also for the inability of the French government to achieve a coherent and peaceful administration. Theorists could turn to Aquinas, who saw homosexuality as an offence against right reason, for it excludes the possibility of procreation, which is the proper end of carnal copulation.[61] Those with a taste for history need not have looked as far back as Sodom. Henry of Huntingdon knew that the wreck of the *White Ship* in 1120 in which King Henry I's heir was lost was a consequence of the sin of sodomy with which almost all on board were associated.[62]

The accusation also has associations with the two other themes that run through this collection of charges: that the Templars had been infiltrated by Islam or Catharism or both. It was generally believed in the west that homosexuality was common in Moslem society, especially since Catholic traders were actively involved in a commerce concerned with the sale of young boys to various Moslem rulers.[63] The Cathars were also accused of homosexuality, particularly as the *Bonhommes* travelled in pairs of the same sex while on their preaching missions.[64]

It has been seen that the idea that the Templars sought gain by whatever means came to hand can be linked with current superstitions about witchcraft and sorcery, as well as the omission of the words of consecration during the mass. The success of the Templars as bankers and landowners would make those less well endowed susceptible to this accusation, especially as biblical reference would tell them that Satan tempted Christ in the wilderness with all the kingdoms of the earth if he would give him his allegiance.[65]

Finally, the secrecy with which many – indeed, probably most – of the Templar receptions and chapters were held presented Nogaret with the ideal means of avoiding the necessity of providing any outside proof that these crimes had been committed. This factor, combined with internal confession and absolution, might well explain why the corruption within the Order had remained undetected for so many years.

Magic, sorcery and witchcraft were part both of the popular heritage and of the contemporary intellectual structure, and as a consequence the charges outlined above would strike a response at all levels of society. The attribution of these beliefs to the Templars was a deliberate and successful attempt to vilify them and ruin their reputation, but perhaps in the final analysis it was only partly conscious, for both Philip's lawyers and Clement's inquisitors were themselves part of the age and in some way or another imbued with its ideas and traditions.

8: The Trial in Other Countries

When the Templars in France were suddenly arrested on 13 October 1307, Edward II of England had been king for only four months. He was, as yet, uncrowned. He was young and inexperienced, and all his life he had been overshadowed by the towering personality of his father. Despite his many successes Edward I had left his heir an inheritance full of stresses and strains. Wars with Scotland and France and a lavish programme of castle-building had put the crown heavily in debt, yet had failed to solve the problems which lay behind the wars. Discontent among the baronage, which had been growing during the later years of Edward I's reign, was now very near the surface. On the face of it, it might be expected that when Edward II received news of the arrest of the Templars, he would have seized the opportunity to score an easy success. The Templars' lands in England were by no means as extensive as those in France, but they were still a considerable prize, and their seizure might have helped alleviate immediate financial problems without alienating any important sectional interest. The example of the experienced Philip IV, who, if he had failed to crown all his ventures with success, had for more than twenty years kept the authority of the monarchy intact by such expedients, lay before him. Moreover, opposition from the Templars was likely to be minimal, for although the Order in England was rich in possessions, it was comparatively small in terms of personnel.

However, on 30 October he had told Philip IV that he could not give 'easy credence' to the accusations, but since the charges apparently originated in Guienne, he would write to Guillaume de Dène, his seneschal in Agen, summoning him to come to his presence to give his account.[1] The outcome was that Edward remained unconvinced of the veracity of the charges and instead of arresting the Templars, on 4 December he sent out duplicate letters to the Kings of Portugal, Castile, Aragon and Naples, strenuously defending the Order.[2] Recently there had come before the king 'a certain clerk'[3] who had applied himself 'with full zeal' towards the destruction of the Temple by defaming it through 'certain horrible and detestable matters repugnant to the Catholic Faith'. His aim was to induce the king to arrest the Templars 'without due consideration of the matter'. But the Order had been honourably instituted a long time before and 'shines bright in religion', having defended the Holy Land since its foundation. Therefore, 'ready belief' in such unheard-of accusations 'was hardly to be entertained'. The kings should not listen to such perverse slanderers, who were inspired by cupidity, but leave the Templars unmolested until they were legally convicted. The king then wrote to the pope on 10 December. He had heard 'a rumour of infamy, a rumour indeed full of bitterness, terrible to think of, horrible to hear, and detestable in wickedness', directed against the Templars. But since the Templars had been 'constant in the purity of the faith', he could not give credence to these stories until he knew about these things with greater certainty. In Edward's view the charges had arisen from envious persons who were liars and criminals, and he therefore asked that the pope should not act until the matter had been brought before him in proper legal form and the affair more clearly uncovered.[4]

Since Hugues de Payns had come to the British Isles in 1128–9 the Templars had held a respected, trusted and privileged position in the domains ruled by the Norman and Angevin kings. A case in point can be taken from the year 1158. At that time Marguerite, daughter of King Louis VII of France, was espoused to Henry, eldest son of King Henry II. Part of Marguerite's dowry was to be the fortress of Gisors in Normandy, together with other castles, and the Templars were entrusted with the task of holding these castles – which were strategically important – until the couple came of age.[5] During the twelfth and thirteenth centuries the Order's banking and loan service had eased the financial burdens of successive English monarchs, including Richard I, John and Henry III.[6] On the Third Crusade in 1190–3, the Order had given Richard I valuable military and political support, and was sufficiently closely associated with the Angevin monarchy for Richard to have secured the appointment of Robert de Sablé, one of his Angevin vassals and a former fleet commander for the royal armies during the crusade, as Grand Master.[7] The Order's many lands were scattered over most counties; the details of those held in the twelfth century were recorded between 1185 and 1195 in an inquest or survey ordered by the new Master in England, Geoffrey Fitz Stephen. The financial character of the Templar administration, based on the New Temple in London, can be

seen in this 'Domesday of the Templars' for the Order was not simply a passive recipient of donations, but an active agent in the land
market, buying, selling and exchanging property on a considerable
scale.[8] The extent to which the Order had entrenched itself in England can be gauged from a comprehensive confirmation of its property and privileges granted by King Henry III in February 1227. On
their property the Templars exercised jurisdictional rights like sac
and soc, covering the pleas of free peasants, and toll and team, giving the right to take a tax on the sale of cattle and to hold a court for
those accused of cattle thefts. They were freed from paying royal
aids, scutages and a host of other financial exactions; they were
allowed to cut timber where they wished on their lands without
penalty; they received freedom from tolls in all markets and fairs,
and upon crossing bridges, roads and ferries throughout the kingdom. Any penalties of forfeiture incurred by any of their brethren
would belong to the Order whatever the court to which the matter
appertained. They even possessed the right to animals, lost by their
owners, which should wander on to Templar lands.[9]

Edward II clearly did not find it easy to effect a sudden reversal of
this policy, and perhaps, if he had tried to balance the short-term
gains of seizure against the long-term advantage of steady service,
what seems in essence to have been an emotional reaction to the
arrests might have been stiffened by practical considerations as well.
But if the king was not inclined to act at the behest of Philip IV, he
changed his mind when, on 14 December, he received the bull *Pastoralis praeeminentiae*, authorising the arrest of the Templars in the
name of the papacy.[10] The bull left little room for argument, and
on 26 December Edward replied that the matters concerning the
affair of the Templars would be expedited in 'the quickest and best
way'.[11] Royal instructions ordered that the Templars be arrested on
10 January.[12]

In the event 'the quickest and best way' proved to be very cumbersome. No concerted attempt to bring the Templars into custody
was made which was in any way comparable with the arrests in
France in October 1307, even though it must have been well within
the administrative capacities of the English crown to make one.
Many of the Templars seem to have been allowed to remain in their
preceptories, some of them until they were actually brought before
the pontifical inquiries, which did not begin until the autumn of

1309. William de la More, the Master in England, was arrested on 9 January at the New Temple in London. William was imprisoned at Canterbury, but was allowed the company of two brethren and the material comforts of bed, robes and various personal possessions and utensils. In addition he received an allowance of 2 shillings 6 pence per day. On 27 May he was actually released, and on 23 July a royal order granted six Templar manors to him for the sustenance of himself and his suite. Other Templars also received allowances, generally 4 pence per day, drawn from Templar lands. However, the Master was rearrested on 28 November 1308 and the manors taken from him. At the same time the king ordered that the Templars be guarded more strictly.[13]

At last, on 13 September 1309, two representatives of the Inquisition arrived in England: Dieudonné, Abbot of Lagny in the diocese of Paris, and Sicard de Vaur, a canon of Narbonne. Edward ordered that the inquisitors and their staff be provided with every facility and be protected from any injury or molestation wherever they wished to travel in the kingdom. All the Templars were to be sent to London, York or Lincoln, where they would be examined by the inquisitors.[14] The inquisitors were joined by English prelates, including the Archbishop of York, and the Bishops of London and Lincoln.[15] Edward also wrote to his Justiciar in Ireland, John Wogan, ordering that the Templars not yet arrested be taken into custody without delay and sent to Dublin castle. John de Segrave, Edward's governor in Scotland, received similar instructions.[16]

Between 20 October and 18 November 1309, the two inquisitors, together with the Bishop of London, questioned forty-three Templars at the Church of the Holy Trinity in London on a schedule of eighty-seven articles which included all the main accusations which had been brought in France, but none of the Templars was prepared to admit any of the charges. The responses of a knight, William Raven, who was questioned on 23 October, are typical. He and another knight, since dead, had been received about five years before at Coombe in the diocese of Bath by William de la More. When the hardships of the Order had been explained to him he swore the usual vows of poverty, chastity and obedience, and not to lay violent hands on anyone except in self-defence or against the Saracens. Two other brothers were present but, unusually, he also stated that about a hundred secular persons had also witnessed the ceremony.[17] Several other brothers confirmed this basic mode of reception and indicated that they had seen others received in the same orthodox way, except that no secular persons had been present. Imbert Blanke, Preceptor of the Auvergne, was examined on 28 October. He was a man of experience and authority, a Templar for thirty-seven or thirty-eight years, during which he had served in Outremer under the Grand Master Guillaume de Beaujeu who had died at Acre in 1291. Imbert seems to have been visiting England at the time of the arrests. When he was asked about the secrecy of chapter-meetings and receptions, he replied that the only reason for this was 'on account of foolishness'. In fact they had done nothing in secret that was not fit for the whole world to see. He denied all the accusations, saying concerning the confessions of the leaders that he did not know what they had said, 'but if they had confessed the aforesaid errors, they had lied'.[18] One of the few lines of enquiry taken up was the matter of the rather mysterious death of a Templar called Walter Bacheler, a former Preceptor of Ireland. But this yielded no more than the account given by a Templar called Ralph de Barton, who said that he knew nothing about this except that the preceptor had been imprisoned in fetters and died there, and that he had heard that he underwent great hardship while in prison. He said that he was not buried in a cemetery because he had disobeyed the Order's rules and was therefore considered excommunicate.[19]

The contrast to the mass confessions so quickly obtained in France emphasises the differences in the legal systems of the two countries. In France the Inquisition had been accepted and used as a tool of the monarchy, indeed almost as an arm of government. Where inquisitors had acted contrary to the interests of the crown, they had been checked, but in general the later Capetians found that the machinery of the Inquisition could be usefully employed. In England, however, the Norman and Angevin kings had developed a sophisticated and uniform legal machinery applying to all free men of the land, which left no room for an Inquisition which was sometimes seen as an agent of foreign popes. Consequently, the Inquisition had never functioned in England and had no machinery or tradition upon which to rely. The Abbot of Lagny and Sicard de Vaur were its first and only representatives in the British Isles. Immediately, they came upon a barrier to their activities, for English law relied upon the opinion of local jurors and did not employ torture.

Given the nature of the charges and the admitted secrecy of the Templars, it seemed almost impossible for any evidence to be gathered by the traditional processes of English law. Outside witnesses were extensively used, but however fantastic their imaginations, they could hardly be expected to provide the inquisitors with any really effective ammunition. When the provincial Council of Canterbury met in London on 24 November therefore, the inquisitors began pressing for the use of torture as was customarily allowed by the Inquisition. On 9 December they asked the king if they could proceed 'according to ecclesiastical constitutions', which meant the use of torture. The king replied the next day, rather ambiguously, that they were permitted 'to act and proceed against the Templars as related to their office, although nothing should be done against our crown or the state of our kingdom', which was taken to mean that the use of torture was permitted.[20]

Fresh proceedings therefore began in the New Year, 1310, strengthened by the framing of a new set of articles on which the Templars were to be examined.[21] The disappointment of the inquisitors at their almost total lack of success at this second hearing is reflected in the constant attempts to bring further pressure to bear on the prisoners. In March Guillaume de Dène was appointed to organise the work of torture, and it was ordered that individual Templars be kept separate.[22] In April and May 1310 the Templars questioned at York and Lincoln were no more forthcoming.[23] In late May a council of the northern province at York which had met to consider, among other matters, the affair of the Templars, decided to postpone discussions until the next year.[24]

On one small point only was there any indication of an irregularity. Several Templars seem to have believed that the Grand Master or regional preceptor could give them a general absolution for their sins in chapter.[25] This had not even originally been included among the articles of accusation, but it proved to be the only area in which the inquisitors were able to shake the Templars before there had been any extensive use of torture. However, even on this point the leaders and more experienced Templars drew a distinction which suggests that many brothers simply misunderstood rather than wilfully contravened ecclesiastical law. William de la More described what took place in chapter. A brother who admitted an offence entered the chapter, stripped to the waist, and was struck three times with whips. He was told to ask God to forgive him, and the other brothers were told to support this plea. More then warned the offender not to repeat his act, but he denied that he said, 'I absolve you in the name of the Father, Son, and Holy Spirit. Amen.' Other sins which they dared not confess, either as a result of their own weakness or because of fear of the Order's justice, he remitted as far as he was able, according to the power granted him by God and the pope.[26] It seems that some brothers erroneously believed that the Master was giving them a general absolution, rather than that he was simply dealing with their offences against the Order's rules.

Nobody therefore could have found the evidence collected very convincing. This was tacitly admitted by the inquisitors in a letter of 16 June 1310 to the Archbishop of Canterbury, in which they complained that they could find no one to carry out tortures properly and that the procedure ought to be by ecclesiastical law as in France. They protested that they had done their duty as well as possible and claimed the right to return to the Holy See, and leave the remainder of the task to the archbishop and the other English prelates. The body of the letter however dealt with eight ways in which the inquisitors thought proceedings could be speeded up, a matter which now must have seemed urgent in view of the spectacular results achieved by the burnings in France that spring. The inquisitors wanted the guard of the prisoners removed from the king and his officers, ostensibly to relieve the crown of the expense but in practice to facilitate the use of torture, and they wanted the stipend of 4 pence per day to be given to the ordinaries. The admission about supposed absolution in chapter they wanted to use as a lever to secure the condemnation of individual brethren, while giving the Templars every opportunity of purgation to prove their innocence. The pressure could be increased by feeding the prisoners bread and water on alternate days and by providing really appalling lodgings, but most sweeping was the idea that all the English Templars be sent to the County of Ponthieu, just across the Channel, which, although part of the lands of the English king, did not suffer from the disadvantage of English law; that is, the same methods could be employed as in the rest of France. They suggested too that the confessions of the French brethren be widely publicised in England in an effort to stifle any potential popular protest, and that the clergy of other countries be asked to provide testimonies of witnesses from their areas to condemn some of the English Templars.[27]

It now seems that a more concerted effort was made by the king to enforce the demands for torture; on 26 August and 6 and 23 October he ordered procedure 'according to ecclesiastical law'.[28] On 23 September the adjourned provincial Council of Canterbury decided that the Templars from London and Lincoln should be separated and again examined so that 'some truth might be elicited from them'. It was decided that 'if through the various methods and separations they wished to confess nothing more than before, that then they should be put to the question, in such a way that these questions should be made without mutilation or permanent injury to any members and without violent effusion of blood'.[29] Nevertheless, a letter from Clement V to Edward II on 23 December 1310 suggests that torture was still not being systematically applied, for the pope offered the king remission of sins and the eternal mercy of God if the trial could be transferred to Ponthieu.[30]

A measure of the difficulties which the inquisitors were experiencing can be seen in the extensive use of witnesses from outside the Order. In France, where a large number of confessions had been rapidly extracted by torture, only six of the 231 extant depositions were made by persons outside the Order, whereas in the British Isles, where the numbers of Templars were much smaller, there were sixty such witnesses in England, forty-one in Ireland and forty-nine in Scotland. No attempt seems to have been made to find a representative selection of witnesses, for only six of the sixty outside witnesses in England were not ecclesiastics, and of these only two were knights of the social standing which would entitle them to sit on local juries.[31]

However, some witnesses did tell colourful stories.[32] William de la Forde, rector of Crofton in the diocese of York, for instance, had been told by a William de Reynbur, an Augustinian, now dead, that he had heard the confession of the late Patrick de Ripon, a Templar. He was told to deny God and Christ and to spit on a crucifix, and then he was ordered 'to pull down his breeches [and] turn his back to the crucifix'. Afterwards he was shown an image of a calf placed upon an altar, and he was told to kiss and venerate this. All these things he did. Then finally, with his eyes covered, he was ordered to kiss each of the brothers present, 'although he did not know on which part'.[33] Another witness, a knight called Ferinsius Mareschal, recounted how his uncle had entered the Order 'strong, healthy and cheerful, with his birds and dogs, and three days after he was dead, and, as he now suspected, he had died on account of the crimes which he had heard concerning the Templars, since he did not wish to consent to the evil deeds perpetrated by the other brothers'.[34] In Scotland and Ireland the witnesses seem simply to have stated their opinion, with very little substance to back it. A typical deposition was that of a monk called William le Botiller who had been present when the Templars had celebrated mass at their church at Clonfert. When the host had been elevated, the Templars had looked towards the ground and had not lifted their eyes towards it, nor had they attended to the reading of the gospels.[35] One further method was tried. Two depositions, from Templars arrested in France but who had originally been received into the Order in England, were read out in an attempt to implicate others received in the British Isles. The better-known of them was Geoffroi de Gonneville, Preceptor of Aquitaine, who, in 1307, had said that he had been received in London.[36]

It was a small result for so much effort. However, just as the trial in England seemed to be petering out without any substantial confessions, early in June 1311 the king's officers captured a fugitive Templar called Stephen de Stapelbrugge at Salisbury. He and another fugitive, Thomas de Thoroldeby, who had earlier escaped from prison at Lincoln, but afterwards had surrendered, provided the first confessions comparable to those in France. On 23 June at Newgate, before the Bishops of London and Chichester, Stephen de Stapelbrugge deposed that there were two receptions in the Order, one 'licit and good' and the other 'against the faith'. He was received by both methods, in the first place in an honest manner, but two years later according to the second mode. The receptor on the second occasion was Brian le Jay, then Master in England. A cross was brought and then, in the presence of two brothers with drawn swords, the receptor said to him, 'It is necessary for you to deny that Jesus Christ is God and man, and to deny Mary, his mother, and to spit on this cross.' Stephen was frightened and made the requisite denials, although like the French brethren, it was only 'by the mouth, and not in the heart', and he spat on a hand next to the cross rather than on the cross itself. The reception had taken place at dawn, and he believed that such receptions were general in the Order. He also admitted that he had been told not to believe in the sacrament of the altar, that the Grand Master gave a general absolution from sins, and that homosexuality was allowed. He knew that the Templar Walter Bacheler, about whom other Templars had been questioned, had died 'in prison through tortures'. He thought that the Order's errors had originated in the diocese of Agen.

> And then bending with knees to the ground, with eyes uplifted and hands clasped together, with tears, sighs and laments, he devotedly asked for the mercy and grace of the Holy Church; and that there should be enjoined on him a salutary penance for what he had done, saying that he did not care about the death of the body, nor about other torments, but only for the safety of his soul.[37]

Thomas de Thoroldeby was examined on 26 June, also by the Bishops of London and Chichester. He had previously appeared before the Archbishop of Canterbury and had denied all the articles. But since then he had fled, 'from fear of death', for when, at Lincoln, the Abbot of Lagny, the inquisitor, had asked him if he wished to confess, he replied that he had nothing to say unless 'he would admit falsehood', at which the abbot placed his hand on his chest and swore 'that he would deliver his confession, before he should escape from his hands'. Thomas had then bribed his gaoler with 40 florins and had been let free. Afterwards, disguised in secular clothes, he had travelled to France and had visited the papal Curia, apparently on some kind of spying mission for the Master in England. However, while abroad he had heard about many confessions, including those of four brothers who said that they had been received by Imbert Blanke, Preceptor of the Auvergne then held in England, with denial and spitting. On 29 June he was examined again, and made a more incriminating statement, perhaps as a result of torture in the intervening period. He described a reception very similar to that of Stephen de Stapelbrugge, even to the point of having two brothers present with drawn swords. He told stories about the former Master, Brian le Jay, who he claimed treated the poor with contempt, for he had received a request for alms for the love of the Virgin by throwing a farthing into the mud so that the people had to grovel for it. When he was in the east, he had seen the Saracens let the Templars depart in peace, even though they attacked other Christians, and he had never been able to gain a satisfactory explanation from the Order's officials as to why this was so. As for himself, he had not been able to look upon the host for three years without thinking of the devil, an idea which even prayer would not remove, 'but on this day he had heard mass with great devotion, thinking of nothing else except Christ'. There was nothing in the Order which could save his soul 'unless it reformed itself', since all its members were guilty either of illicit absolution or of some other unlawful act. This accorded with what others had told him after he had entered the Order. A Brother John de Moun had said to him, 'If you sit above the bell-tower of St Paul's in London, you could not see greater misfortune than the things which will concern you before you die.' Another brother, Thomas de Toulouse, had told him and other brothers that they would never have a good day in the Order.[38]

By this time a third witness had been found. John de Stoke, a Templar priest, who had previously denied the accusations, appeared on 1 July and made a limited confession. He had been received in an orthodox way about eighteen years before, but about a year after this, at the preceptory of Garway in the diocese of Hereford, he was called into the presence of Jacques de Molay and other brothers. A crucifix had been brought and Molay had asked whose image it was; John de Stoke replied that it was Jesus Christ who had suffered for the redemption of the human race. To this, the Grand Master had said, 'You speak badly, and you are in error; for he was the son of a certain woman, and since he said that he was the Son of God, he was crucified.' Molay then ordered that he deny Christ, and when John showed reluctance threatened to put him in prison. The threat was backed by the drawn swords of two of the brothers present, and since he feared that they were about to kill him, he made the denial, but with the usual formula that he did not mean this in his heart. Asked in what Molay had told him to believe since he should deny Christ, he replied 'in the great omnipotent God, who created heaven and earth, and not in the Crucifixion'.[39]

Much capital was made out of these confessions. The provincial Council of Canterbury which had been sitting intermittently since November 1309 was once more assembled at St Paul's, London, and on 27 June Stephen de Stapelbrugge and Thomas de Thoroldeby appeared before it to make public abjuration of their errors. The Archbishop of Canterbury formally reconciled the penitents and enjoined the Bishop of Chichester to absolve them. On 3 July John de Stoke was also absolved and reconciled.[40]

Between 9 and 13 July another fifty-seven brothers either abjured certain heresies which they had confessed, such as the belief in lay absolution in chapter, or if they had confessed nothing, admitted that they had been so defamed by the articles concerning the denial of Christ and the spitting on the cross that they could not purge themselves from them. Individual brothers were then sent to various monasteries where they would do penance. There were two outstanding exceptions: William de la More, Master in England, and Imbert Blanke, Preceptor of the Auvergne. On 31 July it was said in the council that William de la More had spoken with the Archbishop of Canterbury and 'it was hoped by many that he wished . . . to be reconciled'. On the 5th the Bishop of Chichester had gone to All Saints Church at Barking and the Master appeared before him, but he confessed nothing 'in a most full interrogation'. He insisted that he had never committed the heresies of which the Order was accused and he did not wish to abjure crimes which he had never committed. He was therefore returned to prison. Imbert Blanke exhibited similar determination, despite extensive interrogations concerning receptions he had made in Clermont, so 'it was ordered that he be shut up in the most vile prison bound in double irons, and there to be kept until it was otherwise ordained, and meanwhile to be visited for the purpose of seeing if he wished to confess anything further'.[41] William de la More was sent to the Tower of London to await papal judgement; he was dead by February 1313.[42] At York, on 29 July, a council of the northern province publicly reconciled another twenty-four Templars who had similarly admitted that they had been 'so vehemently defamed by the articles in the papal bull that they could not purge themselves'.[43]

The proceedings in Scotland and Ireland added little or nothing. Indeed, in Scotland, there appear to have been only two Templars, both of whom came from England. They were examined by William Lamberton, Bishop of St Andrews, and John de Solerio, a papal clerk, on 17 November 1309, but admitted nothing, except that the Grand Master and the other leaders could absolve brothers from certain sins, except for murder and assaults on priests.[44] In Ireland, the Templars were more numerous, for here fourteen were questioned, some as many as four times. Again, their depositions had little substance, although six of them believed that their preceptors could absolve them from sin, while three said that they had sworn to work for the increase of the Order, right or wrong.[45]

The trial in the British Isles contrasts markedly with the proceedings in France. In England, despite the demands of the papal inquisitors, it seems clear that torture was not properly applied (if at all) until the summer of 1311, nearly two years after the inquisitorial proceedings had begun in England. Until this time extensive interrogation and, in some cases, threats and prolonged imprisonment, could not produce more than the admission that some brothers had failed to grasp the difference between sacramental absolution by priests and absolution by the Master for breaking the Order's rules and regulations. This is despite the fact that relations between the English and French Templars would be expected to be close; indeed the papal inquisitors tried to emphasise this themselves by the use of depositions of French Templars who had been received in England in an attempt to incriminate the English Templars, and by their report which argued that the practices followed by the Order were universally applied. Even after torture and intimidation had been used, the two leading figures among those tried in England, William de la More and Imbert Blanke, persisted in their denials. By the same token, however, it must be accepted that many brothers did believe that they were receiving a general absolution for their sins in chapter. This feature of the trial has been fully examined in an article by H. C. Lea.[46] The problem really arose from the passage of time. In the Cistercian Rule (upon which that of the Templars was based) monks had to confess to the abbot or one of the older monks, and later this was developed into public confession in chapter. However, nothing was said about absolution, because these rules originated in the early twelfth century, and it was not really until the advent of the refined scholasticism of the thirteenth century that its sacramental character was fully developed. Penance as a sacrament appears only at this time. Therefore, in the twelfth-century Rule the Master in chapter gave brothers a penance to perform for their sins, and even though he was not a priest, nothing strange was seen in this. The real mistake of some of the Templars seems to have been their failure to adapt these early practices to the Church's sacramental theory, something which could have been done once they were granted their own priests in 1139. Nevertheless, the relative numbers of priests in England remained low – there were only eight among the 144 Templars examined – and in small preceptories it is unlikely that a priest was always available. The effect was that many Templars thought that their Master was giving them a general absolution for their sins, even if they had not confessed them, and some admitted this, apparently without being aware of the development of theological opinion on the whole subject. Even so, William de la More strongly denied that he used the formula 'I absolve you' in these chapter-meetings, so in his case even this rather slight transgression could not be proved. The proceedings in the British Isles show the general failure to make the charges stick, except with the aid of torture, and indeed it is significant that the charge of unauthorised absolution in chapter was not included among the original accusations of 1307.

Late in October 1307 three Aragonese Templars travelled across the frontier to Tudela in Navarre, which was ruled by Louis, eldest son of Philip the Fair. Louis had, on 23 October, arrested the Templars of the kingdom residing at Pamplona, and the three men, perhaps recklessly or perhaps with an imperfect understanding of the situation, proposed to petition the prince on behalf of their brethren. They were promptly arrested and imprisoned. James II, King of Aragon, a man deeply sensitive to the preservation of his rights, felt obliged to protest, and asked for the immediate release of the three men, since they were native-born Aragonese, as well as asking for the release of the Templars taken at Pamplona, who had also originated in his lands. It seems that the king gained the release of the three men, but there was little hope that Louis would relinquish the Templars from Pamplona. Indeed, the French authorities in Navarre expressed some surprise that King James had not received a papal order for the arrest and seizure of the Templars in his own lands.[47]

But King James was no more enthusiastic than Edward II. Philip IV's letters of 16 and 26 October had caused him to express his 'astonishment' and 'disquiet', and he stressed that the Order had always laboured for his predecessors towards 'the exaltation of the faith and the laying low of the enemies of the cross'. As a result, his predecessors, believing that the Order was without error and that it had been instituted for the service of God, had conceded to it many

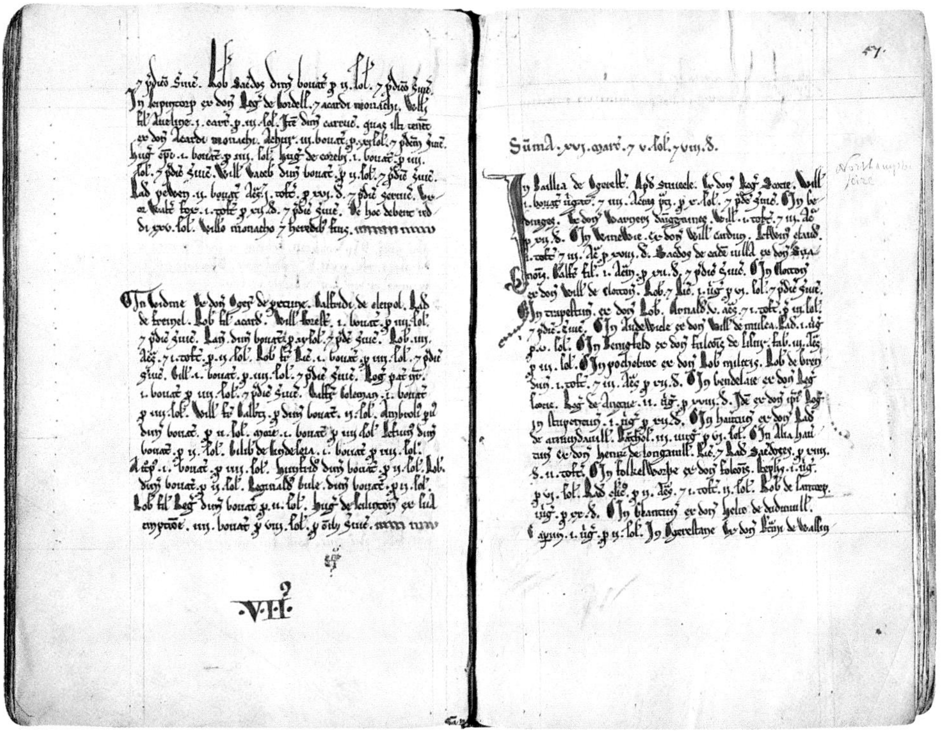

In 1185 Geoffrey Fitz Stephen, Master in England (1185–95), ordered a survey of the extent and value of the Order's estates throughout the kingdom. This information, which took five years to gather, was collected by local juries. This 'Templar Domesday' showed not only the considerable wealth of the Order in England, but also its administrative sophistication. *Right*, Edward II had initially been shocked by the accusations against the Templars. However, he was not prepared to gainsay the pope and, in December 1307, ordered their arrest in the name of the papacy

The establishment of the
Temple encouraged the foundation of new Military Orders
in the Iberian peninsula. One
of these was Calatrava,
founded in Castile in 1158,
when the Templars said they
could no longer defend the
castle. *Right*, among the
Templar preceptories in
Portugal was that of Tomar,
established in 1160. In 1319
it was occupied by the new
Order of Christ, which the
pope had conceded could be
created to take over the
property of the Temple

strong castles, towns and other places, together with other gifts. The Order was held in high regard in his part of Christendom, where no error had arisen against it; on the contrary, it had rendered the greatest service against the infidel. He would only proceed if commanded to do so by the Church and if there were clear and vehement suspicion.[48] On 19 November, two days after replying to the French king, James wrote to tell the pope of the news that he had received from Philip IV, assuring him that he did not wish to act until he knew the truth from the pope himself, and asking that if Clement knew of any error in the Temple, he would send the information to him.[49] The same attitude is shown by his contacts with the Kings of Castile and Portugal, with whom he may have been seeking a common policy, for he sent Ramón de Montros, Archdeacon of Guarda, to stress to the kings the high repute and important services of the Order and to explain that he himself would not act without papal instruction. He asked that the other two monarchs should similarly stay their hands.[50]

Suddenly however, towards the end of November, the king abruptly changed his policy. On 1 December, contrary to his protestations that he was awaiting papal instruction, he ordered his procurator in Valencia to seize the Templars and appropriate their goods there. On 5 December, Juan de Lotger, papal Inquisitor in Aragon, cited the Templars of Valencia to appear within ten days because of 'the most vehement and violent suspicion' which had arisen against the Order, and on the same day the king fixed 6 January for an assembly of bishops to consider the matter. Meanwhile, the royal forces took over the important Templar coastal fort of Peníscola without resistance, together with most of the Order's other Valencian strongholds. Some Templars fled, but large numbers were captured, including Exemen de Lenda, Master of Aragon.[51] The speed of the operation easily outpaced the papal bull, *Pastoralis praeeminentiae*, which, although it had been issued on 22 November, did not reach Aragon until 18 January.[52]

The reason for this may well have been tactical. Early in November, Exemen de Lenda wrote to his local preceptors telling them that he had had an audience with the king in which he had asked for shelter and counsel in view of the seizures which had already taken place in Navarre and France. The king had declared that he did not believe the charges to be true, but on the other hand he had to consider whether the French king, equipped as he was with excellent counsel, could have proceeded without grounds; he would therefore give his answer later. Meanwhile, the king wanted to know why the Templars were rumoured to be preparing their castles for action, but he was apparently satisfied with the explanation that this was simply a precaution against those who would seek to despoil the Order, for they had already heard of a letter from a Gascon knight to an Aragonese correspondent urging just this course. The Master nevertheless advised the Preceptor of Peníscola and the other fortress commanders to continue discreet guard upon their castles, although he hoped that the affair would eventually result in the honour of the Order.[53] The obvious anxiety of the Aragonese Master cannot have been allayed during the next few days by the persistent report that the king was leaving Daroca in order to go to besiege Peníscola.[54] Throughout November, the Templars picked up scraps of information about possible royal activity and distorted versions of events in France, and they warned each other to take care.[55] Exemen de Lenda began to change Templar property into gold so that it could be hidden with sympathisers.[56]

Cause and effect are not easy to disentangle here, but in Aragon two circumstances coincided which did not coincide in France or England. Firstly, the Aragonese Templars had warning of the possible course of events, and secondly, being in an area of active service, had considerable numbers of fighting men. James II must have decided that if he delayed too long he would lose the opportunity of gaining any tangible benefits for himself from the affair, yet would have to face the problem of possible armed Templar resistance at his own expense. Certainly he was developing an eye for the Templar property; as early as 29 December he wrote to the pope requesting that if the Order should be suppressed, certain Templar property should be made over to the monastery of Sexena where his daughter Blanche resided.[57] By 5 February he was instructing his procurator at the Roman Curia to try to secure a disreputable deal with Clement whereby James promised to enrich two of the papal nephews in his own lands in return for control over the question of the Templar property. Moreover, if the King of France received the whole of the Templar goods, then he, James, wanted a favour as well, for he was in no way prepared to allow the clergy to take over the property, as the spiritual power could not defend the land, nor would he greet with favour the intrusion of any new or existing Order. No one could have the castles, especially those on the frontiers or by the sea. In this case, the procurator could ask if the pope was interested in a division in which the king would gain the territories without the movable goods.[58] Whatever his scruples when he first heard of the arrests in France, expediency and greed had now overcome them. In these circumstances the temporary displeasure of the pope at James's precipitate action was but a minor irritation, and it cost the king nothing to apologise.[59]

But, despite the arrest of the Master in Aragon and the capture of Peníscola, James II had not been totally successful. Large and important castles, especially in Aragon itself, remained in Templar hands, and were rapidly being strengthened to resist him. Miravet, Monzón, Ascó, Cantavieja, Villel, Castellote and Chalamera had not fallen,[60] while the leadership of the Order had been taken over by the vigorous Preceptor of Mas Deu in Roussillon, Ramón Sa Guardia, who had entrenched himself at Miravet. On 8 December Ramón appealed to Queen Blanche to intervene on behalf of the Templars.[61] On the same day he wrote to the king, pointing out that the situation of the Aragonese Templars was quite different from those in France. The Aragonese Templars had shed their blood for his predecessors and for him, and in return the kings had granted them many privileges and immunities, and had made over property to them for the conflict with Christ's enemies. Everyone knew that the Templars were the first to the defence in time of war; only recently in the march against Granada and Ruhon they had spilt much blood, and the Master, Pedro de Moncada, had himself perished. As well as being active in war, the Order gave out large sums in alms, both on a daily basis and in times of famine, as when they fed twenty thousand persons at Gardeny and another six thousand at Monzón. In the terrible situation in which the Temple now found itself he thought it appropriate to remind the king too of the Order's patriotism and loyalty, pointing out how, in the time of the king's father, Pedro the Great, when the French had invaded and all the defenders of Barcelona and the surrounding districts had fled, the Templars stayed at their posts, ready to die for the king or to recover the land which had been lost. For these reasons the king should release the Master and brothers, for 'we are loyal, Catholic and good Christians'. He therefore asked for nothing but justice and a proper hearing before they were convicted. The king replied briefly and generally. 'What we have now done, we have done as a most Catholic prince and in the future we will also act in accordance with truth and justice.'[62]

This seems to have induced a hardening of resolve at Miravet. 'God knows', wrote Ramón Sa Guardia on 26 January, 'that I pity you, the King of France, and all Catholics in relation to the harm which arises from all this, more than ourselves who have to endure the evil.' He had every reason to suspect that great misfortune would result from the delusion, shared by King James, King Philip and the other Catholic princes, that they were serving God, when in fact they were serving the devil. He was willing to demonstrate the Order's method of admission by reference to the Rule which had been given by the Church to the Temple. Why else would so many noble and well-bred men, from the time of the Order's foundation, have been willing to enter it for sixty years or more for their salvation? How could anyone imagine that such people would have remained in the Order, if the things which had been said about it were true? Ramón offered to come to the king under a safe-conduct, and to show him how he could withdraw from the affair with honour, profit and dignity.[63]

King James now decided to besiege the castles, having failed to persuade the Templars to respond to the inquisitorial citation.[64] On 1 February there seem to have been about two hundred defenders of Miravet, including some young nobles who were not Templars, but who had joined them in the castle, perhaps from bravado or a sense of chivalry. The besiegers were initially seventy in number, there being only forty before Miravet, while at Ascó there were only ten during the day and twenty at night. This was hardly a serious effort, but on 13 February it was decided to construct a siege engine at Miravet, a move which perhaps marked the beginning of a more concerted attack. Certainly when, early in March, the king offered free passage to all non-Templars in Miravet, most seem to have departed. Even so, the king, perhaps mindful of the expense, never threw his full force behind the siege, and no frontal assault was therefore possible, most of the fighting being confined to skirmishing, leaving supplies the Templars' chief worry.[65]

Meanwhile, the king and Ramón Sa Guardia continued to maintain contact, which suggests that both sides still hoped to end the fighting by negotiation; certainly the siege seems to have been half-hearted. On 21 April, Bernart Cespujades, *Viguier* of Tortosa, wrote to tell the king that Ramón Sa Guardia had repeatedly stated his willingness to surrender, provided that the king would give the Templars protection while Pope Clement remained under the domination of the King of France. If King James would then speak to the pope on their behalf, they would hand over to the king the castle of Monzón and provide the queen with an equivalent gift from their salt tax, together with an annual rent of 30,000 *solidi*. If the king would meet with Ramón Sa Guardia at Tortosa, then the preceptor would show him how he could emerge from this affair with honour.[66] Three days after, Ramón wrote direct to the king, having apparently failed to gain a satisfactory answer. This time his tone was much more aggressive. If the king wished to take Miravet by force, it would be very costly in terms of lives and money. The pope had not ordered that they should be attacked or killed, nor 'did he will that our goods be sold and dissipated through all the world, as the royal officials are doing'. They stood by their defence, as they stood without blame or guilt, and were prepared to die as martyrs.[67]

On 10 May a royal representative, Pedro de Queralt, reported that he had seen Ramón Sa Guardia the day before, and had been told that the defenders of Miravet were prepared to accept the dissolution of their Order or to transfer to another Order or to a new Order, but they could not accept a situation in which the pope declared them heretics, in which case they would defend themselves honourably and die in their castles. In the meantime, they asked if an armistice could be arranged in which the Templars would remain in Miravet, but the king would have the guard of the castle outside the keep. In return they requested supplies of fresh meat and money for bread and drink.[68] But James was not prepared to accept conditions of the kind proposed by Ramón Sa Guardia during April and May. There were still the suspicion of heresy and the infamy of the Order to be considered, together with the danger that they would be convicted of contumacy. There was nothing that he could do concerning the pope. 'The pope possesses all omniscience and is the deputy of God; he also rules all creatures . . . we can place on him no stipulations.'[69] At the end of June, with the king's permission, a Majorcan noble, Ramón de Canet, who was a relative of Ramón Sa Guardia, visited the Templars at Miravet. He reported to the king that all the knights remained true to their Order and their honour. Next to God, King James was everything to them, but nevertheless the Templars would not allow Sa Guardia out to talk to the king without a safe-conduct.[70]

So the Templars struggled on, their situation slowly deteriorating as the months passed. By the end of October they seem to have reached crisis point. Ramón Sa Guardia made one more effort to involve the pope in some direct interest in their fate when he wrote to Arnold, Abbot of Fontfroide and papal vice-chancellor, recalling the nine months of siege and telling him that they would defend the fortress to the death. He asked the abbot to plead their case with the pope so that he would persuade the king to raise the siege. The tone is still defiant: 'As for the crimes and abominations which have been imputed to us, we choose to justify ourselves, us and our brothers, as true Christian and Catholic knights, by arms, or otherwise accord-ing to canonical and legitimate rules, or in such manner as the lord pope would wish it.'[71] But in reality they were on the verge of surrender. On 18 October Berenguer de San Justo, commander of Miravet, had already written to the king, reminding him once more of the services rendered to him and his family, but also describing the increase in suffering and sickness in the castle, and asking for meat, wine and vegetables in return for some costly gifts, including two rings. But the king now realised his advantage and declined the offer, saying that he sympathised with their condition, but there was nothing that he could do about it.[72] Miravet finally capitulated at the end of November 1308; sixty-three men were still in the almost completely bare castle, most of whom were sent to Tortosa, where they were kept in a reasonably tolerant captivity.[73] Some of the other Templar castles had already fallen: Cantavieja in August, Villel in October, and Castellote shortly before Miravet in early Novem-ber.[74] The most valuable, Monzón, with an estimated income of between 40,000 and 50,000 *solidi* per annum, excluding the tithe of wine, oil and meat, held out until May 1309, when it eventually fell by treachery.[75] Hostilities finally came to an end in July 1309 with the fall of Chalamera and the intervention of the papal envoy, Bertrand, Prior of Saint-Cassiano in Béziers, who had been sent in response to the Templar offer to submit to the pope.[76]

An attempt was now made to proceed in the manner set out by

the papal bulls of August 1308. The Archbishop of Tarragona and the Bishop of Valencia had been named as custodians of the Templar lands and goods in Aragon,[77] and the appropriate inquiries were initiated. Some fragments of a hearing of thirty-two Aragonese Templars, together with some outside witnesses, held at the house of the Dominicans at Lérida, have survived for February 1310.[78] None of the Templars themselves admitted the charges, but the outside witnesses were divided in their opinions. Pedro Olivonis, Dominican prior of the convent at Lérida, said that he had heard from a certain Ferrario de Bigleto, the king's vicar at Tarragona at the time of the Templars' arrest, that it was said that they adored heads. When he had dined with Ferrario de Lileto, his uncle, who was a Templar priest, he had many times seen a cord which the priest had worn above his shirt, attached to which was a silver head with a beard, and from this 'he presumed that it was true that the Templars adored heads'. In contrast Pedro de Podio, warden of the Franciscan convent at Lérida, 'had heard the confessions of many Templars, many times, and they seemed to him to be good Christians'. Several witnesses 'believed evil' of the Templars, especially because of the secrecy of their receptions and because of chance remarks that they had heard individual Templars make, but none could muster any concrete evidence.

From the papal point of view the proceedings were hindered, as in England, by the almost complete prohibition on torture under Aragonese law. For many of the Templars their freedom was restricted for more than three years while the inquiries were going on, but conditions seem to have been considerably better than in France. Diet included meat three days a week as well as fish and eggs, although there were complaints about the insufficiency of clothing. At certain periods irons seem to have been used, causing swollen joints and inflammation, especially among the older Templars, but there is no evidence to suggest systematic cruelty of the kind applied in France.[79] Accordingly, the pope wrote from Avignon in March 1311 ordering that the Archbishop of Tarragona and the Bishop of Valencia arrange for some of the Templars to be tortured in order to obtain 'the full truth'.[80] Torture seems to have been applied to eight Templars at Barcelona in August 1311, but it failed to produce any confessions.[81] Eventually the hearings in Aragon seemed to peter out, the fate of individual Templars being left to local councils such as that of Tarragona, which on 4 November 1312 declared the Templars innocent of the crimes charged to them, and free of all infamy, 'although they were put to the torture towards the confession of the crimes'.[82]

The kingdom most closely associated with the Aragonese crown was that of Majorca, which was ruled by a cadet branch of the Aragonese royal family. Majorca was much smaller than Aragon and its lands more scattered, consisting not only of the Balearic Islands but also including the mainland Counties of Roussillon and Cerdagne and the Lordship of Montpellier. King James I was in no position to challenge the King of France or to resist papal authority in this matter, even had he been inclined to do so, and the arrests of the Templars seem to have been carried out reasonably promptly following the issue of *Pastoralis praeeminentiae* on 22 November 1307.[83] Most of the documentation for this kingdom comes from Roussillon, which was in the diocese of the Bishop of Elne, and relates to the Templars of the important Preceptory of Mas Deu, of which Ramón Sa Guardia was the commander. Mas Deu had command of seven subsidiary preceptories, and the personnel were scattered, mostly in ones and twos, in these dependencies. At the time of the arrest, twenty-six members were taken into custody, to which number was added Ramón Sa Guardia in August 1309 after he had been extradited from Aragon. Probably these men were little different from those arrested in the Kingdom of France, mostly following peaceful agricultural pursuits.

Despite the reasonably efficient arrests, no hearings began before 1310. Ramón Costa, Bishop of Elne, was the suffragan of Gilles Aicelin, Archbishop of Narbonne, from whom Ramon received the relevant documents, including a copy of *Faciens misericordiam* and the 127 articles. The archbishop ordered that the papal commands be carried out in a letter dated 5 May 1309, but the Bishop of Elne did not begin his inquiry until Wednesday 14 January 1310, explaining that the delay had been caused by his illness and that even now he was not fully recovered. In accordance with the papal instructions the bishop assembled a commission, consisting of two canons from his cathedral, and two Dominicans and two Franciscans from Perpignan.[84]

During the second half of January the episcopal commission heard the depositions of twenty-five Templars, whose years of service ranged from four to thirty-seven. All these men unambiguously asserted their innocence. Bartholomé de Turri, a priest with twenty-nine years' service, was the first to appear and his replies are typical.

> He believed firmly and in no way doubted that the Lord Jesus Christ was and will be the Word of God the Father, and had assumed human nature and proceeded from the sacred womb of the most holy Mary for ever the Virgin, his mother, in whom he was conceived by the Holy Spirit and without male insemination, and suffered not for his sins, but for ours, and had arisen from death on the third day.

He denied the charge of homosexuality, nor did he believe that any Templars followed such practices, 'as on to the sons of defiance, there descends and comes the wrath of God'. He agreed that they wore cords above their shirts, 'because it is written in the gospel of Luke: *Sint lumbi vestri precincti*, etc.', adding that a cord was worn by all the brothers from the day of reception and that it was an observance of the Order. They did not touch idols with it. His reception and those of others which he had seen, including four priests and two knights, had been entirely orthodox.

Other witnesses were equally assertive. Pierre Bleda said that if the Grand Master had confessed to the charges then 'he lied in his gullet in a false manner'. No suspicions should arise from the secrecy of the chapters, and 'if by chance they suspected the contrary, he believed them to have sinned, and may the Lord spare them'. Béren-ger de Collo, a knight, said that

> on account of reverence of the crucified Lord Jesus, all brothers of the Order wore a cross on their cloaks. And as Jesus Christ shed his own blood on the cross on our behalf, in significance of that the brothers of the Order wore a cross of red cloth on their cloak, as they shed their own blood against the enemies of Christ, the Saracens in the lands beyond the sea, and against other enemies of the Christian faith.

Ramón Sapte, a priest from Mas Deu, maintained that 'if by chance some should have confessed . . . he believed that they are and were not men, but wholly infernal demons who were naturally accustomed to speak falsely'.

Ramón Sa Guardia himself appeared on 20 January. He had been received thirty-five years before by Pedro de Moncada, then Master in Aragon and Catalonia. The crimes contained in the first article, which concerned the denial of Christ, were 'horrible, exceedingly heinous and diabolical'. Receptions were entirely orthodox, and the knights followed the proper observances of the Church with regard to confession, mass and the cross. Concerning the accusation of homosexuality,

> according to the statute of the said Order any brother committing sin against nature ought to lose the habit of his religion, and should be delivered into perpetual imprisonment, being placed with great shackles on the feet and chains on the neck, and iron fetters on the hands, where he should have for sustenance the bread of sadness and the water of tribulation and should finish the remaining time of his life.

Brothers who confessed were liars. He believed that the errors 'never originated from a good spirit, but had a malign and diabolical spirit', nor did he believe that any of them had existed in the Order.

This picture of devout observance was only slightly marred by two Templars whose grasp of the questions and recall of past events were sufficiently faulty to raise doubts about the extent to which they were able to follow the Order's observances. Ramón Rulli could not answer the questions about his reception, since 'he did not know what was meant by *habentur pro professis*, since he was a simple man, rude and lay', while Arnold Calis, a venerable Templar of thirty-seven years' service, could not remember the observances and method of his reception, 'since he was an old man and always given to the country and the custody of the animals of the said house [Mas Deu]. Moreover, his ignorance was because of the very long lapse of time since the aforesaid.' However, both denied the charges presented to them. The proceedings were officially closed by the Bishop of Elne on 31 August 1310, with nothing more concrete against the Order and its individuals than in Aragon.

In the Kingdoms of Castile–León and Portugal, arrests must have been made some time in 1308, for two commissions were set up following the issue of *Faciens misericordiam* in August. In Castile the leading members were the Archbishops of Toledo and Compostela and the Bishop of Palencia. At Medina del Campo the Archbishop of Compostela questioned thirty Templars and three other witnesses. For Portugal, the Bishop of Lisbon presided over an inquiry at Orense, before which appeared twenty-eight Templars and six other witnesses.[85] In neither inquiry could anything incriminating be found, and once again the provincial councils – like that of Salamanca in October 1310 – failed to find any substance in the charges.[86] It has sometimes been argued that the Iberian rulers favoured a verdict which cleared the Templars, at least partly because it gave these rulers a better chance of acquiring the Order's lands – a verdict of guilty might have sent these possessions straight into the hands of the Holy See – but it must also be stressed that, with the exception of Navarre, which was decisively within the French sphere of influence, the proceedings in Iberia failed to dredge up as much against the Templars as even the pitifully small result in England.

In Italy and Germany, which also contained Templar preceptories, although on a considerably smaller scale than in France and Spain, political fragmentation brought varied results and inconsistent application of papal directives. In Italy there were seven papal and episcopal commissions set up, divisions which reflect the political diversity of the peninsula rather than give any indication of the number of Templars present, which appears to have been quite small.[87] Fragmentary material from some of these inquiries survives. The only unified monarchy of these regions was that of Charles II, King of Naples, who was the uncle of Philip IV and could therefore be expected to follow the French line. Presumably torture and other forms of pressure were used in the Neapolitan lands, but there are few depositions extant. In April 1310, at Luceria, six Templars appeared and confessed to the main charge of denial of Christ. The first of these, Galcerand de Teus, who had been received in Catalonia, added an elaborate explanation for the practice of lay absolution in chapter. The terms of the absolution were as follows: 'I pray God that he will pardon you your sins as he pardoned them to Saint Mary Magdalene and the thief who was put on the cross.' By 'the thief', it ought to be understood that according to the Templar statutes, this referred to 'that Jesus or Christ' who was crucified by the Jews, and who said that 'he was God and King of the Jews in contempt of him who is the true God in Heaven'. For Jesus, as he approached death, was pierced in the side by a lance from Longinus, and

> he repented that he had said that he was God the King of the Jews, and having in this way repented concerning his sin, he asked pardon from the true God and thus the true God spared him and therefore we know concerning that Christ crucified these words: As God pardoned the thief who was hung on the cross.

This witness had also heard of a cat who, in the time of the mastership of Philippe de Nablus (1169–71), had appeared in chapters and had been adored, although this cat had not been seen recently.[88] An inquiry presided over by Bartolomeo, Archbishop of Brindisi, contains the depositions of only two serving brothers, who appeared on 4 June 1310. Giovanni di Nardò, preceptor of a local house, admitted that he had denied a cross, and that the assembled company had trampled on it. Nardò joined with them, but when they had urinated on the cross, he claimed that he was not able to do so because he had urinated only a short while before. He agreed with the inquisitor that he would have done so had he been able. He had done these things because he had been threatened that he would be thrown into a latrine if he refused. He confessed also to kissing, on his bare stomach, the Master who had received him and to the adoration of a grey cat which had appeared in chapters. He agreed that he had been negligent in not reporting these errors to the proper authorities, but claimed in mitigation that he was 'simple and rustic'. The other serving brother, Hugo de Samaya, reported nothing amiss about his reception, but admitted that later, while he was serving in Cyprus, he had been forced to deny Christ, having been told that it was the custom of the Order.[89]

In the Papal State there is no record of the initial seizures, but a commission under the Bishop of Sutri and Master Pandolfo di Sabello did perambulate the region, visiting Rome, Viterbo, Spoleto, Aquila, Penne, Chieti, Albano, Segni, Castel Fajole, Tivoli and Palombara between October 1309 and July 1310. The results of this protracted travelling were negligible. Most of the imprisoned Templars refused to defend the Order or to testify, while outside witnesses were not very informative. Torture brought some confessions of denial and spitting and talk of idol worship.[90]

In Lombardy many of the prelates were openly favourable towards the Templars and it is not surprising that many found the courage to declare their innocence in these circumstances. In 1309, in the Mark of Ancona, the Bishop of Fano heard only one Templar and nineteen outside witnesses, but could find no incriminating evidence. The Archbishop of Ravenna and the Bishop of Rimini interrogated two Templars at Cesena, and both stated their innocence. One of these, Andrea di Siena, said that he had heard that many brothers had confessed because they were afraid of torture, but he knew nothing of the articles of accusation, nor had he heard anything about them before. If he had heard any such thing he would have left the Order and denounced it to the Inquisition. He maintained that 'he would rather have gone begging, asking for bread, than remain with such men, and indeed would rather have died, because the safety of the soul is to be preferred before all things'.[91] After some postponements and changes of venue, a council was assembled at Ravenna under the archbishop on 18 June 1311. Seven Templars appeared before it, all denied the charges, and a proposal that torture be employed was voted down. It was ruled that the innocent be freed and the guilty punished. 'Innocence' was interpreted in a way unique for the trial, being taken to include those who had confessed for fear of torture, but had then revoked. Finally, the council recommended that the Order as a whole should be preserved if the majority of its members were found innocent.[92]

The inquiries relating to the province of Tuscany were held at Florence by the Archbishop of Pisa and the Bishop of Florence in September 1311. Earlier in the year the pope had ordered the use of torture in Lombardy and Tuscany, and the inquisition was conducted with this in mind.[93] Thirteen Templars were examined, of whom six made comprehensive confessions, led by Egidio, Preceptor of San Gimignano. However, the other seven had denied the articles, and these depositions the inquisitors decided not to insert in the record, since some witnesses were agricultural labourers and not Templars, while others, having only recently joined the Order, did not properly know the Order's secrets, even although tortured.[94]

Action in Germany was equally confused, and much depended upon the political inclinations of local rulers and the speed with which local groups of Templars reacted. A typical series of events took place in the summer of 1308, when Burchard, Archbishop of Magdeburg, took energetic measures against the Templars, imprisoning a number of them, including Frederick von Alvensleben, Preceptor of Germany. But this brought him into conflict with the Bishop of Halberstadt, who believed that his rights had been infringed and therefore took it upon himself to excommunicate the archbishop. Clement V himself was forced to intervene when he revoked the excommunication in September 1310.[95]

In response to the pope's demands, several provincial councils were called in the Rhineland in 1310 and 1311. At Trier, for instance, the archbishop heard a number of witnesses and ended by acquitting the Order.[96] Peter von Aspelt, Archbishop of Mainz, had a less easy passage. On 14 May 1310, while his council was in session, he was suddenly confronted by Hugo von Salm, Templar Preceptor at Grumbach, who burst in accompanied by twenty fully armed knights. The archbishop, clearly frightened, asked the preceptor to be seated and if he had anything that he wished to put to them. Hugo said that he and his brothers understood that this council had been assembled on the orders of the pope for the purpose of destroying the Order, and that the Templars had been charged with enormous crimes. This was most harsh and intolerable, especially since they had been condemned without a proper hearing or conviction, which was why, in the presence of the fathers assembled there, they appealed to a future pope and all his clergy. He also publicly protested that those who had constantly denied these enormities had been delivered up to the fire, but that God had shown their innocence by a miracle, for the red cross and white mantle which they wore would not burn. The archbishop, frightened that there would be a riot, admitted their protest and replied that he would take the matter up with the pope.[97]

It seems that the effect of this was to break up the council, which did not reassemble until 1 July. This family clearly had a taste for the dramatic gesture, for when Frederick von Salm, Hugo's brother and Preceptor of the Rhine province of the Templars, appeared, he offered to prove the Order's innocence by submission to the red-hot-iron ordeal. He told the council that he had been twelve years in the Order and had had extensive experience in Outremer, where he knew Jacques de Molay well. The Grand Master he 'held and still held to be a good Christian, as good as any Christian could be'. In all, thirty-seven Templars deposed and asserted their innocence. Twelve outside witnesses, three of whom were counts, also spoke in favour of the Order, including a priest who, recalling a time of great famine when a measure of grain, which commonly sold for 10 *sous* or less, was fetching 33 *sous*, asserted that during that period the Templars at the local preceptory of Masteire fed a thousand paupers each day.[98] The result was that the archbishop gave a judgement favourable to the Templars, much to the irritation of Pope Clement, who annulled the decision, claiming that it appertained to him alone.[99]

Although there were scattered Templar preceptories in, for instance, the parts of Greece which still remained in Latin hands, the one major trial of the Templars which took place outside western Europe was in Cyprus, which remained the headquarters of the Order. The position of the Templars on the island was greatly complicated by the unstable political situation, in which the Templars were much more deeply involved than they were in any other country. Jacques de Molay had never been very friendly with Henry II, King of Cyprus, whom he regarded as an opponent of his efforts to revive the crusade and to establish a base on the Palestinian mainland.[100] Molay had not been alone in his opposition to the king. On 26 April 1306 a revolt led by the king's brother, Amaury de Lusignan, and supported by a number of powerful lords, deposed Henry and set up Amaury as Governor of the island, and local chroniclers claimed that Jacques de Molay was party to this revolt.[101]

Certainly when the papal orders to arrest the Templars arrived in the island on 6 May 1308,[102] Amaury seems to have been reluctant to move against them in any strength. On 12 May, Balian d'Ibelin, titular Prince of Galilee, was sent to Limassol, where the leading officials of the Order were staying, to ask them to comply with the papal order that they and their goods should be placed under guard. They should give up their arms and horses, and accept what seems to have been envisaged as a kind of house-arrest in the palace of the Archbishop of Nicosia. The chief Templar official left on the island was Ayme d'Oselier, the marshal, and he felt strong enough to negotiate. Although he was prepared to allow the Templar estates to be removed from his direct control, he would not give up his arms, nor would he let the Order's treasure out of his sight, asking that it be kept wherever the Templars themselves were to be placed. He had a suggestion for this too: they should retreat to one of their estates, where they would be guarded by a force of secular knights, until papal judgement was received.

There was little Balian d'Ibelin could do and he returned to Nicosia to deliver the reply to Amaury de Lusignan. This seems to have stiffened the Governor's attitude, and he forbade all financial dealings with the Templars, and on 19 May sent another emissary, Baldwin, a canon of the Cathedral of Nicosia, with the threatening message that unless the Templars obeyed he would cause them to be put to death and entirely annihilated. But the Templars now proposed that the whole matter should wait until September, during which time a galley should be sent to carry messages from the two sides to Pope Clement, who it was expected would then send them his decision. Amaury could not accept this proposal either, and he tried once more, this time sending Andrea Tartarol, a canon of Famagusta. He found the Templar leaders, including the marshal and the turcopolier, at the castle of Nisso, which was about five leagues from Nicosia and which belonged to Raymond Visconte, a local lord. Here a meeting was arranged and, on 24 May, agreement was reached. Three days later Ayme d'Oselier, together with the other Templar leaders, presented himself before Amaury de Lusignan in Nicosia. Then the Templars read a public statement of belief before an assembly of clergy and people, which was translated into French by Canon Baldwin so that all the hearers would understand. Baldwin stated that the Templars were good Christians who had always fought hard for the Christian faith, especially at the castle of Safed and in many other places. The Order's leaders, together with two sergeants, then swore an oath adhering to their statement on behalf of all the other brothers in Cyprus, who numbered eighty-three knights and thirty-five sergeants or serving brothers.

Meanwhile, the Governor had secretly sent a force of knights and foot-soldiers to Limassol, while on the night of 28 May he held his own assembly of clergy, knights and people, at which he had the contents of the papal letters, with the accounts of the trial in France and the articles of accusation, read out. The next day, his officials began to inventory the Templar property at Nicosia, although the Templars had already secretly removed most of the valuables to

This illustration from the *Libro de Acedrex, Dados e Tablas* of King Alfonso X of Castile (1252–84) shows two Spanish Templars playing chess, although, according to the French Rule, brothers were not allowed to play board games. *Below*, at the Council of Vienne in May 1312, Clement V granted the Templar lands to the Hospitallers. However, the Spanish kings argued that they constituted a special case and, in 1317, James II of Aragon obtained papal permission to form the new Order of Montesa, which received both Templar and Hospitaller lands in Valencia. This altarpiece of the *Madonna of Mercy* was painted by Antonio Peris for the Masters of Montesa in *c.*1410

Like other religious Orders, the Templars maintained representatives at the papal Curia. Here the Order's lobbying for further help against the infidel is satirised by the Flemish poet Jacquemart Giélée in his *Renart le Nouvel* (1289). *Left*, this marginal sketch from the Memoranda Rolls of the English Exchequer shows the profiles of Edward I and Philip IV, whose confrontations over Gascony contributed to the financial problems of both monarchs

Limassol. Similar action was taken at the Templar houses at Paphos and Famagusta. Ayme d'Oselier left Nicosia with most of his men, returned to Limassol, and on 29 May took up arms ready to fight. He appears however to have been outmanoeuvred by Amaury's forces, for the Templars were caught and besieged at Limassol and, on Saturday 1 June, surrendered. The usual inventories were taken, and the arms and various food supplies were seized. The total amount of money found was about 120,000 white *besants*, but apparently much larger sums had been hidden in a secret place. Some of the Templars, under the marshal, were confined in the castle of Khirokitia, while the remainder, under the commander, were sent to Yermasoyia. However, the leaders are reported to have plotted their escape by trying to procure an armed galley from Genoa, and as a consequence, the marshal, the commander, the draper, the turcopolier, the treasurer and the commander of Apulia were taken to the castle of Lefcara, where presumably they were more secure.[103]

There followed a long delay, for there were no hearings in Cyprus until May 1310. Probably the two papal representatives, Bartholomé, Abbot of Alet, and Thomas, Arch-Priest of St John of Rieti, did not arrive until the spring of that year. Together with the Bishops of Limassol and Famagusta, they heard their first witness on 1 May, depositions being taken from twenty-one witnesses in all during a sitting lasting five days. None of these witnesses were Templars: sixteen were knights (including Philippe d'Ibelin, seneschal of the kingdom, and Renaud de Soissons, the marshal); there were two abbots, and three burghers.[104] In view of the Templars' political activity over the previous two decades, it might have been expected that at least some of these witnesses would have vented stored-up grievances, perhaps in the form of malicious stories, yet this was not the case. Some commented on the secrecy of their receptions, which was an occasion for suspicion, or they remembered rumours that the Templars promised to augment the goods of the Order by whatever means came to hand, but they had nothing substantially hostile to say. Most spoke positively in favour of the Order. Renaud de Soissons 'had seen them in churches and in the divine offices devoted to the faith'. Aygue de Bessan, a prominent noble who supported King Henry II,[105] said that he knew nothing about the accusations against the Order 'under peril of his soul, except all good'. Jacques de Plany, a knight who was present at the fall of Acre in 1291, testified that he had seen many Templars spill their blood that day on behalf of the Christian faith, and Guillaume de Beaujeu, the Grand Master of that time, died fighting for the Christian faith, unlike many other knights, who fled. The Templars were 'good and honest religious, as ever any other religious of the world, as far as he could see and perceive'.

Two knights, Pierre Isan and Raymond de Bentho, had been among those deputed to guard the Templars during the two years since they had surrendered, and had therefore had an opportunity to observe them at close quarters. Pierre Isan had seen a young Templar who was gravely ill, many times hold in his hands a cross on which was depicted Christ's image, saying, 'You are the true God, the son of God, O my Saviour, and the Creator of me and of the whole world; I invoke you, Christ alone, to my aid, that you can save me at this time and others.' And saying this 'he crossed over to the Lord'. Raymond de Bentho had seen the Templars fight against the Saracens as well as or better than other Christians, and he had seen them revere the cross in Syria and in Cyprus. But he had been sent by Amaury de Lusignan to guard the Templars at the castle of Khirokitia, and because of what he had heard in the papal letters his mind had been very much turned against them. He did not wish to hear mass with the Templars, nor to participate in anything with them; on the contrary he avoided their company as much as he was able. But he lacked a priest with whom he could conveniently hear mass and so one day he joined with the Templars to hear the divine offices. But when the priest lifted the body of Christ to the altar, the host appeared to him as great as an *oblea* and white as snow. He told no one, but afterwards went to the priest and asked him to show him the hosts that had been used, and he saw that they were smaller than a *gros tournois*. He believed therefore that there had been a divine miracle which had occurred because of his wrong presumptions against the Templars. Thereafter, he began to join the Templars at meals and divine services.

Between 5 and 21 May the Templars themselves were questioned. There are seventy-six extant depositions, reflecting the high proportion of fighting men that would be expected in Cyprus. At least thirty-eight of these men were knights, but there was only one priest and one other man – a smith – of the twenty-three designated as sergeants or serving brothers who had a specifically non-military occupation.[106] There is nothing in this piece of evidence to suggest that the Order in its front-line province was suffering from an accretion of too many members seeking merely a comfortable living, a fatal sign of internal decline for any monastic Order. Their years of service ranged from three up to forty-three, but none would admit the crimes of which they were accused. Ayme d'Oselier maintained that 'there never were any errors'. Between 1 and 4 June, another batch of thirty-five non-Templar witnesses seemed to confirm this assertion of innocence.[107] These witnesses included a wide sector of society, taking in priests, canons, friars, monks, knights and burghers, but none recounted anything incriminating about the Templars. Many of them had known the Templars for years and had seen nothing wrong: they had always celebrated the divine offices properly, they gave large quantities of alms in the form of bread, meat and money, they provided hospitals, and many of them had been decapitated by the Saracens rather than renounce Christ. Perocius, a burgher from Famagusta, said that he did not believe article ten, which concerned the abuse of the cross, because he had seen a Templar priest in Nicosia, with cross in hand, excommunicate devils from the body of a woman from Montaro.

These proceedings were dramatically interrupted on the evening of Friday 5 June, when the mutilated body of Amaury de Lusignan, the Governor, was discovered stuffed beneath the stairs in his house at Nicosia. There is no clear evidence to indicate that partisans of King Henry II were responsible for this, but, in any event, it did pave the way for the king's restoration in August 1310.[108] The new regime could hardly be expected to be favourable to the Templars, but there is no apparent connection between the return of Henry II and the letters of Clement V of August 1311, which ordered a new trial for the Templars, backed by the use of torture.[109] Clement was evidently dissatisfied with the results of the inquiry of May and June 1310, and he instructed Pierre de Plaine-Cassagne, Bishop of Rodez and papal legate in the east, to act with the inquisitors.[110] Nothing is known about these new proceedings, but the chronicler Francesco Amadi records under the year 1316 that Ayme d'Oselier, the marshal, and many other Templars died in the dungeon of the castle of Kerynia.[111] The marshal may have been put there because of his supposed complicity in a plot against the king in June 1311,[112] but the presence of other Templars does suggest that the new trial found against the knights, with or without the complicity of King Henry II.

The trial of the Templars outside France demonstrates very clearly the ineffectiveness of both French and papal pretensions beyond certain limits, and emphasises the broader developments of European history in the later middle ages. Christendom was becoming a group of separate political units, in which even the most powerful of those units had great difficulty in exercising a decisive influence beyond its own sphere. On a narrower front, the weakness of the proof and the dependence upon torture to secure the condemnation of the Templars is clearly demonstrated and must form an important part of any discussion concerning the veracity or otherwise of the charges laid against the Order by the French king.

9: The Suppression

Clement V opened the first session of his great ecumenical council with a sermon in the Cathedral at Vienne on Saturday 16 October 1311. The assembled clergy were to consider the three great matters of the Order of the Temple, aid to the Holy Land, and reform of the Church.[1] Injunctions to attend had been sent out to at least 161 prelates, apart from the clergy of the papal Curia itself and the suffragans of these prelates. Representatives were to come from all over Christendom, from Italy, France, the Empire, the Iberian peninsula, the British Isles, Scandinavia and eastern Europe, as well as the four great patriarchs of the Church after the pope. The council was to be truly universal, for it encompassed the Irish sees in the west at one extreme, and the Archbishopric of Riga in the east at the other.[2] The great princes had been invited: the King of the Romans, and the Kings of France, England and the Iberian peninsula, as well as the Kings of Sicily, Hungary, Bohemia, Cyprus and Scandinavia.[3] But even as the official opening was completed and the blessing given to the congregation, the project was already turning sour. More than a third of the prelates did not come in person, a contemporary placing the number at 114.[4] No kings appeared except for Philip the Fair, who did not come until the following spring, and who was in attendance not to participate in the work of reform, but to pressurise the pope on the specific issue of the Templars. He stayed only long enough to achieve his object. Some clergy, although specifically summoned, failed to appear at all or to give sufficient excuse, and the next year Clement was obliged to suspend them from their duties for disobedience.[5] The Parisian chronicler the canon Jean de Saint-Victor commented, 'It was said by many that the council was created for the purpose of extorting money.'[6] The chosen town was not well liked. On 9 November Ramón, the Bishop of Valencia, wrote to King James II of Aragon, 'It is very tedious here, since the land is cold beyond measure, and for that reason it is not suited to my age. The place is small, with a multitude of people, and therefore crowded. As a result many remain inconvenienced, but it is necessary to endure it with patience.' The pope had authorised certain persons to look into the affair of the Templars, but Ramón was not sanguine about the speed with which the proceedings could be completed, for there were so many facets to examine.[7] This is hardly the language of the Church militant, staffed by prelates eager to participate in the work of reform and moral regeneration. The cynicism, both lay and clerical, which had accumulated during the thirteenth century weighed heavily upon the pontificate of Clement V, and it was not to be allayed by the conduct of affairs at Vienne, where the French ascendancy in the Church was all too visible.[8] The course of the Council of Vienne was to justify fully the attitude of those who approached the proceedings with less than unqualified enthusiasm.

In the months preceding the council Clement had been active in gathering the evidence against the Templars which he intended to present at Vienne. But the inquiries in countries other than France had not been terminated so abruptly, and as late as August 1311 Clement was still hastily sending out instructions for the torture of recalcitrants in Castile, Aragon, Portugal, Tuscany, Lombardy, Cyprus and Latin Greece so that the expected confessions could be sent to Vienne.[9] The material which was received was examined by the pope at the Priory of Grazean, where he was staying with some of his cardinals immediately prior to the council, and by a special group of prelates and other educated men sitting at Malaucène, near Orange, in the same region.[10] It was probably this group which produced the *rubricae* or summaries of the proceedings in a convenient form for the council.

Only the summary of the trial in England has survived, but if this example is any way typical, then it would be difficult to argue that Clement's commission had done its work without bias, for the emphasis is heavily on the gossip and hearsay from outside witnesses to the exclusion of the consistent denials of the charges made by the great majority of the Templars in the British Isles. The articles concerning the denial of Christ, for instance, are considered to have been proved by the confessions of two Templars, one of whom, Geoffroi de Gonneville, Preceptor of Aquitaine, had originally been received in London, but whose confession was made in the very different circumstances of the trial in France, although no mention is made of this in the summary. Thirteen other witnesses, only one of whom was a Templar, are quoted as corroboratory evidence. None could provide direct evidence, although all had heard about the denial. One, a lord called John de Heure, claimed that he had read in the book of a certain Templar that Christ was not the Son of God, nor born of a virgin, but was from the seed of Joseph, the husband of Mary, conceived in the same way as other men, and that he was not Christ, but a false prophet, not crucified for the redemption of the human race, but because of his own shameful acts.

Similar stories are quoted in proof of other charges. Thomas de Redemer, a Dominican, seems to have been particularly useful. Concerning the accusations centred on the spitting, trampling and urinating on the cross, he told a story of how

a certain Templar, mortally ill in the house of his sister, had forbidden this sister in any way to allow his body to be stripped after death. However, she, being curious, believing that she would find a sign of sanctity, stripped the body and found an image of a crucifix hanging on the bare flesh next to the anus.

On the charge relating to the Templars' supposed lack of belief in the sacrament of the altar, Thomas de Redemer had heard from one Reginald de Braybof, a Dominican, that a Templar who had recently died at Lincoln had 'received the body of Christ from the hand of the priest, and preserving it intact in his mouth until he had left this priest, he spat it into a urinal'. This pattern was repeated on the other major charges. On the matter of indecent kissing, a Richard Berard said that he had heard, twenty-five years before, that a certain Hospitaller, after quarrelling with the Templars, called them 'anus kissers'. On homosexuality, a London notary, Robert de Dorturer, claimed that Guy de Foresta, Master of England, 'wished to seize him for sodomy; however, he fled'.[11] The fathers at the council would certainly have been aware that they were only receiving digests of the proceedings, and it does appear that the full depositions of the witnesses in various countries were available for perusal if they were wanted,[12] but it is equally evident that in the time available no detailed reading of trial records was possible.

In addition to presenting the council with the summaries, the pope had also invited the clergy to submit their own views in writing, rather as Pope Gregory X had done in the last great church council at Lyons in 1274. Only two of the reports survive: they are by Jacques Duèze, Bishop of Avignon, who succeeded Clement V as Pope John XXII in 1316, and Guillaume Le Maire, the elderly Bishop of Angers. Jacques Duèze felt that there was enough evidence available for a judgement to be made on guilt or innocence, and that if it was decided to suppress the Order, then the pope should do this in his capacity as sovereign pontiff. The tone of the report clearly reflects the bishop's feeling that the Order should be condemned, for he argued that suppression would not cause any serious prejudice to the interests of the faith, since the Templars had apostasised from their vocation and by their arrogance and riches had provoked hatred. Although the pope should ask the assent of the council for this action as a matter of courtesy, he was in fact entitled to abolish the Order through his own legitimate authority.[13]

Guillaume Le Maire was more overtly hostile to the Order. Some asserted 'that the Order ought to be given a defence, nor ought so noble a member of the Church to be cut off from its body without the rigour of justice and great discussion'. But others took the view that the Order should be destroyed without delay, since grave scandal had arisen against it throughout Christendom, 'especially since many errors and heresies have been found to be clearly proved against them by the proceedings and inquisitions as well as by two thousand witnesses'. Guillaume's solution was much the same as that suggested by Jacques Duèze: the pope should suppress the Order *ex officio* 'either through the rigour of justice or the plenitude of power', since this Order 'has already caused the Christian name to smell among unbelievers and infidels and has shaken some of the faithful in the stability of their faith'. The 'frivolous and vexatious allegations concerning a defence' should be rejected, and the Order's goods reserved for the Holy See. It was not a valid argument to assert that it was a good Order at the time of its foundation, for this took no account of what had happened since. The suppression should take place without delay 'in case from delay the capricious spark of this error ignites in flames, which could burn the whole world'. There could be no discussion about an Order which had caused so much scandal, and could cause a further weakening of the Church if it was allowed to exist any longer.[14]

Clement V had, however, formally invited the Templars to come to Vienne to defend their Order,[15] although it seems unlikely that he expected them actually to do so. Then suddenly, in late October, a dramatic event occurred which must have done much to counter the arguments of those who urged the Order's swift abolition. On 4 December Clement wrote to King Philip describing what had happened. One day, while the fathers of the council were deliberating and the pope was absent, seven Templars appeared, and soon after they were followed by two others, who presented themselves for the defence of the Order, asserting that there were 1,500 or two thousand brothers in Lyons and the surrounding region ready to support them. The pope, however, ordered their detention before summoning 'the gaoler customarily most skilful in diligence'.[16] If Clement really believed that there were as many Templars as this roaming the Lyonnais, he may have thought that an armed attack was possible, in the manner of the group of German Templars who had burst into the provincial Council of Mainz. It is more likely however that the pope wished to remove this embarrassment as quickly as possible and hoped that it would be overlooked.

Indeed, the pope's conduct both during and after this first session of the council suggests that he had finally determined to end the affair of the Templars. Perhaps he feared that a far greater scandal would be provoked if the proceedings against Boniface VIII were revived, for witnesses had already been heard in this case in Avignon and Rome during the year 1310 and the early months of 1311.[17] Perhaps too he hoped that the way would be cleared for a new crusade, a project for which he always maintained his enthusiasm and in which he clearly had a genuine interest. In any event, at some time during this first session, he announced that, 'since it was difficult, indeed almost impossible' for the affair of the Templars to be discussed by the entire assembly, a commission would be selected, consisting of leading prelates from a number of countries, who would consider the evidence. This was done and they spent several days in the Cathedral at Vienne listening to the depositions and summaries of the trial, 'as much of these as they wished to hear'. From this commission, a smaller group was elected by the council, under the presidency of the Patriarch of Aquileia.[18] Quite possibly Clement expected that this small group would be easily persuaded to accept the view that suppression was the best course. The pope's confidence is reflected in letters of the Aragonese ambassadors of 12 and 27 December 1311, in which they reported to King James II that Clement had been sounding opinion in the council about the disposal of the Templars' property. The pope had found that most of the fathers favoured a new Order, although Clement personally preferred that the goods be transferred to the Hospital, a solution which would avoid the creation of a new Rule and which would prevent the property being annexed by any Order which had a more specifically national or regional character. Despite this potential difference of opinion, the ambassadors told the king that the pope was confident that the council would be finished by 20 January.[19]

But Clement was beginning to find that the incident of the seven Templars was not being overlooked, and that a very large majority of the Church fathers were beginning to make what Guillaume Le Maire had called 'frivolous and vexatious allegations concerning a defence'. Tolomeo da Lucca, Dominican Bishop of Torcello and contemporary biographer of the pope, wrote that

> the prelates were called to confer with the cardinals about the Templars. The acts relevant to this were read among the prelates, and they were summoned individually about this to be asked by the pontiff whether the Templars should be given a hearing or a defence. All the prelates from Italy, except for one, from Spain, Germany, Sweden, England, Scotland and Ireland, concurred in this opinion. Item, [so did] the French, except for the three metropolitans, namely Rheims [Robert de Courtenay], Sens [Philippe de Marigny] and Rouen [Gilles Aicelin].

Ptolemy dates these events early December.[20] The Aragonese ambassadors confirm this account. At the beginning of December, four questions had been posed: should the Order be allowed a defence? should the six or seven Templars who had recently come forward be given the chance to make a defence? should the Templars be allowed a procurator? if this was too difficult, should the pope nominate a defender for them? Only the Archbishop of Rouen, the Abbot of Cluny and three other French bishops were opposed to a defence.[21] The English chronicler Walter of Hemingborough was scornful:

> In the second [session] there was a long dispute about the Order of the Temple, as to whether it ought to remain or be destroyed *de jure*. And almost all the prelates were for the Order of the Templars, except the prelates of France, who, on account of fear of

the King of France, by whom, it was said, all that scandal had been caused, did not dare to do otherwise.'[22]

But at the council some were beginning to feel apprehensive. Henry Ffykeis, an English procurator at the Roman Curia, sent news of the council to John Salmon, Bishop of Norwich, on 27 December 1311. There had been a spate of deaths and serious illnesses. The Cardinal of Albano had died at Lucca, Etienne de Suisy had died during the council, and the Cardinal of Sabina, the legate in Italy, 'remains as if dead without hope of evasion'. Bérenger Frédol had been in the same state, 'but God delivered him'. This was fertile ground for the prophets of doom, one such foretelling that by Easter ten cardinals would have died and another with them, 'whom I do not dare to name', presumably meaning the pope.

> Concerning the matter of the Templars there is great debate as to whether they ought in law to be admitted to the defence. The larger part of the prelates, indeed all of them, excepting five or six from the council of the King of France, stand on their behalf. On account of this the pope is strongly moved against the prelates. The King of France more so; and he is coming in a rage with a great following. We are frightened of this action and we tremble on account of this event. It is believed that on this account there was at least to be a prorogation of the council, in case it became worse if the king did not have his way. In short it is certainly hoped that the pope will transfer himself elsewhere, especially on account of the insufficiencies of this place. Nevertheless it is not known what he intends. Concerning other things with which the council is concerned, nothing is transacted, but everything remains in suspense.

Henry Ffykeis was very miserable. One of the 'insufficiencies of the place' was provisions. 'In a few words all things here are dear. Indeed more goods are to be had in Avignon for one black *denarius* than here for a *sterling*.'[23]

Henry Ffykeis's fears had some justification, for Philip the Fair could see Clement's tenuous control of the council slipping away from him. After more than four years of effort the whole affair was once more in jeopardy, and Philip therefore resorted to well-tried methods of intimidation. On 30 December he convoked a meeting of the Estates at Lyons, only a short distance upriver from Vienne, for 10 February 1312. No record of this assembly survives, but it seems to have met in the second half of March and to have condemned the Temple in the terms required.[24] The Aragonese envoys noted that on 17 February a special embassy had arrived from the king, consisting of Louis d'Evreux, the Counts of Saint-Pol and Boulogne, Enguerrand de Marigny, the royal Chamberlain and effectively the king's first minister by this time, Nogaret and Plaisians. Together with four French cardinals (including Bérenger Frédol and Nicolas de Fréauville) and one Italian, they held daily meetings with the pope in the greatest secrecy. These meetings went on for twelve days until, on 29 February, they returned to the king, who was staying at Mâcon.[25] At the time, the Aragonese suspected that an agreement had been negotiated, but on 7 March Marigny returned to the council alone, and began a further series of meetings with the pope, convincing the Aragonese that no final agreement had been reached.[26]

The Aragonese proved to be correct, for on 2 March Philip himself had written to the pope from Mâcon, the next important town along the River Saône north of Lyons. The pope must have felt a powerful sensation that the king was about to descend upon him. The letter was a thinly disguised ultimatum. It was, according to the king, manifest that because of the crimes and heresies of its members the Order ought justly to be suppressed.

> Which is why, burning with zeal for the orthodox faith and in case so great an injury done to Christ should remain unpunished, we affectionately, devotedly and humbly ask Your Holiness that you should suppress the aforesaid Order and wish to create anew another Military Order, on which be conferred the goods of the above-mentioned Order with its rights, honours and responsibilities.

Alternatively, the goods could be transferred to another of the Military Orders, as would seem to the pope 'to be profitable to the honour of God and to the use of the Holy Land'. Whatever the pope decided the king would 'devotedly receive and observe ... saving whatever rights remain to us, the prelates, barons, nobles and various others in our kingdom, which appertained to us and the other persons aforementioned before the aforesaid arrests'.[27] On 8 March Clement replied vaguely that if the Order were suppressed, then its property would be used for the defence of the Holy Land.[28]

These events had been closely observed by the Aragonese ambassadors, who felt that it was now time to press the claims of their own king. James II had sent representatives to the council for the specific purpose of protecting what he regarded as his rightful claims to the Order's goods in Aragon. In a letter of 12 January to Pierre Boyl and Guillermo Olomar, who were acting for him at the council, James had spelt this out. The goods of the Temple in Aragon were not to be transferred to the Hospital, but to the Aragonese Order of Calatrava,

> in which are established our natural brothers, as the brothers of the Temple were, in which we have the service of *regalia* and other rights, which we had on the Templars and their other goods. And that, if it cannot be obtained otherwise, the lord pope should have responsions from the Master of Calatrava, which the Master of the Temple of our kingdom made to the Grand Master of the Order of the Temple.

The ambassadors should stress that these goods were given for the defence of the Church against the Saracens in Spain and, for this reason, the king could not allow them to be transferred elsewhere contrary to the use for which his ancestors had granted them.[29] In early March therefore, when matters seemed to be coming to a head, the Aragonese were also involved in negotiations with the pope, Enguerrand de Marigny, and the Priors of the Hospital from France and the Auvergne.[30]

Clement flapped about. On the one hand the council wanted to give the Templars a hearing, while on the other, the demands of the French and the Aragonese became ever more insistent. On 20 March Clement did not know, he said, whether the Order would be destroyed or conserved.[31] But on the same day his mind was clarified. The king, with his brothers, Charles and Louis, and his three sons, together with a considerable armed force, arrived at Vienne.[32] On 22 March Clement held a secret consistory in which his special commission, together with some of the cardinals, participated. Now four-fifths of those present voted for suppression, perhaps because they realised that opposition was now little use or perhaps because they had been bribed or intimidated by the French.[33] In any event, Ramón, Bishop of Valencia, was almost alone when he protested that the decision was 'against reason and justice'.[34]

The decision to suppress the Order was made public in a solemn session of the council on 3 April. Walter of Hemingborough described the scene.

> The lord pope sat for the purpose of judgement, and on one side was the King of France, and on the other was the King of Navarre, his son, and a certain cleric arose and forbade, under pain of major excommunication, anyone to say a word in the council, except with the permission or at the request of the pope.[35]

The anonymous monk who continued the chronicle of Guillaume de Nangis noted that King Philip sat on the pope's right 'in some degree lower'. Secure from any inconvenient argument, Clement addressed the assembly on the theme from the Psalms, 'The impious shall not stand in judgement, nor sinners in the council of the just.'[36] The bull of suppression, *Vox in excelso*, dated 22 March, was then read out.

> Considering therefore the infamy, suspicion, noisy insinuation and the other things above which have been brought against the Order, and also the secret and clandestine reception of the brothers of this Order, and the difference of many of these brothers from the general custom, life and habits of the others of Christ's faithful, in that especially when receiving others among the brothers of their Order, in this reception they made those being received make profession and swear to reveal to no one the manner of the reception, nor to leave that Order, as a result of which presumption evidently arose against them; considering moreover the grave scandal which has arisen from these things against the Order, which it did not seem could be checked while this Order remained in being, and also the danger both to faith and souls, and that many horrible things have been done by very many of the brothers of this Order ... who have lapsed into the sin of wicked apostasy against the Lord Jesus Christ himself,

the crime of detestable idolatry, the execrable outrage of the Sodomites . . . considering also that the Roman Church has sometimes caused other illustrious Orders to be suppressed from causes incomparably less than those mentioned above, even without blame being attached to the brothers: not without bitterness and sadness of heart, not by way of judicial sentence, but by way of provision or apostolic ordinance, we abolish the aforesaid Order of the Temple and its constitution, habit and name by an irrevocable and perpetually valid decree, and we subject it to perpetual prohibition with the approval of the Holy Council, strictly forbidding anyone to presume to enter the said Order in the future, or to receive or wear its habit, or to act as a Templar. Which if anyone acts against this, he will incur the sentence of excommunication *ipso facto*. Furthermore, we reserve the persons and goods of this Order to the ordinance and disposition of our Apostolic See, which, by the grace of divine favour, we intend to make for the honour of God and the exaltation of the Christian faith and the prospering state of the Holy Land, before the present council is ended.

The pope added that he judged any further interference in the matter, knowingly or unknowingly, from this time as 'vexatious and worthless'.[37] Walter of Hemingborough offered a rather sour gloss to this bull.

> The pope added that although from the above proceedings he could not destroy the Order *de jure*, nevertheless he suppressed the Order from the plenitude of his power, conferring, adding and uniting their lands and possessions to the Hospitallers. Also a tenth from the universal Church was granted for six years to the King of the French; so that at the end of six years he could go personally to the Holy Land, the holy council neither consenting nor expressly contradicting.[38]

Clement had succeeded in suppressing, although not in condemning, the Templars, with the help of a vow of silence imposed upon dissident voices within the council, but after *Vox in excelso* opinion throughout Christendom was no longer restrained. There is no doubt that many genuinely believed in the Templars' guilt; however,

it soon became evident that many others, especially observers outside the Kingdom of France, were either shocked or cynically
amused at the blatant methods used by the pope at the council and
the open menace applied to him by the French government. Similar
circumstances had prevailed at Poitiers in 1308, and with similar
results, but these meetings, although well known, were not in such
full public view as a great ecumenical council in which it was evident
that a large majority were opposed to the pope's chosen course of
action. For Walter of Hemingborough the assembly at Vienne 'did
not merit being called a council, since the lord pope did everything
on his own authority, the holy council not replying or consenting'.[39]
The Florentine Giovanni Villani, not always strictly accurate in the
stories which he gathered about events in France, nevertheless is an
interesting example of contemporary foreign opinion. He had no
doubts about the sordid circumstances which had led to the destruction of the Order. Villani describes how two men, the Prior of
Montfaucon and Noffo Dei, who he thought had been the original
denunciators of the Order, had gone to the king, who

> was moved by his avarice, and made secret arrangements with the
> pope and caused him to promise to destroy the Order of the Tem-
> plars laying to their charge many articles of heresy; but it is said
> that it was more in hope of extracting great sums of money from
> them, and by reason of offence taken against the Master of the
> Temple and the Order.[40]

A less polemical and calmer opinion was expressed by a Cistercian monk, Jacques de Thérines, a professor of theology at the
University of Paris. He was an independent-minded man, unafraid
of the government of Philip the Fair, and, together with thirteen
other masters, he had already told the king that, even if the confessions proved to be true, he had no legal right to arrest, examine or
punish members of the clergy, who were exempt, nor to touch the
property, which was reserved for the defence of the Holy Land. At
Vienne, he spoke up for the rights of exempt Orders, and in 1312
wrote a tract, *Contra Impugnatores Exemptorum*, which reflected
his opinions on the fate of the Templars. If the doings ascribed to the
Templars were true, he said, they were indeed to be execrated, and
should excite the horror of all Christendom. The Templars had

Coins of Amaury, James II and Pope Clement V. When the Templars were arrested in October 1307, their frontline was Cyprus, at that time ruled by Amaury de Lusignan, Lord of Tyre and brother of King Henry II. The Templars had helped him to power in a *coup* in April 1306 and, not surprisingly, he was slow to follow up the papal order to arrest them. James II of Aragon was equally sceptical of the charges, for the Templars had been prominent in the wars against the Moors. Moreover, the task of arresting them was made more difficult because they had been forewarned and thus had been able to retreat to their castles. Clement V, often portrayed as a weak pope, in fact manoeuvred quite skilfully in difficult circumstances. Ultimately, he was unable to prevent the dissolution of the Order, although he avoided outright condemnation. *Below,* the seals of Andreas de Colours, showing the Temple at Jerusalem (1214), William de la More, Master in England, showing the *Agnus Dei* or Lamb of God (1304), and Fulk de Villaret, Grand Master of the Hospital. Fulk and Jacques de Molay, Grand Master of the Temple, both received requests from Clement V for their views on the best means of continuing the holy war and a proposed union of the two Orders. However, only Molay appeared in person to present his advice

ent de la partie de leuesque mais ils furent al
les tost deliures de prison par paiant vne grât
fôme dargent. De la mort du maistre du tem
ple.

Neest an auisi ou moys de mars
ou temps de karsme. le general
maistre du temple et vn autre
giant maistre apres lui en lordre si côme len dit
visiteur. a paris en lisle deuant les augustins

The end for the Templars finally came with execution of Jacques de Molay and
Geoffroi de Charney, Preceptor of Normandy, as relapsed heretics on the Ile-des-
Javiaux in the Seine in March 1314, an event recorded in *Les Grandes Chroniques*

fallen into a shameful and criminal error both from the point of view of faith and natural morals. He was however in very considerable doubt. He wondered how these heresies could have entered the Order in the first place, since there were so many men of noble birth, devoted to the defence of the Holy Land, contained within it; why some retracted their confessions, even though this meant death by burning, and why there were so many contradictory points in the results of the inquiries which were read out at Vienne. Doubt remained with him, for he could find no clear answer to the questions that he asked himself.[41]

But whatever the doubts, the pope had suppressed the Order and he was now faced with the practical questions of how to dispose of its property and personnel. The question of the property naturally dominated. Here too, the fathers of the council made sure that the pope's path was not easy, for their opposition both to the idea that a new Order should be created and to the plan to grant the property to the Hospital prolonged the third session of the council until 6 May. According to the Aragonese report, Clement found himself in opposition to most of the cardinals and the Church fathers as well as to Philip the Fair's own counsellors, with the notable exceptions of Charles of Valois and Enguerrand de Marigny, in his wish to transfer the property to the Order of the Hospital. Neither threats nor the reading of letters reporting a recent great victory of the Hospitallers over the Turks were sufficient to persuade the majority that such a transfer was desirable. Certainly the fathers were still opposing the papal will on 15 April. Again Clement was driven to act on his own authority, for he told the prelates that if they would not agree to the transfer, he would nevertheless make it himself.[42]

The pope's hand was strengthened by the fact that Charles of Valois and Marigny seem to have convinced Philip IV that it was expedient to settle for this arrangement. Probably Marigny in particular favoured a quick end to a long-drawn-out affair which had not been of his making. Ideally, the king would probably have liked to see the formation of a new Order,[43] possibly with a member of the French royal house at its head, but in the end he was persuaded that the transfer to the Hospital was an acceptable compromise, an arrangement which would undoubtedly be subject to certain conditions favourable to the French crown. A letter of Philip IV to the pope, dated 24 August 1312, confirms this. The king accepted the decision to transfer the goods to the Hospital, but indicated that it had been agreed that the Order 'should be regulated and reformed by the Apostolic See both in its head and its members', a concession which provided a potential lever against the Hospital in the future, for in many ways it was as vulnerable as the Templars. Moreover, the transfer of the goods was only to be made 'after the deduction of necessary expenses for the custody and administration of these goods' and saving 'all the rights on the aforesaid goods previously appertaining to us and the prelates, barons, nobles and others of our kingdom', the implementation of which must have been made all the easier by the threat of 'reform'.[44]

The papal decision was embodied in the bull *Ad providam* of 2 May 1312. The property had been given originally to support the interests of the Holy Land and for the conflict against the infidels, and therefore the pope and the council had decided that the best course was to join the goods in perpetuity to the Hospitallers. In consequence, the pope, with the assent of the council, had transferred everything which the Templars had possessed in October 1307, the time of their capture, to the Order of the Hospital. The only exception was the property outside France in the lands of the Kings of Castile, Aragon, Portugal and Majorca, the disposition of which the pope reserved. Finally, the pope threatened excommunication and interdict to those who, in this affair, occasioned any wrong to the Hospitallers.[45]

On 21 March 1313, Léonard de Tibertis, Prior of the Hospital at Venice, acting on behalf of his Grand Master, agreed to pay the French royal treasury the sum of 200,000 *livres tournois* in order to compensate losses which the crown claimed to have incurred as a result of the deposit of royal treasure at the house of the Temple in the years before the trial, 'since afterwards the said people of the lord king were said to have received less in the final account'. The payment was to be made in three equal parts over the following three years. 'And thence the said Order . . . will remain in perpetuity quit and completely freed . . .'[46] However, despite the apparently final nature of this payment, the representatives of the Hospital experienced some difficulty in gaining full possession of the lands. Indeed, the French government adopted an aggressive stance when the Hospitallers tried to take action, accusing them of interfering. On 8 June 1313 Clement V wrote a soothing letter to Philip IV after

just such a protest against Albrecht von Schwarzburg, Grand Preceptor of the Hospital in the west. The preceptor had been called to
the papal presence and explained that he had not intended to interfere, but only to ask for subventions from the Hospitaller priors in
France which had been delayed, with the result that the Master and
chapter overseas, 'not without expense in the affairs of the Holy
Land, were suffering great need'. Otherwise, he was humbly grateful
'for the benevolence and gracious favours which you have bestowed
. . . especially at the Council of Vienne', and he wanted only to come
into the royal presence to bring 'certain precious objects' to the king
and to his son, Louis. When he had done this, he would leave for
business in other parts.[47]

Even after the death of Philip IV in November 1314 the French
monarchy still refused to slacken its grip. On 14 February 1316,
Léonard de Tibertis was forced to make a new series of proposals,
the agreement of March 1313 notwithstanding. The document
acknowledges that the officials of Philip IV and now those of his
son, Louis X, had claimed that 'great and diverse sums of money'
were still outstanding to the crown from the Templar property, but
points out that 200,000 *livres tournois* had already been settled for
deposits made at the Temple, and that an additional 60,000 *livres
tournois* had been granted for the expenses incurred by the crown
during the trial. The Hospital now proposed to concede all the
goods of the Temple which had been converted to the usage of the
crown since the time that the Order had been proscribed in France,
to cancel the debts of the French royal family to the Temple, to offer
quittance for everything that the royal administrators had taken
since the time of the arrests and of two-thirds of the arrears of
farms owed, and quittance of the movables and chattels held by the
king's men till this time.[48] Broadly, these proposals were accepted
by Philip V, who came to the throne in 1316, in an *arrêt* of *Parlement* dated 11 October 1317.[49] The French monarchy seems to
have been finally shaken off with yet another lump sum of 50,000
livres tournois to be paid over three years by the Hospital as a final
quittance (6 March 1318).[50] Giovanni Villani went so far as to
claim that the Hospital was 'poorer than it was before in its property'.[51] While the accession of the extensive Templar estates must
ultimately have enriched the Hospital, the transfer may well have
created short-term financial embarrassment. Such calculations must

surely have influenced Enguerrand de Marigny when he had recommended that the king accept the plan to transfer the property to the
Hospital, for the creation of a new Order under French auspices
would certainly have been costly even with the Templar properties
to draw on, while, in contrast, the Hospital could be squeezed for
compensation which would help to cover the financial problems
which continued to plague the reign.

Nor was the position any easier elsewhere, although in other
countries the Hospitallers faced a problem smaller in scope. The bull
Ad providam had specifically excluded the Order's property in
Iberia from its major provisions, which shows the effectiveness of
the Aragonese envoys, who, as Bishop Ramón of Valencia wrote on
7 May 1312, had obtained this 'not without clamour and labour'.[52]
This in turn reflected the constant pressure exercised on the envoys
by James II to ensure that the property, and especially the fortresses,
should not be transferred to the Hospital, but instead should go
to the Aragonese Order of Calatrava. As recently as 1 April, James
had written to his representatives to stress that if a general transfer
to the Hospital was ordered, then they must at once obtain an audience with the pope and 'explain to him humbly and devotedly on
our behalf, in accordance with the instruction to which you have
been bound by us, the extent to which you have to dissent from
his order'.[53]

But the bull *Ad providam* had made no final decision regarding
the property in Iberia, and, after the council, Clement V invited representatives of the kingdoms concerned to meet him at Avignon for a
final judgement in February 1313.[54] King James sent three representatives to negotiate on his behalf, who were at the Curia in Avignon
by the beginning of the year 1313, when they received detailed
instructions from the king. If the union of the Templar goods with
those of the Hospital were allowed it would put the kingdom in the
greatest danger, for if the Hospitallers, holding castles on the frontiers and the coasts, did not observe fidelity to the king, then they
could not be prevented from bringing into the land 'whatever power
they wished'. Even if they remained faithful, the kingdom would still
be scandalised by the power which the Hospitallers held. Special
provision ought to be made, because the Templars had a far higher
proportion of the land in Aragon than in any other kingdom. The
dangers of this were clearly apparent, as the Templar resistance to

arrest had shown. If they had had sufficient supplies they could have fought much longer than they did. Since many of these castles were given to the Temple by the king and his predecessors in fief, 'it could not be reasonable to dispose [of them] to other persons without the wish and assent of the king'. The king was not moved by avarice, 'since he does not wish to retain any of the said goods; indeed he is prepared to make offering from his own'. However, if it was finally necessary to agree to the union, then there had to be special conditions. The king should retain all the fortresses, all the former Templars must swear an oath of fidelity to the king, the Hospital could not acquire more goods than the Temple had had, and the Templar property in Valencia should be conceded to a newly created branch of the Order of Calatrava. Continued papal resistance should be contradicted as much as possible, and the negotiators should say that they would appeal to the pope's successor or to a general council if necessary.[55]

Discussions with the pope began on 14 February 1313. According to the Aragonese, the pope listened sympathetically to their arguments and agreed that there were certain dangers to the king inherent in the union, but he could not make individual provision concerning the goods without scandal. The Aragonese should return with fresh proposals. Meanwhile, Cardinal Bérenger Frédol had told them that he agreed with their point of view, but had secretly urged them to accept the union and then make regulations about the acquisition of property by the Hospital in the king's own lands afterwards, as other kings did. But 'if we asked this from the Church, we should never obtain it!'[56] Nevertheless, the Aragonese appear to have asked for this concession, but succeeded only in angering the pope, for he told them that such a request was 'against God and against justice and all reason'.[57]

The Aragonese had made no further progress by 28 March, when Albrecht von Schwarzburg, Grand Preceptor of the Hospital in the west, arrived at the Curia with six brethren. When the Hospitallers were granted audience the pope explained to them why he had made the grant of Templar property to their Order, in terms which seem to have been meant for public consumption and were especially to be noted by the Aragonese. He had not created the union on account of any special affection for the Hospital beyond that of any other Order, but because he thought that this would be the best way of

ensuring that the Templar goods were used for their original purpose. Recently, messengers from the King of France had fully agreed
with him, but now 'he had to manage and order something else with
certain others, not naming us expressly nor others, but [that] finally
everything would go to his wish'. The Hospitallers thanked the
pope, saying effusively that he had made a greater donation than
any other 'beyond the donation which the Emperor Constantine
made to the Church of Rome'. They were prepared to receive the
goods, but they wished to do so without 'a quarrel with any prince,
since there could be great danger to them'.[58]

In the hope presumably of having impressed the Aragonese, the
pope called them to his presence again on 1 April. He told them that
he had deliberated fully on their arguments and, the ambassadors
told James II, 'had found that our reasons were not strong either *de
jure* or *de facto*'. He had been informed by some former Templars
that the kings of Aragon had never had any jurisdiction or service on
the goods of the Temple, except for a *cens* which had been taken by
force and 'always with protests and contradictions from them'. The
pope told the envoys not to persist with their arguments, since by
doing so they placed their souls in great danger. The Aragonese
replied that their reasons were 'just and good', but Clement said that
he would recall them after some days and then would expressly tell
them his intention. 'However,' said the envoys, 'he has not yet called
us concerning this, but we wait for it daily.' The following day, they
consulted Bérenger Frédol. He was not very hopeful, telling them
that the best they could obtain was an agreement to an oath of
fidelity for the king, 'if we remained here for ever'. He suggested that
they would do better to return to the king and take fresh advice, but
they did not believe that the pope wished to break off negotiations
completely and were staying on since they knew perfectly the king's
intentions. Berengar Frédol, however, suggested secretly that they
accept the idea of union, and then the king should simply break the
papal order as he thought fit![59] But James II had no intention of giving in on this issue. In his reply to the envoys' letters, dated 16 April,
he told them to make a public instrument indicating his express dissent from the union.[60] Persistence had some success, for Clement in
the end decided to suspend the matter, and on 24 April sent the
envoys back to Aragon having replied to them, as they said, 'in a
very skilful and cunning manner'. Before saying anything to them he

made them swear on oath that they would say nothing about his reply, except to the king alone. 'And thus, lord, the affair is to be prorogued and meanwhile the pope will not proceed until he has your reply.' For the time being, the pope intended to leave Avignon and go to Châteauneuf where he would remain in secret.[61]

The matter remained unresolved until Clement's death in April 1314. On hearing of his fatal illness, James II warned that none of his envoys were to speak to the pope on the issue of the Templar goods,[62] clearly fearing that Clement would be provoked into an unfavourable decision. Negotiations might be more fruitful with the next pope, and in fact a compromise solution was eventually reached with John XXII on 10 June 1317. A new Order, based at Montesa, was to be founded, following the observances of Calatrava and subject to the rule of the Master of Calatrava. It was to have the former possessions of the Templars and the lands of the Hospitallers in the region, an arrangement which created a new fighting Order, closely tied to the Aragonese monarchy, on the southern frontier. On the other hand, the Templar possessions in Aragon and Catalonia were to be granted to the Hospital, although the Hospitaller Castellan of Amposta would be obliged to pay homage to the king when he entered office.[63]

King Ferdinand IV of Castile had been equally keen to secure the Templar property, and there are indications that the Aragonese, Castilian and Portuguese monarchies kept in close contact during and after the Council of Vienne.[64] Ferdinand prematurely sent the news of the suppression of the Temple to Johan Osorez, Grand Master of the Order of Santiago, in July 1308,[65] presumably in anticipation of seizing the goods, and in 1309 and 1312 there are records of the king's sale of Templar goods to the Order of Alcántara.[66] But the king's death in 1312 plunged the country into anarchy, and the new monarch, Alfonso XI, was in no position to pursue the pope with the assiduity of the Aragonese. Some lands were taken by the crown, others seized by the stronger lords, and a small part was received by the Military Orders of Ucles and Calatrava. Theoretically, by a bull of 14 March 1319, the property should have gone to the Hospital, but the usurpations forced the Order into a series of negotiations with individuals, some of which dragged on for many decades.[67] In 1331 the king asked for a new Order, but the pope told him that he was too late. In 1366 Pope Urban V was still complaining that the

Castilian kings had not fulfilled their obligations to the Hospital.[68] King Diniz of Portugal had, in contrast, ensured that he was well represented at the Curia, and in March 1319 the Portuguese were granted permission to form a new military Order – the Order of Christ – with the goods of the Templars in Portugal.[69] King Sancho of Majorca was also opposed to the idea of union and sent his envoys to protest. However, eventually he had to settle for some movable property together with a lump sum. 'Through devotion for the Order of the Hospital, through personal consideration for brother Arnold de Soler [the Hospitaller representative], whom he cherished and loved extremely, and ceding also to proceed in this affair with all goodness and kindness', he agreed to receive an annual rent of 9,000 *sols majorquins* and 2,000 *sols barcelonais* for his rights over Templar property, and a lump sum of 22,500 *sols* of royal *majorquins*. The king had already appropriated a large proportion of the movable property, but he graciously abandoned the church ornaments provided that they were used only in the churches and chapels.[70]

In England the position was complicated by the fact that Edward II had farmed out some of the Templar lands, and initially, in August 1312, he blocked the attempts of the Prior of the Hospital to take over the property, since, he said, it was to the manifest prejudice of the crown.[71] It was not until 28 November 1313 that he actually ordered the official transfer to the Hospital.[72] The baronage however was not inclined to relinquish the hold which it had established during the trial. In 1317 it was necessary for Pope John XXII to send legates to order restitution of the property. In 1322 the pope had to write to the king drawing attention to the continued existence of usurpers in the former Templar lands.[73] In the summer of 1324, the king did order the royal keepers in the various counties to permit the sheriffs to hand over the Templar lands, in compliance with royal statute.[74]

The Hospitallers themselves pressed their claims. The papal frontal assaults were supplemented with the judicious distribution of bribes. In 1324, for instance, the king received three manors worth £432 per annum,[75] while an extent of the Hospitaller lands in England, made in 1338, shows that robes were distributed twice a year, in winter and summer, to 140 officials in the royal treasury at a cost of £10 per annum, and 200 marks per annum was spent on, among other things, 'gifts given in the courts of the lord king and of other magnates, for the purpose of receiving favours'.[76]

But neither papal legates nor Hospitaller bribery had immediate effect. The extent of 1338 shows that the Order still had not laid its hands on much of the Templar property. The king himself was among the usurpers, for among the properties listed were 'water mills at York, occupied by the king, valued at 20 marks'. Among other occupiers, the Countess of Pembroke held the manor of Strode, 'a gift of the king', as well as those at Deneye, Hurst and Newsom, valued in total at 279 marks. The total value of the usurped lands was calculated to be 1,259 marks, 3 shillings and 1 penny.[77] Even when property had been recovered it was often in a poor condition and involved costly restoration. At Thornton in Northumbria for instance, one messuage had had to be rebuilt by the last prior, Leonard, since after the suppression 'all the houses were destroyed and taken away by the feudal lords'.[78] Clearly the occupiers were reluctant to give up these valuable supplementary incomes, but the position was complicated by the fact that the Templar lands, built up piecemeal over many generations, were often held under various tenures from many different lords. In Lincolnshire alone, in 1303, the Templars had held forty-seven different knights' fees or fractions of a fee from twenty-three different lords, a figure which includes only those lands held by military tenure.[79] The delay in sorting out this mosaic of rights and jurisdictions was compounded by the fact that the Hospitallers did not gain possession of the relevant documents – deeds, charters and rolls – by means of which they could prove their claims, until July and August 1324.[80] At the same time, although the English rulers were ostensibly co-operative, seemingly prepared to issue orders to the sheriffs to complete the transfer, in fact the royal officials created many difficulties in the day-to-day problems which continually occurred. Frequently, the Prior of the Hospital in England was forced to attend the Exchequer concerning debts allegedly owed to the crown, and although delays in payment were granted it was not until 1336 that the Hospital was finally quit of these extortions.[81] Finally, extra expenses had been incurred by the Exchequer, which, even before papal judgement on the disposal of the goods, had been settling claims on Templar property from other parties, in particular retainers of the Order who, since they were not actually members, were not involved in the proceedings.[82]

In Germany and Italy the fate of the property varied in accordance with the disturbed political circumstances of those regions. By the autumn of 1317 the Hospital had taken possession in the dioceses of Magdeburg and Halberstadt, and in the Kingdom of Bohemia, but at Hildesheim the Templars had to be expelled by force, a pattern repeated in other parts of southern Germany. Local rulers, like Thibaut, Duke of Lorraine, and Waldemar, Margrave of Brandenburg, took a proportion of the goods before conceding to the Hospital. In Italy, it took the papacy until 1319 to induce Robert, King of Naples, to hand over the Templar property in his dynastic lands in Provence, and it is therefore probable that similar delays occurred in his south Italian lands. In Cyprus, however, the transfer was completed by November 1313 with relatively few problems, perhaps because here the needs of the crusade were more clearly evident.[83] In some cases therefore the transfer of the Templar property met costly difficulties, and this placed a great strain on Hospitaller finances, especially as it coincided with the consolidation of the Order's position on the island of Rhodes;[84] nevertheless, the Order did succeed in gaining the greater part of the property within ten years of the Council of Vienne, which in the circumstances, would seem to be a relatively rapid solution of an immensely complicated problem.

In relation to the property, the persons of the Templars were much less important; there were unlikely to be any unseemly squabbles over the possession of these men. Their fate had been decided at the end of the Council of Vienne in the constitution *Considerantes dudum* of 6 May 1312. The leaders were to be reserved for papal judgement, while the rank and file received judgement at the provincial councils. Those who were found innocent or had submitted to the Church were to be given a pension drawn on the property of the Order, which would cover 'subsistence' and would be proportionate to the respective condition of the persons concerned. They could reside either in former Templar houses or in other monasteries, although not in too great a number. Those who relapsed or remained impenitent were however to be treated with the full rigour of canon law. All fugitives were ordered to appear before the relevant provincial council within a year, failing which they were to be declared heretics.[85]

Many Templars did indeed receive pensions, some on a generous scale. Ramón Sa Guardia, Preceptor of Mas Deu in Roussillon, was absolved and allowed to live in his old preceptory

> without paying any rent or hire, with the enjoyment of the pro-
> duce of the garden and fruits of the fruit trees, but for his food
> only; beyond this, that he can freely take from the wood for him-
> self and his company in the forests of Mas Deu or in other places
> which depend upon it, without however causing any damage.

He was assigned 350 *livres* annually on the property of the preceptory to see to the needs of the company, to commence at the end
of October 1313.[86] A Hospitaller agreement concerning Templar
pensions of October 1319 shows that he was still receiving 350
livres (or 7,000 *sols*), and a Templar called Dalmau de Rochaberti,
brother of a former Archbishop of Tarragona, was receiving 1,000
sols more than this. Sums of 1,400 and 2,000 *sols* were not uncom-
mon, and the lowest given, apparently to ordinary serving brothers,
was 500 *sols* per annum.[87] In England, pensions were still being
granted to twelve former Templars in 1338.[88] Letters of John XXII
in December 1318 show that pensions were being paid apparently
on too generous a scale. The pope ordered that the rate of allocation
be restricted, naming dioceses in France, Flanders, the British Isles,
Germany, Italy, Cyprus and Aragon.[89] As the memory of the trial
faded and the major participants disappeared, it was even possible
to show mercy to some of the imprisoned Templars. On 1 May 1321
the pope declared that the priest Pons de Buris, from the diocese of
Langres, who had suffered prison under 'harsh' conditions for the
previous twelve years following his condemnation at the Council of
Sens, had shown sufficient penitence, and was therefore authorised
to celebrate the divine offices.[90]

Pope John did however state specifically that the suppression did
not release former Templars from their monastic vows.[91] Templars
who were not imprisoned were expected to live quiet lives on their
pensions in scattered ones and twos in various monasteries. But
many found this difficult, for their strongest motivation for a life of
this kind had been effectively removed. For many there must have
been a powerful temptation to embark upon another career, an
ambition which could be most easily achieved outside Christian
lands. In September 1313 Bernard de Fontibus, former Preceptor of

Corberis, turned up at the court of James II in Barcelona as the ambassador of the Moslem ruler of Tunis.[92]

Unfortunately not all the former Templars were so constructive. On 26 October 1314 James II felt compelled to write to the Archbishop of Tarragona about the conduct of one Berenguer de Pulcronisu, who was living at the former Templar preceptory of Gardeny 'on condition that he should lead his life honestly', but who 'publicly holds a concubine . . . and has also shamefully committed many other dishonest acts'. As a consequence, the local chapel, previously held in great devotion by the people, was seldom visited. The king asked the archbishop to stop this, 'since you least of all ought to pass over such things with closed eyes'.[93] Even earlier, in 1313, another Aragonese Templar, Martín de Frígola, had been imprisoned for rape and other 'enormous crimes'.[94] These were not apparently unique cases. In August 1317 the pope had to write to the Archbishop of Tarragona telling him to ensure that ex-Templars retired to the prescribed places with the shortest possible delay and to stress that they owed complete obedience to the ordinaries. If the archbishop encountered any difficulties he was to call on the secular power for help.[95] Early the next year the archbishop forbade Templars to take part in wars or involve themselves in secular affairs and ordered them to stop wearing gaudy and expensive clothing inappropriate to their monastic status.[96]

The malaise was not confined to Aragon. In December 1318 Pope John issued a general order to all patriarchs, archbishops and bishops concerned with the problems of renegade Templars. Some Templars 'were living as laymen in danger of their souls', and some had married and were living publicly with their wives, not appreciating that their vows on entry to the Temple had been in perpetuity and had not been dissolved by the suppression. The pope therefore instructed each ordinary to give the offenders a warning within the next month, ordering them to enter an approved monastery within three months. In the monastery clerks would be treated in accordance with their clerical status, and laymen as *conversi*. Failure to do this within this prescribed time would lead to the cancellation of pensions. To ensure that these remedies were carried out the pope asked for reports on the execution of his order.[97] The effectiveness of this decree is difficult to gauge. Individual cases can be found, such as that of Guillaume de Roussillon, Bishop of Valence and Die in Provence, who on 16 April 1319 compelled three Templars to put aside their wives and enter a monastery.[98] In Aragon, a few years later, in 1325, a Berenguer de San Marcial had his pension stopped for refusing to enter a religious house.[99]

Martín Pérez de Orós, Hospitaller Castellan of Amposta, argued that the root cause of the trouble was what he saw as the great and immoderate provision which the Templars received,[100] and in 1318 the pope ordered that pensions be reduced so that Templars could not accumulate money or live luxuriously, but should only receive enough income to provide them with food and clothing commensurate with the life of a monk.[101] With nothing else to do, the provision of more than adequate means may well have been a possible reason for the disintegration of the remaining vestiges of Templar discipline, but this was a two-way process. In Portugal, the Master of the Knighthood of Christ, which had been founded from Templar property, refused to receive a former Templar, Velasco Fernandez. The pope intervened and ordered, in August 1321, that this man have either a house or a preceptory conferred on him for life.[102] There are no further papal decrees on the subject after 1324, which may indicate that they were being enforced, but more likely suggests that the scale of the problem was gradually diminishing as the numbers of former Templars dwindled and the memory of the trial and the Council of Vienne became blurred.

The real conclusion of the trial had occurred in 1314. Pope Clement had been slow to implement his decision to reserve judgement on the leaders, a judgement in which Molay and the others had for so long placed their faith. It was not until 22 December 1313 that he appointed a commission of three cardinals to deal with the matter. These were Nicolas de Fréauville, Arnaud d'Auch and Arnaud Nouvel.[103] On 18 March 1314 the cardinals convoked a special council at Paris in the presence of Philippe de Marigny, Archbishop of Sens, and many prelates and doctors of theology and canon law. Jacques de Molay, Hugues de Pairaud, Geoffroi de Gonneville and Geoffroi de Charney were brought before them. The scene was described by a contemporary, the monk who continued the chronicle of Guillaume de Nangis.

Since these four, without any exception, had publicly and openly confessed the crimes which had been imputed to them and had persisted in these confessions and seemed finally to wish to persist in them, after the council had with expedition considered many things in the courtyard of the communal precinct of the church of Paris, on the Monday after the Feast of St Gregory, they were adjudged to be thrust into harsh and perpetual imprisonment. But lo, when the cardinals believed that they had imposed an end to the affair, immediately and unexpectedly two of them, namely the Grand Master and the Master of Normandy, defending themselves obstinately against the cardinal who had preached the sermon and against the Archbishop of Sens, returned to the denial both of the confession as well as everything which they had confessed.[104]

The clouds of confusion which had hung over the Grand Master throughout the trial now cleared. He was an old man, probably into his seventies by this time, and he had spent nearly seven years in prison. The pathetic reliance which he had placed in papal judgement, even to the exclusion of some kind of defence of the Order, had failed him.

The surprising reaction of Molay and Charney left the cardinals temporarily at a loss. The continuator of Guillaume de Nangis writes:

And then they were simply delivered from the cardinals into the hand of the *prévôt* of Paris, who was present at that time, until they should have fuller deliberation upon this the following day: as soon as this news came to the ears of the king, who was then in the royal palace, he, having communicated with the prudent men of his council, although not calling upon the clergy in the same manner, around the hour of vespers on the same day, on a certain small island in the Seine, situated between the royal garden and the church of the hermit brothers of St Augustine, ordered both to be burned to death. They were seen to be so prepared to sustain the fire with easy mind and will that they brought from all those who saw them much admiration and surprise for the constancy of their death and final denial; the other two were shut up in prison in accordance with the judgement.[105]

The action had been taken in such haste that it was later discovered that the Ile-des-Javiaux, on which the two men were burnt, was under the jurisdiction, not of the king, but of the monks of Saint-Germain-des-Prés, and Philip was obliged to issue letters confirming that this execution did not in any way prejudice their rights on the island.[106]

The heroic deaths of the two leaders quickly gave rise to a series of legends. Pope Clement died in the early hours of the morning of Saturday 20 April.[107] Philip the Fair died on 29 November in the same year.[108] It was said that Jacques de Molay had called them both to appear with him within the year before the tribunal of God.[109] Giovanni Villani was equally picturesque.

And the King of France and his sons had afterwards much shame and adversity, both because of this sin and of the capture of Pope Boniface . . . And note, that the night after the said Master and his companion had been martyred, their ashes and bones were collected as sacred relics by the friars and other religious persons, and carried away to holy places.[110]

10: Conclusion

Few people, surveying the events of the twentieth century, can have any illusions about the capability of the state to oppress organisations, groups or individuals, indeed, even to effect a complete change in mental outlook in those in its power. It would now be difficult to argue, as some nineteenth-century historians did, that the Templars were guilty of the accusations made against them by the regime of Philip the Fair, or that the confessions demonstrate anything more than the power of torture over the mental and physical resistance of all but the most extraordinary persons. The direct relationship between the confessions and torture can be clearly shown by a survey of the countries in which the trial of the Templars took place; the contrast is especially evident in a comparison between the results of the trial in France and England, two countries which in so many other ways retained close connections in the middle ages. Little is gained by a minute survey of the confessions in a vain search for a consistency which might indicate guilt, or an inconsistency which might show proof of individual veracity, or vice versa, for such an approach is essentially circular, while the widespread application of torture makes any such analysis inevitably inconclusive. If the internal evidence of the depositions is unproductive, so too is the search for material evidence of guilt, for no idols have been found, nor a secret rule, despite the detailed inventories of the king's officers and the equally diligent investigations of nineteenth-century antiquarians and historians.[1] An examination of the charges themselves is more fruitful, for if viewed within the wider context of the heretical accusations current in the twelfth and thirteenth centuries, they show the guilt of the Templars to be intrinsically unlikely. The accusations represent an attempt to play upon the deep-seated fears of contemporaries, especially concerning unexplained forces in the world around them. These fears were often focused upon an 'out-group' such as the Jews. In the case of the Templars the accusations were calculated to exploit a certain degree of residual hostility to the Order after the disasters of 1291, so that the Templars too became an 'out-group'. However, as H. C. Lea has pointed out, in contrast to the Cathars, not one Templar was prepared to be martyred for the heresies which members of the Order were supposed to have guarded so fiercely for so long,[2] yet many, including finally the Grand Master himself, died asserting the Order's innocence.

The issue of whether or not the Temple was an Order in decline at the beginning of the fourteenth century, as opposed to being heretical, is more complex and elusive. There is no doubt that extensive preoccupation with administration and finance represents a major threat to the spiritual dynamism of any monastic Order, and that from an early date after the foundation, the Templars were especially concerned with such matters. Strictures from the papacy from 1179 onwards reflect the Order's concern for its lands and privileges, while in the course of the thirteenth century, there are signs of a growing general hostility to the arrogant conduct of some Templars. All monastic Orders run the risks of success, which brings increased donations and therefore responsibility for new lands, jurisdictions and dependants, and increased membership which may dilute the quality of the original zealots. On the other hand, the very nature of a Military Order demanded that it have an efficient back-up organisation to provide finance for equipping soldiers, maintaining and building castles, and protecting pilgrims. So high were the costs of such activities, especially when the logistics of the crusades are taken into account, that this back-up organisation needed to be very large, making it necessary for the Order to contain a higher number of non-combatant members than actual fighters at any given time. Moreover, the inventories made by the servants of Philip the Fair in October 1307 do not suggest that these non-combatant members had fallen into the ways of luxury. Even the lack of flexibility of the Order after the loss of Acre in 1291 is not really a ground for condemnation, for while the Hospitallers took Rhodes and the Teutonic Knights consolidated their hold in Prussia, the Templars tried to stick to their original mandate, which, as both the Rule and the reception ceremony stressed, demanded that they strive to conquer and defend the Holy Land. In comparison, the island of Rhodes, held by the Greeks, was an easy mark. Only hindsight revealed that the Latins would never regain their position on the Palestinian mainland; the Templars were unaware of their obsolescence, and indeed they continued to attract recruits right up to the eve of the trial.[3]

These considerations do, however, suggest that the Templars

were more vulnerable than more conventional Orders. The necessary military, financial and sometimes political functions of the Templars attracted men who would have been less suited to a more contemplative and studious Order. If the Templars were to live up to the ideals of their founders, then the functional role of the Order needed to be pursued with some intensity, for there was no other substitute. While some of the practices of the Cistercians or the Franciscans in the early fourteenth century may not have met with the approval of their founders and certainly did not always follow the spirit of their respective Rules, nevertheless they still performed useful functions in society and they still provided outlets for men to whom contemplation, education and community service were of solid value.[4] But the Templars without the Holy Land were an empty Order, having no substance, no inner life, which could carry them through difficult periods and perhaps provide a foundation for a later reformation. In this sense, the seeking of new military outlets by the leaders of the Hospitallers and the Teutonic Knights proved to be shrewder than perhaps even they realised.

The internal organisation of the Templars increased the inherent risks of decline, especially in the west, for in the inventories taken in 1307 and 1308 it can be seen that the Templars rarely lived in monastic communities of any size in which they could participate in the full monastic life and in which the routines of a large community could impose discipline. Many Templar houses in the west were on a small scale, with perhaps two or three brothers only, a fact which must have encouraged a merging with the social environment until it was difficult to distinguish these supposed monks from their secular neighbours. The problems which stemmed from this are shown by the one charge which was pressed successfully, that some Templars were not aware of the Church's sacramental theory concerning lay absolution. The changes which had taken place in the Church's position on this issue since the first half of the twelfth century should have been made evident to the Templars by their priests, yet this does not seem to have been the case. The likely reasons for this support the belief that the spiritual life of the Temple was not as strong as that of many other Orders. It seems probable that the Temple was not in a position to attract priests of talent and ambition, for Orders like the Cistercians or the Dominicans were better able to cater for both. The aspiring priest does not seem to have viewed the Temple as a means to a promising career in the Church hierarchy; possibly the dislike of other Orders and of the secular clergy encouraged them to block promotion from the Temple, for few Templar priests seem to have become prelates of the Church.

There is here, however, little positive proof of internal decline: the elderly Arnold Calis of the Preceptory of Mas Deu who could not remember what observances had been enjoined upon him at his reception, the mysterious 'sisters' of the Order described by Ponsard de Gizy, and the dissolute activities of some former Templars after the suppression might hint at problems, but they are not in themselves decisive evidence of the state of the Temple in general before 1307. To set against criticisms, it can be seen that although the first confessions were obtained rapidly enough, nearly six hundred Templars retained sufficient loyalty to their Order to support a vigorous defence early in 1310, and even after the burnings of May of that year, it cannot be shown that all of them were cowed or that their morale was completely crushed, for less than a fifth of the Templars who had offered to defend the Order can definitely be proved to have retreated from the defence after the burnings.[5] In any case, whatever problems may have beset the Temple, other contemporary Orders had their problems too,[6] problems which might have assumed a different significance to historians had any of these Orders been unlucky enough to fall foul of the regime of Philip the Fair.

If the accusations of heresy are unproven and the evidence for internal decline impossible to assess, then this inevitably concentrates attention upon the motivation of Philip the Fair in causing the arrest and trial of the Templars in the first place. The most immediate and obvious motive was financial, for in both its general financial position and in the specific matter of the lack of specie to return to the 'good money' of Saint Louis, the monetary problems of the government are evident. However, while this remains the prime reason for the attack on the Templars, it does not exclude the possibility that there were other factors in the arrests. The Templars were a military organisation responsible not to the king directly but to the papacy, and they possessed considerable immunities within the French kingdom. Possibly a man of Philip's temper saw them as posing a threat to his concept of the Capetian kingdom. At first sight this argument looks rather thin, if the numbers and age-structure of the largely unarmed guardians of the scattered rural preceptories are taken into account. Despite the exposure of the fragility of the French army at Courtrai and despite the fact that relatively small numbers of determined men, if well armed and properly motivated, could achieve considerable military success in the thirteenth century, it stretches credibility indeed to portray the Templars in France as a direct military threat to the crown. But, more plausibly, it could be suggested that the existence of any immunity of the kind represented by the Templars was objectionable to Philip IV's lawyers, and that what was at stake was a matter of principle rather than any military threat. If, as Professor J. R. Strayer believes, Philip IV was striving to unite the two ideas of a sacred king ruling over a holy country as a basis for the concentration of the people's loyalty upon the French monarchy,[7] then the Templars, especially if portrayed as heretics and therefore as a dire threat to this holy unity, could justifiably be suppressed. The utterances of the government during the trial certainly support Professor Strayer's view of the regime's image of itself, but in this affair it is to be suspected that this largely represents a high-flown justification for an action with more sordid motives. The Templars' position was not after all unique in France; the Hospitallers, for instance, were equally a privileged Order responsible to the papacy. Perhaps it is enough to say that the Templars were particularly obnoxious to Philip the Fair as a wealthy, exempt and predominantly aristocratic enclave in a country whose king had made considerable progress towards subduing the pretensions of the feudal nobility. Whereas the Hospitallers, like others whose wealth lay predominantly in landed property, had been adversely affected by rising prices while rents remained fixed, the liquid wealth of the Templars, deeply involved in banking as well as land, was both an affront and a temptation to the monarchy. Finally, there remains the possibility that Philip and his government really believed in the accusations of heresy that they levelled against the Templars; this would distinguish the Templars from similarly placed elements within the kingdom such as the Hospitallers. Despite the propaganda element in the charges this cannot be ruled out completely. The 'Most Christian king' displayed considerable powers of self-deception during his reign, while neither he nor his advisers can be so completely detached from their environment that they should be seen absolutely as its manipulators.

The trial of the Templars can be explained in terms of factors

external to the Order, rather than through any of its internal fail-
ings: the financial needs of Philip the Fair, the weakness of the
papacy after the defeat of Boniface VIII, the loss of Acre and its
impact upon the attitudes of western Christendom, and the chance
that led Clement V to request Jacques de Molay's presence in France
during one of the recurrent financial crises of Philip IV's government. However, while these practical circumstances were of immediate relevance, the social context of the trial should not be ignored.
Contemporaries believed that the devil was constantly seeking to
spread corruption throughout Christian society, and, by attacking
the weak points of the structure, aimed to break down its functional
unity. The task of the faithful was to be ever vigilant to this threat
and when these evil activities were exposed, ruthlessly to cut out the
canker, lest the whole be threatened. The arguments used against the
Templars during the trial both play upon and reflect these fears. At
Poitiers, Plaisians warned the pope that 'the devil comes as a robber
for the purpose of breaking into your house';[8] the anonymous jurist
of 1310 justified his view that the Templars should be condemned by
reference to Scripture, for he pointed out that a whole city had been
brought down because many of, although not all, its inhabitants,
had committed the sins of idolatry and sodomy, which had also been
proved against the Templars;[9] while at the Council of Vienne, Guillaume Le Maire had seen the course of action against the Order,
paraphrasing Matthew 5 and 18, 'If your right eye or right limb
offend you, cut them off and throw them away. For it is better that
one of your limbs should be destroyed than the whole body.'[10] The
trial cannot therefore be viewed in the conventional sense of a test of
guilt or innocence, but as a medieval tragedy in which society, by
creating the circumstances which enabled the government of Philip
IV to act as it did, crushed the life from an Order which it had once
been proud to raise up.

Appendix A

THE ARTICLES OF ACCUSATION,
12 AUGUST 1308*

These are the articles on which enquiry should be made against the Order of the Knighthood of the Temple.

Firstly that, although they declared that the Order had been solemnly established and approved by the Apostolic See, nevertheless in the reception of the brothers of the said Order, and at some time after, there were preserved and performed by the brothers those things which follow:

Namely that each in his reception, or at some time after, or as soon as a fit occasion could be found for the reception, denied Christ, sometimes Christ crucified, sometimes Jesus, and sometimes God, and sometimes the Holy Virgin, and sometimes all the saints of God, led and advised by those who received him. – Item, [that] the brothers as a whole did this. – Item, that the majority [of them did this].

Item, that [they did this] also sometimes after the reception.

Item, that the receptors said and taught those whom they were receiving, that Christ, or sometimes Jesus, or sometimes Christ crucified, is not the true God.

Item, that they told those whom they received that he was a false prophet.

Item, that he had not suffered nor was he crucified for the redemption of the human race, but on account of his sins.

Item, that neither the receptors nor those being received had a hope of achieving salvation through Jesus, and they said this, or the equivalent or similar, to those whom they received.

Item, that they made those whom they received spit on a cross, or on a representation or sculpture of the cross and an image of Christ, although sometimes those who were being received spat next [to it].

Item, that they sometimes ordered that this cross be trampled underfoot.

* *Procès*, vol. i, pp. 89–96.

Item, that brothers who had been received sometimes trampled on the cross.

Item, that sometimes they urinated and trampled, and caused others to urinate, on this cross, and several times they did this on Good Friday.

Item, that some of them, on that same day or another of Holy Week, were accustomed to assemble for the aforesaid trampling and urination.

Item, that they adored a certain cat, [which] sometimes appeared to them in their assembly.

Item, that they did this in contempt of Christ and the orthodox faith.

Item, that they did not believe in the sacrament of the altar. – Item, that some of them [did not believe]. – Item, that the majority [of them did not believe].

Item, that nor [did they believe] in the other sacraments of the Church.

Item, that the priests of the Order by whom the body of Christ is consecrated did not speak the words in the canon of the mass. – Item, that some of them [did not]. – Item, that the majority [did not].

Item, that the receptors enjoined this upon them.

Item, that they believed, and thus it was told to them, that the Grand Master could absolve them from sin. – Item, that the Visitor [could]. – Item, that the preceptors [could], of whom many were laymen.

Item, that they did this *de facto*. – Item, that some of them [did].

Item, that the Grand Master of the aforesaid Order confessed this, in the presence of important persons, before he was arrested.

Item, that in the reception of the brothers of the said Order or at about that time, sometimes the receptor and sometimes the received were kissed on the mouth, on the navel, or on the bare stomach, and on the buttocks or the base of the spine. – Item, [that they were kissed] sometimes on the navel. – Item, [that they were kissed] sometimes on the base of the spine. – Item, [that they were kissed] sometimes on the penis.

Item, that in that reception they made those who were being received swear that they would not leave the Order.

Item, that they regarded them straightway as professed brethren.

Item, that they held these receptions secretly.

Item, that there was no one present except the brothers of the said Order.

Item, that on account of this, vehement suspicion had, for a long time, worked against the said Order.

Item, that it was generally held.

Item, that they told the brothers whom they received that they could have carnal relations together.

Item, that it was licit for them to do this.

Item, that they ought to do and submit to this mutually.

Item, that it was not a sin for them to do this.

Item, that they did this, or many of them [did]. – Item, that some of them [did].

Item, that in each province they had idols, namely heads, of which some had three faces, and some one, and others had a human skull.

Item, that they adored these idols or that idol, and especially in their great chapters and assemblies.

Item, that they venerated [them].

Item, that [they venerated them] as God.

Item, that [they venerated them] as their Saviour.

Item, that some of them [did].

Item, that the majority of those who were in the chapters [did].

Item, that they said that that head could save them.

Item, that [it could] make riches.

Item, that it gave them all the riches of the Order.

Item, that it made the trees flower.

Item, that [it made] the land germinate.

Item, that they surrounded or touched each head of the aforesaid idols with small cords, which they wore around themselves next to the shirt or the flesh.

Item, that in his reception, the aforesaid small cords or some lengths of them were given to each of the brothers.

Item, that they did this in veneration of an idol.

Item, that it was enjoined on them that they should wear the small cords around themselves, as is set out, and wear them continually, and they did this even by night.

Item, that the brothers of the said Order were generally received in the aforesaid manner.

Item, that [it was done] everywhere.

Item, that [it was done] by the majority.

Item, that those who were not willing to do the aforesaid at their reception or afterwards were killed or imprisoned.

Item, that some of them [were].

Item, that the majority [were].

Item, that they enjoined them, on oath, that they should not reveal the aforesaid.

Item, that [this was done] under punishment of death, or of imprisonment.

Item, that nor should they reveal the manner of reception.

Item, that neither should they dare speak about the aforesaid among themselves.

Item, that if any were found to have revealed [these things], they were punished by death or prison.

Item, that they enjoined them not to confess to anyone except a brother of their Order.

Item, that the said brothers of the Order, knowing the said errors, neglected to correct them.

Item, that they neglected to inform Holy Mother Church.

Item, that they did not retreat from the observance of the aforesaid errors and the community of the aforesaid brothers, although they had the opportunity for retreating and for doing the aforesaid.

Item, that the aforesaid things were done and preserved beyond the sea, in places in which the Grand Master and chapter of the said Order were at the time staying.

Item, that sometimes the aforesaid denial of Christ was done in the presence of the Grand Master and the chapter of the aforesaid.

Item, that the aforesaid things were done and observed in Cyprus.

Item, that [they were done] on this side of the sea in all kingdoms and in other places in which receptions of the aforesaid brothers were made.

Item, that the aforesaid things were observed in the whole Order generally and communally. – Item, that [they were] of long and general observance. – Item, that [they were] of ancient custom. – Item, that [they were] from the statute of the aforesaid Order.

Item, that the aforesaid observances, customs, ordinances and statutes were made and observed in the whole Order, beyond the sea and on this side of the sea.

Item, that the aforesaid were from points of the Order, having been introduced by their errors after the approval of the Apostolic See.

Item, that the receptions of the brothers of the said Order were made generally in the aforesaid manner in the whole Order aforesaid.

Item, that the Grand Master of the said Order enjoined that the aforesaid be thus observed and done. – Item, that the Visitors [did]. – Item, that the preceptors [did]. Item, that other leaders of the said Order [did].

Item, that these self-same men observed this, and taught that it be done and preserved. – Item, that others of them [did].

Item, that the brothers did not preserve another mode of reception in the said Order.

Item, that it is not within the memory of anyone of the Order who is living that there has been observed in their time another mode [of reception].

Item, that the Grand Master, the Visitors, the preceptors and the other Masters of the said Order, having power in this, punished gravely [those] not preserving nor willing to preserve the aforesaid manner of reception and the other things above, when a complaint was brought to them.

Item, that charitable gifts in the said Order were not made as they ought, nor was hospitality offered.

Item, that they did not reckon [it] a sin in the said Order to acquire properties belonging to another by legal or illegal means.

Item, that it was authorised by them that they should procure increase and profit to the said Order in whatever way they could by legal or illegal means.

Item, that it was not reckoned a sin to commit perjury on this account.

Item, that they were accustomed to hold their chapters in secret.

Item, that [they were held] secretly, either at the first sleep or in the first vigil of the night.

Item, that [they were held] secretly, since all the other *familia* of the house had been sent out and the house had been closed, as they sent out all the *familia* on those nights when they held chapters.

Item, that [they were held] secretly, because in this way they shut themselves up when a chapter was held, as all the doors of the house and church in which they were holding the chapter they fortified so firmly that no one might nor could gain access to them or near them, nor could anyone see or hear what they were doing or saying.

Item, that [they were held] so secretly that they were accustomed to place a guard on the roof of the house or church in which they were holding the chapter, in case anyone approached the place in which they were holding the chapter.

Item, that they observed and were accustomed to observe similar secrecy, as was usual in the receiving of brothers.

Item, that this error flourishes and has flourished in the Order for a long time, since they hold the opinion, and held in the past, that the Grand Master can absolve the brothers from their sins.

Item, that the greater error flourishes and has flourished, that these hold and have held in the past that the Grand Master can absolve the brothers of the Order from sin, even [sins] not confessed which they omitted to confess on account of some shame or fear of the penance to be enjoined or inflicted.

Item, that the Grand Master has confessed these aforesaid errors before capture, spontaneously, in the presence of ecclesiastics and laymen dignified in the faith.

Item, that the majority of the preceptors of the Order were present.

Item, that they hold and have held the aforesaid errors, not only through the opinions and beliefs of the Grand Master, but from other preceptors and especially from leading Visitors of the Order.

Item, that whatever the Grand Master, especially with his chapter, made, ordained and legislated, the whole Order had to hold and to observe and also was observed.

Item, that this power appertained to him and has resided in him from of old.

Item, that the aforesaid depraved habits and errors had lasted for such a time that the Order could have been renewed in personnel once, twice or more from the time of the introduction or observation of the aforesaid errors.

Item, that . . . all or two-thirds of the Order, knowing the said errors, neglected to correct them.

Item, that they neglected to inform Holy Mother Church.

Item, that they did not retreat from the observance of the aforesaid errors and from the community of the said brothers, although they had the opportunity to retreat and do the aforesaid.

Item, that many brothers of the said Order, because of the filth and errors of their Order, departed, some transferring to another Order and others remaining in secular life.

Item, that on account of each of the aforesaid, great scandals have arisen against the said Order in the hearts of elevated persons, even of kings and princes, and have been generated in almost the whole of the Christian population.

Item, that all and each of the aforesaid have been observed and manifest among the brothers of the said Order.

Item, that concerning these things there is public talk, general opinion and repute both among the brothers of the Order and outside. – Item, that [there is] concerning the majority of the aforesaid. – Item, that [there is] concerning others.

Item, that the Grand Master of the Order, the Visitor and the Grand Preceptors of Cyprus, Normandy and Poitou, as well as many other preceptors and some other brothers of the said Order, have confessed what is written above, both in judicial inquiry and outside, in the presence of appointed persons and also before public persons in many places.

Item, that some brothers of the said Order, knights as well as priests, also others, in the presence of our lord pope and of the lords cardinal, have confessed the aforesaid or a great part of the said errors.

Item that [they have confessed] through the swearing of oaths by them.

Item that also they have certified the aforesaid in full consistory.

Appendix B

AN ORTHODOX RECEPTION: THE DESCRIPTION OF GERARD DE CAUX, 12 JANUARY 1311*

He had been received into the said Order at about the time of the Feast of the Holy Apostles Peter and Paul, twelve or thirteen years ago, in a room of the house of the Temple at Cahors, in the morning, after high mass, by Brother Guigo Ademar, formerly a knight, then preceptor of the province, in the presence of Brothers Raymond de la Costa, priest, Raymond Robert, the Preceptor of Basoez, Pierre, then Preceptor of the said house of Cahors, of whose family name he was ignorant, and a former knight companion of the said Brother Guigo, whose names and family names he said that he could not remember, and Ger. Barasci and Bertrand de Longa Valle, knights, who, at the same day and time, with the same persons present, were received with him in this way.

For, when he and the said Ger. Barosa and Bertrand de Longa Valle, who, together with the witness himself, had, five days before, been newly knighted, were waiting in a certain room next to the chapel of the said house, the said Brother Raymond Robert and a certain other knight, whom he had not noticed, as it seemed to him, came to them and spoke to them the following words: Do you seek the company of the Order of the Temple and participation in the spiritual and temporal goods which are in it? and when these men had replied that they did, the said two men who had come to them had said: You seek what is a great thing, and you do not know the strong precepts which are [observed] in the said Order; for you see us from the outside, well dressed, well mounted, and in great apparel, but you cannot know the austerities of the Order, and the strong precepts which are in it; for when you wish to be on this side of the sea, you will be beyond [it], and the converse, and when you wish to sleep it will be necessary for you to be awake, and to go

* *Procès*, vol. 1, pp. 379–86.

hungry when you wish to eat. Can you sustain all these things for the honour of God and the safety of your souls?

And when they had replied yes, if it should please God, they had continued: We wish to know from you if you are free from those things which we wish to ask from you. For the first: we wish to know if you believe well in the Catholic faith according to the faith of the Roman Church, if you are in holy orders or tied by the bond of matrimony, if you are bound by oath to another Order, if you are of the knightly class and born from legitimate wedlock, if you are excommunicate on account of your own fault or otherwise, if you have promised anything or made a gift to any of the brothers of the Order of the Temple or others that you might be received into this Order, if you have any secret infirmity on account of which you might be unable to serve the house and to bear arms, if you are burdened by debt on your own behalf or on behalf of others of which you cannot discharge yourself or with your friends without the goods of the Temple. To which it was replied by those being received that they believed well in the faith, and that they were free, noble, fit and of legitimate birth, nor did they suffer from any of the aforesaid impediments.

After which the two receptors had said to them that they should turn themselves towards the said chapel, and ask God, the Blessed Virgin and all the saints of God that if their entry should work towards the safety of their souls, and the honour of their persons and their friends, that God should bring to completion their petition and intention; and when they had turned themselves for the purpose of making the said prayer, the two brothers had retreated from them, going, as the witness believed, to tell the said Brother Guigo about their reply and intention.

After a short delay, the two brothers, returning to them in the same place, had asked if they had thought well concerning the aforesaid, and if they persisted in the same intention as before; when these men had answered yes, they retreated from them, returning, as he believed, to the said Brother Guigo to refer the aforesaid, and after a while had come back to them, saying that they should remove from their heads their caps and coifs, and having clasped hands, they should come into the presence of the said Brother Guigo, and that, with knees bent, they should ask from him and say what is written below: Lord, we come here to you and to these lord brothers who

are with you, and ask for the companionship of the Order and participation in the spiritual and temporal goods which are in it, and we
wish in perpetuity to be the serving slaves of the said Order and to
put aside our will for that of another; and the said Brother Guigo
answered that they were asking a great thing, repeating the words
spoken above to them by the aforesaid two brothers, and they, having replied, as is written above, through an oath on a certain book,
which they took on bended knees, in his presence, that there were
not upon them the impediments named above, he said to them: You
should understand fully what we are saying to you; you should
swear and promise to God and the Blessed Mary that you will
always be obedient to the Master of the Temple, and to whichever
brother of the said Order is put above you, and that you will preserve chastity, the good usages and the good customs of the Order,
and you will live without property, except that it may be conceded
to you by your superior, and that you will always help as far as you
can to conserve what is acquired in the Kingdom of Jerusalem, and
to conquer what is not yet acquired, and that you will never be in
any place in which, from your desire or inclination, any Christian
man or woman is killed, or disinherited unjustly, and if goods of the
Temple are committed to you, that you will return a good and lawful account from them on behalf of the Holy Land, and you will not
leave this Order for better or for worse without the permission of
your superiors.

When they had sworn these things, he said to them: We receive
you, your fathers and mothers, and two or three of your friends
whom you will have chosen to participate in the spiritual works
done or to be done in the Order from the beginning to the end. And
these things having been said, he put the mantles on them, and
blessed them, and for the blessing the said Brother Raymond de la
Costa, the priest, spoke the psalm: *Ecce quam bonum et quam
jocundum habitare fratres in unum*; and the versicles: *Mitte eis aux-
ilium de sancto, et nichil proficiat inimicus in eis*, with the prayer of
the Holy Spirit: *Deus, qui corde fidelium*, etc. And then the Master,
raising them upwards by their hands, kissed them on the mouth, and
it seemed to him that the said priest and the knights present kissed
them on the mouth in the same way.

After which the said Master, having sat down, made them sit near
his feet, and when the said brothers who were present had sat down,

he said to them that they should be very joyful, because the Lord had led them to so noble an Order as was the Knighthood of the Temple, and that they should especially pray that they should not do anything on account of which they might lose the said Order, and that this was not pleasing to God, adding that there were some reasons on account of which they could lose the said Order, and some on account of which they could lose the habit of the said Order, and some on account of which they might be subjected to some punishments, concerning which he explained to them those which they should remember, and they should diligently ask others among the brothers of the said Order. And, among other things, he said to them that they would be ejected from the house: if they made entry to the said Order by simony; if they revealed the secrets of the chapters at which they were present to any brothers of the Order, or to others who were not present at them; if they were convicted of grievously killing a Christian man or woman, and as a result of this they would also be placed in perpetual imprisonment; if convicted of theft, by which they also understood that they should not go out except by customary doors, [and] that they should not make 'counter keys'; if they were convicted of the crime of sodomy, on account of which they could also be imprisoned perpetually; if two, or three, or more of them by common counsel and false faction should bring any charge against brothers of the Order, and concerning this they were convicted by their confessions, or by two or more brothers of the Order, or by their patrons; if they should visit the Saracens with the intention of remaining with them, although afterwards they might return and do penance; if they were convicted of not believing properly in the Catholic faith; if they took flight, being in arms against the enemies of the faith, having deserted their standard and their leader; and if, without permission of their superiors, they should cause themselves to be promoted to holy orders.

Item, the aforesaid Brother Guigo said to them that they would lose the habit, if they disdained to obey their superiors, and were rebellious against them, and [their expulsion] notwithstanding, if they should persevere in rebellion, they should be placed in fetters; if they should maliciously thrust at or strike a brother, so that he was forced to move both feet, and if a shedding of blood should result, they could be imprisoned; if they should strike a Christian man or woman with stone, stick or iron, as a result of which he could, with

one blow, be mutilated or injured; if they should have carnal intercourse with a woman, or had been in a suspicious place with her; if
they should make accusation against other brothers concerning some
reason by which they should lose the habit, and they should fail in
proof; if they should fraudulently impute to others things which were
not true, which if such things had been true they [the accused] would
have been expelled from the Order; if they should say in the presence
of other brothers, even in the heat of anger, that they would cross
over to the Saracens, even though they did not; if when carrying the
banner of arms, they should fight with it, without the order of their
superiors, or others follow, or should lay it aside, and if there followed damage from the aforesaid, they could be imprisoned as a
result of this; if, being in arms, they should go to attack enemies without the order of the leader, except that they should do this for the
help of any Christian man or woman; if they should receive money
belonging to another as their own, so that temporal lords should lose
their customary tolls; if they maliciously contrived to deny any temporal lord *census*, or a certain service, to the performance of which
they were held responsible; if they refused to receive any travelling
brother of the Order in the houses of the Order which they held, and
to refresh [him]; if they should receive anyone into the brotherhood
of the Order without authority, [without] the presence of the chapters or their superiors, or otherwise than they ought; if they should
receive an ignoble person into the said Order; if they should open letters which were sent to others by the Master and maliciously break
the seal; if they should break someone else's lock or fastening of bags
in which were carried money or similar things, or other things, and if,
from the said breakage there should follow damage, they should be
held as for theft; if they should give away the goods of the houses of
the Order which were not committed to them, or if they should dissi-
pate the goods of the houses conceded to them, or if they should
stand surety to such [persons] that by standing surety, or by accom-
modating them, they could likely be lost, or if they gave away any
animal of the Order except a dog, or a cat, which was not in their
power; if by hunting or by following the hunt they lost or destroyed
any horses, or in any other way they should bring damage to the
Order from this particular activity; if, wishing to prove arms without
the authority of their superiors, they should destroy [the horses];
if they should cause damage to their house beyond the value of 4

deniers. If moreover with the intention of putting aside the Order they should stay one night outside the houses of the Order, but if for two nights or more they should stay outside the house, they should not be able to recover the habit for one year; if, moved by anger, in the presence of other brothers, they should throw aside their habit, and do not resume [it] at once at the admonition, prayer or request of those present, or if another brother throws aside the mantle in this way, and not wishing to resume it, at the admonition, prayers or request of those present he places this mantle on his shoulder, in the said three last cases he could not recover the mantle except after a year, but in other cases it will be left to the decision of the Master and brothers when the said mantle should be returned, when, on account of the aforesaid cases, it was lost.

Item, after the aforesaid the said receptor said to them that since they had come to the Order he should teach them how they ought to come to church and to table, and he told them that when matins was struck they should arise and, entering quietly into the church, they should say twenty-eight *Pater nosters*, fourteen for the hours of the day and fourteen for the hours of the Blessed Mary, and they ought to maintain silence from when they arose until after prime, and for each hour of the day they should say fourteen *Pater nosters*, namely seven for the hours of the day and seven for the hours of the Blessed Mary, and, when they were in a place in which they could do this, they ought to hear to be spoken or sung in church, matins, prime, terce, midday prayers (*meridiem*) and mass; afterwards, at the striking of the bell, they ought to assemble at table and at the meal, and if there was a brother priest in the house, before they sat at table, they ought to wait for him to make benediction at table, and each brother should say *Pater noster* at least once; also before they sat, they ought to see if there was on the table bread and salt, wine, and water when they did not have wine, and at table they ought to speak little; having eaten the meal, they ought to return to the church, if it was near, to give thanks, and the priest returned thanks by saying prayers and *Miserere mei*, and the brothers said *Pater noster* once; and if there was not a church there or it was a long way away, they did this in the refectory or in the house in which they were, standing and not sitting. Afterwards, at the striking of nones, they ought to re-enter the church, and for it to say fourteen *Pater nosters*, and at vespers eighteen; nevertheless they were not held to say the said number of *Pater nosters* for each hour when they heard them spoken or sung in church, unless they wished; and at all hours they were to begin first to say *Pater noster* for the hours of the Blessed Mary; but at compline they said the said *Pater noster* for the hours of the Blessed Mary, ultimately for the purpose of signifying, as the said receptor said to them, that their Order was begun to the honour of the Blessed Mary and would be finished in her honour when God pleased. And beyond the aforesaid, he ordered them that every day before a meal, they should say sixty *Pater nosters*, namely thirty for the living, that God might lead and preserve them to a good end, and thirty for the dead; and thus, as he said, it was ordered from a general precept of the Order to other brothers when they were received. Item, the said receptor told them that, at supper, which they ought to eat before compline, they ought to do those things aforesaid concerning lunch, and after compline, speak little, and that they should visit their horses, and when they were on an armed expedition, they should see to their harness, and afterwards enter their beds and lie in their clothing and linen hose; and that they should wear around themselves some small cords, as a sign that they ought to live chastely and to restrain their carnal desires; and that they should maintain a light during the night in the place in which they lay, lest an evilly disposed enemy should give them occasion for transgressing, and also in the stable if they have [one]. Item, the said receptor said that they ought not to be godfathers, nor to enter a house in which a woman was lying in confinement, nor to permit women to serve them personally, except in cases of illness, when other servants were not present, and then with the authority of their superiors; nor to kiss any woman even of their own family. Nor ought they to say to any persons anything improper, and to make reference to any obscene speech, nor to swear concerning God, since all courteous things were permitted to them and all impolite things forbidden them. And then the said receptor said to them: Go, God make you worthy men.

Chronology
of the Trial of the Templars

Late February: Seven questions to the masters of theology at Paris

24–9 March: Convocation of the Estates-General

25 March: Reply of the masters of theology

5–15 May: Meeting of the Estates-General at Tours

26 May: Philip IV arrives at Poitiers for a meeting with the pope

29 May: First discourse of Guillaume de Plaisians in the papal consistory

14 June: Second discourse of Guillaume de Plaisians

27 June: Philip IV sends the pope seventy-two picked Templars

5 July: *Subit assidue*

12 August: *Faciens misericordiam* and *Regnans in coelis*

13 August: Clement V departs from Poitiers

17–20 August: Cardinals' hearing of the leaders of the Order at Chinon

1309   *March*: Clement V takes up semi-permanent residence at Avignon

Spring (?): Beginning of the episcopal inquiries

8 August: Papal commission opens inquiry into the Order

22 November: First hearings of the papal commission

26 November: Jacques de Molay's first appearance before the commission

28 November: Molay's second appearance before the commission; papal commission closes its first session

1310   *3 February*: Papal commission reassembles for second session

2 March: Molay's third appearance before the commission

14 March: 127 articles of accusation read to the Templars who are prepared to defend the Order

28 March: Mass meeting of the Templars prepared to defend the Order convened in the episcopal garden in Paris

4 April: *Alma mater*

7 April: Defence of the Order led by Pietro di Bologna and Renaud de Provins

12 May: Burning of fifty-four Templars near Paris

30 May: Papal commission adjourns proceedings

3 November: Papal commission begins third session

1311   *26 May*: Last depositions before the papal commission

      5 June: Papal commission closes proceedings

      16 October: Opening of the Council of Vienne

      Late October: Seven Templars appear at Vienne offering to defend the Order

1312   *20 March*: Philip IV arrives at Vienne

      22 March: *Vox in excelso*

      2 May: *Ad providam*

      6 May: *Considerantes dudum*

1313   *21 March*: Hospitallers agree to pay Philip IV 200,000 *livres tournois* compensation

1314   *18 March*: Burning of Jacques de Molay and Geoffroi de Charney

      20 April: Death of Clement V

      29 November: Death of Philip IV

Notes

(See Bibliography for abbreviations used in the Notes.)

I THE PARTICIPANTS

1 See the following accounts of pilgrim experiences: Saewulf, *An Account of the Pilgrimage of Saewulf to Jerusalem and the Holy Land in the Years 1102 and 1103*, tr. W. R. B. Brownlow, in *PPTS*, vol. 4 (London, 1892), pp. 8–9; Daniel the Higumene, *The Pilgrimage of the Russian Abbot Daniel in the Holy Land, 1106–7 AD*, tr. C. W. Wilson, in *PPTS*, vol. 4, pp. 9, 26, 42–3, 48–50, 56–7, 59, 61, 65–6, 72–3; Ekkehard of Aura, *Ekkehardi Hierosolymita*, ed. H. Hagenmeyer (Tübingen, 1877), p. 309; Albert of Aix, *Alberti Aquensis Historia Hierosolymitana*, bk XII, chap. 33, in *RHCr.: Historiens occidentaux*, vol. 4 (Paris, 1879), pp. 712–13.

2 William of Tyre, *Historia Rerum in Partibus Transmarinis Gestarum*, bk XII, chap. 7, in *RHCr.: Historiens occidentaux*, vol. 1 (Paris, 1844), p. 520.

3 H. de Curzon (ed.), *La Règle du Temple* (Paris, 1886), pp. 11–70.

4 *Ibid.*, cl. 14 (62), p. 25.

5 *Ibid.*, cl. 70 (56), p. 69.

6 *Ibid.*, cl. 17 (20), pp. 27–8.

7 *Ibid.*, cl. 68 (21), pp. 67–8.

8 *Ibid.*, cl. 69 (55), p. 68.

9 *Ibid.*, cl. 268–78, pp. 164–9.

10 *Ibid.*, cl. 57 (51), 58 (66), pp. 58–61.

11 Marquis d'Albon (ed.), *Cartulaire général de l'ordre du Temple, 1119?–1150* (Paris, 1913), no. 7, p. 5; no. 17, pp. 11–12; *The Anglo-Saxon Chronicle*, ed. and tr. D. Whitelock (London, 1961), year 1128, pp. 194–5.

12 See J. Riley-Smith, *The Knights of St John in Jerusalem and Cyprus, c.1050–1310* (London, 1967), chap. 2.

13 Bernard of Clairvaux, *Liber ad Milites Templi de Laude Novae Militiae*, in *Sancti Bernardi Opera*, vol. 3, ed. J. Leclercq (Rome, 1963), pp. 213–39.

14 D'Albon (ed.), *Cartulaire*, 'Bullaire', no. 5, pp. 375–9; no. 8, p. 381; no. 10, p. 382. The tithe exemption in *Omne datum optimum* was not, however, complete, nor was independence from the Patriarch of Jerusalem; see Riley-Smith, 'The Templars and the Castle of Tortosa in Syria: An Unknown Document concerning the Acquisition of the Fortress', *English Historical Review*, LXXXIV (1969), pp. 278–88.

15 A. Luchaire, *Etude sur les actes de Louis VII* (Paris, 1885), no. 230, p. 173; see J. Piquet, *Des banquiers au Moyen Age: Les Templiers* (Paris, 1939), pt II, chap. 1.

16 *Theoderich's Description of the Holy Places circa 1172 AD*, tr. and ed. A. Stewart, in *PPTS*, vol. 5 (London, 1891), pp. 30–2.

17 Gervase of Canterbury, *Opera Historica*, vol. 1, ed. W. Stubbs (Rolls Series, vol. 73; London, 1879), pp. 239, 298. A similar grant was made by Philip II of France in 1222, who left the Orders 2,000 marks each, plus a sum of 50,000 marks on condition that they kept three hundred knights in service for three years in the Holy Land: M. A. Teulet (ed.), *Layettes des trésors des chartes*, vol. 1 (Paris, 1863), no. 1547, p. 550.

18 See Riley-Smith, *The Feudal Nobility and the Kingdom of Jerusalem, 1174–1277* (London, 1973), esp. pp. 28–30, for the acquisition of lay fiefs and castles by the Military Orders during the last years of the Kingdom of Jerusalem.

19 For an idea of the resources needed to build and maintain Safed, see R. B. C. Huygens (ed.), 'De Constructione Castri Saphet', *Studi Medievali*, 3rd ser., vi (1965), pp. 355–87.

20 Odo of Deuil, *De Profectione Ludovici VII in Orientem*, ed. and tr. V. G. Berry (New York, 1948), pp. 115–27, 134–5.

21 Jacques de Vitry, *Historia Hierosolimitana*, in J. Bongars, *Gesta Dei per Francos*, vol. 2 (Hanover, 1611), pp. 1083–4.

22 Ibn al-Athir, *Extrait de la Chronique intitulée Kamel-Altevarykh*, in *RHC: Historiens orientaux*, vol. 1 (Paris, 1872), p. 679, where the French translation is *les charbons de Francs*.

23 *Ibid.*, p. 688. On another occasion the chronicler records that it was Saladin's custom to slaughter the Templars and Hospitallers, 'because of the violent hatred which they bore towards the Moslems and because of their bravery' (p. 736).

24 Curzon (ed.), *Règle*, cl. 77–181, pp. 75–134.

25 *Ibid.*, cl. 198–223, pp. 142–52.

26 *Ibid.*, cl. 386–543, pp. 216–84.

27 *Ibid.*, cl. 657–86, pp. 337–50. There is also a very detailed account of an orthodox reception in a deposition by the knight Gérard de Caux on his appearance before the papal commission during the trial (12 January 1311): *Procès*, vol. 1, pp. 379–86. See also appendix B, pp. 300–6.

28 William of Tyre, bk xii, chap. 7, p. 521.

29 *Ibid.*, bk xxi, chap. 26, p. 1049; C.-J. Hefele, *Histoire des Conciles*, tr. H. Leclercq, vol. 5, pt 2 (Paris, 1912), canon 9, pp. 1095–6. For further examples of conflict with the secular clergy, see Paris, Bibliothèque Nationale, *Nouvelles Acquisitions latines*, vol. 1, fols 165–7 (1160); vol. 2, fol. 71 (1198).

30 H. Prutz (ed.), *Malteser Urkunden und Regesten zur Geschichte der Tempelherren und der Johanniter* (Munich, 1883), no. 4, p. 38. He cites a further twenty-one renewals of this bull.

31 Paris, Bibliothèque Nationale, *Nouvelles Acquisitions latines*, vol. 2, fols 42, 68.

32 William of Tyre, bk xvii, chap. 27, pp. 804–6; bk xix, chap. 11.

pp. 900–2; bk xx, chap. 5, pp. 948–9; bk xx, chaps 29–30, pp. 995–9. For the behaviour of the Assassins, M. G. S. Hodgson, *The Order of the Assassins* (The Hague, 1955), esp. pp. 148ff.

33 See A. C. Krey, 'William of Tyre: The Making of an Historian in the Middle Ages', *Speculum*, xvi (1941), p. 164, and F. Lundgreen, *Wilhelm von Tyrus und der Templerorden* (Berlin, 1911), pp. 89–93, 101, 104–5, 150–3. Lundgreen presents a rather extreme case against William of Tyre which seems unlikely.

34 Letter of Innocent III, 13 September 1207, in *PL*, vol. 215, cols 1217–18. The pope's condemnation of the Templars for the sin of pride may here be in conscious contrast to the praise which St Bernard had originally been able to bestow on them for their lack of concern with knightly pomp. Moreover, William of Tyre had said that the Templars had neglected humility, 'the guardian of all the virtues'; this contrasts with pride, the first of man's sins. Other sins stemmed from pride, or in Innocent's phrase, they added 'sin to sin like a long rope'. The accusations of 1307 may have some connection with such attacks, since pride led men to put aside their function within the universal scheme, a neglect which could be seen as a repudiation of God. The theme that the Templars had denied Christ and disrupted the functional unity of medieval society runs very strongly through the trial. Pride naturally became avarice, as seen in the Templars' quest for material wealth. In their defence, the Templars argued that their Order had been 'founded in charity' (see above, chap. 5, p. 162), which again represents a conscious opposite, in this case to avarice.

35 Clement IV, *Les Registres de Clément IV (1265–8)*, ed. E. Jordan, vol. 1 (Paris, 1904), no. 836, pp. 326–7.

36 Matthew Paris, *Chronica Majora*, ed. H. R. Luard, vol. 5 (*Rolls Series*, vol. 57; London, 1880), p. 148. Matthew Paris also claimed that the Temple and the Hospital deliberately stirred up trouble between Christians and Moslems in order to obtain money from pilgrims (*ibid.*, vol. 4, p. 291), and that in 1241 rivalry between the Orders led the Templars to besiege the houses of the Hospitallers in Acre, and to drive the Teutonic Knights from the city (*ibid.*, pp. 167–8, 256).

37 *Gestes des Chiprois*, ed. G. Raynaud (Geneva, 1887), pp. 234–7; *Ludolph von Suchem's Description of the Holy Land, and of the Way Thither, Written in the Year 1350*, tr. A. Stewart, in *PPTS*, vol. 12 (London, 1895), pp. 55–6. Guillaume de Beaujeu was particularly resented as a representative of the claims of Charles of Anjou, King of Sicily until 1285, to the throne of Jerusalem. Beaujeu was a former commander of the Templars in Apulia (*Gestes des Chiprois*, p. 202), and was related to the Capetian family. He acted on Charles's behalf in the east, e.g. in the sale of grain (8 November 1277); N. Nicolini, *Codice diplomatico sui rapporti Veneto-Napoletani durante il regno di Carlo I d'Angio* (Rome, 1965), no. 205, pp. 217–18.

38 See M. C. Barber, 'James of Molay, the Last Grand Master of the

Temple', *Studia Monastica*, XIV (1972), pp. 95–6, 98–9. For the career of Molay, see M. L. Bulst-Thiele, *Sacrae Domus Militiae Templi Hierosolymi-tani Magistri* (Göttingen, 1974), pp. 295–359. This book contains biographies of all the Grand Masters of the Temple.

39 James I of Aragon, *The Chronicle of James I of Aragon*, ed. and tr. J. Forster, vol. 2 (London, 1883), p. 649.

40 Clement V, *Regestum Clementis Papae V . . . nunc primum editum cura et studio Monachorum Ordinis S. Benedicti*, year 1 (Rome, 1885), no. 1033, cols 190–1, is the order to the Grand Master of the Hospital. The order to Molay has not survived, but was probably sent at the same time.

41 Baluze, vol. 3, p. 85.

42 *Procès*, vol. 1, p. 475; vol. 2, p. 279.

43 Baluze, vol. 3, pp. 145–9.

44 *Ibid.*, pp. 150–4.

45 Pierre Dubois, *De Recuperatione Terre Sancte*, ed. C. V. Langlois (Paris, 1891), pp. 13–15.

46 *Ibid.*, p. 134. Dubois wanted action taken against Boniface VIII at the same time, for he asserted that Boniface had received 50,000 florins for keeping quiet about the errors of the Temple. The paragraph is not included in the Langlois edition, but was printed by Mollat in his edition of Baluze, vol. 3, p. 162, after consulting the original manuscript.

47 Jean de Saint-Victor, *Excerpta e Memoriali Historiarum Auctore Johanne Parisiensi, Sancti Victoris Parisiensis Canonico Regulari*, in *RHG*, vol. 21, p. 645; Tolomeo da Lucca, *Historia Ecclesiastica*, in Baluze, vol. 1, pp. 24–5; Bernard Gui, *Flores Chronicorum*, in Baluze, vol. 1, p. 60.

48 Bernard Gui, *Flores Chron.*, pp. 59–60; for details of his earlier career, see G. Lizerand, *Clément V et Philippe IV le Bel* (Paris, 1910), pp. 23ff.

49 Tolomeo da Lucca, p. 52. Mollat believed that Clement was suffer-ing from cancer of the bowel or stomach; Baluze, vol. 2, p. 93.

50 For the political theories of the canonists, see W. Ullmann, *Medieval Papalism* (London, 1949).

51 See S. Runciman, *The Sicilian Vespers* (Cambridge, 1958).

52 See W. L. Wakefield, *Heresy, Crusade and Inquisition in Southern France, 1100–1250* (London, 1974), for a summary of Cathar history in Languedoc.

53 See, for example, Pierre Garcias of Toulouse, accused of Cathar belief in 1247, who is reported as saying that 'he held matrimony to be of no worth and that he had not had sexual relations with his wife for two years'; C. Douais (ed.), *Documents pour servir à l'histoire de l'Inquisition dans le Languedoc au XIIIᵉ et au XIVᵉ siècle* (Paris, 1900), p. 106, also pp. 90–114.

54 See E. Griffe, *Les Débuts de l'aventure cathare en Languedoc (1140–90)* (Paris, 1969), chap. 2.

55 See H. C. Lea, *A History of the Inquisition of the Middle Ages*, vol. 1 (New York, 1889), esp. pp. 310–11, and H. Maisonneuve, *Etudes sur les origines de l'Inquisition*, 2nd edn (Paris, 1960).

56 E. Friedberg (ed.), *Corpus Iuris Canonici*, vol. 2 (Graz, 1959), cols 780–2.

57 See A. Fliche, C. Thouzellier and Y. Azais, *La Chrétienté romaine (1198–1274)* (*Histoire de l'Eglise*, ed. A. Fliche and V. Martin, vol. 10; Paris, 1950), pp. 304–24, for the repression of heresy under Gregory IX; A. Potthast, *Regesta Pontificum Romanorum*, vol. 2 (Berlin, 1875), no. 14592 (15 May 1252) for Innocent IV's bull.

58 Bernard Gui, *Practica Inquisitionis Heretice Pravitatis*, ed. C. Douais (Paris, 1886), pp. 3–12. There is a text and translation of the fifth part, concerned primarily with the different types of heresy likely to be encountered by an inquisitor at this time, in Bernard Gui, *Manuel de l'Inquisiteur*, 2 vols, ed. and tr. G. Mollat (Paris, 1926).

59 Bernard Gui, *Practica*, p. 214.

60 *Ibid.*, pp. 189–91, 214–15. This is not meant to imply that secular proceedings were somehow fairer, for in contemporary secular criminal trials in France, both the names of the witnesses and the depositions were withheld from the defendant; see A. C. Shannon, 'The Secrecy of Witnesses in Inquisitorial Tribunals and in Contemporary Secular Trials', in *Essays in Medieval Life and Thought Presented in Honor of Austin P. Evans*, ed. J. H. Mundy, R. W. Emery and B. N. Nelson (New York, 1955), p. 69.

61 Bernard Gui, *Practica*, p. 284.

62 *Ibid.*, pp. 101–2, 159 (prison); pp. 150–9 (signs of infamy); pp. 60, 100 (molestation of heretics); pp. 37–9, 40–1, 94–8, 165–6 (pilgrimage); pp. 218–19 (the secular arm).

63 *Ibid.*, pp. 120–3.

64 See T. S. R. Boase, *Boniface VIII* (London, 1933), chap. 2.

65 Boniface VIII, *Les Registres de Boniface VIII*, ed. G. Digard *et al.* (Paris, 1884), vol. 1, no. 2354, cols 941–3.

66 See Boase, chap. 9; for *Ausculta fili*, see Boniface VIII, *Reg. de Bon. VIII*, vol. 3, no. 4424, cols 328–35.

67 P. Dupuy, *Histoire du différend d'entre le pape Boniface VIII et Philippe le Bel, Roy de France* (Paris, 1655), pp. 68–9.

68 G. Picot (ed.), *Documents relatifs aux Etats Généraux et Assemblées réunis sous Philippe le Bel* (Paris, 1901), no. 5, p. 11.

69 Friedberg, vol. 2, cols 1245–6; Dupuy, *Histoire du différend*, pp. 182–6.

70 Dupuy, *Histoire du différend*, pp. 102–6.

71 Picot, pp. xiv–xliv.

72 See Boase, chap. 13.

73 Dupuy, *Histoire du différend*, pp. 207–8, 227–9; see Lizerand, *Clém. V*, chap. 1.

74 Tolomeo da Lucca, p. 25; Bernard Gui, *Flores Chron.*, pp. 60–1; *Chronographia Regum Francorum*, ed. H. Moranville, vol. 1 (Paris, 1891), p. 176.

75 See Lizerand, *Clém. V*, pp. 376–80.

76 Dupuy, *Histoire du différend*, p. 86.

77 Baluze, vol. 2, p. 71; vol. 3, no. 43, p. 237.

78 C. Wenck, *Clemens V und Heinrich VII* (Halle, 1882), no. 1, p. 169; Clement V, *Reg. Clem. V*, year 1, no. 940, p. 174; see Lizerand, *Clém. V*, pp. 46–7.

79 See Lizerand, *Clém. V*, pp. 51–4.

80 See Baluze, vol. 2, pp. 120–1, 107–11; vol. 3, no. 27, p. 139.

81 See Lizerand, *Clém. V*, pp. 56–7, 71–4.

82 *Ibid.*, pp. 74–5.

83 See R. Fawtier, *The Capetian Kings of France*, tr. L. Butler and R. J. Adam (London, 1960), pp. 55–6. Legends were encouraged which showed Hugh Capet receiving the crown from the last Carolingian, Louis V.

84 See F. Lot and R. Fawtier, *Histoire des institutions françaises au Moyen Age*, vol. 2 (Paris, 1958), pp. 29–34, and M. Bloch, *The Royal Touch: Sacred Monarchy and Scrofula in England and France*, tr. J. E. Anderson (London, 1973), esp. bk I, chaps 1 and 2; bk II, chap. 1.

85 See W. Ullmann, *Principles of Government and Politics in the Middle Ages* (London, 1961), pt II, chap. 4.

86 Guillaume de Nangis, *Gesta Sanctae Memoriae Ludovici Regis Franciae*, in *RHG*, vol. 20, p. 311.

87 See J. R. Strayer, 'France: The Holy Land, the Chosen People, and the Most Christian King', in *Medieval Statecraft and the Perspectives of History: Essays by Joseph R. Strayer*, ed. J. F. Benton and T. H. Bisson (Princeton, NJ, 1971), p. 313.

88 See E. Boutaric, *La France sous Philippe le Bel* (Paris, 1861), bk XIV, chap. 1.

89 See F. J. Pegues, *The Lawyers of the Last Capetians* (Princeton, NJ, 1962), and J. Favier, 'Les Légistes et le gouvernement de Philippe le Bel', *Journal des savants* (1969), pp. 92–108.

90 See Favier, *Un Conseiller de Philippe le Bel: Enguerran de Marigny* (Paris, 1963), pp. 64ff.

91 Ives de Saint-Denis, *Chronicon*, in *RHG*, vol. 21, p. 205.

92 H. Bordier, 'Une Satire contre Philippe le Bel (vers 1290)', *Bulletin de la Société de l'histoire de France*, 2nd ser., 1 (1857–8), pp. 198–9.

93 Dupuy, *Histoire du différend*, pp. 643–4.

94 *Ibid.*, p. 518.

95 See, for instance, Fawtier, *Histoire du Moyen Age*, vol. 6, *L'Europe occidentale de 1270 à 1380*, pt 1 (*Histoire générale*, ed. G. Glotz, Paris 1940), p. 299; Strayer, 'Philip the Fair – a "Constitutional" King', in *Medieval Statecraft*, pp. 195–212.

96 See G. P. Cuttino, 'Historical Revision: The Causes of the Hundred Years War', *Speculum*, XXXI (1956), pp. 463–77; C. V. Langlois, *Saint Louis, Philippe le Bel: Les Derniers Capétiens directs (1226–1328)* (*Histoire de France*, ed. E. Lavisse, vol. 3, pt 2 (Paris, 1901), pp. 295–303.

97 See Langlois, *Saint Louis, Philippe le Bel*, pp. 295–311; J. Le

Patourel, 'The King and the Princes in Fourteenth-Century France', in *Europe in the Later Middle Ages*, ed. J. Hale, R. Highfield and B. Smalley (London, 1965), pp. 169–73.

98 See Strayer, 'The Crusade against Aragon', in *Medieval Statecraft*, pp. 113–14. Even allowing for exaggeration, this is still a huge sum, and a large part of it must have been outstanding at the time of Philip III's death.

99 See Strayer, *Studies in Early French Taxation* (Cambridge, Mass., 1939), pp. 8–11, 21–3; Langlois, *Saint Louis, Philippe le Bel*, pp. 254–8.

100 See Langlois, 'Les Doléances des communautés du Toulousain contre Pierre de Latilli et Raoul de Breuilli (1297–8)', *RH*, XCV (1907), pp. 23–53.

101 *Ibid.*, pp. 29–38.

102 *Ibid.*, pp. 51–2.

103 Strayer, *Studies in Early French Taxation*, pp. 7–8, 25–33.

104 See, for instance, Langlois, 'Doléances du clergé de France au temps de Philippe le Bel', *Revue bleue*, 5th ser., IV (1905), pp. 329–33, 486–90.

105 C. Port (ed.), *Livre de Guillaume Le Maire*, in *Mélanges historiques: Choix de documents*, vol. 2 (Paris, 1877), pp. 323–5.

106 *Ibid.*, pp. 360–1.

107 *Ibid.*, pp. 370–1.

108 Langlois, *Saint Louis, Philippe le Bel*, p. 244; Strayer, *Studies in Early French Taxation*, pp. 33–8.

109 F. Ehrle, 'Ein Bruchstück der Acten des Concils von Vienne', *Archiv für Literatur- und Kirchengeschichte des Mittelalters*, IV (1888), pp. 368, 374, 384.

110 Boutaric (ed.), *Documents relatifs à l'histoire de Philippe le Bel*, in *Notices et extraits des manuscrits de la Bibliothèque Impériale*, XX (1862), no. 14, pp. 142–3.

111 Strayer, *Studies in Early French Taxation*, pp. 19–21; Langlois, *Saint Louis, Philippe le Bel*, p. 252.

112 Strayer, *Studies in Early French Taxation*, pp. 11–16; Langlois, *Saint Louis, Philippe le Bel*, p. 253, for the *maltôte*.

113 See L. L. Borrelli de Serres, *Les Variations monétaires sous Philippe le Bel* (Chalon-sur-Saône, 1902), pp. 293–4, 329.

114 E. de Laurière (ed.), *Ordonnances des roys de France de la troisième race*, vol. 1 (Paris, 1723), p. 325.

115 See Borrelli de Serres, pp. 338–9.

116 Jean de Saint-Victor, pp. 646–7.

117 *Ibid.*, p. 647; *Cont. Nangis*, vol. 1, pp. 354–6.

118 A. de Beugnot (ed.), *Les Olim*, vol. 3, pt 1 (Paris, 1844), pp. 610–11.

119 *Cont. Nangis*, vol. 1, pp. 387–8, 399.

120 See Strayer, 'Italian Bankers and Philip the Fair', in *Medieval Statecraft*, pp. 239–47; Langlois, *Saint Louis, Philippe le Bel*, pp. 227–30.

121 Laurière, vol. 1, p. 489.

122 C. Devic and J. Vaissète, *Histoire générale de Languedoc*, ed. A. Molinier, vol. 10 (Toulouse, 1885), 'Preuves', cols 315–16.

123 *Les Grandes Chroniques de France*, ed. J. Viard, vol. 8 (Paris, 1934), p. 249, gives 'environ le Magdalene'; *Cont. Nangis*, vol. 1, p. 355, says the month of August. See Boutaric, *La France*, pp. 302–3, for an account of the seizures.

124 See L. Delisle, *Mémoire sur les opérations financières des Templiers* (*Mémoires de l'Institut national de France, Académie des inscriptions et belles-lettres*, vol. 33; Paris, 1889), pp. 40–86.

125 A. Baudouin, *Lettres inédites de Philippe le Bel* (*Mémoires de l'Académie des sciences, inscriptions et belles-lettres de Toulouse*, 8th ser., VIII; 1886), no. 184, pp. 211–13; H. Prutz, *Entwicklung und Untergang des Tempelherrenordens* (Berlin, 1888), pp. 302–3.

126 Baudouin, no. 148, pp. 163–4; see Piquet, pt II, chap. 1.

127 Picot, no. 14, p. 50; no. 15, p. 53; Prutz, *Entwicklung*, pp. 307–8.

128 Delisle, *Mém. sur les opérations financières*, no. 33, p. 226.

129 See Lot and Fawtier, bk 1, chaps 2 and 4.

130 The meetings of 1302 and 1308 are reasonably well documented, but the details of the assemblies of 1290, 1312 and 1314 are rather vague, while it is doubtful if the 1303 assembly can be called an Estates-General in the full sense, since, although a meeting was convened, it was divided between groups meeting at Paris in March and June, and several provincial assemblies, especially in the south, held throughout the summer; see Picot, pp. xiv–xliv.

131 *Ibid.*, no. 10, p. 25; no. 11, pp. 25–6.

132 *Ibid.*, no. 22, pp. 62–3.

133 *Ibid.*, nos. 39 and 40, pp. 78–80; no. 30, pp. 69–70. See also no. 29, pp. 68–9; no. 38, pp. 77–8.

134 See, for instance, *Antequam Essent Clerici*, in Dupuy, *Histoire du différend*, pp. 21–3; *Disputatio inter Clericum et Militem*, in M. Goldast, *Monarchia S. Romani Imperii*, vol. 1 (Hanover, 1611), pp. 13–18.

135 Jean de Paris, *Tractatus de Potestate Regia et Papali*, in J. Leclercq, *Jean de Paris et l'ecclésiologie du XIIIᵉ siècle* (Paris, 1942), pp. 176, 178–9, 199.

136 See Strayer, 'France: The Holy Land', p. 312.

137 See Fawtier, 'Comment, au début du XIVᵉ siècle, un roi de France pouvait-il se représenter son royaume', *Comptes rendus des séances de l'Académie des inscriptions et belles-lettres* (1959), pp. 117–23.

2 THE ARRESTS

1 Lizerand, *Le Dossier de l'affaire des Templiers* (Paris, 1923; repr. 1964), p. 16.

2 *Cont. Nangis*, vol. 1, p. 360.

3 H. Finke, *Papsttum und Untergang des Templerordens*, vol. 2

(Münster, 1907), p. 74, for the official list; *Procès*, vol. 1, pp. 30, 509; vol. 2, pp. 1, 33, 144, 147, 157, 159, 241, 263, 265, 266, for others mentioned as having fled, either in their own depositions or in the depositions of other Templars.

4 *Procès*, vol. 1, p. 412.

5 *Ibid.*, vol. 2, pp. 263, 265.

6 *Ibid.*, p. 267.

7 For the trial in England, see above, chap. 8.

8 Finke, vol. 2, p. 75. It seems unlikely that any such plot existed, for there is no other mention during the trial of such an important accusation. Nevertheless, it is interesting to note that two of the escapees, Pierre de Modies and Falco de Milly, were related to Hugues de Châlons, the former being described as his nephew and the latter as the kinsman of Pierre de Modies, while a fourth Templar, Jean de Chali, fled in company with Pierre de Modies. Such a close grouping suggests a planned flight, perhaps with some forewarning of the arrests. Jean de Chali was in fact asked directly why he had fled, but he gave the predictable answer: he had been afraid of arrest and he had wanted to leave the Order a long time before because of the illicit things that were done in it, but he had not done so because he feared that the Templars would recapture him. *Procès*, vol. 2, p. 265.

9 *Procès*, vol. 1, p. 30.

10 *Cont. Nangis*, vol. 1, p. 360.

11 *Procès*, vol. 1, p. 74.

12 *Ibid.*, pp. 30, 77–8, 83.

13 Finke, vol. 2, p. 46.

14 *Ibid.*, vol. 1, pp. 147–8.

15 *Ibid.*, vol. 2, p. 149. Finke (vol. 1, p. 148) says that there is no record of this authorisation under Boniface VIII or Benedict XI.

16 *Ibid.*, vol. 2, p. 49.

17 *Ibid.*, p. 36.

18 *Ibid.*, p. 149.

19 In the bull *Pastoralis praeeminentiae* (22 November 1307), the pope recalled that rumours had first reached him at about the time of his coronation. See above, chap. 3, pp. 84–5.

20 Finke, vol. 2, p. 149.

21 *Ibid.*

22 Baluze, vol. 3, pp. 58–60.

23 Finke, vol. 2, p. 58.

24 Lizerand, *Clém. V*, appendix, no. 6, p. 434.

25 Finke, vol. 2, p. 142. See above, chap. 3, pp. 107, 109.

26 Finke, vol. 1, p. 146. See also above, chap. 4, pp. 122–3, in the papal bull *Subit assidue* (5 July 1308) in which Clement refers to the failure of Guillaume de Paris to tell him of the plans for the arrests.

27 Boutaric, 'Clément V, Philippe le Bel et les Templiers', *RQH*, x (1871), pp. 332–3.

28 Finke, vol. 2, pp. 46–7.

29 Giovanni Villani, *Cronica*, vol. 2 (*Collezione di storici e cronisti italiani*; Florence, 1845; facs. repr. 1969), pp. 124–5 (bk VIII, chap. 92).

30 See A. Rigault, *Le Procès de Guichard, évêque de Troyes (1308–13)* (Paris, 1896), pp. 23, 41, 103, 219.

31 Finke, vol. 2, p. 318 (6 November 1307).

32 *Procès*, vol. 1, p. 458. The Gascons had perhaps been captured by the French king's forces during the warfare over the fief; see above, chap. 1, pp. 35–6. Néry claimed to have read the letters, but could not remember how they had been sealed.

33 *Procès*, vol. 1, pp. 36–9. See above, chap. 1, p. 24, for this aspect of inquisitorial procedure.

34 See above, chap. 8, pp. 225–6.

35 Finke, vol. 2, pp. 83–4.

36 *Ibid.*, p. 145.

37 *Procès*, vol. 2, p. 278.

38 K. Schottmüller, *Der Untergang des Templer-Ordens*, vol. 2 (Berlin, 1887; repr. 1970), pp. 35–8.

39 Finke, vol. 2, p. 336.

40 *Ibid.*, p. 143.

41 *Ibid.*, pp. 44–6. The language suggests that the letter was drafted by the French chancery. It was sent from Pontoise, and Guillaume de Nogaret was there on 22 September to receive the great seal.

42 Lizerand, *Dossier*, pp. 24–8.

43 *Ibid.*, pp. 46–55.

44 *Procès*, vol. 2, pp. 293, 306, 320, 324, 330, 350, 353, 368, 370, 381, 396, 415, 418.

45 *Ibid.*, vol. 2, pp. 320, 330.

46 *Ibid.*, pp. 385, 407.

47 *Ibid.*, pp. 369, 375, 386, 394, 374, 409.

48 Prutz, *Entwicklung*, pp. 324–7, 334–5; Finke, vol. 2, pp. 313–24. There were six from Bayeux, two from Chaumont, ten from Renneville, two from Troyes, thirteen from Caen, all held in October; forty-four from Cahors, held in October and November; six from Carcassonne, held in November; six from Bigorre, held in December; and another five from Cahors, in January.

49 Prutz, *Entwicklung*, pp. 334–5; Finke, vol. 2, pp. 315–16.

50 Prutz, *Entwicklung*, p. 327. Letter of 23 November.

51 Schottmüller, vol. 2, p. 69.

52 *Ibid.*, p. 67.

53 *Ibid.*, p. 49.

54 W. Sargant, *Battle for the Mind: A Physiology of Conversion and Brain-Washing* (London, 1957). The quotation comes from p. 181. See also J. A. C. Brown, *Techniques of Persuasion: From Propaganda to Brainwashing* (Harmondsworth, 1963), esp. chap. 11, where it is denied

that the effects of brainwashing are permanent, except in cases 'where the new belief is a perfect substitute for the old ones' (p. 293). Both Sargant and Brown provide many examples of situations similar to those experienced by the Templars, in which the victims have broken down and confessed. Their main difference seems to be on the permanence of the change of mind.

55 *Procès*, vol. 1, p. 218 (April 1310).

56 *Ibid.*, p. 75.

57 *Ibid.*, vol. 2, p. 293, for his first deposition; Schottmüller, vol. 2, p. 62, for his deposition in 1308.

58 *Procès*, vol. 2, pp. 306–7; Schottmüller, vol. 2, pp. 41–2.

59 Schottmüller, vol. 2, p. 48.

60 *Ibid.*, p. 65.

61 *Procès*, vol. 1, p. 69.

62 *Ibid.*, vol. 2, pp. 277–315.

63 *Ibid.*, vol. 1, p. 296.

64 *Ibid.*, vol. 2, p. 309.

65 *Ibid.*, pp. 409 and 370.

66 *Ibid.*, pp. 352 and 390.

67 *Ibid.*, vol. 1, p. 532.

68 *Ibid.*, vol. 2, p. 353.

69 From 132 and 111 depositions respectively.

70 *Procès*, vol. 2, pp. 355–7.

71 *Ibid.*, p. 403.

72 See Bloch, *Feudal Society*, tr. L. A. Manyon (London, 1961), p. 146.

73 *Procès*, vol. 2, pp. 391, 403.

74 *Ibid.*, pp. 290, 294.

75 *Ibid.*, pp. 279, 290, 299, 300, 313, 315, 363, 367.

76 *Ibid.*, p. 364.

77 Finke, vol. 2, p. 316.

78 *Ibid.*, pp. 321–3.

79 *Ibid.*, pp. 323–4.

80 *Procès*, vol. 2, pp. 295–6.

81 There is a story that Molay was secretly offered the opportunity to flee, but had indignantly refused this means of escape, asserting that there was no reason for flight because the Templars were without sin and the Order was good and honourable. They were all believing Catholics, just like the pope, the cardinals and other Christians (Finke, vol. 2, pp. 58–9). This information is contained in a letter, written in November 1307, from an anonymous person at the papal Curia at Poitiers to the Templar commander of the Aragonese preceptory of Ascó. The news had originally come from another anonymous correspondent in Paris. Although it seems unlikely that an offer of this kind would have been known to an outsider, it is possible that the persons giving these details were themselves Templars, since the Parisian report adds that the Grand Master had told the brothers not to despair, a

detail which suggests that Molay could have made known such an offer to the members of the Order in Paris. However, there is no corroboration of the story and its first documentary appearance is already at least third-hand.

82 *Procès*, vol. 2, pp. 305–6.

83 See above, chap. 7.

84 Finke, vol. 2, p. 307.

85 Jean de Saint-Victor, p. 649; *Cont. Nangis*, vol. 1, p. 361.

86 Jean de Saint-Victor, p. 651; *Cont. Nangis*, vol. 1, p. 362.

87 Finke, vol. 2, pp. 310–12. See also above, chap. 2, p. 60.

88 Finke, vol. 2, p. 49. Letter of the Parisian university master, Romeus de Brugaria, to King James II.

89 *Ibid.*, pp. 116–17. There is no evidence to suggest that there had been any public assemblies of this kind since 25 October. On the reliability of this letter, see Finke, vol. 1, p. 187. See also above, chap. 3, pp. 87–8.

90 Finke, vol. 2, p. 102. See above, chap. 5, pp. 175–7. A story of this kind seems to have been in general circulation; see Jean de Saint-Victor, p. 658, and also Villani, *Cronica*, vol. 2, p. 126 (bk VIII, chap. 92), who has Molay confessing *per paura di tormento, e per lusinghe del papa, e del re*, a line which also implies that Molay may have been offered some inducement if he complied.

91 See above, chap. 1, p. 24.

92 See Sargant, chap. 7.

93 *Procès*, vol. 1, pp. 32–3. See above, chap. 5, p. 143.

94 Finke, vol. 2, p. 46.

95 *Ibid.*, p. 47.

96 *Procès*, vol. 2, pp. 362, 116; Finke, vol. 2, p. 75. See above, chap. 2, pp. 53–4 on Hugues de Châlons; Pierre was probably the Pierre de Modies mentioned above.

97 *Procès*, vol. 2, pp. 297, 298, 306–7, 309, 335, 336, 337, 343, 344, 359, 364, 386, 391, 409, 412, 314, 324, 366.

98 The only exception was Jean de Paris; see *ibid.*, p. 386.

99 *Ibid.*, p. 300.

100 *Ibid.*, p. 285.

101 *Ibid.*, pp. 361–3.

102 *Ibid.*, pp. 374–5.

103 *Ibid.*, pp. 398–400. The line which suggests a previous, probably unofficial, interrogation is *Requisitus quare tardavit dicere tantum, quia alias requisitus fuerat dicere veritatem* ... See Finke, vol. 1, p. 161, for a discussion of this point.

104 *Procès*, vol. 2, pp. 369, 375, 385–6, 394–5. They were interrogated between 9 and 15 November. The deposition of Jean de Châteauvillars was typical. He was a knight, aged thirty, and had been received four years before at Mormant in the diocese of Troyes. He had made many promises concerning the good statutes of the Order; then his receptor received him by a kiss on the mouth, and 'nothing else was enjoined or

ordered him'. Only Jean de Paris and Lambert de Toysi appear in the records of the trial again, between February and April 1310, when, together with a large number of other Templars, they indicated their willingness to help in defending the Order. *Procès*, vol. 1, pp. 64, 97, 107, 153, for Jean de Paris; and pp. 64, 103, for Lambert de Toysi.

105 See above, chap. 2, pp. 61–2. L. Delisle, *Etudes sur la condition de la classe agricole et l'état de l'agriculture en Normandie au Moyen Age* (Paris, 1903), pp. 721–8, gives five examples, including the house of Baugy discussed above.

106 Boutaric, *Docs. rel. à l'hist. de Ph. le Bel*, no. 23, pp. 161–2.

107 Finke, vol. 2, p. 56.

108 *Ibid.*, p. 51.

109 *Ibid.*, pp. 94–8. He told James that he had recently written to Clement V a pointed letter about the pope's own conduct, and given him warning of serious consequences if he did not begin church reform.

110 Boutaric, 'Clém. V, Ph. le Bel et les Templiers', pp. 332–3.

3 THE PAPAL INTERVENTION

1 Finke, vol. 2, p. 114. The witness was the procurator at the papal court of Pedro, Bishop of Lérida, March 1308.

2 *Ibid.*, pp. 58–60. This is the letter of an anonymous correspondent at the papal Curia to the Templar Preceptor of the house of Ascó (see also above, pp. 320–1, n. 81. Both the tone of the letter, which speaks of the writer's great sadness of heart at the general arrest of the Templars, and its recipient, an Aragonese Templar, suggest that the author belonged to the Order. That he was one of the treasurers is suggested both by his presence in Poitiers in November 1307 (the date of the letter), and by his warning to the Preceptor of Ascó not to transmit any money to the Grand Master, which is contained in the opening sentences.

3 T. Rymer, *Foedera, Conventiones, Literae et Cuiuscunque Generis Acta Publica*, vol. 1 (The Hague, 1745), pt IV, pp. 99–100, which is the bull sent to Edward II of England. The texts sent to the King of Aragon and to Robert of Calabria, the son of Charles II, King of Naples, also survive.

4 Baluze, vol. 3, p. 90.

5 *Ibid.*, pp. 91–2.

6 *Ibid.*, pp. 92–4.

7 Finke, vol. 2, pp. 110–11.

8 *Ibid.*, pp. 114–19. See also above, chap. 2, p. 76.

9 Finke, vol. 2, p. 102. For the dating of this document, see above, chap. 5, p. 175.

10 Schottmüller, vol. 2, p. 37.

11 Finke, vol. 2, pp. 338–9.

12 See Dupuy, *Traitez concernant l'histoire de France* (Paris, 1685), no. 34, pp. 91–2.

13 The exact date of the suspension is not known, but it was probably operative by February 1308. See Finke, vol. 2, pp. 90ff, in which correspondents seem to be talking of inquisitorial proceedings as if in the past. For the pope's reasons, see the bull by which Clement revoked the suspension on 5 July 1308, above, chap. 4, p. 122.

14 Finke, vol. 2, p. 114. Letter of Pedro, Bishop of Lérida, to King James II, 11 March 1308.

15 *Ibid.*, p. 123. Anonymous letter to the commanders of the houses of Gardeny and Ascó, 21 April(?) 1308.

16 It should however be said that there appears to have been some counter-propaganda in circulation. An anonymous letter, purporting to be to the doctors and scholars of the University of Paris, which was probably written in February 1308, strongly defends the Order, complaining that the confessions had been extracted by torture and cruel imprisonment from motives of envy and cupidity. The conduct of the Templars in defending the Christian faith, in continuing to attract recruits, and in refusing to abjure the faith even when captured by the Saracens and offered the strongest temptations, simply could not be reconciled with the absurdity of the charges. The author of this work seems to have had contact of some kind with the imprisoned Templars, for certain parts of this letter were later employed by the defenders of the Order before the papal commission in April 1310; see above, chap. 5, pp. 161–4. See C. R. Cheney, 'The Downfall of the Templars and a Letter in Their Defence', in *Medieval Miscellany Presented to Eugène Vinaver*, ed. F. Whitehead, A. H. Divernes and F. E. Sutcliffe (Manchester, 1965), pp. 65–79.

17 See above, chap. 1, p. 18. Lizerand, *Dossier*, pp. 84–5, believes that the author was Dubois because of the use of certain characteristic phrases.

18 The nephew to whom the pamphlet refers was Bernard de Fargues, who became Archbishop of Rouen in June 1306. Gaillard de Preissac, the Bishop of Toulouse, was also related to the pope, but the Bishopric of Poitiers was not held by a relative of Clement V. See Lizerand, *Dossier*, p. 87, nn. 3, 4, 5.

19 *Ibid.*, pp. 84–94.

20 *Ibid.*, pp. 96–100.

21 *Ibid.*, pp. 56–62.

22 See above, chap. 3, p. 90.

23 Lizerand, *Dossier*, pp. 62–70. The masters of theology were largely adhering to the orthodox papal view on this subject. The theologian Agostino Trionfo (d. 1328), for instance, argued that no king or prince had the right to take over heretics directly subject to the Church, nor to take a final decision on the matter without the orders of the Church. The only possible exception to this was if the heresy had developed very suddenly and was running strongly, so that the prince could not wait for the Church's permission without danger of infection for his subjects. Naturally,

however, he was to hand over the matter to the Church as soon as possible. For a discussion of this and relevant references, see Finke, vol. 1, p. 195.

24 Picot, no. 657, pp. 487–8; no. 658, pp. 488–9; no. 747, p. 547; no. 749, pp. 548–9. There are records of provincial councils for the dioceses of Rheims and Rouen.

25 *Ibid.*, no. 659, pp. 489–90.

26 *Ibid.*, no. 660, pp. 490–1.

27 *Ibid.*, no. 661, pp. 491–2. Dated 29 March.

28 *Ibid.*, no. 664, pp. 494–5; no. 665, pp. 495–6.

29 *Ibid.*, p. liv. See, for instance, no. 845, p. 600: *Comme vous aiés mandé par vos lettres que de totes lez communes et de toutes les viles où il a ferez ou marchiés* ... Also no. 861, p. 605; no. 862, p. 606; no. 941, p. 643; no. 952, p. 649.

30 See A. Petel, 'Le Diocèse de Troyes dans le différend entre Boniface VIII et Philippe le Bel et dans l'affaire des Templiers', *Mémoires de la Société académique d'agriculture, des sciences, arts et belles-lettres du Département de l'Aube*, 3rd ser., LXX (1906), p. 75; Picot, no. 929, p. 637.

31 Picot, p. lvi.

32 *Ibid.*, no. 973, pp. 658–9.

33 *Ibid.*, no. 792, p. 575; no. 794, p. 576; no. 783, p. 570; no. 790, p. 574.

34 *Ibid.*, no. 787, p. 572; no. 793, p. 575; no. 795, p. 576; no. 796, p. 577; no. 801, p. 579; no. 802, p. 580; no. 816, p. 587; no. 797, p. 577; no. 805, p. 582; no. 812, p. 585; no. 786, p. 571.

35 *Ibid.*, no. 804, p. 581.

36 *Ibid.*, no. 709, p. 525; no. 719, pp. 531–2.

37 *Ibid.*, no. 668, pp. 498–9.

38 *Ibid.*, p. xlix.

39 *Ibid.*, no. 735, p. 541; no. 766, p. 557. See also no. 721, p. 532 *et passim.*

40 *Ibid.*, no. 691, pp. 513–14. Picot, p. xlix, suggests that this reflects the uncertainty about the final meeting place shown by the misleading instructions sent out by the Archbishop of Narbonne, but this seems to be a misinterpretation.

41 *Ibid.*, no. 1076, p. 720.

42 Jean de Saint-Victor, pp. 650–1. Almost (*fere*) all those present, says the chronicler.

43 *Philippi Quarti Mansiones et Itinera*, in *RHG*, vol. 21 (Paris, 1855), p. 449.

44 Picot, no. 1076, p. 720.

45 Finke, vol. 2, pp. 134, 141 and 143.

46 Tolomeo da Lucca, p. 29; Baluze, vol. 3, pp. 95–6.

47 Finke, vol. 2, p. 134.

48 See G. Mollat, *The Popes at Avignon, 1305–78*, tr. J. Love (London, 1963), pp. 294–303.

49 Finke, vol. 2, pp. 134–5.

50 *Ibid.*, pp. 140–1, 147. The text is in Latin.

51 See *ibid.*, vol. 1, p. 208.

52 The use of the opening words *Christus Vincit, Christus Regnat, Christus Imperat!* appears to be a calculated attempt to emphasise Philip the Fair's descent from Saint Louis, who was the first French king to use them on gold currency. Already the motto was becoming a symbol of the *Rex Christianissimus* and was taking its place as an element in the cult of the French kings so assiduously fostered by the later Capetians. See E. H. Kantorowicz, *Laudes Regiae: A Study in Liturgical Acclamations and Mediaeval Ruler Worship* (Berkeley, Calif., 1958), p. 4.

53 Finke, vol. 2, pp. 135–40.

54 *Ibid.*, pp. 141–7. For the question of Molay's confession to lay absolution, see above, chap. 2, p. 60.

55 Finke, vol. 2, pp. 147–8. There are three other versions of this consistory, none of which are as detailed as that of Jean Bourgogne. Tolomeo da Lucca, pp. 29–30, summarises Plaisians's speech by saying that, on behalf of the king, he told the pope that the Templars had been found heretics and should be punished as such. There followed seven more orations reinforcing the same point. There is an account in English, apparently a sixteenth-century translation of a French manuscript, in L. Blancard, 'Documents relatifs au procès des Templiers en Angleterre', *Revue des sociétés savantes*, 4th ser., VI (1867), pp. 416–20, which also briefly summarises Plaisians's speeches, but includes additional material on the pope's replies; see above, chap 3, p. 112. Lastly, there is a version in a fragment of the chronicles of St Albans. See William Rishanger, *Chronica Monasterii S. Albani: Willelmi Rishanger, Quondam Monachi S. Albani, et Quorundam Anonymorum, Chronica et Annales, Regnantibus Henrico Tertio et Edwardo Primo, AD 1259–1307*, ed. H. T. Riley (*Rolls Series*, vol. 28; London, 1865), pp. 492–7. The author is not known, but his account follows the main outlines of those given by the official version and by Jean Bourgogne, differing in some details. The speeches of the Archbishops of Narbonne and Bourges are also mentioned, and the papal reply. It is possible that this version also comes from an eye-witness, perhaps an emissary of the English crown, but unlike Jean Bourgogne, it is here retailed at least second-hand, and in a briefer form.

56 Finke, vol. 2, pp. 148–50.

57 Lizerand, *Dossier*, pp. 124–36. For the dating of this document, see Finke, vol. 1, p. 208.

58 Blancard, pp. 417–18.

4 THE PAPAL AND EPISCOPAL INQUIRIES

1 Lizerand, *Clém. V.*, appendix, no. 10, pp. 440–1.

2 Schottmüller, vol. 2, pp. 13–71; bull *Faciens misericordiam*, in Port (ed.), *Guillaume Le Maire*, pp. 437–8.

3 Schottmüller, vol. 2, pp. 13–71, contains thirty-three depositions, and Finke, vol. 2, pp. 329–40, contains another seven depositions plus two names. The remaining two can probably be counted as confessions also. See *Procès*, vol. 1, pp. 70 and 73, for an additional four names of those who state that they have previously appeared before the pope; *ibid.*, p. 174, for the remaining eight names. These do not state explicitly that they had appeared before the pope, but the papal commissioners before whom they were appearing later state with reference to these names, 'since the witnesses who had been sworn in above and had not been examined by the lords commissioners were said to have been at another time [examined] by the lord pope or by the lord cardinals deputed by him . . . the commissioners resolved to omit from examination the aforesaid witnesses sworn and examined by the lord pope or the aforesaid cardinals, until they had deliberated more fully on these things' (*ibid.*, pp. 231–2). There are fifteen names which fall into this category, but seven can be identified among the names given by Schottmüller and Finke. The total figure of seventy-two is given in the bull *Faciens misericordiam*.

4 *Procès*, vol. 1, pp. 73–4.

5 See above, chap. 2, p. 60.

6 Schottmüller, vol. 2, pp. 35–8.

7 See above, chap. 2, p. 60.

8 Finke, vol. 2, pp. 334–7. It is possible that the head mentioned was in fact a reliquary of Hugues de Payns, containing his actual head. It may be that the additional details concerning the candelabra, the drapery and the precious stones owe something to the descriptions of the image of Mahomet, supposed to have been worshipped by Moslems, as described in the *Chansons de Geste*. See C. M. Jones, 'The Conventional Saracen of the Songs of Geste', *Speculum*, XVII (1942), pp. 211–12. This is also reminiscent of the exotic statuary of eleventh-century Christian art. Some contemporary clerics were shocked at what they regarded as 'idols'. Invented 'idols' described by the Templars may have been based on statues of this kind which they had seen. See G. Duby, *The Making of the Christian West, 980–1140* (Geneva, 1967), pp. 97–8.

9 Finke, vol. 2, pp. 337–9.

10 *Ibid.*, p. 331.

11 Schottmüller, vol. 2, pp. 28, 30, 50, 59, 68, 70.

12 *Ibid.*, pp. 18, 20, 22, 45, 51; Finke, vol. 2, p. 329. Concerning the two who had not been captured: Guillaume de Reses had left and been given quittance by the Master of the Auvergne, and Jacques de Bregecuria had evaded the Templars so that he could go to the Flemish wars.

13 Schottmüller, vol. 2, pp. 31, 39, 40, 42, 47, 48, 50, 52, 59, 61, 63, 64, 66, 67, 68, 70; Finke, vol. 2, p. 332.

14 Schottmüller, vol. 2, p. 49.

15 *Procès*, vol. 1, pp. 70, 73.

16 Port (ed.), *Guillaume Le Maire*, p. 438 (*Faciens misericordiam*).

17 Finke, vol. 2, p. 333; *Procès*, vol. 1, p. 622.

18 *Grosser historischer Weltatlas*, vol. 2, *Mittelalter* (Munich, 1970), pp. 82, R2, R3, R4.

19 Schottmüller, vol. 2, pp. 64, 60.

20 Port (ed.), *Guillaume Le Maire*, p. 451. Elsewhere, 'not of mean condition' (*reputacionis non modice*); *Faciens misericordiam, ibid.*, p. 437. See Finke, vol. 1, p. 217.

21 See above, chap. 4, p. 113.

22 Port (ed.), *Guillaume Le Maire*, p. 420, *nonnulli eorum*; Finke, vol. 2, p. 340, *paucis exceptis*. See Finke, vol. 1, p. 217, where he speculates that there may have been as many as thirty who had not confessed, based on the fact that he and Schottmüller had found only forty-two names, the same number given in the papal abstract for the Council of Vienne in 1311–12, where the Order was suppressed. However, this needs to be modified in view of the notarial record of the papal commission in *Procès*, vol. 1, p. 70, which shows three more Templars who had confessed before the pope, beyond the forty-two names given in Finke and Schottmüller. Perhaps 'excepting a few' is closer to the truth, given the apparently careful selection of the Templars who appeared at Poitiers, and the figure of forty-two is either a coincidence or it represents the only material available to the papacy by 1311.

23 Port (ed.), *Guillaume Le Maire*, p. 420. The bull *Subit assidue*.

24 Finke, vol. 2, pp. 152–3.

25 Lizerand, *Clém. V*, appendix, no. 11, p. 442.

26 Boutaric, 'Clém. V, Ph. le Bel et les Templiers', p. 9.

27 *Ibid.*, pp. 11–12. See also Finke, vol. 1, p. 213.

28 Port (ed.), *Guillaume Le Maire*, pp. 418–23.

29 *Ibid.*, p. 424.

30 *Ibid.*, pp. 423–4.

31 Finke, vol. 2, p. 152.

32 Baluze, vol. 3, pp. 82–3 (13 July 1308).

33 *Ibid.*, pp. 78–81; see also Lizerand, *Clém. V*, appendix, no. 12, p. 443; no. 13, p. 444; no. 14, pp. 444–6.

34 *Faciens misericordiam* describes the interrogation of the leaders at Chinon which was not completed until 20 August. Many bulls of about this time are dated 12 August, and it appears that a scribe in the papal chancery, perhaps working through a large number of undated bulls a few days later, dated them *en bloc*, probably choosing 12 August because it was the day before Clement left Poitiers. See above, chap. 4, p. 126.

35 See above, chap. 3, p. 85.

36 Port (ed.), *Guillaume Le Maire*, pp. 435–41.

37 *Procès*, vol. 1, pp. 1–7.

38 Port (ed.), *Guillaume Le Maire*, pp. 426–35.

39 Rigault, pp. 57–8. See also above, chap. 7, p. 209.

40 See above, chap. 1, p. 28.

41 Tolomeo da Lucca, p. 30; Blancard, pp. 419–20.

42 Tolomeo da Lucca, p. 30.

43 Blancard, pp. 417–18.

44 *Philippi Quarti Mansiones et Itinera*, p. 450, says that the king left Poitiers between 24 and 27 July; Blancard, pp. 417–18, says St Margaret's Day (20 July).

45 Finke, vol. 2, p. 157.

46 *Ibid.*, p. 155.

47 *Ibid.*, p. 157. In fact he did not arrive until March 1309.

48 *Ibid.*, p. 155.

49 *Ibid.*

50 There is no proper transcription of these hearings. The information derives from a letter of the cardinals to King Philip (Baluze, vol. 3, pp. 98–100); an extract from the Vatican Archive register of the Avignon popes given in Finke, vol. 2, pp. 324–8; and the bull *Faciens misericordiam*, Port (ed.), *Guillaume Le Maire*, pp. 438–40.

51 Port (ed.), *Guillaume Le Maire*, pp. 439–40. *Faciens misericordiam*.

52 Finke, vol. 2, pp. 171–2.

53 *Ibid.*, p. 158. The whole tone of the ambassador's letter suggests that he was continuing to find it difficult to gain an audience with the pope.

54 *Ibid.*, pp. 189–201.

55 Port (ed.), *Guillaume Le Maire*, pp. 446–8. The existence of a copy of these instructions in this collection of the acts relating to the Bishopric of Angers suggests that other episcopal inquiries followed this pattern of interrogation.

56 For similar procedures see, for instance, Bernard Gui, *Manuel de l'Inquisiteur*. Comparison with modern methods is also instructive; see Sargant, pp. 204–11.

57 Prutz, *Entwicklung*, pp. 327–34.

58 *Procès*, vol. 1, pp. 498–9; see Finke, vol. 1, p. 244. *Subit assidue* and *Faciens misericordiam* are entered in Guillaume Le Maire's register on 11 and 25 February 1309 respectively (Port (ed.), pp. 418, 435).

59 Prutz, *Entwicklung*, p. 334.

60 *Procès*, vol. 1, pp. 42, 557, 514.

61 *Ibid.*, pp. 264, 270.

62 *Ibid.*, vol. 2, pp. 13–14, 15–16, 19.

63 *Ibid.*, vol. 1, p. 230.

64 *Ibid.*, pp. 71–2.

65 See Lizerand, *Clém. V*, p. 396.

66 Port (ed.), *Guillaume Le Maire*, pp. 450–3.

67 *Ibid.*, pp. 425–6; Baluze, vol. 3, p. 141.

68 Petel, 'Templiers et Hospitaliers dans le diocèse de Troyes: Le Temple de Bonlieu et l'Hôpital d'Orient', *Mémoires de la Société académique d'agriculture, des sciences, arts et belles-lettres du Département de l'Aube*, 3rd ser., LXXIV (1910), pp. 284–8; no. 37, pp. 341–6.

69 J. Schwalm, 'Reise nach Frankreich und Italien im Sommer 1903, mit Beilagen', *Neues Archiv der Gesellschaft für Ältere Deutsche Geschichtskunde*, XXIX (1904), p. 618.

70 Finke, vol. 2, p. 196. See also *ibid.*, vol. 1, pp. 232–4, which shows that Philip also had in mind determining the composition of commissions set up in countries other than France.

71 See Lizerand, *Clém. V*, p. 148; *Procès*, vol. 1, p. 1, for list of the commissioners.

72 *Procès*, vol. 1, pp. 9–11, 21.

73 *Ibid.*, pp. 12–18.

74 *Ibid.*, pp. 18–19.

75 *Ibid.*, pp. 22–6.

5 THE DEFENCE OF THE ORDER

1 *Procès*, vol. 1, pp. 26–7. The bishop was to provide him with 'the necessities of life and the other things which were kept for other fugitive brothers of the Order'.

2 *Ibid.*, pp. 27–8.

3 *Ibid.*, pp. 28–9.

4 *Ibid.*, pp. 29–31.

5 *Ibid.*, pp. 32–5.

6 *Ibid.*, pp. 36, 39, 40, 41.

7 See above, chap. 1, p. 24, and chap. 2, pp. 58–9.

8 This statement presents a problem, for, with the exception of a very limited number of references to devils in female form made by a specific group of Templars (see above, chap. 7, p. 214), there is no other reference in the trial records to women at Templar receptions, nor is Ponsard's allegation included in the articles of accusation. Lizerand, *Dossier*, p. 159, n. 1, suggests that these women were *femmes de charge* or housekeepers of the Order, but it seems unlikely that Ponsard would designate them as 'sisters', or that they would actually be entering the Order *pour les ames sauver*. Perhaps therefore an incident of this kind had really occurred, albeit isolated and unknown to the denunciators of the Order.

9 *Procès*, vol. 1, pp. 36–9.

10 See above, chap. 1, p. 15.

11 *Procès*, vol. 1, pp. 42–5.

12 *Ibid.*, p. 45.

13 *Ibid.*, pp. 50–2 (26 November).

14 *Ibid.*, pp. 46–53. The commission still lacked replies from certain archbishops and bishops.

15 *Ibid.*, pp. 53–8.

16 *Ibid.*, p. 81.

17 *Ibid.*, pp. 58–87.

18 *Ibid.*, pp. 60, 68, 69.

19 *Ibid.*, pp. 75, 76, 77–8, 80, 83, 81–2, 82.

20 *Ibid.*, pp. 87–8.

21 Including the leaders, eight Templars had refused to offer any defence on 2 and 13 March, bringing the total to twenty-three.

22 *Procès*, vol. 1, pp. 89–98. See above, chap. 7, p. 208, and appendix A, pp. 293–9, for the details of the 127 articles.

23 *Procès*, vol. 1, pp. 98–9.

24 *Ibid.*, pp. 65, 108, 114.

25 *Ibid.*, pp. 79, 108.

26 *Ibid.*, pp. 42, 80, 108, 114.

27 *Ibid.*, pp. 71, 98, 109, 115, 138.

28 *Ibid.*, pp. 99–111.

29 *Ibid.*, pp. 112–26, 129–39, 147–52, 155–64.

30 *Ibid.*, pp. 150–1.

31 e.g. those held at the house of Guillaume de la Huce; *ibid.*, pp. 113–14.

32 *Ibid.*, pp. 116–17.

33 *Ibid.*, pp. 119–24.

34 *Ibid.*, pp. 134–5.

35 *Ibid.*, pp. 138–9.

36 *Ibid.*, pp. 114–16.

37 *Ibid.*, pp. 126–8; see above, chap. 1, pp. 23–6.

38 *Procès*, vol. 1, pp. 139–45.

39 *Ibid.*, pp. 146–7.

40 *Ibid.*, pp. 147–8.

41 *Ibid.*, pp. 150–1.

42 *Ibid.*, pp. 148–64.

43 *Ibid.*, pp. 164–9. See also above, p. 323, n. 16, for a possible source of some of these arguments.

44 *Procès*, vol. 1, pp. 169–71.

45 *Ibid.*, pp. 171–4.

46 He is referred to as *de Bononia* or *de Bononie* which could also mean Boulogne, but the other circumstances, especially his reception by the Preceptor of Lombardy, suggest that Bologna is much more likely.

47 *Ibid.*, vol. 2, pp. 348–9.

48 See above, chap. 2, pp. 69–70, for this deposition. See also chap. 3, p. 89, for a priest called Renaud who, in December 1307, persuaded more than sixty Templars to revoke their confessions by 'secret writings'. This may also have been Renaud de Provins.

49 *Procès*, vol. 2, pp. 355–7.

50 See above, chap. 4, pp. 133–4, for this inquiry.

51 Prutz, *Entwicklung*, pp. 332, 333; *Procès*, vol. 1, p. 562.

52 *Procès*, vol. 1, p. 175; see Pegues, p. 54.

53 *Procès*, vol. 1, pp. 176, 177.

54 *Ibid.*, p. 186; Devic and Vaissète, vol. 10, *preuves*, pp. 344, 384,

528, which shows that he was a former *sénéchal* of Toulouse; *Procès*, vol. 1, pp. 135, 148, for the house where the Templars were kept; *ibid.*, p. 276, for torture.

55 *Procès*, vol. 1, p. 174; see above, p. 326, n. 3.

56 *Procès*, vol. 1, p. 67.

57 *Ibid.*, p. 216.

58 *Ibid.*, p. 232.

59 See above, chap. 4, pp. 130–1.

60 *Procès*, vol. 1, pp. 175–7.

61 *Ibid.*, pp. 182–7.

62 *Ibid.*, pp. 187–93.

63 *Ibid.*, pp. 193–201.

64 *Ibid.*, pp. 201–5.

65 Finke, vol. 2, p. 74.

66 *Procès*, vol. 1, pp. 229–31. Two others from Chartres were prepared to make a defence if they were restored to freedom.

67 *Ibid.*, pp. 253–9.

68 e.g. Finke, vol. 2, p. 107; Lizerand, *Dossier*, p. 71.

69 Finke, vol. 2, pp. 102–7.

70 N. Valois, 'Deux Nouveaux Témoignages sur le procès des Templiers', *Comptes rendus des séances de l'Académie des inscriptions et belles-lettres* (1910), pp. 230–8. Again, this cannot be easily dated.

6 THE END OF RESISTANCE

1 Favier, *Enguerran de Marigny*, p. 131.

2 *Ibid.*, p. 132.

3 Clement V, *Reg. Clem. V*, year 5, no. 6293, p. 397.

4 See above, chap. 4, p. 122.

5 *Procès*, vol. 1, pp. 259–62.

6 Pegues, pp. 92–8.

7 See above, chap. 3, p. 108.

8 *Procès*, vol. 1, p. 262.

9 *Ibid.*, pp. 263–4.

10 *Ibid.*, pp. 274–5.

11 *Ibid.*, p. 281.

12 *Cont. Nangis*, vol. 1, pp. 377–8.

13 *Les Grandes Chroniques de France*, vol. 8, pp. 272–3.

14 Jean de Saint-Victor, p. 655.

15 *Cont. Nangis*, vol. 1, pp. 377–8, 381; Jean de Saint-Victor, p. 655; Bernard Gui, *E Floribus Chronicorum Auctore Bernardo Guidonis*, in *RHG*, vol. 21, p. 719; there may also have been some burnings in the south; see Lea, *Hist. of the Inquisition*, vol. 3, p. 295.

16 *Procès*, vol. 1, pp. 363, 509, 535, 538, 575, 591.

17 *Ibid.*, p. 274.

18 *Ibid.*, pp. 83, 106, 153; 85, 105; 70; 69, for the defenders; 70, for the other two.

19 The two volumes of *Procès* are apparently complete, for the evidence is internally consistent. Reading through them reveals no obvious lacunae, and all the 231 witnesses which the notaries state at the close of the proceedings as the total which had been heard can be accounted for (*ibid.*, vol. 2, p. 271). This figure is in fact one short of the total given by J. Gmelin, *Schuld oder Unschuld des Templerordens* (Stuttgart, 1893), who compiled tables of these witnesses from the evidence given in *Procès* (tables ix to xx), but Gmelin included Jean de Juvignac (*Procès*, vol. 1, p. 229), who appeared before the commission, but did not in fact depose, since he had already confessed before the pope at Poitiers in 1308. The notaries do not therefore seem to have included him.

20 Friedberg (ed.), *Corpus Iuris Canonici*, vol. 2, pp. 780–2. *Ad abolendam.*

21 See above, chap. 5, pp. 177–8.

22 *Procès*, vol. 1, pp. 275–7.

23 *Ibid.*, pp. 277–80.

24 *Ibid.*, pp. 281–5.

25 *Ibid.*, pp. 283–5.

26 *Ibid.*, pp. 285–7.

27 See above, chap. 5, pp. 151–3.

28 *Procès*, vol. 1, pp. 282–3.

29 *Ibid.*, pp. 287–367.

30 *Ibid.*, vol. 2, pp. 3–4. In these circumstances they could not, of course, be called upon to testify in defence of the Order.

31 e.g. *ibid.*, vol. 1, pp. 460, 512.

32 *Ibid.*, pp. 534, 641; vol. 2, p. 68.

33 *Ibid.*, vol. 2, p. 323; vol. 1, pp. 86, 133.

34 *Ibid.*, vol. 1, pp. 556–8.

35 *Ibid.*, pp. 70, 582; 63, 97, 107, 116; vol. 2, p. 119; vol. 1, pp. 67, 110; vol. 2, p. 178.

36 *Ibid.*, vol. 1, p. 463.

37 *Ibid.*, vol. 2, pp. 203, 212.

38 *Ibid.*, pp. 192–3.

39 *Ibid.*, vol. 1, p. 502; vol. 2, p. 218. For the legend of the eleven thousand virgins, see G. G. Coulton, *Five Centuries of Religion*, vol. 3 (Cambridge, 1936), pp. 93–4.

40 *Procès*, vol. 1, pp. 591–5.

41 *Ibid.*, vol. 2, pp. 205–9.

42 *Ibid.*, pp. 258–61.

43 *Ibid.*, vol. 1, pp. 35–6, 82, for his previous appearances before the commission; p. 254, for his kinship with Ponsard de Gizy. There seem to be two others from this family also in the Order at this time: Jean, a priest, and Baudouin, a serving brother; pp. 566, 575.

44 *Ibid.*, pp. 394–402.

45 *Ibid.*, pp. 454–9. Néry also described a conversation with an Hugues Achoti, who told him a very similar story about a man called Berlio d'Illino. For Néry's story about the letters being carried by the clerk warning about impending accusations against the Order, see above, chap. 2, p. 58.

46 *Procès*, vol. 1, pp. 78, 494; 71, 506; 89, 109, 512; 75; vol. 2, p. 171.

47 *Ibid.*, vol. 2, pp. 278–9; vol. 1, pp. 78, 115, 283.

48 *Ibid.*, vol. 1, pp. 494–7.

49 *Ibid.*, vol. 2, pp. 6–23.

50 *Ibid.*, p. 23.

51 *Ibid.*, pp. 9, 12.

52 *Ibid.*, p. 17.

53 *Ibid.*, pp. 82–5, 96–9, 101–3.

54 *Ibid.*, pp. 209–11.

55 *Ibid.*, pp. 88–96.

56 *Ibid.*, p. 89.

57 *Ibid.*, pp. 107–9.

58 *Ibid.*, vol. 1, pp. 368–70, 377–9.

59 See above, chap. 6, p. 189.

60 *Procès*, vol. 1, pp. 520–2, 527–9.

61 *Ibid.*, vol. 2, pp. 195–6. Pierre had two stories of his own to contribute: one was apparently based on the well-known seal of the Templars, which showed two men riding upon one horse, which seems to have been a symbol of the Order's early poverty, but was interpreted by some as a Templar with a devil riding behind, seducing him from his duty, and the other concerned the former Grand Master, supposedly released from a Moslem prison on condition that he introduced various errors into the Order. Pierre did not himself know if these stories were true or not.

62 *Ibid.*, vol. 1, p. 285. See above, chap. 6, p. 186.

63 *Procès*, vol. 1, p. 285.

64 *Ibid.*, vol. 2, pp. 269–74.

7 THE CHARGES

1 Lizerand, *Dossier*, pp. 16–24. See above, chap. 2, p. 52.

2 See above, chap. 3, p. 90; chap. 4, pp. 121–3.

3 *Procès*, vol. 1, pp. 89–96; vol. 2, p. 423. See also above, appendix A, pp. 293–9.

4 See Boase, chap. 14. The arrest and trial of Bernard Saisset, the Bishop of Pamiers, in 1301, had been one element in this struggle. At this time Pierre Flote was Chancellor and in this case pioneered the methods which later so characterised Nogaret. Saisset was accused of simony, blasphemy, heresy, fornication and sorcery. His goods were seized and his servants tortured to force testimony against him. See also above, chap. 1, p. 27.

5 See Rigault.

6 See S. Reinach, 'La Tête magique des Templiers', *Revue de l'histoire des religions*, LXIII (1911), pp. 25–6; J. Loiseleur, *La Doctrine secrète des Templiers* (Orléans, 1872).

7 C. Rodenberg (ed.), *Epistolae Saeculi XIII e Regestis Pontificum Romanorum*, in *Monumenta Germaniae Historica, Epistolae*, vol. 1 (Berlin, 1883), no. 537, pp. 432–4. Recipients of the letters included Emperor Frederick II; his son, Henry; Siegfried, Archbishop of Mainz; Conrad, Bishop of Hildesheim; and Conrad of Marburg. Full crusading indulgences were granted to those who would arm themselves against the heretics.

8 Adémar de Chabannes, *Ademari S. Cibardi Monachi Historiarum Libri Tres*, bk III, chap. 59, in *PL*, vol. 141, pp. 71–2.

9 *Vetus Aganon*, in *Cartulaire de l'Abbaye de Saint-Père-de-Chartres*, ed. B.-E.-C. Guérard (*Collection de documents inédits sur l'histoire de France*, vol. 1, *Collection de cartulaires de France*; Paris, 1840), p. 112.

10 Guibert de Nogent, *Histoire de sa vie (1053–1124)*, ed. G. Bourgin (Paris, 1907), pp. 212–13.

11 Walter Map, *De Nugis Curialium*, ed. M. R. James (*Anecdota Oxoniensia, Medieval and Modern Series*; Oxford, 1914), dist. 1, chap. 30, p. 57.

12 Alain de Lille, *Alani de Insulis De Fide Catholica contra Haereticos Sui Temporis*, bk 1, in *PL*, vol. 210, p. 366.

13 *Gesta Treverorum Continuatio IV*, ed. G. Waitz, in *Monumenta Germaniae Historica, Scriptores*, vol. 24 (Berlin, 1879), p. 401.

14 Guillaume de Paris, *De Legibus*, in *Opera Omnia*, vol. 1 (Amiens, 1674), p. 83.

15 Bernard Gui, *Manuel de l'Inquisiteur*, vol. 1, p. 48.

16 See H. L. Strack, *The Jew and Human Sacrifice*, tr. H. Blanchamp (London, 1909), with reference to similar accusations against the Gnostics in the third century. For recent modern discussions which set this subject in a wider context, see J. B. Russell, *Witchcraft in the Middle Ages* (Ithaca, NY, 1972), and N. Cohn, *Europe's Inner Demons: An Enquiry Inspired by the Great Witchhunt* (London, 1975), in which chap. 5 is devoted to the trial of the Templars.

17 See, for instance, J. J. I. von Döllinger (ed.), *Beiträge zur Sekten-geschichte des Mittelalters*, vol. 2 (Munich, 1890), pp. 293–6. There is also one instance, in a *Chanson de Geste*, in which some of these practices are associated with the Moslems. In this case, conversion to Islam involves, among other things, spitting on the name of Jesus and kissing an anus. See Jones, p. 224, n. 5.

18 *Les Grandes Chroniques de France*, vol. 8, pp. 274–6.

19 See Russell, pp. 88–93.

20 Finke, vol. 2, pp. 342–64.

21 Jean de Pollencourt said that he had heard of a cat which came into

assemblies of the Templars, but that this story had only been told to him after the arrests. See above, chap. 6, p. 202.

22 See above, chap. 7, p. 216.

23 Finke, vol. 2, pp. 363–4, shows that it can only be 1308 or 1310. If this really is an episcopal inquiry, then the dates of April to June on the depositions mean that 1308 is impossible, for the episcopal inquiries had not been instituted as early as this. See above, chap. 4, pp. 122–3.

24 J. Hansen, *Quellen und Untersuchungen zur Geschichte des Hexen-wahns und der Hexenverfolgung in Mittelalter* (Bonn, 1901), p. 1.

25 Saint Augustine, *De Civitate Dei*, in *Œuvres de Saint Augustin*, vol. 36, ed. and tr. G. Bardy and G. Combès (Paris, 1960), bk XVIII, chap. 18, pp. 534–42.

26 Hansen, pp. 38–9.

27 Saint Thomas Aquinas, *Quaestiones Quodlibetales*, intr. P. Mandonnet (Paris, 1926), bk XI, art. 10, pp. 420–1.

28 See G. L. Burr, 'The Literature of Witchcraft', in *George Lincoln Burr: His Life and Selections from His Writings*, ed. R. H. Bainton and L. O. Gibbons (New York, 1943), p. 172.

29 Constitution *Super illius specula*, in Hansen, pp. 5–6.

30 Moneta of Cremona, *Adversus Catharos et Valdenses*, ed. T. A. Ricchini (Rome, 1743), pp. 2–5. Moneta was writing *c*.1241. See also above, chap. 1, p. 22.

31 See N. Daniel, *Islam and the West: The Making of an Image* (Edinburgh, 1960), pp. 111–12.

32 Fidenzio of Padua, *Liber Recuperationis Terrae Sanctae*, chap. 15, in G. Golubovich (ed.), *Biblioteca Bio-Bibliografica della Terra Santa*, vol. 2 (Florence, 1913), p. 21.

33 See Daniel, pp. 39–40, 309, who shows that the idea of the Moslem as idolater was simply a literary convention. Nevertheless, the belief was well established at a popular level.

34 Caesarius of Heisterbach, *Caesarii Heisterbacensis Monachi Ordinis Cisterciensis Dialogus Miraculorum*, vol. 1, ed. J. Strange (Cologne, 1851), bk IV, chap. 33, p. 203; bk VI, chap. 36, pp. 388–9. See 1 Peter 5:8, 'Be sober, be vigilant; because your adversary the devil, as a roaring lion, walketh about, seeking whom he may devour.'

35 See above, chap. 2, p. 71; chap. 6, p. 190.

36 Reinach, pp. 31–8.

37 *Procès*, vol. 1, p. 645.

38 *Ibid.*, vol. 2, pp. 223–4.

39 *Ibid.*, p. 238.

40 Map, dist. IV, chap. 12, pp. 183–5.

41 Roger of Howden, *Chronica*, ed. W. R. Stubbs, vol. 3 (*Rolls Series*, vol. 51; London, 1870), pp. 158–9.

42 Gervais of Tilbury, *Des Gervasius von Tilbury Otia Imperialia*, ed. F. Liebrecht (Hanover, 1856), secunda decisio, XII, p. 11.

43 See E. S. Hartland, *The Legend of Perseus: A Study of Tradition in Story, Custom and Belief*, vol. 1 (London, 1894), pp. 1–13.

44 Hartland, *Ritual and Belief: Studies in the History of Religion* (London, 1914), pp. 194–234.

45 See F. T. Elworthy, *The Evil Eye: An Account of This Ancient and Widespread Superstition* (London, 1895), chap. 1 and *passim*; E. S. Gifford, *The Evil Eye: Studies in the Folklore of Vision* (New York, 1958), chap. 1. See L. Thorndike, *A History of Magic and Experimental Science*, vol. 2 (New York, 1929), pp. 169, 202, 385, 553, 558, 574–5, 608, 664–5, 710, 901–2, for medieval belief in the power of fascination as expressed by John of Salisbury, Alexander Neckham, Thomas of Cantimpré, Albertus Magnus, Thomas Aquinas, Roger Bacon and Peter of Abano. For a discussion of the subject in a wider context, see H. Webster, *Magic: A Sociological Study* (Stanford, Calif., 1948), pp. 151–7.

46 Proverbs 23:6; Matthew 6:23; Mark 7:21, 22; Luke 11:34.

47 Elworthy, p. 13; Thorndike, vol. 1, pp. 83, 217.

48 See J. Guiraud, *Histoire de l'Inquisition au Moyen Age*, vol. 1 (Paris, 1935), p. 145; Döllinger (ed.), vol. 2, p. 36.

49 Moneta of Cremona, pp. 2–5. See also above, chap. 1, p. 22.

50 Bernard Gui, *Manuel de l'Inquisiteur*, vol. 1, p. 12.

51 *Ibid.*, p. 24.

52 See above, chap. 4, p. 115, for instance, the deposition of Etienne de Troyes.

53 Giraldus Cambrensis, *Liber de Principis Instructione*, in *Giraldi Cambrensis Opera*, vol. 8, ed. G. F. Warner (*Rolls Series*, vol. 21; London, 1891), p. 301.

54 The same principle was involved in 964 when the Emperor Otto I brought a parallel charge against Pope John XII, accusing the pope of celebrating mass, but not communicating, similarly invalidating the mass. See Liudprand of Cremona, *Liber de Ottone Rege*, in *Quellen zur Geschichte der Sächsischen Kaiserzeit*, ed. A. Bauer and R. Rau (Darmstadt, 1971), p. 508.

55 See above, chap. 8, pp. 237–8. In fact, confession to a layman is implicit in the Rule of St Benedict itself. The abbot will not normally be a priest, but appears to have powers of absolution. See *The Rule of Saint Benedict*, ed. J. McCann (London, 1952), chap. 46, pp. 108–9.

56 See D. S. Bailey, *Homosexuality and the Western Christian Tradition* (London, 1955), chap. 1. The historical background of this subject, outlined in this paragraph, is based upon this penetrating study. See also the arguments of an anonymous jurist concerning the Templar case (1310), above, chap. 10, p. 291, and the deposition of Hugues de Narsac, chap. 6, pp. 191–2.

57 Saint Basil, *Sermo de Renuntiatione Saeculi*, in J. P. Migne (ed.), *Patrologiae . . . Graeca* (162 vols, Paris, 1857–1912), vol. 31, p. 638; Saint Augustine, *Epistolae*, ed. A. Goldbacher (*Corpus Scriptorum*

Ecclesiasticorum Latinorum, vol. 57; Leipzig, 1911), no. 211, pp. 368–9. See Bailey, pp. 84–5.

58 R. Schoell (ed.), *Iustiniani Novellae* (*Corpus Iuris Civilis*, vol. 3; Berlin, 1928), no. 77, pp. 331–3; no. 141, pp. 703–4.

59 Saint Peter Damian, *Liber Gomorrhianus*, in *PL*, vol. 145, col. 162.

60 J. D. Mansi, *Sacrorum Conciliorum Nova et Amplissima Collectio*, vol. 21 (Venice, 1774), col. 264.

61 Saint Thomas Aquinas, *Summa Theologica*, in *PL*, 2nd ser., vol. 3, ques. CLIV, arts 1–2, pp. 1075–8.

62 Henry of Huntingdon, *The History of the English*, ed. T. Arnold (*Rolls Series*, vol. 74; London, 1879), bk VII, pp. 242–3.

63 See Daniel, pp. 142–5.

64 See above, chap. 1, p. 23, on Christian ideas about Cathar sexual practices.

65 Luke 4:1–14.

8 THE TRIAL IN OTHER COUNTRIES

1 See above, chap. 2, p. 81. Edward wrote to the seneschal on 26 November, Rymer, vol. 1, pt IV, p. 100.

2 Rymer, vol. 1, pt IV, p. 101. Letter to King Diniz of Portugal.

3 Bernard Pelet, one of the original denunciators of the Temple, had apparently brought the letters to England. See above, chap. 2, p. 59.

4 Rymer, vol. 1, pt IV, p. 102.

5 William of Newburgh, *Historia Rerum Anglicarum*, in *Chronicles of the Reigns of Stephen, Henry II, and Richard I*, vol. 1, ed. R. Howlett (*Rolls Series*, vol. 82; London, 1884), p. 159; see Delisle, *Mém. sur les opérations financières*, pp. 10–11.

6 See Delisle, *passim*; Piquet, chap. 2; T. W. Parker, *The Knights Templars in England* (Tucson, Ariz., 1963), pp. 58–80. A Templar called Geoffrey was responsible for the wardrobe accounts of Henry III between 1236 and 1240, a position comparable to that held by the Templar treasurers in Paris under Louis IX; see T. F. Tout, *Chapters in the Administrative History of Mediaeval England*, vol. 1 (Manchester, 1920), p. 245.

7 See L. Landon, *The Itinerary of King Richard I* (London, 1935), p. 34, which shows Robert de Sablé as fleet commander; G. Müller, *Documenti sulle relazioni delle città Toscane coll'Oriente* (Florence, 1879), pp. 58ff, which shows him as Grand Master of the Temple.

8 For the text and analysis of the inquest, see B. A. Lees, *Records of the Templars in England in the Twelfth Century* (London, 1935); see D. Knowles and R. N. Hadcock, *Medieval Religious Houses: England and Wales* (London, 1953), pp. 234–9, for a list of Templar houses and their incomes at the time of the suppression.

9 W. Dugdale, *Monasticon Anglicanum*, ed. J. Caley, H. Ellis and B. Bandinel, vol. 6, pt 2 (London, 1846), p. 844.

10 See above, chap. 3, pp. 84–5.

11 Rymer, vol. 1, pt IV, p. 106.

12 *Calendar of Close Rolls, 1307–13* (London, 1892), pp. 14, 48–9.

13 See C. Perkins, 'The Trial of the Knights Templars in England', *English Historical Review*, XXIV (1909), p. 433. The administration of the custody of the Templars nevertheless remained exceedingly slack, for on 14 December 1309 it was still necessary for the king to order the sheriff of Kent to seize Templars wandering about the region in secular clothes, while in 1310 and 1311, the sheriff of York was reprimanded for allowing Templars in his custody to wander at liberty; Rymer, vol. 1, pt IV, pp. 163, 166, 182. This was still a problem in 1312; see *Registrum Roberti Winchelsey Cantuariensis Archiepiscopi*, vol. 2, ed. R. Graham (*Canterbury and York Society*, vol. 52; Oxford, 1956), pp. 1240–1. The registers of those prelates in England involved in the trial contain many scattered references to local problems which arose.

14 Rymer, vol. 1, pt IV, pp. 152, 154.

15 *Ibid.*, p. 152.

16 *Ibid.*, pp. 157, 158.

17 D. Wilkins, *Concilia Magnae Britanniae et Hiberniae*, vol. 2 (London, 1737), p. 334. This is a summary of the Templar proceedings based upon Bodleian MS. 454.

18 *Ibid.*, pp. 337–8.

19 *Ibid.*, p. 337.

20 F. M. Powicke and C. R. Cheney (eds), *Councils and Synods with Other Documents Relating to the English Church*, vol. 2, AD 1205–1313, pt 2, 1265–1313 (Oxford, 1964), pp. 1267–9.

21 Wilkins, vol. 2, pp. 349–50.

22 Rymer, vol. 1, pt IV, p. 165.

23 Wilkins, vol. 2, pp. 365–7, 371–3.

24 Powicke and Cheney (eds), vol. 2, pt 2, pp. 1278–9, 1284.

25 See Lea, 'The Absolution Formula of the Templars', in *Minor Historical Writings and Other Essays by Henry Charles Lea*, ed. A. C. Howland (London, 1942), pp. 97–112, and above, chap. 8, pp. 237–8.

26 Wilkins, vol. 2, pp. 356–7.

27 See Perkins, 'Trial of the Knights Templars', pp. 437–8.

28 Rymer, vol. 1, pt IV, pp. 174, 176.

29 Powicke and Cheney (eds), vol. 2, pt 2, p. 1290.

30 Clement V, *Reg. Clem. V*, year 5, no. 6670, pp. 84–6.

31 Wilkins, vol. 2, pp. 358–64, 378–80, 381–3; see Perkins, 'Trial of the Knights Templars', p. 440.

32 See also above, chap. 9, p. 261.

33 Wilkins, vol. 2, p. 359.

34 *Ibid.*, p. 360.

35 *Ibid.*, pp. 373–8, 381–2.

36 *Ibid.*, pp. 359–60; see above, chap. 2, pp. 79–80.

37 Wilkins, vol. 2. pp. 383–4.

38 *Ibid.*, pp. 384–7.

39 *Ibid.*, pp. 387–8.

40 The ceremony of absolution is fully described in the notarial record; see next note.

41 Powicke and Cheney (eds), vol. 2, pt 2, pp. 1307–17. For examples of the assignment of Templars to various monasteries in the diocese of Salisbury, together with details of their penances and the provisions for their maintenance, see *Registrum Simonis de Gandavo Diocesis Saresbiriensis*, vol. 2, ed. C. T. Flower and M. C. B. Dawes, *Canterbury and York Society*, vol. 41; Oxford, 1934), pp. 403–8.

42 Rymer, vol. 2, pt 1, p. 27.

43 Powicke and Cheney (eds), vol. 2, pt 2, pp. 1331–9.

44 Wilkins, vol. 2, pp. 380–1. See D. E. Easson, *Medieval Religious Houses: Scotland* (London, 1957), pp. 131–2, where only two houses are listed.

45 Wilkins, vol. 2, pp. 373–8. See A. Gwynn and R. N. Hadcock, *Medieval Religious Houses: Ireland* (London, 1970), pp. 327–31, for Templar preceptories.

46 See Lea, 'Absolution Formula'.

47 Finke, vol. 2, p. 50. See also vol. 1, pp. 283–4.

48 *Ibid.*, vol. 2, p. 55 (17 November 1307). See above, chap. 2, p. 81.

49 Finke, vol. 2, p. 63n.

50 *Ibid.*, vol. 1, pp. 286–7, n. 3.

51 *Ibid.*, vol. 2, pp. 63–6, 66–7; Prutz, *Entwicklung*, p. 348.

52 Finke, vol. 2, p. 77. See above, chap. 3, pp. 84–5.

53 Finke, vol. 2, pp. 52–3.

54 *Ibid.*, pp. 54–5.

55 *Ibid.*, pp. 60–2, 62–3.

56 *Ibid.*, pp. 56–7. See also vol. 1, p. 285.

57 *Ibid.*, vol. 2, pp. 73–4.

58 *Ibid.*, p. 89.

59 *Ibid.*, p. 77.

60 *Ibid.*, p. 78.

61 *Ibid.*, pp. 69–70.

62 *Ibid.*, pp. 70–3.

63 *Ibid.*, pp. 79–81.

64 *Ibid.*, p. 78.

65 *Ibid.*, pp. 85–6.

66 *Ibid.*, pp. 125–6.

67 *Ibid.*, p. 127.

68 *Ibid.*, pp. 128–9.

69 *Ibid.*, p. 130 n.

70 *Ibid.*, pp. 151–2.

71 B. Alart, 'Suppression de l'ordre des Templiers en Roussillon',

Bulletin de la Société agricole, scientifique et littéraire des Pyrénées-Orientales, xv (1867), p. 38.

72 Finke, vol. 2, pp. 172–3.

73 *Ibid.*, pp. 176–7. See also vol. 1, pp. 300–1.

74 See *ibid.*, vol. 1, p. 305.

75 According to Pedro, Bishop of Lérida, it was said that James's father, Pedro the Great, had called the original donor, the Count of Barcelona, 'old and decrepit and out of his mind' to make such a gift to the Templars, and said that it was done to the manifest prejudice of the kingdom. *Ibid.*, vol. 2, p. 154.

76 Clement V, *Reg. Clem. V*, year 4, nos. 5012–17, pp. 435–8.

77 *Ibid.*, year 3, no. 3515, pp. 312–15.

78 Finke, vol. 2, pp. 364–76.

79 *Ibid.*, pp. 159–64.

80 Clement V, *Reg. Clem. V*, year 6, no. 7497, p. 408.

81 A. Mercati, 'Interrogatorio di Templari a Barcellona (1311)', *Gesammelte Aufsätze zur Kulturgeschichte Spaniens*, vi (1937), pp. 246–51.

82 Mansi, vol. 25, cols 515–16.

83 See Alart, pp. 33–4, who provides a detailed account of the proceedings in Roussillon, with frequent quotation from the original documents. His references are, however, arbitrary and erratic.

84 *Procès*, vol. 2, pp. 423–515, contains the transcript of the proceedings in Roussillon under the Bishop of Elne.

85 M. Raynouard, *Monumens historiques relatifs à la condamnation des chevaliers du Temple* (Paris, 1813), pp. 264–7, 313–15.

86 Mansi, vol. 25, cols 297–8.

87 See Finke, vol. 1, p. 234n.

88 Raynouard, pp. 280–4.

89 Schottmüller, vol. 2, pp. 108–39.

90 *Ibid.*, pp. 405–19.

91 Raynouard, pp. 273–5.

92 Mansi, vol. 25, cols 293–6; Raynouard, pp. 276–7.

93 Clement V, *Reg. Clem. V*, year 6, nos. 7527, 7528, p. 439.

94 Loiseleur, 'Pièces just.', no. 3, pp. 172–212. The notarial record could be read to mean that the six who confessed were not tortured, but this would seem unlikely in the circumstances. It probably means that they were not tortured when they were examined a second time.

95 Clement V, *Reg. Clem. V*, year 5, no. 5888, pp. 271–2.

96 Raynouard, pp. 126, 270.

97 Mansi, vol. 25, cols 297–9.

98 Raynouard, pp. 268–70.

99 Clement V, *Reg. Clem. V*, year 6, nos. 6666–8, pp. 83–4 (23 December 1310).

100 Probably some time before 1306, the king had complained to the pope about the Grand Master, claiming that the hostility of the Templars

towards his predecessor, Hugh III, had, since Hugh's death, been directed against him. L. de Mas-Latrie, *Histoire de l'île de Chypre*, vol. 2, pt 1 (Paris, 1852), pp. 108–9.

101 See G. Hill, *A History of Cyprus*, vol. 2 (Cambridge, 1948), pp. 216–24, for an account of the revolt. Molay's part, if any, in the initial moves against the king is obscure, but he is on the list of signatories to a charter of 26 April 1306, the day of the coup, which details the complaints of Amaury's party against the king. The charter said that the country was defended inadequately, that there was poverty and famine, that there was almost no diplomatic activity, and that justice was not properly administered. Mas-Latrie, 'Allocution au Roi Henri II de Lusignan', *RQH*, XLIII (1888), pp. 524–41.

102 Baluze, vol. 3, pp. 84–6.

103 Francesco Amadi, *Chroniques d'Amadi et de Strambaldi*, ed. R. de Mas-Latrie (Paris, 1891), pp. 283–91; Florio Bustron, *Chronique de l'île de Chypre*, ed. R. de Mas-Latrie (Paris, 1886), pp. 164–71.

104 Schottmüller, vol. 2, pp. 147–65.

105 See Hill, vol. 2, pp. 248–56.

106 Schottmüller, vol. 2, pp. 166–218.

107 *Ibid.*, pp. 376–400.

108 For these events, see Hill, vol. 2, pp. 245–60.

109 Clement V, *Reg. Clem. V*, year 6, nos. 7595, 7596, 7599, pp. 457–8; nos. 7603–5, p. 463.

110 *Ibid.*, year 6, no. 7612, p. 465 (25 August 1311).

111 Amadi, p. 398.

112 *Ibid.*, pp. 392–3; Bustron, pp. 244–5.

9   THE SUPPRESSION

1 *Cont. Nangis*, vol. 1, p. 388; Bernard Gui, *Flores Chron.*, p. 71.

2 Finke, vol. 2, pp. 303–5; Tolomeo da Lucca, p. 42.

3 Clement V, *Reg. Clem. V*, year 3, nos. 3626, 3627, pp. 386–91; Lizerand, *Clém. V*, appendix, no. 28, p. 467.

4 *Cont. Nangis*, vol. 1, p. 388.

5 Clement V, *Reg. Clem. V*, year 7, nos. 8843, 8850, pp. 329–30.

6 Jean de Saint-Victor, p. 656.

7 Finke, vol. 2, pp. 251–2.

8 According to the Aragonese ambassadors, the French clergy, with over fifty members present, took the most active part in the proceedings, followed by the Italians. The small contingents from Spain, England and Germany seem mainly to have been observers. *Ibid.*, p. 299.

9 Clement V, *Reg. Clem. V*, year 6, nos. 7524–8, p. 439; no. 7597, p. 458; no. 7605, p. 463; no. 7611, p. 464.

10 J. L. Villanueva, *Viaje literario a las iglesias de España*, vol. 5 (Madrid, 1806), no. 6, p. 216, the text of the bull of suppression, *Vox in excelso*.

11 Schottmüller, vol. 2, pp. 78–102, who heads the document *Deminutio laboris examinantium processus contra ordinem templi in Anglia, quasi per modum rubricarum.* It is undated, but Schottmüller believes that it is a summary prepared for the Council of Vienne. This assumption has been challenged by Perkins, 'Trial of the Knights Templars in England', p. 440, n. 51. There is a second summary of the evidence given in England in *Annales Londonienses,* in *Chronicles of the Reigns of Edward I and Edward II,* vol. 1, ed. W. Stubbs (*Rolls Series,* vol. 76; London, 1882), pp. 180–98, which Perkins believes is largely a summary of the *Deminutio,* which he says was evidently made after the inquisitors had succeeded in obtaining the three full confessions gained in England in late June 1311; see above, chap. 8, pp. 233–5. The content of these three confessions is not included in the *Deminutio,* but surely would have been if it had been compiled after late June 1311. For Perkins, this invalidates Schottmüller's conclusion. However, Perkins's arguments seem far from decisive, for there is no reason to assume that the passage in the *Annales Londonienses* is a condensation of the *Deminutio*; indeed the mention of confessions which seem to be those of late June 1311 in *Annales Londonienses* seems itself to contradict this. Even this is unclear, for the summary in *Annales Londonienses* is headed 22 April 1311, which is before the capture and confession of the three Templars. Moreover, the material upon which the summaries for the Council of Vienne were based would almost certainly have had to be sent to the commission sitting at Malaucène before late June 1311. These arguments do not prove that Schottmüller is correct, but the balance of probability must lie with his conclusion.

12 For the evidence for this, see Finke, vol. 1, pp. 348–9. The Aragonese ambassadors at the council call these *rubricae, Translat deles inquisicions* (*ibid.,* vol. 2, p. 239). The bull *Vox in excelso* of the following March recalls that the prelates had seen and examined *dicte attestationes ac rubrice.*

13 See V. Verlaque, *Jean XXII, sa vie et ses œuvres* (Paris, 1883), pp. 52–3.

14 Port (ed.), *Guillaume Le Maire,* pp. 471–4.

15 Clement V, *Reg. Clem. V,* year 3, nos. 3584–5, pp. 363–6: *Faciens misericordiam.*

16 Lizerand, *Clém. V,* appendix, no. 30, p. 472.

17 See Boase, pp. 360–3.

18 Villanueva, vol. 5, pp. 216–19.

19 Finke, vol. 2, pp. 260, 264–5.

20 Tolomeo da Lucca, p. 42.

21 Finke, vol. 2, pp. 258–9.

22 Walter of Hemingborough, *Chronicon Domini Walteri de Hemingburgh, De Gestis Regum Angliae,* ed. H. C. Hamilton, vol. 2 (London, 1868), p. 292.

23 Langlois, 'Notices et documents relatifs à l'histoire du xiiie et du xive siècle', *RH*, LXXXVII (1905), pp. 75–6.

24 Boutaric, *La France*, p. 38, n. 2; *Philippi Quarti Mansiones et Itinera*, p. 459, shows that the king was in Lyons on 16 March, but had moved on to Vienne by 22 March.

25 Finke, vol. 2, pp. 276–9.

26 *Ibid.*, pp. 280–5.

27 Lizerand, *Dossier*, no. 11, pp. 196–8.

28 Dupuy, *Traitez concernant l'histoire de France*, pp. 199–202.

29 Finke, vol. 2, pp. 265–8.

30 *Ibid.*, p. 284.

31 *Ibid.*, p. 285.

32 *Ibid.*, p. 286; *Cont. Nangis*, vol. 1, p. 389.

33 Villanueva, vol. 5, p. 219; Bernard Gui, *Cathalogo Brevi Romanorum Pontificum*, in Baluze, vol. 1, p. 56.

34 Finke, vol. 2, p. 287.

35 Walter of Hemingborough, vol. 2, pp. 293–4.

36 *Cont. Nangis*, vol. 1, pp. 389–92.

37 Villanueva, vol. 5, pp. 219–21; see also C. Mirbt, *Quellen zur Geschichte des Papsttums und des Römischen Katholizismus* (Tübingen, 1911), no. 310, p. 164, for the text of this section of *Vox in excelso*.

38 Walter of Hemingborough, vol. 2, pp. 293–4.

39 *Ibid.*, p. 293.

40 Villani, *Cronica*, vol. 2, p. 125 (bk VIII, chap. 92). The translation is from *Selections from the First Nine Books of the Croniche Fiorentine of Giovanni Villani*, tr. R. E. Selfe and P. H. Wicksteed (London, 1896), p. 378. See also above, chap. 2, p. 58.

41 N. Valois, pp. 238–41.

42 Finke, vol. 2, pp. 298–300. The letters said that 1,500 of the enemy had been killed for the loss of only seventy-five Hospitallers.

43 See above, chap. 9, p. 266, letter of 2 March 1312.

44 Lizerand, *Dossier*, no. 11, pp. 198–201.

45 Clement V, *Reg. Clem. V*, year 7, no. 7885, pp. 65–8. On the same day the pope named commissioners to execute the decree (no. 7886, pp. 68–71); on 16 May he informed the administrators and curators of the Templar property of the decision (no. 7952, pp. 82–3).

46 Delisle, *Mém. sur les opérations financières*, appendix, no. 35, pp. 228–9.

47 Lizerand, *Clém. V*, appendix, no. 35, pp. 482–3.

48 Delisle, *Mém. sur les opérations financières*, no. 36, pp. 229–33.

49 Beugnot (ed.), *Les Olim*, vol. 2, pp. 643–5.

50 Delisle, *Mém. sur les opérations financières*, appendix, no. 37, pp. 234–8.

51 Villani, *Cronica*, vol. 2, p. 127; tr. Selfe and Wicksteed, p. 381.

52 Finke, vol. 2, p. 302.

53 *Ibid.*, pp. 289–91. The king had been determined to gain his share of the Templars' property almost from the beginning of the trial; see above, chap. 8, pp. 240–1.

54 Clement V, *Reg. Clem. V*, year 7, no. 8862, pp. 334–6 (23 August 1312).

55 Finke, vol. 2, pp. 213–16. The representatives were Vidal de Villanova, the royal Chancellor, Dalmatius de Pontonibus, and the knight Bernard de Ponte.

56 *Ibid.*, pp. 218–19.

57 See *ibid.*, vol. 1, p. 377, n. 3.

58 *Ibid.*, vol. 2, pp. 219–20.

59 *Ibid.*, pp. 221–3.

60 *Ibid.*, pp. 223–4.

61 *Ibid.*, pp. 224–5.

62 *Ibid.*, p. 228.

63 Baluze, vol. 3, nos. 49 and 50, pp. 256–66.

64 Villanueva, vol. 5, no. 5, pp. 206–7; no. 8, pp. 225–6.

65 A. Benavides, *Memorias de D. Fernando IV de Castilla*, vol. 2 (Madrid, 1860), no. 409, p. 607.

66 *Ibid.*, no. 452, pp. 667–8; no. 567, pp. 828–9.

67 See Finke, vol. 1, p. 380; Mollat, *Lettres communes de Jean XXII*, vol. 2 (Paris, 1905), no. 9057, p. 342.

68 See J. Delaville le Roulx, 'La Suppression des Templiers', *RQH*, XLVIII (1890), pp. 57–8, for the history of the suppression in Castile.

69 Mollat, *Lettres communes*, vol. 2, no. 9053, p. 342.

70 Alart, pp. 86–8; Clement V, *Reg. Clem. V*, year 8, no. 9383, pp. 201–3; no. 9496, pp. 233–4.

71 Rymer, vol. 2, pt 1, p. 10. See also Tout, vol. 2, pp. 316–24, for the administration by the king's chamber of the Templar lands during the trial.

72 Rymer, vol. 2, pt 1, pp. 55–7.

73 Mollat, *Lettres communes*, vol. 1, no. 5179, p. 469; Rymer, vol. 2, pt 11, p. 48.

74 *Calendar of Close Rolls, 1323–7* (London, 1898), pp. 111, 117.

75 Rymer, vol. 2, pt 11, p. 109.

76 L. B. Larking and J. M. Kemble, *The Knights Hospitallers in England* (*Camden Society* os, vol. 65; London, 1857), pp. 210–11. For other examples, see Perkins, 'The Wealth of the Knights Templars in England and the Disposition of It after Their Dissolution', *American Historical Review*, XV (1909–10), pp. 260–1; on this subject see also A. M. Leys, 'The Forfeiture of the Lands of the Templars in England', in *Oxford Essays in Medieval History Presented to H. E. Salter*, ed. F. M. Powicke (Oxford, 1934), pp. 155–63.

77 Larking and Kemble, pp. 212–13.

78 *Ibid.*, p. 133.

79 Perkins, 'Wealth of the Knights Templars', p. 259.

80 *Calendar of Close Rolls, 1323–7*, pp. 126, 219.

81 *Ibid., 1330–3* (London, 1898), p. 112; *1333–7* (London, 1898), pp. 638, 661.

82 A typical settlement was that made on 8 March 1312, when a William Lambert and his wife, Caorsetta, were granted an annual pension of 100 shillings on the New Temple in London in quit-claim of a corrody they had in that house. *Ibid., 1307–13*, p. 409, also p. 422.

83 See Delaville le Roulx, pp. 53–5; Lea, *Hist. of the Inquisition*, vol. 3, pp. 330–1.

84 See, for instance, *Calendar of Close Rolls, 1323–7*, p. 545.

85 Clement V, *Reg. Clem. V*, year 7, no. 8784, pp. 303–5; Bernard Gui, *Flores Chron.*, p. 73.

86 Alart, p. 83.

87 Villanueva, vol. 5, no. 9, pp. 226–32. An agreement by the Hospital concerning Templar pensions in parts of the Iberian peninsula.

88 Larking and Kemble, p. 209.

89 Mollat, *Lettres communes*, vol. 2, nos. 8721–3, pp. 310–11.

90 *Ibid.*, vol. 3, no. 13307, p. 277.

91 Dupuy, *Histoire de l'ordre militaire des Templiers* (Brussels, 1751), no. 137, pp. 511–13.

92 Finke, vol. 2, pp. 226–7.

93 Prutz, *Entwicklung*, p. 316.

94 See Finke, vol. 1, p. 383.

95 Mollat, *Lettres communes*, vol. 1, no. 4670, pp. 429–30.

96 Finke, vol. 1, p. 384, n. 1.

97 Prutz, *Entwicklung*, pp. 293–4.

98 *Ibid.*, p. 294.

99 Finke, vol. 1, pp. 385–6. This may have been the result of a new papal complaint on this subject in 1324; Mollat, *Lettres communes*, vol. 5, nos. 20015, 20016, p. 169.

100 Mollat, *Lettres communes*, vol. 1, no. 4670, pp. 429–30 (12 August 1317).

101 C. Eubel (ed.), *Bullarium Franciscanum*, vol. 5 (Rome, 1898), no. 347, pp. 160–2.

102 Mollat, *Lettres communes*, vol. 3, no. 14027, p. 342. This was also a problem in England. The Templar sent to the Abbey of Kirkstall escaped, apparently because of the deliberate negligence of the abbot and convent; see *The Register of William Greenfield, Lord Archbishop of York*, pt v, ed. W. Brown and A. Hamilton Thompson (*Surtees Society*, vol. 153; London, 1940), no. 2354, pp. 1–3.

103 Clement V, *Reg. Clem. V*, year 8, no. 10337, p. 482.

104 *Cont. Nangis*, vol. 1, pp. 402–3.

105 *Ibid.*, pp. 403–4.

106 Beugnot (ed.), *Les Olim*, vol. 2, p. 599.

107 Tolomeo da Lucca, p. 52; see Lizerand, *Clém. V*, p. 373.

108 See Boutaric, *La France*, pp. 424–6.

109 See Lea, *Hist. of the Inquisition*, vol. 3, p. 326, on these legends.

110 Villani, *Cronica*, vol. 2, p. 127; tr. Selfe and Wicksteed, p. 381.

10 CONCLUSION

1 For the main arguments concerning these issues see Lea, *Hist. of the Inquisition*, vol. 3, pp. 264–76; Finke, vol. 1, pp. 326–44; Mollat, *Popes at Avignon*, pp. 242–6.

2 Lea, *Hist. of the Inquisition*, vol. 3, p. 265.

3 See above, chap. 2, p. 67; chap. 5, pp. 152, 153.

4 See, for instance, the comments of D. Knowles, *The Religious Orders in England*, vol. 1 (Cambridge, 1960), pp. 317–19.

5 See above, chap. 6, pp. 187–8.

6 See, for instance, Coulton, *Five Centuries of Religion*, vol. 2 (Cambridge, 1927), chap. 13, on the Friars.

7 Strayer, 'France: The Holy Land', pp. 300ff.

8 Lizerand, *Dossier*, p. 130. See above, chap. 3, pp. 109–10.

9 Finke, vol. 2, p. 106. See above, chap. 5, pp. 175–7.

10 Port (ed.), *Guillaume Le Maire*, pp. 473–4. See above, chap. 9, p. 262.

Bibliography

There are two thorough bibliographies of the Order, which cover publications up to 1965: M. Dessubré, *Bibliographie de l'ordre des Templiers* (Paris, 1928; repr. 1966), and H. Neu, *Bibliographie des Templer-Ordens 1927–1965* (Bonn, 1965). There is a survey of the chief documentary sources of the trial and a critical examination of the important secondary works published before 1889, in C. V. Langlois, 'Livres sur l'histoire des Templiers', *Revue historique*, XL (1889), pp. 168–79.

This section is primarily intended to describe the works that I have found most useful in writing this book, and to provide a reference list of works cited in the Notes. There are two basic collections of printed sources. J. Michelet, *Le Procès des Templiers*, 2 vols (*Collection de documents inédits sur l'histoire de France*; Paris, 1841–51), is the notarial record of the hearings at Paris in October and November 1307, and of the hearings of the papal commission between 1309 and 1311, based upon the copy deposited at Paris at the close of the papal commission. Michelet also printed the record of a local episcopal inquiry at Roussillon in 1310 at the end of vol. 2. The second important work is that of H. Finke, *Papsttum und Untergang des Templerordens*, vol. 2 (Münster, 1907). This is an extensive collection derived primarily from the Barcelona Archive, but also including material from the Archives Nationales and the Bibliothèque Nationale at Paris, and the Vatican Archive. It is divided into three parts: (1) letters, reports and opinions on the trial; (2) reports of the ambassadors of the Aragonese king, James II, at the Council of Vienne (1311–12), including the king's replies; (3) proceedings of the trial, including those in which the papacy or its representatives played a direct role. In addition, K. Schottmüller, *Der Untergang des Templer-Ordens*, vol. 2 (Berlin, 1887; repr. 1970), published the records of proceedings at Poitiers, Brindisi, Cyprus and the Papal State, together with a summary of the trial in England, apparently intended for the Council of Vienne – materials which he derived from research in the Vatican Archive. The appendices of H. Prutz, *Entwicklung und Untergang des Tempelherrenordens* (Berlin, 1888), include, among other Templar records, fragments from local French inquiries against the Templars. Finally, there is a convenient compilation of sources on the trial, together with a French translation, in G. Lizerand, *Le Dossier de l'affaire des Templiers* (Paris, 1923; repr. 1964).

Papal collections, although not primarily concerned with the trial, nevertheless provide a great deal of relevant material. E. Baluze, *Vitae Paparum Avenionensium*, ed. G. Mollat, 4 vols (Paris, 1914–27), includes extensive documentation of the pontificate of Clement V. Vol. 1 covers the chronicle sources appertaining to the pope's life and vol. 3 has many of his letters and bulls. The texts of many of the major bulls issued by the pope concerning the trial can be found in *Livre de Guillaume Le Maire*, ed. C. Port, in *Mélanges historiques: Choix de documents*, vol. 2 (*Collection de documents inédits sur l'histoire de France*; Paris, 1877). The main source for the acts of Clement's reign is *Regestum Clementis Papae V . . . nunc primum editum cura et studio Monachorum Ordinis S. Benedicti*, years 1–9 (Rome, 1885–92). There is also an invaluable collection of translated documents on heresy between the eleventh and the fourteenth centuries in *Heresies of the High Middle Ages*, ed. and tr. W. L. Wakefield and A. P. Evans (*Columbia Records of Civilization*; New York, 1969), which, although it does not deal with the Templars as such, is very helpful in setting the trial in the wider context of the heresies of this period.

There are three balanced and detailed secondary accounts of the trial: vol. 1 of Finke, *Papsttum*; vol. 3 of H. C. Lea, *A History of the Inquisition of the Middle Ages* (New York, 1889); and G. Lizerand, *Clément V et Philippe IV le Bel* (Paris, 1910), which includes a useful appendix of documents. The best short summary is that of G. Mollat, *The Popes at Avignon, 1305–78*, tr. J. Love (London, 1963), pp. 229–46. These books can be supplemented by the aids to study provided by the volume of tables of the depositions of the Templars during the trial in J. Gmelin, *Schuld oder Unschuld des Templer ordens* (Stuttgart, 1893), and the map and list of Templar houses in *Grosser historischer Weltatlas*, vol. 2, *Mittelalter* (Munich, 1970).

Periodical literature examines specific aspects of the trial. E. Boutaric, 'Clément V, Philippe le Bel et les Templiers', *Revue des questions historiques*, x and xi (1871–2), is a study of the relevance of the trial to the papal/monarchical relations of the period based upon original source material. There is a review article of Finke's book by C. V. Langlois, 'L'Affaire des Templiers', *Journal des savants* (1908), pp. 417–35, which supplements his earlier article,

'Le Procès des Templiers', *Revue des deux mondes*, CIII (1891), pp. 382–421. There are two articles which examine the problems created by the various depositions of Jacques de Molay during the trial: P. Viollet, 'Les Interrogatoires de Jacques de Molay, Grand Maître du Temple: Conjectures', *Mémoires de l'Académie des inscriptions et belles-lettres*, XXXVIII, pt 2 (1911), pp. 121–36, and G. Lizerand, 'Les Dépositions du Grand Maître, Jacques de Molay, au procès des Templiers (1307–14)', *Le Moyen Age*, 2nd ser., XVII (1913), pp. 81–106. The question of idol worship is analysed in S. Reinach, 'La Tête magique des Templiers', *Revue de l'histoire des religions*, LXIII (1911), pp. 25–39. For the trial outside France there is the detailed study of C. Perkins, 'The Trial of the Knights Templars in England', *English Historical Review*, XXIV (1909), pp. 432–47, and a more general survey by J. Delaville le Roulx, 'La Suppression des Templiers', *Revue des questions historiques*, XLVIII (1890), pp. 29–61.

WORKS CITED

Abbreviations

Baluze	Baluze, E., *Vitae Paparum Avenionensium*, ed. G. Mollat, 4 vols (Paris, 1914–27)
Cont. Nangis	Guillaume de Nangis, *Chronique latine de Guillaume de Nangis, de 1113 à 1300 avec les continuations de cette chronique de 1300 à 1368*, ed. H. Géraud, vol. 1 (Paris, 1843)
PL	Migne, J. P. (ed.), *Patrologiae Cursus Completus, Series Latina*, 221 vols (Paris, 1844–6); ... *Series Secunda*, 4 vols (Paris, 1845–6)
PPTS	*Palestine Pilgrims' Text Society*, 14 vols (London, 1887–97)
Procès	Michelet, J. (ed.), *Le Procès des Templiers*, 2 vols (*Collection de documents inédits sur l'histoire de France*; Paris, 1841–51)
RH	*Revue historique*
RHCr.	*Recueil des historiens des Croisades: Historiens occidentaux*, 5 vols (Paris, 1844–95); ... *Historiens orientaux*, 5 vols (Paris, 1872–1906).

RHG   Bouquet, M. *et al.* (eds), *Recueil des historiens des Gaules et de la France*, 23 vols (Paris, 1738–1876)

RQH   *Revue des questions historiques*

Adémar de Chabannes, *Ademari S. Cibardi Monachi Historiarum Libri Tres*, in *PL*, vol. 141.

Alain de Lille, *Alani de Insulis De Fide Catholica contra Haereticos Sui Temporis*, in *PL*, vol. 210.

Alart, B., 'Suppression de l'ordre des Templiers en Roussillon', *Bulletin de la Société agricole, scientifique et littéraire des Pyrénées-Orientales*, xv (1867), pp. 25–115.

Albert of Aix, *Alberti Aquensis Historia Hierosolymitana*, in *RHCr: Historiens occidentaux*, vol. 4.

Albon, Marquis d' (ed.), *Cartulaire général de l'ordre du Temple, 1119?–1150* (Paris, 1913).

Amadi, Francesco, *Chroniques d'Amadi et de Strambaldi*, ed. R. de Mas-Latrie (Paris, 1891).

Anglo-Saxon Chronicle, The, ed. and tr. D. Whitelock (London, 1961).

Annales Londonienses, in *Chronicles of the Reigns of Edward I and Edward II*, vol. 1, ed. W. Stubbs (*Rolls Series*, vol. 76; London, 1882).

Aquinas, Saint Thomas, *Summa Theologica*, in *PL*, 2nd ser., vol. 3.

——*Quaestiones Quodlibetales*, intr. P. Mandonnet (Paris, 1926).

Augustine, Saint, *Epistolae*, ed. A. Goldbacher (*Corpus Scriptorum Ecclesiasticorum Latinorum*, vol. 57; Leipzig, 1911).

——*De Civitate Dei*, in *Œuvres de Saint Augustin*, vol. 36, ed. and tr. G. Bardy and G. Combès (Paris, 1960).

Bailey, D. S., *Homosexuality and the Western Christian Tradition* (London, 1955).

Barber, M. C., 'James of Molay, the Last Grand Master of the Temple', *Studia Monastica*, xiv (1972), pp. 91–124.

Basil, Saint, *Sermo de Renuntiatione Saeculi*, in J. P. Migne (ed.), *Patrologiae Cursus Completus, Series Graeca* (162 vols, Paris, 1857–1912), vol. 31.

Baudouin, A., *Lettres inédites de Philippe le Bel* (*Mémoires de l'Académie des sciences, inscriptions et belles-lettres de Toulouse*, 8th ser., viii; 1886).

Benavides, A., *Memorias de D. Fernando IV de Castilla*, vol. 2 (Madrid, 1860).

Benedict, Saint, *The Rule of Saint Benedict*, ed. J. McCann (London, 1952).

Bernard Gui, *E Floribus Chronicorum Auctore Bernardo Guidonis*, in *RHG*, vol. 21.

——*Practica Inquisitionis Heretice Pravitatis*, ed. C. Douais (Paris, 1886).

——*Cathalogo Brevi Romanorum Pontificum*, in Baluze, vol. 1.

——*Flores Chronicorum*, in Baluze, vol. 1.

——*Manuel de l'Inquisiteur*, 2 vols, ed. and tr. G. Mollat (Paris, 1926).

Bernard of Clairvaux, *Liber ad Milites Templi de Laude Novae Militiae*, in *Sancti Bernardi Opera*, vol. 3, ed. J. Leclercq (Rome, 1963).

Beugnot, A. de (ed.), *Les Olim*, vol. 2 and vol. 3, pt 1 (Paris, 1844).

Blancard, L., 'Documents relatifs au procès des Templiers en Angleterre', *Revue des sociétés savantes*, 4th ser., VI (1867), pp. 414–23.

Bloch, M., *Feudal Society*, tr. L. A. Manyon (London, 1961).

——*The Royal Touch: Sacred Monarchy and Scrofula in England and France*, tr. J. E. Anderson (London, 1973).

Boase, T. S. R., *Boniface VIII* (London, 1933).

Boniface VIII, *Les Registres de Boniface VIII*, ed. G. Digard *et al.*, vols 1 and 3 (Paris, 1884).

Bordier, H., 'Une Satire contre Philippe le Bel (vers 1290)', *Bulletin de la Société de l'histoire de France*, 2nd ser., 1 (1857–8), pp. 197–201.

Borrelli de Serres, L. L., *Les Variations monétaires sous Philippe le Bel* (Chalon-sur-Saône, 1902).

Boutaric, E., *La France sous Philippe le Bel* (Paris, 1861).

——(ed.), *Documents relatifs à l'histoire de Philippe le Bel*, in *Notices et extraits des manuscrits de la Bibliothèque impériale*, XX (1862).

——'Clément V, Philippe le Bel et les Templiers', *RQH*, X (1871), pp. 301–421; XI (1872), pp. 5–40.

Brown, J. A. C., *Techniques of Persuasion: From Propaganda to Brainwashing* (Harmondsworth, 1963).

Bulst-Thiele, M. L., *Sacrae Domus Militiae Templi Hierosolymitani Magistri* (Göttingen, 1974).

Burr, G. L., 'The Literature of Witchcraft', in *George Lincoln Burr: His Life and Selections from his Writings*, ed. R. H. Bainton and L. O. Gibbons (New York, 1943), pp. 166–89.

Bustron, Florio, *Chronique de l'île de Chypre*, ed. R. de Mas-Latrie (Paris, 1886).

Caesarius of Heisterbach, *Caesarii Heisterbacensis Monachi Ordinis Cisterciensis Dialogus Miraculorum*, vol. 1, ed. J. Strange (Cologne, 1851).

Calendar of Close Rolls, 1307–13 (London, 1892); . . . *1323–7*; . . . *1330–3*; . . . *1333–7* (London, 1898).

Cheney, C. R., 'The Downfall of the Templars and a Letter in Their Defence', in *Medieval Miscellany Presented to Eugène Vinaver*, ed. F. Whitehead, A. M. Divernes and F. E. Sutcliffe (Manchester, 1965), pp. 65–79.

Chronographia Regum Francorum, ed. H. Moranville, vol. 1 (Paris, 1891).

Clement IV, *Les Registres de Clément IV (1265–8)*, ed. E. Jordan, vol. 1 (Paris, 1904).

Clement V, *Regestum Clementis Papae V . . . nunc primum editum cura et studio Monachorum Ordinis S. Benedicti*, years 1–9 (Rome, 1885–92).

Cohn, N., *Europe's Inner Demons: An Enquiry Inspired by the Great Witchhunt* (London, 1975).

Coulton, G. G., *Five Centuries of Religion*, vols 2 and 3 (Cambridge, 1927–36).

Curzon, H. de (ed.), *La Règle du Temple* (Paris, 1886).

Cuttino, G. P., 'Historical Revision: The Causes of the Hundred Years War', *Speculum*, XXXI (1956), pp. 463–77.

Damian, Saint Peter, *Liber Gomorrhianus*, in *PL*, vol. 145.

Daniel the Higumene, *The Pilgrimage of the Russian Abbot Daniel in the Holy Land, 1106–7 AD*, tr. C. W. Wilson, in *PPTS*, vol. 4 (London, 1892).

Daniel, N., *Islam and the West: The Making of an Image* (Edinburgh, 1960).

Delaville le Roulx, J., 'La Suppression des Templiers', *RQH*, XLVIII (1890), pp. 29–61.

Delisle, L., *Mémoire sur les opérations financières des Templiers* (*Mémoires de l'Institut national de France, Académie des inscriptions et belles-lettres*, vol. 33; Paris, 1889).

——*Etudes sur la condition de la classe agricole et l'état de l'agriculture en Normandie au Moyen Age* (Paris, 1903).

Devic, C., and Vaissète, J., *Histoire générale de Languedoc*, ed. A. Molinier, vol. 10 (Toulouse, 1885).

Disputatio inter Clericum et Militem, in M. Goldast, *Monarchia S. Romani Imperii*, vol. 1 (Hanover, 1611).

Döllinger, J. J. I. von (ed.), *Beiträge zur Sektengeschichte des Mittelalters*, vol. 2 (Munich, 1890).

Douais, C. (ed.), *Documents pour servir à l'histoire de l'Inquisition dans le Languedoc au XIIIᵉ et au XIVᵉ siècle* (Paris, 1900).

Dubois, Pierre, *De Recuperatione Terre Sancte*, ed. C. V. Langlois (*Collection de textes pour servir à l'etude et à l'enseignement de l'histoire*; Paris, 1891).

Duby, G., *The Making of the Christian West, 980–1140* (Geneva, 1967).

Dugdale, W., *Monasticon Anglicanum*, ed. J. Caley, H. Ellis and B. Bandinel, vol. 6, pt 2 (London, 1846).

Dupuy, P., *Histoire du différend d'entre le pape Boniface VIII et Philippe le Bel, Roy de France* (Paris, 1655).

——*Traitez concernant l'histoire de France* (Paris, 1685).

——*Histoire de l'ordre militaire des Templiers* (Brussels, 1751).

Easson, D. E., *Medieval Religious Houses: Scotland* (London, 1957).

Ehrle, F., 'Ein Bruchstück der Acten des Concils von Vienne', *Archiv für Literatur- und Kirchengeschichte des Mittelalters*, IV (1888), pp. 361–470; V (1889), pp. 574–84.

Ekkehard of Aura, *Ekkehardi Hierosolymita*, ed. H. Hagenmeyer (Tübingen, 1877).

Elworthy, F. T., *The Evil Eye: An Account of This Ancient and Widespread Superstition* (London, 1895).

Eubel, C. (ed.), *Bullarium Franciscanum*, vol. 5 (Rome, 1898).

Favier, J., *Un conseiller de Philippe le Bel: Enguerran de Marigny* (Paris, 1963).

——'Les Légistes et le gouvernement de Philippe le Bel', *Journal des savants* (1969), pp. 92–108.

Fawtier, R., *Histoire du Moyen Age*, vol. 6, *L'Europe occidentale de 1270 à 1380*, pt 1 (*Histoire générale*, ed. G. Glotz; Paris, 1940).

——'Comment, au début du XIVᵉ siècle, un roi de France pouvait-il se représenter son royaume', *Comptes rendus des séances, de l'Académie des inscriptions et belles-lettres* (1959), pp. 117–23.

——*The Capetian Kings of France*, tr. L. Butler and R. J. Adam (London, 1960).

Fidenzio of Padua, *Liber Recuperationis Terrae Sanctae*, in G. Golubovich (ed.), *Biblioteca Bio-Bibliografica della Terra Santa*, vol. 2 (Florence, 1913).

Finke, H., *Papsttum und Untergang des Templerordens*, vols 1 and 2 (Münster, 1907).

Fliche, A., Thouzellier, C., and Azais, Y., *La Chrétienté romaine (1198–1274)* (*Histoire de l'Eglise*, ed. A. Fliche and V. Martin, vol. 10; Paris, 1950).

Friedberg, E. (ed.), *Corpus Iuris Canonici*, vol. 2 (Leipzig, 1881; repr. Graz, 1959).

Gervais of Tilbury, *Des Gervasius von Tilbury Otia Imperialia*, ed. F. Liebrecht (Hanover, 1856).

Gervase of Canterbury, *Opera Historica*, vol. 1, ed. W. Stubbs (*Rolls Series*, vol. 73; London, 1879).

Gesta Treverorum Continuatio IV, ed. G. Waitz, in *Monumenta Germaniae Historica, Scriptores*, vol. 24 (Berlin, 1879).

Gestes des Chiprois, ed. G. Raynaud (Geneva, 1887).

Gifford, E. S., *The Evil Eye: Studies in the Folklore of Vision* (New York, 1958).

Giraldus Cambrensis, *Liber de Principis Instructione*, in *Giraldi Cambrensis Opera*, vol. 8, ed. G. F. Warner (*Rolls Series*, vol. 21; London, 1891).

Gmelin, J., *Schuld oder Unschuld des Templerordens* (Stuttgart, 1893).

Grandes Chroniques de France, Les, ed. J. Viard, vol. 8 (Paris, 1934).

Griffe, E., *Les Débuts de l'aventure cathare en Languedoc (1140–90)* (Paris, 1969).

Grosser historischer Weltatlas, vol. 2, *Mittelalter* (Munich, 1970).

Guibert de Nogent, *Histoire de sa vie (1053–1124)*, ed. G. Bourgin (*Collection de textes pour servir à l'étude et à l'enseignement de l'histoire*; Paris, 1907).

Guillaume de Nangis, *Gesta Sanctae Memoriae Ludovici Regis Franciae*, in *RHG*, vol. 20.

Guillaume de Paris, *De Legibus*, in *Opera Omnia*, vol. 1 (Amiens, 1674).

Guiraud, J., *Histoire de l'Inquisition au Moyen Age*, vol. 1 (Paris, 1935).

Gwynn, A., and Hadcock, R. N., *Medieval Religious Houses: Ireland* (London, 1970).

Hansen, J., *Quellen und Untersuchungen zur Geschichte des Hexenwahns und der Hexenverfolgung im Mittelalter* (Bonn, 1901).

Hartland, E. S., *The Legend of Perseus: A Study of Tradition in Story, Custom and Belief*, vol. 1 (London, 1894).

——*Ritual and Belief: Studies in the History of Religion* (London, 1914).

Hefele, C.-J., *Histoire des Conciles*, tr. H. Leclercq, vol. 5, pt 2 (Paris, 1912).

Henry of Huntingdon, *The History of the English*, ed. T. Arnold (*Rolls Series*, vol. 74; London, 1879).

Hill, G., *A History of Cyprus*, vol. 2 (Cambridge, 1948).

Hodgson, M. G. S., *The Order of the Assassins* (The Hague, 1955).

Huygens, R. B. C. (ed.), 'De Constructione Castri Saphet', *Studi Medievali*, 3rd ser., VI (1965), pp. 355–87.

Ibn al-Athir, *Extrait de la Chronique intitulée Kamel-Altevarykh*, in *RHCr.: Historiens orientaux*, vol. 1 (Paris, 1872).

Ives de Saint-Denis, *Chronicon*, in *RHG*, vol. 21.

Jacques de Vitry, *Historia Hierosolimitana*, in J. Bongars, *Gesta Dei per Francos*, vol. 2 (Hanover, 1611).

James I of Aragon, *The Chronicle of James I of Aragon*, ed. and tr. J. Forster, vol. 2 (London, 1883).

Jean de Paris, *Tractatus de Potestate Regia et Papali*, in J. Leclercq, *Jean de Paris et l'ecclésiologie du XIIIe siècle* (Paris, 1942).

Jean de Saint-Victor, *Excerpta e Memoriali Historiarum Auctore Johanne Parisiensi, Sancti Victoris Parisiensis Canonico Regulari*, in *RHG*, vol. 21.

Jones, C. M., 'The Conventional Saracen of the Songs of Geste', *Speculum*, XVII (1942), pp. 201–25.

Kantorowicz, E. H., *Laudes Regiae: A Study in Liturgical Acclamations and Mediaeval Ruler Worship* (Berkeley, Calif., 1958).

Knowles, D., *The Religious Orders in England*, vol. 1 (Cambridge, 1960).

——and Hadcock, R. N., *Medieval Religious Houses: England and Wales* (London, 1953).

Krey, A. C., 'William of Tyre: The Making of an Historian in the Middle Ages', *Speculum*, XVI (1941), pp. 149–66.

Landon, L., *The Itinerary of King Richard I* (London, 1935).

Langlois, C. V., *Saint Louis, Philippe le Bel: Les Derniers Capétiens directs (1226–1328)* (*Histoire de France*, ed. E. Lavisse, vol. 3, pt 2; Paris, 1901).

——'Doléances du clergé de France au temps de Philippe le Bel', *Revue bleue*, 5th ser., IV (1905), pp. 329–33, 486–90.

——'Notices et documents relatifs à l'histoire du XIIIe et du XIVe siècle', *RH*, LXXXVII (1905), pp. 55–79.

——'Les Doléances des communautés du Toulousain contre Pierre de Latilli et Raoul de Breuilli (1297–8)', *RH*, xcv (1907), pp. 23–53.

Larking, L. B., and Kemble, J. M., *The Knights Hospitallers in England* (*Camden Society*, os, vol. 65; London, 1857).

Laurière, E. de (ed.), *Ordonnances des roys de France de la troisième race*, vol. 1 (Paris, 1723).

Le Patourel, J., 'The King and the Princes in Fourteenth-Century France', in *Europe in the Later Middle Ages*, ed. J. Hale, R. Highfield and B. Smalley (London, 1965), pp. 155–83.

Lea, H. C., *A History of the Inquisition of the Middle Ages*, vols 1 and 3 (New York, 1889).

——'The Absolution Formula of the Templars', in *Minor Historical Writings and Other Essays by Henry Charles Lea*, ed. A. C. Howland (London, 1942), pp. 97–112.

Lees, B. A., *Records of the Templars in England in the Twelfth Century* (London, 1935).

Leys, A. M., 'The Forfeiture of the Lands of the Templars in England', in *Oxford Essays in Medieval History Presented to H. E. Salter*, ed. F. M. Powicke (Oxford, 1934), pp. 155–63.

Liudprand of Cremona, *Liber de Ottone Rege*, in *Quellen zur Geschichte der Sächsischen Kaiserzeit*, ed. A. Bauer and R. Rau (Darmstadt, 1971).

Lizerand, G., *Clément V et Philippe IV le Bel* (Paris, 1910).

——*Le Dossier de l'affaire des Templiers* (Paris, 1923; repr. 1964).

Loiseleur, J., *La Doctrine secrète des Templiers* (Orléans, 1872).

Lot, F., and Fawtier, R., *Histoire des institutions françaises au Moyen Age*, vol. 2 (Paris, 1958).

Luchaire, A., *Etude sur les actes de Louis VII* (Paris, 1885).

Ludolph von Suchem's Description of the Holy Land, and of the Way Thither, Written in the Year 1350, tr. A. Stewart, in *PPTS*, vol. 12 (London, 1895).

Lundgreen, F., *Wilhelm von Tyrus und der Templerorden* (Berlin, 1911).

Maisonneuve, H., *Etudes sur les origines de l'Inquisition*, 2nd edn (Paris, 1960).

Mansi, J. D., *Sacrorum Conciliorum Nova et Amplissima Collectio*, vols 21 and 25 (Venice, 1774–82).

Map, Walter, *De Nugis Curialium*, ed. M. R. James (*Anecdota*

Oxoniensia, Medieval and Modern Series; Oxford, 1914).

Mas-Latrie, L. de, *Histoire de l'île de Chypre*, vol. 2, pt 1 (Paris, 1852).

——'Allocution au Roi Henri II de Lusignan', *RQH*, XLIII (1888), pp. 524–41.

Mercati, A., 'Interrogatorio di Templari a Barcellona (1311)', *Gesammelte Aufsätze zur Kulturgeschichte Spaniens*, VI (1937), pp. 240–51.

Mirbt, C., *Quellen zur Geschichte des Papsttums und des Römischen Katholizismus* (Tübingen, 1911).

Mollat, G., *Lettres communes de Jean* XXII (10 vols, Paris, 1904–28), vols 1, 2, 3 and 5.

——*The Popes at Avignon, 1305–78*, tr. J. Love (London, 1963).

Moneta of Cremona, *Adversus Catharos et Valdenses*, ed. T. A. Ricchini (Rome, 1743).

Müller, G., *Documenti sulle relazioni delle città Toscane coll'Oriente* (Florence, 1879).

Nicolini, N., *Codice diplomatico sui rapporti Veneto-Napoletani durante il regno di Carlo I d'Angio* (Rome, 1965).

Odo of Deuil, *De Profectione Ludovici VII in Orientem*, ed. and tr. V. G. Berry (New York, 1948).

Paris, Bibliothèque Nationale, Nouvelles Acquisitions latines, vols 1 and 2.

Paris, Matthew, *Chronica Majora*, ed. H. R. Luard, vols 4 and 5 (*Rolls Series*, vol. 57; London, 1880).

Parker, T. W., *The Knights Templars in England* (Tucson, Ariz., 1963).

Pegues, F. J., *The Lawyers of the Last Capetians* (Princeton, NJ, 1962).

Perkins, C., 'The Trial of the Knights Templars in England', *English Historical Review*, XXIV (1909), pp. 432–47.

——'The Wealth of the Knights Templars in England and the Disposition of It after Their Dissolution', *American Historical Review*, XV (1909–10), pp. 252–63.

Petel, A., 'Le Diocèse de Troyes dans le différend entre Boniface VIII et Philippe le Bel et dans l'affaire des Templiers', *Mémoires de la Société académique d'agriculture, des sciences, arts et belles-lettres du Département de l'Aube*, 3rd ser., LXX (1906), pp. 9–100.

——'Templiers et Hospitaliers dans le diocèse de Troyes: Le Temple de Bonlieu et l'Hôpital d'Orient', *Mémoires de la Société académique d'agriculture, des sciences, arts et belles-lettres du Département de l'Aube*, 3rd ser., LXXIII (1909), pp. 257–358; LXXIV (1910), pp. 11–350.

Philippi Quarti Mansiones et Itinera, in *RHG*, vol. 21 (Paris, 1855), pp. 430–64.

Picot, G. (ed.), *Documents relatifs aux Etats Généraux et Assemblées réunis sous Philippe le Bel* (Paris, 1901).

Piquet, J., *Des banquiers au Moyen Age: Les Templiers* (Paris, 1939).

Port, C. (ed.), *Livre de Guillaume Le Maire*, in *Mélanges historiques: Choix de documents*, vol. 2 (*Collection de documents inédits sur l'histoire de France*; Paris, 1877).

Potthast, A., *Regesta Pontificum Romanorum*, 2 vols (Berlin, 1874–5).

Powicke, F. M., and Cheney, C. R. (eds), *Councils and Synods with Other Documents Relating to the English Church*, vol. 2, AD *1205–1313* (Oxford, 1964).

Prutz, H. (ed.), *Malteser Urkunden und Regesten zur Geschichte der Tempelherren und der Johanniter* (Munich, 1883).

——*Entwicklung und Untergang des Tempelherrenordens* (Berlin, 1888).

Raynouard, M., *Monumens historiques relatifs à la condamnation des chevaliers du Temple* (Paris, 1813).

Register of William Greenfield, Lord Archbishop of York, The, pt v, ed. W. Brown and A. Hamilton Thompson (*Surtees Society*, vol. 153; London, 1940).

Registrum Roberti Winchelsey Cantuariensis Archiepiscopi, vol. 2, ed. R. Graham (*Canterbury and York Society*, vol. 52; Oxford, 1956).

Registrum Simonis de Gandavo Diocesis Saresbiriensis, vol. 2, ed. C. T. Flower and M. C. B. Dawes (*Canterbury and York Society*, vol. 41; Oxford, 1934).

Reinach, S., 'La Tête magique des Templiers', *Revue de l'histoire des religions*, LXIII (1911), pp. 25–39.

Rigault, A., *Le Procès de Guichard, évêque de Troyes (1308–13)* (Paris, 1896).

Riley-Smith, J., *The Knights of St John in Jerusalem and Cyprus, c.1050–1310* (London, 1967).

——'The Templars and the Castle of Tortosa in Syria: An Unknown Document concerning the Acquisition of the Fortress', *English*

Historical Review, LXXXIV (1969), pp. 278–88.

——*The Feudal Nobility and the Kingdom of Jerusalem, 1174–1277* (London, 1973).

Rodenberg, C. (ed.), *Epistolae Saeculi XIII e Regestis Pontificum Romanorum*, in *Monumenta Germaniae Historica, Epistolae*, vol. 1 (Berlin, 1883).

Roger of Howden, *Chronica*, ed. W. R. Stubbs, vol. 3 (*Rolls Series*, vol. 51; London, 1870).

Runciman, S., *The Sicilian Vespers* (Cambridge, 1958).

Russell, J. B., *Witchcraft in the Middle Ages* (Ithaca, NY, 1972).

Rymer, T., *Foedera, Conventiones, Literae et Cuiuscunque Generis Acta Publica*, vols 1 and 2 (The Hague, 1745).

Saewulf, *An Account of the Pilgrimage of Saewulf to Jerusalem and the Holy Land in the Years 1102 and 1103*, tr. W. R. B. Brownlow, in *PPTS*, vol. 4 (London, 1892).

Sargant, W., *Battle for the Mind: A Physiology of Conversion and Brain-Washing* (London, 1957).

Schoell, R. (ed.), *Iustiniani Novellae* (*Corpus Iuris Civilis*, vol. 3) (Berlin, 1928).

Schottmüller, K., *Der Untergang des Templer-Ordens*, vol. 2 (Berlin, 1887; repr. 1970).

Schwalm, J., 'Reise nach Frankreich und Italien im Sommer 1903, mit Beilagen', *Neues Archiv der Gesellschaft für Ältere Deutsche Geschichtskunde*, XXIX (1904), pp. 571–640.

Shannon, A. C., 'The Secrecy of Witnesses in Inquisitorial Tribunals and in Contemporary Secular Trials', in *Essays in Medieval Life and Thought Presented in Honor of Austin P. Evans*, ed. J. H. Mundy, R. W. Emery and B. Nelson (New York, 1955), pp. 59–69.

Strack, H. L., *The Jew and Human Sacrifice*, tr. H. Blanchamp (London, 1909).

Strayer, J. R., *Studies in Early French Taxation* (Cambridge, Mass., 1939).

——'Philip the Fair – A "Constitutional" King', in *Medieval Statecraft and the Perspectives of History: Essays by Joseph R. Strayer*, ed. J. F. Benton and T. H. Bisson (Princeton, NJ, 1971), pp. 195–212.

——'The Crusade against Aragon', *ibid.*, pp. 107–22.

——'France: The Holy Land, the Chosen People, and the Most Christian King', *ibid.*, pp. 300–14.

——'Italian Bankers and Philip the Fair', *ibid.*, pp. 239–47.

Teulet, M. A. (ed.), *Layettes des trésors des chartes*, vol. 1 (Paris, 1863).

Theoderich's Description of the Holy Places circa 1172 AD, tr. and ed. A. Stewart, in *PPTS*, vol. 5 (London, 1891).

Thorndike, L., *A History of Magic and Experimental Science*, vols 1 and 2 (New York, 1929).

Tolomeo da Lucca, *Historia Ecclesiastica*, in Baluze, vol. 1.

Tout, T. F., *Chapters in the Administrative History of Mediaeval England*, vols 1 and 2 (Manchester, 1920).

Ullmann, W., *Medieval Papalism* (London, 1949).

——*Principles of Government and Politics in the Middle Ages* (London, 1961).

Valois, N., 'Deux nouveaux témoignages sur le procès des Templiers', *Comptes rendus des séances de l'Académie des inscriptions et belles-lettres* (1910), pp. 229–41.

Verlaque, V., *Jean XXII, sa vie et ses œuvres* (Paris, 1883).

Vetus Aganon, in *Cartulaire de l'Abbaye de Saint-Père-de-Chartres*, ed. B.-E.-C. Guérard (*Collection de documents inédits sur l'histoire de France*, vol. 1, *Collection de cartulaires de France*; Paris, 1840).

Villani, Giovanni, *Cronica*, vol. 2 (*Collezione di storici e cronisti italiani*; Florence, 1845; facs. repr. 1969).

——*Selections from the First Nine Books of the Croniche Fiorentine of Giovanni Villani*, tr. R. E. Selfe and P. H. Wicksteed (London, 1896).

Villanueva, J. L., *Viaje literario a las iglesias de España*, vol. 5 (Madrid, 1806).

Wakefield, W. L., *Heresy, Crusade and Inquisition in Southern France, 1100–1250* (London, 1974).

Walter of Hemingborough, *Chronicon Domini Walteri de Hemingburgh, De Gestis Regum Angliae*, ed. H. C. Hamilton, vol. 2 (London, 1868).

Webster, H., *Magic: A Sociological Study* (Stanford, Calif., 1948).

Wenck, C., *Clemens V und Heinrich VII* (Halle, 1882).

Wilkins, D., *Concilia Magnae Britanniae et Hiberniae*, vol. 2 (London, 1737).

William of Newburgh, *Historia Rerum Anglicarum*, in *Chronicles of the Reigns of Stephen, Henry II, and Richard I*, vol. 1, ed. R. Howlett (*Rolls Series*, vol. 82; London, 1884).

William of Tyre, *Historia Rerum in Partibus Transmarinis Gestarum*, in *RHCr.: Historiens occidentaux*, vol. 1.

William Rishanger, *Chronica Monasterii S. Albani: Willelmi Rishanger, Quondam Monachi S. Albani, et Quorundam Anonymorum, Chronica et Annales, Regnantibus Henrico Tertio et Edwardo Primo*, AD *1259–1307*, ed. H. T. Riley (*Rolls Series*, vol. 28; London, 1865).

Supplementary Bibliography

SOURCES

Le Procès des Templiers d'Auvergne (1309–11): *Edition de l'inter-rogatoire de juin 1309*, ed. R. Sève and A. M. Chagny-Sève (Mémoires et documents d'histoire médiévale et de philologie, nouvelle collection; Paris, 1987).

The Trial of the Templars in Cyprus. A Complete English Edition, ed. A. Gilmour-Bryson (Leiden, 1998).

The Trial of the Templars in the Papal State and the Abruzzi, ed. A. Gilmour-Bryson (Studi e Testi, 303; Vatican City, 1982).

SECONDARY WORKS

Barber, M., *The New Knighthood. A History of the Order of the Temple* (Cambridge, 1994).

——'The Trial of the Templars Revisited', in *The Military Orders*, vol. 2, *Welfare and Warfare*, ed. H. Nicholson (Aldershot, 1998), pp. 329–42.

Bautier, R.-H., 'Diplomatique et histoire politique: ce que la critique diplomatique nous apprend sur la personnalité de Philippe le Bel', *Revue Historique*, CCLVI (1978), pp. 3–27.

Beck, A., *Der Untergang der Templer. Größter Justizmord des Mittelalters?* (Freiburg, 1993).

Bramato, F., *Storia dell'Ordine dei Templari in Italia*, vol. 2, *Le Inquisizioni. Le Fonti* (Rome, 1994).

Brown, E. A. R., '*Persona et Gesta*: The Image and Deeds of the Thirteenth-Century Capetians. The Case of Philip the Fair', *Viator*, XIX (1988), pp. 219–46.

Bulst-Thiele, M., 'Warum wollte Philipp IV. den Templeorden ver-nichten? Ein neuer Aspekt', in *I Templari: Mito et storia*, ed. G. Minnucci and F. Sardi (Sinalunga-Siena, 1989), pp. 29–35.

Demurger, A., *Vie et mort de l'ordre du Temple, 1118–1314* (Paris, 1985).

——*Jacques de Molay. Le Crépuscule des Templiers* (Paris, 2002).

Elm, K., 'Der Templerprozess, 1307–1312', in *Macht und Recht. Grosse Prozesse in der Geschichte*, ed. A. Demandt (Munich, 1990), pp. 81–101.

Favier, J., *Philippe le Bel* (Paris, 1978).

Forey, A., *The Military Orders from the Twelfth to the Early Fourteenth Centuries* (London, 1992).

——'Towards a Profile of the Templars in the Early Fourteenth Century', in *The Military Orders: Fighting for the Faith and Caring for the Sick*, ed. M. Barber (Aldershot, 1994), pp. 196–204.

——*The Fall of the Templars in the Crown of Aragon* (Aldershot, 2001).

——'Letters of the Last Two Templar Masters', *Nottingham Medieval Studies*, XLV (2001), pp. 145–71.

Frale, B., *L'Ultima Battaglia dei Templari* (Rome, 2001).

Fried, J., 'Wille, Freiwilligkeit und Geständnis um 1300. Zur Beurteilung des letzen Templergrossmeisters Jacques de Molay', *Historisches Jahrbuch*, CV (1985), pp. 388–425.

Gilmour-Bryson, A., 'Age-Related Data from the Templar Trials', in *Aging and the Aged in Medieval Europe*, ed. M. M. Sheehan (Toronto, 1990), pp. 130–42.

——'The London Trial Testimony: Truth, Myth or Fable?' in *A World Explored. Essays in Honour of Laurie Gardiner*, ed. A. Gilmour-Bryson (Melbourne, 1993), pp. 44–61.

——'Sodomy and the Knights Templar', *Journal of the History of Sexuality*, VII (1996), pp. 151–83.

——'The Templar Trials: Did the System Work?' *The Medieval History Journal*, III (2000), pp. 41–65.

Housley, N., *The Avignon Papacy and the Crusades, 1305–1378* (Oxford, 1986).

——*The Later Crusades. From Lyons to Alcazar, 1274–1580* (Oxford, 1992).

Luttrell, A., 'Gli Ospitalieri e l'eredità dei Templari', in *I Templari: Mito e storia*, ed. G. Minnucci and F. Sardi (Sinalunga-Siena, 1989), pp. 67–86.

Melville, M., *La Vie des Templiers* (Paris, 1951; 2nd edn, 1974).

Menache, S., 'Contemporary Attitudes concerning the Templars' Affair: Propaganda's Fiasco?' *The Journal of Medieval History*, VIII (1982), pp. 135–47.

——'The Templar Order: A Failed Ideal?' *Catholic Historical Review*, LXXIX (1993), pp. 1–21.

——*Clement V* (Cambridge, 1998).

Nicholson, H., *The Knights Templar. A New History* (Stroud, 2001).

Partner, P., *The Murdered Magicians. The Templars and Their Myth* (Oxford, 1981).

Riley-Smith, J., 'Were the Templars Guilty?' *Sewanee Review* (forthcoming).

—'The Structures of the Orders of the Temple and the Hospital in *c*.1291', *Sewanee Review* (forthcoming).

Sans y Trave, J. M., *El Procès dels Templers Catalans* (Lérida, 1991).

Strayer, J. R., *The Reign of Philip the Fair* (Princeton, NJ, 1980).

Ward, J. O., 'Review Article. The Fall of the Templars', *The Journal of Religious History*, XIII (1983), pp. 92–113.

NOVELS

Eco, U., *Foucault's Pendulum*, tr. W. Weaver (London, 1989).

Scott, W., *Ivanhoe. A Romance* (London, 1819).

—*The Talisman* (London, 1825).

Index

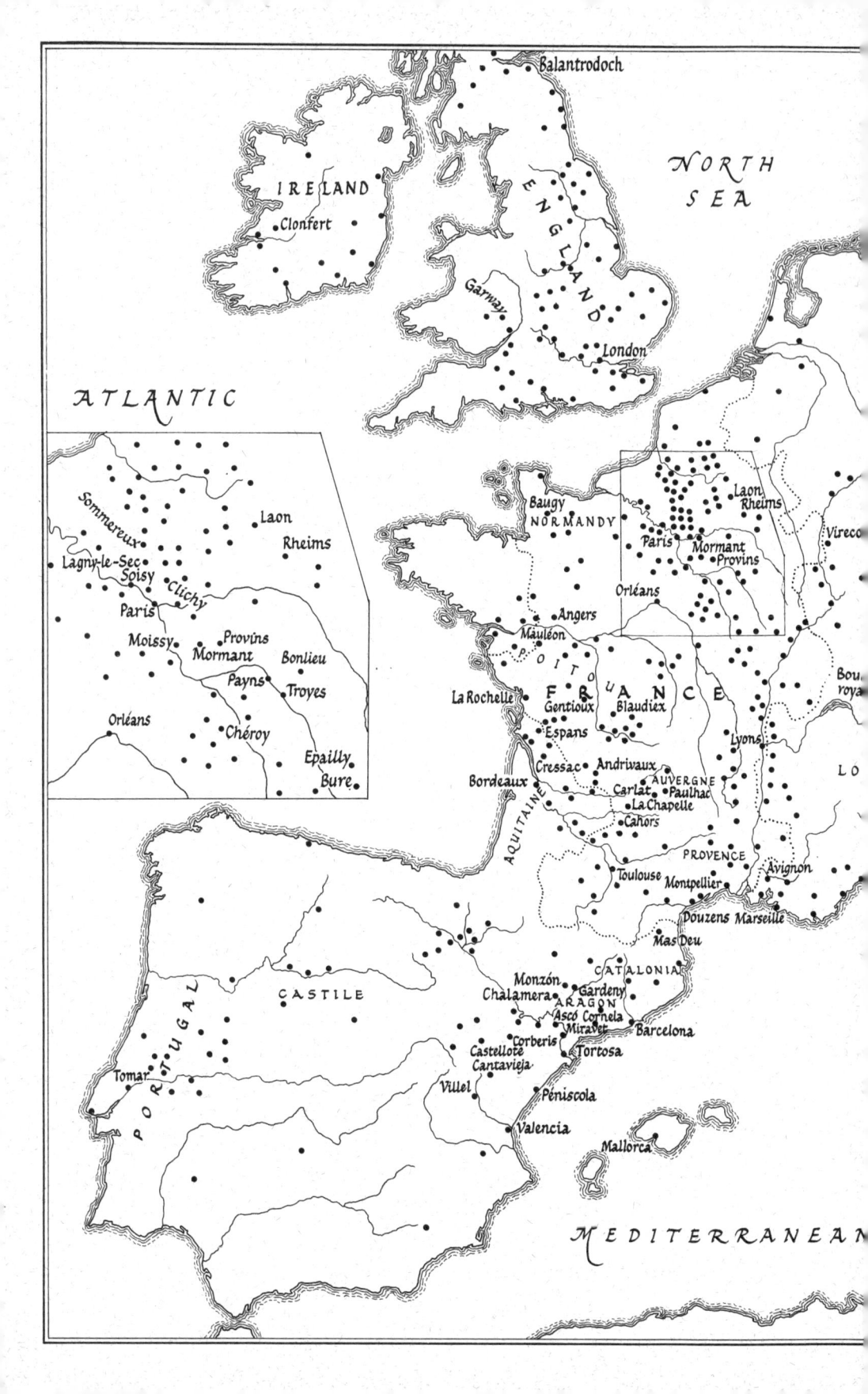